P. 167 modernism

Feminism and Institutions

Feminism and Institutions

Dialogues on Feminist Theory

Edited by

Linda Kauffman

Basil Blackwell

Copyright © Basil Blackwell Ltd, 1989

First published 1989

Basil Blackwell Inc.
3 Cambridge Center
Cambridge, Massachusetts 02142, USA

Basil Blackwell Ltd
108 Cowley Road, Oxford, OX4 1JF, UK

Library of Congress Cataloging in Publication Data
Feminism and institutions : dialogues on feminist theory / edited by
Linda Kauffman.
    p.   cm.
  Bibliography: p.
  Includes index.
  ISBN 0-631-16676-9—ISBN 0-631-16677-7 (pbk.)
  1. Feminism.   2. Feminist literary criticism.   3. Women—Social
conditions.   I. Kauffman, Linda S., 1949-
HQ1154.F4427   1989
305.4′2—dc19   88-36878
                                                      CIP

British Library Cataloguing in Publication Data
A CIP catalogue record for this book is available from the British Library.

Typeset in 11 on 13 pt Garamond
by Downdell Ltd, Oxford
Printed in Great Britain by
The Camelot Press plc, Southampton

Contents

Acknowledgments

The process of producing this collection has been an exhilarating testament to the vitality of collaboration, which has always been one of the greatest strengths of feminist scholarship. In addition to writing their own essays, many of the contributors offered invaluable advice about the structure and content of the entire collection. I especially thank Donna Landry, Elizabeth Meese, Alice Parker, Celeste Schenck, and William Warner. For long hours of intense debate, I have Myra Jehlen, Frank and Melissa Lentricchia, Jane Marcus, Gerald MacLean, and James Thompson to thank.

Thanks are also due to the University of Chicago Press for permission to quote from Catharine MacKinnon's 'Feminism, marxism, method, and the State', Parts I and II, which appeared in *Signs: Journal of Women in Culture and Society* in Spring 1982 and Summer 1983 respectively. Permission to quote from Sherley Anne Williams's 'Meditations on History' in *Midnight Birds*, edited by Mary Helen Washington, was granted by Anchor/Doubleday Books.

The National Endowment for the Humanities awarded me a fellowship in 1987-8; the release time the fellowship provided is gratefully acknowledged. The Department of English, University of Maryland, College Park, provided generous funds in the project's final stages for which I am deeply grateful. I also thank Lorrie Sprecher for excellent sleuthing skills as my research assistant.

The team at Basil Blackwell has been superb; I'm especially indebted to the unflappable Philip Carpenter, my editor, and to Andrew McNeillie, Simon Prosser, and Susan Martin for their tireless efforts on my behalf.

Linda Kauffman
Washington, D.C.
November 1988

Notes on Contributors

Amitai F. Avi-ram was trained at Columbia and Yale. He teaches English at the University of South Carolina and was a Mellon Postdoctoral Fellow at Cornell in 1986-7. He wrote 'Phallic Reflections' while outside the academy.

Bella Brodzki teaches modern fiction, women's studies, and literary theory at Sarah Lawrence College. She and Celeste Schenck have previously collaborated on *Life/Lines: Theorizing Women's Autobiography* (Cornell University Press, 1988). Her current work is a study of the politics of subjectivity.

George P. Cunningham is Associate Professor of Africana Studies at Brooklyn College, where he teaches Afro-American literature and Afro-American intellectual and cultural history. He is the author of *Langston Hughes and the Discourse of the Harlem Renaissance*, (Greenwood Press, 1988).

Bernard Duyfhuizen teaches English at the University of Wisconsin, Eau Claire. He has published in *Comparative Literature*, *Novel*, *Modern Fiction Studies*, *New Orleans Review*, *James Joyce Quarterly*, and *College English*. An earlier version of his essay in this volume appeared in *Tulsa Studies in Women's Literature* (1984).

Gayle Greene is Associate Professor of English at Scripps College, Claremont, California. She is co-editor of *The Women's Part: Feminist Criticism of Shakespeare* (University of Illinois Press, 1980) and *Making a Difference: Feminist Literary Criticism* (Methuen, 1985) and has published articles on Shakespeare, feminist criticism, and contemporary women writers. She is currently working on *Re-Visions: Contemporary*

Women Writers and the Tradition, which will be published by the University of Illinois Press.

Mae G. Henderson holds a joint appointment as Associate Professor in the African American World Studies Program and the Department of English at the University of Iowa. She is the author of several articles on black/women's literature and theatre, and co-editor of the five-volume *Anti-slavery Newspapers and Periodicals: An Annotated Index of Letters, 1817-1871* (G. K. Hall, 1980). Her monograph on black expatriate writers will be published by Oxford University Press. Her work-in-progress develops a black feminist theory of reading.

Linda Hutcheon is Professor of English and Comparative Literature at the University of Toronto. She is the author of *Narcissistic Narrative: The Metafictional Paradox* (1980; 1984); *Formalism and the Freudian Aesthetic* (1984); *A Theory of Parody* (1985); *A Poetics of Postmodernism: Theory, History, Fiction* (1988).

Linda Kauffman is Associate Professor of English at the University of Maryland, College Park. She is the author of *Discourses of Desire: Gender, Genre, and Epistolary Fictions* (Cornell University Press, 1986; 1988), and has published numerous reviews and essays on modern literature and feminist theory in such journals as *Signs*, *Criticism*, *Modern Fiction Studies*, and *Nineteenth Century Literature*. She also edited *Gender and Theory: Dialogues on Feminist Criticism* (Basil Blackwell, 1988). Her work-in-progress is *Special Delivery: Epistolary Modes in Modern Fiction*.

Donna Landry is Assistant Professor of English at the University of Southern California. She has published articles on feminist theory and literary history, and recently completed a book on eighteenth-century British working-class women's poetry, *The Muses of Resistance*. In 1988-9 she was a Fellow at Cornell University's Society for the Humanities, writing a book on feminism, materialism and deconstruction with Gerald MacLean.

Vincent B. Leitch is Professor of English and Co-director of the Philosophy and Literature Program at Purdue University. He is the author of *Deconstructive Criticism: An Advanced Introduction* (Columbia

University Press, 1983), and *American Literary Criticism from the Thirties to the Eighties* (Columbia University Press, 1988).

Elizabeth A. Meese is Professor of English and Adjunct Professor of Women's Studies at the University of Alabama in Tuscaloosa. She has published on nineteenth- and twentieth-century American writers, Southern women writers, and feminist criticism, and is the author of *Crossing the Double-Cross: The Practice of Feminist Criticism* and co-editor (with Alice Parker) of *The Differences Within: Feminism and Critical Theory*.

Alice Parker is Associate Professor of French at the University of Alabama in Tuscaloosa. She has published on eighteenth-century French women writers, Diderot, Francophone writers of the American South, and contemporary French and Canadian lesbian writers. She co-edited *The Differences Within: Feminism and Critical Theory* with Elizabeth Meese.

R. Radhakrishnan teaches critical theory in the English Department at the University of Massachusetts, Amherst. His interests include post-structuralism, feminist theory, cultural studies, post-colonialism and Third World studies. His essays have appeared or are forthcoming in such journals as *boundary 2*, *Works and Days*, *Cultural Critique*, *Poetics Today*, *Melus*, and *Social Text*. He is currently finishing a book on post-structuralist theory and coalitional critical practices.

Celeste Schenck teaches Renaissance literature, women's poetry, and feminist theory at Barnard College. She is a co-founder and director of 'Women Poets at Barnard', a series of readings and publications featuring new women poets, and General Co-editor of 'Reading Women Writing', a series in feminist criticism from Cornell University Press. She co-edited *Life/Lines: Theorizing Women's Autobiography* with Bella Brodzki (Cornell University Press, 1988), and is currently completing *Corinna Sings: Women Poets and the Politics of Genre*.

James J. Sosnoski is Professor of English at Miami University in Oxford, Ohio. In addition to writing essays on literary theory, he is the Executive Director of the Society for Critical Exchange. At present, he is the Executive Editor of its major project, *The Vocabularies of Criticism* *and Theory* (VOCAT), an encyclopedic dictionary to be published by Oxford University Press in the 1990s.

William Beatty Warner is Professor of English at the State University of New York in Buffalo. He is the author of *Reading Clarissa: The Struggles of Interpretation*, and *Chance and the Text of Experience: Freud, Nietzsche and Shakespeare's Hamlet* (1986). He is currently working on *Tactical Engagement: Theories in the Practice of Cultural Studies*.

Introduction

Linda Kauffman

Few in 1969 predicted that feminism would have such lasting effects on civil, legal, economic, political, and educational institutions. Nor did we foresee the feminization of poverty, the failure of the Equal Rights Amendment, or the era of 'post-feminism'. Despite remarkable achievements in the past twenty years, feminism has had to confront numerous dilemmas it did not anticipate: the turn towards neo-conservatism; the humanist backlash against the reconstitution of knowledge; the worldwide resistance among religious fundamentalists; the multiple oppressions of 'Third World' women. The past twenty years have been characterized by stark polarities between dramatic advances and equally dramatic setbacks in family arrangements, reproductive rights, the workplace, and global politics. The essays in this volume, focused on the relation of feminism and institutions, address these stark paradoxes. Rather than approaching feminism as an issue of individual rights, they see the individual as a product of complex power relations and they theorize about the ideological construction of subjects. If feminism can no longer be circumscribed by bourgeois individualism, neither can it be viewed merely as one choice among many theoretical 'perspectives'. It remains first and foremost a political position, cast now within the framework of multi-national economics and politics.

The essays in Part I, 'Transforming Institutions', focus on both the forces of oppression and the seeds of resistance. Despite the oppression of slaves in the American South, they found the means to develop a coded language and to plot insurrection. One such revolt, based on an historical event involving a black woman, is the subject of the first two essays. Mae G. Henderson shows how contemporary black women writers are reconstructing the history of slave women, and George P. Cunningham relates Henderson's position as an Afro-American critic to the institution of feminist literary criticism. The next two essays trace the historical

development of academic professionalization and the contemporary transformation of the academy by feminism. James J. Sosnoski and Gayle
Greene focus on competition in the academy and on feminist contributions
to developing new modes of academic inquiry and collaboration. The
essays by William Beatty Warner and Donna Landry use Catharine
MacKinnon's work as an occasion for analyzing feminism's relation to
marxism and deconstruction, emphasizing that if one suppresses the
conceptual categories with which we think, we remain stuck in the old
modes and systems. At the same time, we are complicitous with the very
discourses and institutions we seek to radicalize.

The essays in Part II, 'Gendering Post-modernism and Post-structuralism', examine the legacy of feminism's encounter with deconstruction.
They consider a certain tendency within post-structuralism toward a
formalist notion of textuality, and suggest alternatives to the disjunction
which that formalist notion creates in relation to feminist politics. Linda
Hutcheon assesses the impact of post-modernism, while Vincent B. Leitch
analyzes some of the impasses in traditional literary historiography and
suggests alternative methodologies. Post-modernism should be studied in
the context of institutional history rather than literary history in order
to expose the concrete operations of power and oppression. Bernard
Duyfhuizen discusses new models for combining deconstructive strategies
with feminist theory, while Bella Brodzki and Celeste Schenck suggest
alternatives to the 'coupling' of feminism and deconstruction.

In Part III, 'Theories of the Body Politic: Global Perspectives', the
essayists discuss multiple forms of oppression around the globe. Alice
Parker examines the lesbian critique of heterosexism in French and
Canadian women's writing, and Amitai F. Avi-ram offers a gay male
critique of phallic economies. Elizabeth A. Meese shows how traditional
notions of individual identity are disrupted by such political struggles as
the fight against South African apartheid, and R. Radhakrishnan compares
the construction of neo-colonialist ideologies in Africa and India. The
contributors analyze their own positions as speaking subjects and examine
the implications of writing in exile, under the shadow of totalitarianism,
imperialism, neo-colonialism. Modes of protest against multiple forms of
oppression are placed in the context of global struggles for liberation. The
essays in this section take into account the social and ideological construction of Otherness around the world – and the material oppression that
such constructions work to disguise.

To fully summarize the heterogeneous quality of this collection would be impossible, but that does not mean that a 'playful pluralism' has guided the selection and editing of these essays. The paired contributors are engaged in similar areas of research in literary studies, and the decision to alternate between male and female essayists and respondents is intended to highlight the arbitrariness of such dichotomies. The men's essays illustrate the profound influence feminism has had on their work, and demonstrate that appropriation and domination are not inevitable male responses. Nor is it the case, of course, that men and women have identical or equivalent experiences of or reactions to sexism.

The motive for structuring the collection in terms of dialogic interventions was not just to break down binary oppositions, but to try to conceptualize other frames of reference. Several of the contributors analyze potentially transforming modes of subjectivity and intersubjectivity. There is a strong emphasis in these pages on the politics of theory and the politics of subjectivity. The very fact that subjectivity is conceived of as having a politics is an attempt to avoid some of the early errors of feminism in the 1960s and 1970s. The objective, after all, is not merely the institutionalization of feminism, but the dismantling of institutional ideologies. That is why so many of the essays focus on disciplinary structures and state apparatuses (civil, legal, educational). The aim is not merely to get institutional endorsement for our practices, but so to shake the institutional foundations that it becomes impossible to replace an 'old Presbyter' with a 'new Priest'. Whether the alternatives they propose are theoretical, utopian, or practical, the contributors suggest fundamental alterations in our discursive practices, in the academy, and in cultural politics. Theory should, after all, lead to reconceptualizations of power that go beyond traditional definitions of politics. This is one of the many areas in which feminism's contribution has been vital. It exposes the falsity of the dichotomy between theory and practice by consistently reminding us that the point of theorizing is to transform human behavior.

I write in a moment when the academy is subject to intense scrutiny. We are witnessing a humanist backlash in the form of accusations that educators are failing to inculcate moral virtue, to police humanistic study, to maintain traditional 'standards'. Such protests (notably those of Allan Bloom, E. D. Hirsch, and William Bennett[1]) represent the conservative credo that education is a function of society and that history comes from the Great Books, which contain the truths that save men's souls. Conversely, leftist critics argue that society is a function of education.[2] Great books come from history; they are never 'above' ideology. But academic theorists are under attack from the Left as well as the Right. In *The Last Intellectuals*, for example, Russell Jacoby maintains that the uncritical professionalism of leftists has turned social commitment into sterile academic entrepreneurship.[3] Despite the political polarity between the Left and the Right, all of these men share an antipathy towards feminism: Bloom and Hirsch acknowledge its impact, but think that it has been overwhelmingly negative. Jacoby, conversely, refuses to acknowledge feminism when he protests that there are no intellectuals in America today who have not fled to academia, who are committed to social change, and who seek to communicate with the American public at large. Jacoby is deaf, dumb, and blind to feminist achievements in the last twenty years. His argument is based on a facile distinction between those 'inside' the academy and those 'outside', distinctions that feminists have been instrumental in dismantling.

The point of the essays in this collection is to show how the act of theorizing is essential to formulate the issues, to expose the invisible mechanisms of ideology, to reveal what is at stake in the struggle of and for discourses, and to explain how that struggle is linked to material oppression. Whether they focus on utopian possibilities or concrete limitations, their aim is to motivate social change and ideological transformations. The collection is marked by an awareness that in terms of political and human rights, the 1980s have been an ignominious decade in this country and around the globe: continued US intervention in Nicaragua, the Middle East, and elsewhere; the Reagan administration's refusal to impose economic sanctions on South Africa; the vocal ascendancy of the 'Moral Majority', have all revealed how rapidly oppression comes to seem 'natural'. The power of the anti-abortionists, the persecution of gays and lesbians, and the fear of AIDS have cast a huge spectre of potential institutional repression on every facet of our existences. Ugly evidence of America's racism abounds in urban centers, in small towns, and on college campuses. The question remains of how to envision and enact the movement towards social justice without complacently submitting to another repressive order. One of the aims of the essays in this volume is to defamiliarize the world around us as the century winds down. From slavery in the American South to South African apartheid, history is a direct reference point in these pages. Rather than nostalgically lamenting the loss of previous generations or epochs or traditions, the intellectuals in this volume are writing a history of the present.

NOTES

1 Bloom 1987; Hirsch 1987; Bennett 1984.
2 On the distinction between the conservative and the radical, see Lentricchia 1983: 1-5; Lentricchia also discusses the falsity of the dichotomy between the academic and the political, pp. 1-7.
3 Jacoby 1987.

REFERENCES

Bennett, William J. 1984. ' "To reclaim a legacy"; text of Report on Humanities in Education', *Chronicle of Higher Education*, 28 November: 16-21.

Bloom, Allan 1987. *The Closing of the American Mind: How Higher Education Has Failed Democracy and Impoverished the Souls of Today's Students*. New York: Simon and Schuster.

Hirsch, Jr, E. D. 1987. *Cultural Literacy: What Every American Needs to Know*. Boston: Houghton Mifflin.

Jacoby, Russell 1987. *The Last Intellectuals: American Culture in the Age of Academe*. New York: Basic Books.

Lentricchia, Frank 1983. *Criticism and Social Change*. Chicago: University of Chicago Press.

Part I

Transforming Institutions

The essays in this section focus both on subjugation and subversion. The first two essayists deal with the institution of slavery, and investigate the intersections of history and narrative, orality and textuality, gender and race. Moving from the slave culture in which knowledge and literacy were crimes, the discussion turns in the next pair of essays to the historical institutionalization of higher education. The essayists examine the ideological foundations underlying academic professionalization, and discuss feminist transformations of the academy. Feminists have also radically altered the legal system; this institution is the focus of the last pair of essays, which analyze Catharine MacKinnon's writing and rhetoric in relation to marxism and deconstruction.

In '(W)Riting *The Work* and Working the Rites', Mae G. Henderson juxtaposes Sherley Anne Williams's 'Meditations on History' (1980) with earlier narratives of the Nat Turner slave revolt in history and fiction. Drawing on texts by Thomas Gray, William Styron, and Angela Davis, Henderson demonstrates that the subjects – the slaves Nat Turner and Dessa Rose – are constituted differently, depending on whether the speaker is a white slave-owning chronicler (Gray), a black slave woman (Dessa), a literary artist (Styron or Williams), or a historian whose own ideology is apparent in the narrative he or she constructs. For example, Stanley Elkins is contrasted to Angela Davis and Herbert Aptheker. Henderson traces the metamorphoses of the formal discourse of nineteenth-century slave narrative, and shows how Williams interrogates the differences between formal and vernacular language, between the 'scholarly', 'objective' account of the revolt by the white slave-owner as opposed to the privately coded, oral communication among the black slaves. Henderson shows how Williams exploits the formal discourse of domination in order to subvert that discourse and resist that domination, a process which results in the reconstruction of both the oral, folk tradition and the formal one. In contrast to the discontinuities of the men's (Nat Turner, Gray, and Styron's) versions of the revolt, Henderson discusses the continuity of purpose shared by Angela Davis, Sherley Anne Williams, and Dessa Rose: in all three of the women's narratives, black women are consistently portrayed as custodians of resistance and insurgency.

George P. Cunningham's 'In No Man's Land: (W)Riting Gender and Race', situates Henderson's essay in relation to current issues in contemporary critical theory, feminist theory, and black literary theory. Henderson's aim is to recover the suppressed subjectivity of a black slave woman, and simultaneously to dismantle notions of unity among the discourses on gender, race, and class. Cunningham approaches Henderson's analysis and Williams's 'Meditations' as a place, a 'no man's land' - a site of struggle for discourse and among discourses. He analyzes Henderson's dialogic method of 'contratextualism' and examines its implications in terms of race and gender, explaining how her method problematizes theoretical distinctions between sexual oppression and racial oppression. The value of Henderson's concept of orality, Cunningham argues, lies in its capacity to free contemporary literary theory from a narrow focus on a Western, male, and literate textual universe.

The remaining essays in Part I focus on historical shifts in literary criticism, the academy, law and society. They trace the complex processes by which we are professionally 'disciplined', often in ways which make it difficult to recognize how our perspectives have been shaped by that disciplinarity. Although we are thus constructed as ideological subjects, some of the essayists insist that it is nevertheless crucial to work at producing concrete suggestions for resisting those constructions and that ideology, in order to initiate social change in both the academy and society.

In 'A Mindless Man-driven Theory Machine: Intellectuality, Sexuality, and the Institution of Criticism', James J. Sosnoski presents a brief history of literary criticism as a profession. He examines the assumptions underlying our approaches to critical argumentation and asks what principles lead us to deem one argument, one book, one colleague, or one theory superior to others. Sosnoski traces the historical processes and theoretical foundations which led to the establishment of academic disciplines and to the rise of professionalization in American universities. As a career, the professing of literary criticism is based on a masculine ideal of mastery, which fosters a spirit of competition rather than collaboration in intellectual life. Sosnoski investigates whether it is possible to change one's belief system, and if so, how that transformation might be effected. While critical theory has traditionally been patriarchal and has been used as an instrument of competition, Sosnoski argues that it can aid in the alterations he proposes: the development of intellectual communities dedicated to interrogating the various public spheres that make up our cultural formation.

What would happen, Gayle Greene asks, if feminists were to stop competing and nobody else did? In 'The Uses of Quarreling', Greene argues that since the university and the institutions it supports are apparatuses of the state, we all contribute to its ideology, whether or not we choose to do so. Competition is the law of the socio-economic system, and knowledge is integrally related not only to power but to capitalism. Whilst attacking the individualism of Sosnoski's proposal, Greene also believes that she has a keener sense than his essay manifests of the kinds of contradictions female feminist academics face every day.

Just as Sosnoski and Greene discuss academic control and competition as a zero-sum game, William Beatty Warner discusses the control over sexuality as another zero-sum game deeply ingrained in capitalism. In 'Treating Me Like an Object: Reading Catharine MacKinnon's Feminism', Warner analyzes Catharine MacKinnon's theories about the dialectical emergence of the feminist subject and the construction of female sexuality. He shows how the subject/object, male/female positions MacKinnon seems to relate dialectically develop, through the political rhetoric of MacKinnon's language, into a pure, ethically charged antithesis. Warner's deconstruction of MacKinnon's rhetoric shows how her arguments become authoritarian and essentialist; the suppression of pleasure, the object, and language make sexuality of any kind unthinkable. In spite of the conceptual lapses he locates, Warner sees MacKinnon's feminism as a cultural machine of value production; the force of her rhetoric helps transform the value of women in our culture.

In 'Treating Him Like an Object: William Beatty Warner's "Di(va)lution" ', Donna Landry argues that Warner's text inscribes within it a sexual exchange that it cannot control. Warner is therefore fascinated but fearful of MacKinnon, whose textuality in his essay comes to stand for feminism as a whole, and thus he fails to read his own text deconstructively. He cannot see how his narrative is grounded in oedipal struggle and he is blind to gendered antagonism. Like many men who are attempting to appropriate or to intervene in feminism, he has failed to analyze critically enough both his own subject position and the historical connections between male violence, (hetero)sexuality and women's oppression, connections he himself criticizes MacKinnon for essentializing.

1

(W)Riting *The Work* and Working The Rites

Mae G. Henderson

For, if it is true that at the heart of power relations and as a permanent condition of their existence there is an insubordination and a certain essential obstinacy on the part of the principles of freedom, then there is no relationship of power without the means of escape or possible flight. Every power relationship implies, at least *in potentia*, a strategy of struggle.

Michel Foucault, 'How is power exercised?'

One day this ole slave name John was walkin' through the woods; and he sees this, this here skeleton . . . laying there in the sun . . . He don't pay them dry bones no mind . . . he done see plenty of them bones in his time . . . he sits down on that rock to rest his weary self; and the next thing you know, he hears somebody eerie say: 'Tongue is the cause of my being here.' John leaped up and ran back to the Master . . . 'Massa . . . Massa' he say, 'there's a talking skeleton in the woods! Old Master say, 'I don't believe that John, you're not trying to make a fool of me are you?' John say: 'No Massa, dem bones is *really* talking.' So the Master called all of his friends from all of the nearby plantations . . . White folks came from all over; and when they arrived at the place of the skeleton - the place of the talking bones - they said to John: 'Make him speak.' But the skeleton wouldn't talk . . . So, and then, they beat John to death with anything that they could get their hands on . . . And left him beside the other skeleton . . . As the sun set redly, the buzzards was tearing into John's liver, and as the waning sun shined through his vacant sockets . . . the bones laying beside him commenced to shake and rattle, and then, chillen, them bones spoke . . . They said: 'Tongue, yes, tongue brought *us* here, and tongue brought you *here* too.'

Old Folk Tale, cited by Larry Neal in
The Glorious Monster in the Bell of the Horn

It would seem that one must be acquainted with darkies from one's birth in order to fully understand what passes for speech amongst them.

Narrator, 'Meditations on History'

There is no doubt about it. White people often undo themselves by such running off at the mouth, and God only knows how many nigger triumphs have been won in total silence.

William Styron's Nat Turner, in *The Confessions of Nat Turner*

And unlike white Americans who could assume literacy and familiarity with existing literary models as norms, the slave found himself without a system of written language – 'uneducated' in the denotative sense of the word. His task was not simply one of moving toward the requisite largeness of soul and faith in the value of his experiences. He first had to seize the word . . . Only by grasping the word could he engage in the speech acts that would ultimately define his selfhood.

Houston A. Baker, *The Journey Back*

'Meditations on History', Sherley Ann Williams's novella about discourse and struggle, achieves much of its meaning through its own struggle with previous modes of discourse.[1] Engaging works by William Styron and Thomas Gray, Williams explores the discourses of history and fiction. Although Williams makes reference neither to Styron nor his work in 'Meditations', her title signals not only that Styron's *Confessions of Nat Turner* is the primary anterior text for her work, but that her purpose is to produce a text which engages Styron as a kind of literary interlocutor.[2] Williams's title, 'Meditations', suggests a formal and thematic revision of Styron's *Confessions of Nat Turner* (a title appropriated from Thomas Gray's earlier document of the same name). Significantly, both titles turn on the notion of discourse (or its absence), silence and utterance, contemplation and revelation, private thought and public language. Williams takes her title from the 'Author's Note' in Styron's *Confessions* where he describes his novel as 'less an [*sic*] "historical novel" in conventional terms than *a meditation on history*'.[3] By unmasking Styron's work as more nearly a personal and authorial 'meditation' than the 'confessions' of his subject, Williams's title constitutes an ironic affirmation of Styron's stated intentions. For both Williams and Styron, the notion of 'meditation' not only implies the priority of the author's imagination and consciousness, but also an ordered reconstruction of history. In the sense that both authors interpose their literary *meditations* into a historical episode, both these works of historical fiction constitute acts of *mediation* as well. Williams's work suggests, however, that Styron's interventions result in the misreading of his historical subject, while her own work represents not only an attempt to reconcile the literary treatment to the historical subject, but, in the process, to deconstruct her predecessor's methods. 'Meditations', then, becomes a gesture of what Henry Louis Gates calls 'critical parody'[4] in that Williams revises and thus problematizes the structuration of Styron's *Confessions*.

Styron structures his *Confessions* in terms of an antithesis curiously appropriate to his subject: freedom and bondage. He declares his intention to 're-create a man and his era', allowing himself as author 'the utmost *freedom* of imagination in reconstructing' the early life and motivations of his protagonist, while remaining 'within the *bounds* of what meager enlightenment history has left us about the institution of slavery'.[5] Although many critics argue that the novelist, even the historical novelist, is entitled to some literary license, others allege that Styron has created a fictional character who reflects the historical Nat Turner less than he represents the author's highly personal and imaginative reconstruction.[6] In her implicit critique of Styron, Williams suggests that the priority of the imagination – especially when it is distantly removed from the historical subject (object) of meditation by race, gender, class, and culture – creates a peculiar dilemma for the writer.[7]

Williams is concerned not only with the problematics of historical fiction, but also with the relationship between discourse, power, and resistance. She explores the critical relationship between power relations and discourse, and the struggle to dominate as well as to resist domination. The central issue for her is not merely the functions, but also the forms, of discourse. The tension between the vernacular discourse of the slave heroine, and the formal discourse of the unnamed white male interviewer who narrates her story raises the issue of spoken versus written language, and their political and ideological functions in racial, sexual, class, and cultural interrelationships.

Williams and Styron follow similar techniques in constructing their works. Both writers take their subjects from an intermediary and create a complex literary personality based upon a historically constituted subject. Styron's narrative is based upon an account told to Thomas R. Gray, who recorded the original *Confessions of Nat Turner* as the convicted slave awaited execution in 1831 for leading a rebellion in which he and his followers killed fifty-five whites. Williams's character, on the other hand, is modelled after a historical figure recorded in Angela Davis's 'Reflections on the black woman's role in the community of slaves'.[8] It is also instructive to note in what ways these two readings of the slave experience are influenced by the work of contemporary historians of slavery. Interpreting the dynamics of the slave community and the character of Nat Turner through Stanley Elkins's controversial work on slavery, Styron concludes that Turner, as a slave rebel, is exceptional in that he initiates 'the only effective, sustained revolt in the annals of American Negro history'.[9] Williams, on the other hand, reads the experiences of her heroine ultimately through Herbert Aptheker's pioneering work on slave resistance, the source for Angela Davis's work on the slave community, which argues that the Nat Turner event 'was not an isolated, unique phenomenon, but the culmination of a series of slave conspiracies and revolts which had occurred in the immediate past.'[10]

Within 'Meditations', Williams's unnamed fictional interviewer, whose narrative role parallels that of Thomas Gray, functions as an amanuensis for the slave, Dessa (as Williams's heroine, Odessa, calls herself). However, as author-to-be of *The Roots of Rebellion and the Means of Eradicating Them* (otherwise referred to as *The Work*), his role also corresponds to Styron's. The narrator in Williams's text is thus a kind of composite character who fulfills the functions of both Gray, as historical investigator/interviewer, and Styron, as literary interpreter. In figuring the Styron/Gray fictional composite within her text, Williams sets up an author–character relationship which gives her the same control over Styron and Gray that they possess over their subject, Nat Turner. The table below illustrates the parallel relationships suggested above between author, Styron; his intermediary, Thomas Gray; and his subject, Nat Turner. It also structures the parallels between the author, Williams; her intermediary, Angela Davis; and her subject, the unidentified female slave rebel. Finally, it suggests the relationship in Williams's narrative between the composite Unnamed Narrator/Author of *The Work* and his subject, Dessa.

SUBJECT	HISTORICAL INVESTIGATOR	INTERPRETER
Nat Turner	Thomas Gray	William Styron
Slave woman	Angela Davis	Sherley Anne Williams
Dessa	Unnamed narrator	Author of *The Work*

I am concerned, however, not only with Williams's replication of Styron's process of composition, but also with her critique of Styron. Like the triptych, above, the elliptical diagram below illustrates the Turner/Gray/Styron and the Slave woman/Davis/Williams relationships, along with their fictional equivalents in Williams's 'Meditations'.

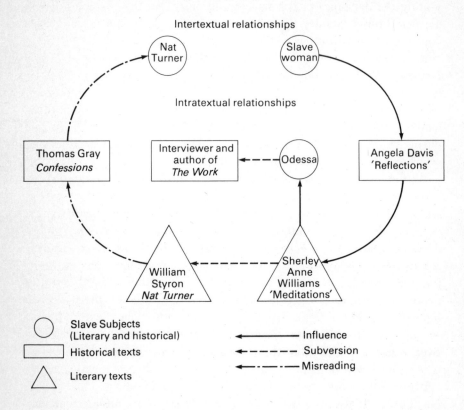

Obviously, no schema can reproduce the complexity of these relationships, but this diagram is meant to suggest some of the interrelationships which I will be examining in the course of this essay. The nature and function of these several relationships are indicated through unbroken lines of influence, or replication; broken lines of difference and subversion, or *re*reading; and parallel broken *and* unbroken lines of influence and subversion, or *mis*reading.[11] The periphery of the diagram inscribes the *inter*textual relationships between Styron/Gray and Williams/Davis, and the center, the *intra*textual relationships depicted in Williams's work. At top left, Nat Turner, the original historical subject, is misread (or constituted and subverted) by Thomas Gray, whose representation is, in turn, appropriated and subverted by William Styron as a literary figure in his novel. In a parallel process of composition, the slave woman at top right is cited by Angela Davis to exemplify her thesis and, in a further development, appropriated by Sherley Anne Williams as a literary subject in her novella. The characters in Williams's text are represented at the center of the diagram in a configuration which both repeats the Styron/Williams technique of composition and, at the same time, plays the dual role of both authenticating Williams's method and revising (subverting) Styron's. In this instance, Dessa is a historical subject falsely constituted (misread) by a historical investigator writing a book on the suppression of slave rebellions, a work which (like Styron's) will be shown to illuminate more about the writer than about his subject.

One finds telling similarities and differences between Williams and Styron in presentation as well as perspective. Both are involved with discourse on the nature of historical fiction, and both assume the role of literary interpreters who meditate on history. Styron's work, however, is meant to be a meditation, or reflection, on history itself, while Williams's can perhaps be more aptly understood as a meditation on historiography – in the sense that it provides the reader with a guide to the contemplation of historical and literary-historical works such as Styron's and Gray's. If, then, Styron's work is a fictional meditation on history, Williams's is a fictional meditation on a fictional meditation on history, as well as a fictional elaboration of a historical incident cited by Angela Davis. Williams's text thus not only gestures toward intertextuality in its relationship to Styron's literary antecedent, but also in its relationship to Davis's historical citation.

Styron's protagonist narrates the events of his life from the first person, inviting a judgment from the reader on Turner as subject/narrator, while Williams's heroine is presented primarily in the third person from the perspective of the white narrator, inviting the reader to distinguish between the narrator's judgment of the subject and the subject (Dessa) herself. When Dessa speaks in her own vernacular voice, she *interdicts* the narrator's discourse. At the same time, the contrast between Dessa's spoken language and the white narrator's written language allows Williams as author, in Gates's apt term, to 'signify' upon her precursors, Styron and Gray.[12] One should perhaps note in passing that the narration of Dessa's story by a white male narrator resolves a technical problem for the author, who must discover a way to present a character who is a victim of an illiteracy enforced by a system which made teaching slaves to read and write a criminal offense. Moreover, it is with a certain appropriateness that Dessa's story is narrated by a white male, representing the class which has historically controlled the print media. It was the historical records of this class (diaries, plantation records, ledgers, etc.) that, until the emergence of modern revisionist scholarship based on the slave's folklore and narratives, provided the primary source materials for the study of slavery.[13]

Williams's concern with signification suggests that the reader must approach the discourse of the 'real' as well as the discourse of the 'imaginary' with a sense of scepticism based on a recognition of the cultural myths inscribed in language and consciousness. It might also suggest that we can assume the truth claim of historical narrative no more than that of literary narrative.[14] Thus, as readers we must beware of what Barbara Johnson describes as the 'interpretive malpractice' that writers (both creative and historical) are subject to.[15]

Because Williams's text repeats in structure and subverts in meaning the Turner/Gray/Styron dynamic, we begin by examining the role of Styron's intermediary, Thomas Gray, whom Styron describes as 'a somewhat enigmatic lawyer . . . who published *Confessions* . . . and then vanished from sight'.[16] In his address 'To the Public' in *The Confessions of Nat Turner*, Gray tells us that what he is about to present is a 'faithful record' of his interview with the subject:

> I have had ready access to him, and finding that he was willing to make a full and free confession of the origin, progress and consummation of the insurrectionary movements of the slaves of which he was the contriver and head; I determined for gratification of public curiosity to commit his statements to writing, and publish them, with little or no variation, from his own words. That this is a faithful record of his confessions, the annexed certificate of the County Court of Southampton, will attest. They certainly bear the stamp of truth and sincerity.[17]

Although Gray's assertions suggest that he locates the authenticity and value of his account in discourse that is presumed to be objective and value-free, a close reading of his prefatory comments would indicate a more complex motivation at work. Turner's actions have, in effect, created moral and social chaos for the narrator and his world. By presenting Turner's story as a cautionary tale, the narrator attempts to restore by simple reaffirmation his own sense of moral and mental order, prerequisite to the reestablishment of the social order which Turner has threatened:

> His [Nat Turner's] own account of the conspiracy is submitted to the public, without comment. It reads an awful, and it is hoped, a useful lesson, as to the operations of a mind like his, endeavoring to grapple with things beyond its reach. How it first became bewildered and confounded, and finally corrupted and led to the conception and perpetuation of the most atrocious and heart-rending deeds. It is calculated also to demonstrate the policy of our laws in restraint of this class of our population, and to induce all those entrusted with their execution, as well as our citizens generally, to see that they are strictly and rigidly enforced. Each particular community should look to its own safety, whilst the general guardian of the laws, keep a watchful eye over all.[18]

The contradiction between the profession of factual objectivity ('without comment') and the editorial imposition of meaning that immediately follows signals Gray's real intentions to the reader. Turner becomes for his amanuensis a symbol of disorder and irrationality. Gray's representation of the events surrounding Turner's activities becomes 'a useful lesson', or rather an instrument or device for restoring psychic order. Furthermore, the policy of restraint and repression which he advocates is aimed at re-establishing public order. His comments also suggest that his findings (like those of the scholar and scientist) have implications for both the formulation of public policy and the machinery designed to enforce that policy.

The ambiguous relationship between Styron and his source, Gray, serves to intensify a clearly problematic relationship between Styron and his subject, Turner. In his essay, 'This Quiet Dust', Styron discounts as 'virtually worthless' the newspaper accounts of the period which he describes as 'sketchy, remote, filled with conjecture'. On the other hand, he appears to affirm the authenticity of Gray's original *Confessions of Nat Turner*, 'a brief pamphlet of some five thousand words, transcribed from Nat's lips as he awaited trial . . . There are several discrepancies in Gray's transcript but it was taken down in haste, and in all major respects it seems completely honest and reliable.'[19] Yet, in his exchange with Herbert Aptheker, published in *The Nation* sometime later, Styron suggests a qualification, if not an actual retraction:

> I have never questioned their authenticity [Gray's *Confessions*], whatever semantic emphasis is placed on that word . . . What I do question . . . is the *accuracy* of the 'Confessions', the overall fidelity to the circumstances of Nat's life and career which Gray maintained during the course of what must have been, considering the hysteria of the moment, an exceedingly difficult and prickly interview.[20]

Continuing, Styron suggests that his primary source, Gray, has in fact subverted and misread his subject:

> The entire pedantic, impossibly elevated and formal tone of the 'Confessions' makes me believe that they were *not* recorded with 'little or no variation' from Nat's words, as Gray states in his prologue; and so how much during that tense encounter was subtly bent and twisted by the narrator? Gray was a man of his time, a Southern racist, and as a functionary of the Commonwealth it may well have been to his advantage (and in spite of his disclaimer to the contrary) to distort many things that the helpless prisoner told him, to add things, to leave things out.[21]

Clearly, Styron is motivated in part by the criticism of detractors who accuse him of inauthenticity, distortion, and historical falsification in his treatment of Turner. Styron's critics have levelled, among others, the charges that the author portrays the slave revolutionary as a weak and irresolute figure; that he associates Turner's liberational impulse to sexual repression, pent-up passion for white women, and latent homosexuality; and that he ignores Turner's wife and the role of his family in the shaping of his character.[22] Styron and his apologists have defended both his artistic and historical integrity on the basis that Styron 'takes liberties with fact, as every novelist does, but he does not do violence to the historical record.'[23] Quoting the marxist critic, Lukács, Styron argues that 'the novelist must be at liberty to treat [historical facts] as he likes, if he is to reproduce the much more complex and ramifying totality with historical faithfulness.'[24]

If Styron's most severe critics indict him for perpetrating 'white

Southern myths, racial stereotypes, and literary cliches', his most astute critics suggest that what is at issue is not Styron's literary license, but his preference for his own imagination over the historical facts of Turner's life.[25] Responding to this issue, Ralph Ellison, for example, would limit the autonomy of the novelist who chooses to write historical fiction. 'The freedom of the fiction writer, the novelist, is one of the great freedoms possible for the individual to exercise,' says Ellison, 'but it is not absolute . . . you don't have the freedom to snatch any and everybody, and completely recreate them.'[26]

Although at a considerably greater remove, Gray is to Styron's *Confessions* what Angela Davis is to Williams's 'Meditations'. And what Turner is to Gray, the unnamed slave woman is to Angel Davis. Dedicating her novella to Davis, Williams opens with a quotation from Davis's 'Reflections on the black woman's role in the community of slaves':

> *The myth [of the black matriarchy and the castrating black female] must be consciously repudiated as myth and the black woman in her true historical contours must be resurrected. We, the black women of today, must accept the full weight of a legacy wrought in blood by our mothers in chains . . . as heirs to a tradition of supreme perseverance and heroic resistance, we must hasten to take our place wherever our people are forging on towards freedom.*[27]

The dedication and quotation contextualizes the Williams/Styron dialogue within a tradition of political insurgency and literary revisionism, as a fuller consideration of Davis's original article will show. At the outset, Davis informs us that her work is a repudiation of the myths of the black woman embodied, for example, in the Moynihan Report. Referring to 'the paucity of literature on the black woman', she writes:

> [W]e must contend with the fact that too many of these rare studies must claim as their signal achievement the reinforcement of fictitious clichés. They have given credence to grossly distorted categories through which the black woman continues to be perceived.[28]

Davis argues that we must examine the biases and presuppositions that the scholar brings to the study of black social structures, warning the reader that the putatively objective discourse of the social scientist and researcher can perpetuate negative stereotypes of black women. She cites the following historical event, upon which Williams bases her story, to demonstrate that black women have been leaders in the struggle for liberation of the black community:

> [A] group of slaves, being led from Maryland to be sold in the South had apparently planned to kill the traders and make their way to freedom. One of the traders was successfully done away with, but eventually a posse captured all the slaves. Of the six leaders sentenced to death, one was a woman. She was first permitted, for reasons of economy, to give birth to her child. Afterwards, she was publicly hanged.[29]

Examining the historical record, Davis concludes that the black woman has been central in the black community from slavery to the present as the 'custodian of resistance'. Davis thus provides Williams with a connecting link to the historical event within a continuum of political insurgency, establishing a continuity of purpose between Davis, Williams, and Dessa - as opposed to the discontinuity between Turner and Gray, Styron and Turner, and even Styron and Gray.

Williams, in effect, gives dramatic expression to Davis's thesis, while simultaneously providing the anonymous historical figure with literary identity. The violence done to the image of the black slave woman by historians corresponds to the violence done to her literary voice by male (black and white) authors. Just as Davis, in her article, seeks to free the black female from historical libel, so Williams seeks to create a text to liberate her protagonist from literary libel. If Williams combines the roles of historian and literary interpreter in the character of the narrator, she represents the black woman's struggle against misrepresentation and misreading in the character of Dessa. What is significant in Williams's treatment is her emphasis on the personal and physical struggles as well as the social and literary struggles of the black woman. Dessa is *literally* imprisoned in a social system controlled by the slaveholders and *literarily* imprisoned in a text controlled by the defenders of that institution.

Williams introduces her story not from the narrator's perspective, but from Dessa's. The main narrative is pre-empted by a prologue that takes the form of a reverie by Dessa. Unlike Styron's Turner, whose early 'meditations' center on his experiences as a house slave pampered by an indulgent master, Dessa's 'meditations' depict her relationships within the slave community, and, more specifically, Dessa's relationship with her husband, Kaine. Dessa's reveries of Kaine allow her a temporary imaginative retreat from the confines of corporeal imprisonment in the root cellar ('It was gone as suddenly as it had come, the memory so strong, so clear it was like being with him all over again' 'Meditations', p. 208). Situated before the main text, narrated by the historical investigator, Dessa's reveries, expressed in the language of private reflection, establish her as a *speaking* (rather than *spoken*) subject, and provide the reader with a subjective and participatory point of reference for understanding the revelation of events which follow. By opening the text with Dessa's reflections, Williams establishes the reader's narrative expectations, promotes identification with her protagonist, and provides clues on how to *read*, or decode, the real meaning of the narrator's ostensibly reportorial journal entries.

In the traditional slave narrative, the prologue or preface to the slave's tale was frequently written by a white guarantor, usually an abolitionist, who assured the reader that the story he was about to read was truthful and reliable.[30] If the prologue was a device for authenticating and validating the traditional slave narrative, then Williams replicates, but, more significantly, reverses this function. The effect of Dessa's prologue in 'Meditations' is to subvert the authority and authenticity of the main narration, while more traditionally, Gray's prologue functions to authenticate Turner's account.

Williams's story, however, inverts not only the structure of the conventional slave narrative, but its social and rhetorical strategies as well. If the original slave narrative had as its goal the condemnation and destruction of the 'peculiar institution', Williams's narrator (like Gray) attempts to use narrative as justification for the suppression of resistance and rebellion. Ironically, despite the narrator's intentions, Dessa's narrative does, in fact, conform in structure to the traditional slave narrative, which culminates in freedom for the ex-slave narrator. Unlike Styron's Turner, Williams's Dessa is not only liberated from the fate of her historical precursor, but assists in the liberation of her fellow slaves.

More subtle perhaps is Williams's subversion of the formal discourse of the nineteenth-century slave narrative. The slave narratives, which inaugurate the black formal and narrative tradition, appropriate the discourse of the dominant white and male culture and, like Gray's *Confessions*, depend for authenticity upon a highly charged public rhetoric in which the slaveholder and the slave system represent a threat to the moral and social order. In *Give Birth to Brightness*, Williams writes,

it is . . . clear from these narratives that whatever descriptions of
Black traditions or 'field of manners' are given are there either to
point up the effects of slavery, or are unintentional by-products. The
major impetus of these men as writers was the need to call attention
to the plight of Black people in this country, to point out the inequities
and horrors of America's caste system, to provide answers and
questions and solutions to America's dilemma.[31]

Williams's insertion of the black vernacular into this discourse, in effect,
writes into history the voices of slaves like Dessa. Although she was illiterate (unlike Nat Turner), she nevertheless represents those slaves who
gained some measure of personal autonomy, despite enforced illiteracy.[32]

The main story, as I have indicated, takes the form of a series of journal
entries recorded by the amanuensis, emphasizing the authority of written
discourse for the narrator. His style, reflecting a 'scholarly' posture, is
impersonal and 'objective', based upon scientific inquiry, reason, logic,
cause and effect. In short, his narration represents white, male, formal
discourse. He is author of *The Complete Guide for Competent Masters in
Dealing with Slaves and Other Dependents*, a work which he dismisses as
'a mere business venture'. More important to the narrator is his forthcoming *magnum opus*. The slave uprising in which Dessa participates, he
believes, will make a 'splendid opening' to his contemplated project:
'. . . she will be brought to recreate that event [the uprising] and all that
led up to it for me. Ah! the work, *The Work* has at last begun' (p. 212).

It is the full title of *The Work - The Roots of Rebellion and the Means
of Eradicating Them* (also referred to as *Roots*) - which reveals the
motivations of the narrator. The ironic allusion to Alex Haley's historical
novel *Roots*[33] suggests a concern not so much with *roots* as with
eradication. Assuming the posture of a historical investigator, the
narrator sets out to 'discover and analyze the motivating factors which
culminated' in what he regards as 'this outrage against the public safety'
(p. 222). *The Work*, then, is projected as a kind of blueprint for the
exercise of power and control by the dominant and privileged over the
dominated and subjected, and thus becomes part of a technology of representation which ensures the ideological dominance and physical
suppression of the slave. Undoubtedly, the rather nice subversion and
parody evoked by the conflation of the abbreviated titles (*Roots* and *The
Work*) will not be lost upon the close reader. As the narrator 'writes' *The
Work* (*Roots*), so Dessa 'works' the 'rites of roots'.[34]

Based upon trial records, the narrator reconstructs the following incident:

Wilson picked up a consignment of slaves in Charleston at the end of March. While in the area, he attended a private sale where he heard of a wench, just entered upon childbearing age, and already increasing, that was being offered for sale on the plantation of Mr. Terrell Vaungham. He inquired at the plantation and was told that the wench was being sold because she had assaulted Vaungham . . . Wilson paid three hundred eighty-five dollars species for her: she would fetch at least twice that much in New Orleans. . . . In the early morning hours of April 29, the wench and the four bucks in her chain group managed to free themselves. . . . Two of these went to subdue the guards and drivers while the other three attacked Wilson and Darkmon [the slavetraders], searching for the keys which would free the rest of the coffle. The negress attacked Darkmon and it was his death screams which awakened Wilson. . . . The darkies then took the horses and pack animals, some provisions and all the firearms and other weapons. . . . A posse was quickly formed and set out in pursuit. . . . After a fierce gun battle in which seven of the posse were wounded . . . the slaves were finally subdued in hand-to-hand combat at a cost to the posse of three dead and numerous minor injuries. . . . Thirty-three blacks were tried (all adults above the age of fifteen): six were hanged and quartered because of the ferocity with which they fought the posse (of these last two totals, six were females); three were whipped only; seven were branded only and three were whipped and branded. . . . The negress still awaits her fate. (pp. 217-21)

Significantly, neither the trial record nor the narrator's text reveals anything of the poignant personal dimension of Dessa's experiences. Although both Dessa and the narrator recount similar experiences, the former's reading is from the perspective of a participant in struggle, while the latter's is from a position of power.

To understand the narrator's text, we must understand his psychic processes, his profession, his values. The narrator opens his journal with the conviction that 'It will be a curious process to delve into the mind of one of the instigators, of this dreadful plot' (p. 211). Ironically, the author's journal reveals more about the narrator's imagination and his sense of self and being-in-the-world than it does about the 'negro savagery' which he proposes to examine. In his journal, Dessa's interrogator explains his intentions:

> Each day I become more convinced of the necessity, the righteousness even of the work I have embarked upon. Think, I say to myself as I sit looking into the negress's face, think how it might have been had there been a work such as I envision after the Prosser uprising of 1800. Would the Vesey conspiracy and all the numerous uprisings which took place in between these two infamous events, would they have occurred? Would this wretched wench even now be huddled before me? No, I say. No, for the evil deed which blossomed forth in her and her companions would never have been planted. (pp. 212-13)[35]

What is interesting here is not only the objective of discourse for the narrator – to restore order by codifying measures of social control – but also the function of his discourse, which is to organize the narrator's world. Like Gray, the narrator believes that the moral and 'natural order of the universe' have been violated by those who do not recognize 'their place':

> Is it merely the untamed, perhaps even *untameable* savagery of their natures which causes them to rise up so treacherously and repudiate the natural order of the universe which has already decreed their place, or is it something more amenable to human manipulation? (pp. 211)

The narrator's text is motivated as much by a sense of outrage as it is by a desire to discover whether or not 'some disciplinary measure or restraining *word*' (my emphasis) might not avert further black uprisings. Moreover, the importance attached to *The Work* not only clearly privileges writing for the narrator, but assumes an added significance in that his prescriptions represent a kind of Nietzschean 'will to power' through the agency of formal discourse, giving credence perhaps to Lévi-Strauss's contention that writing 'seems to be associated with . . . the exploitation of man by man'. The 'necessity' of his work indicates the compulsion with which the narrator approaches his task, while its 'righteousness' suggests his conviction of acting in accordance with divine law. Indeed, in taking Dessa out of doors from the root cellar in which she is incarcerated, the narrator seeks to

> free myself [under the open sky] from the oppressive sense of her eyes casting a spell, not so much upon me (I know that should it ever come to a contest, God will prove stronger than the black devils she no doubt worships). No, not upon me is the spell cast, but upon the whole of the atmosphere from which I must draw breath. (p. 213)

Like Gray's report, the narrator's discourse allows him to impose a kind of Manichean vision on his notion of Self and 'Other', organizing the world according to the dualisms of God/devil, righteousness/evil, order/ disorder.

The objectivity implied by a discourse based upon a presumed neutrality is further undermined by the narrator's white, male, upper-class assumptions. Exploiting all the prevailing stereotypes of the black woman, he describes the fifteen- or sixteen-year-old Dessa as 'this wench scarcely more than a pickaninny', 'the virago', 'this darky' and 'the negress'. Comparing her to 'a wild and timorous animal', 'a beast [crouching] in its lair', and 'a raging nigger bitch', he sees her as 'a cat . . . spitting, biting, scratching, apparently unconcerned about the harm her actions might bring to her child'. More subtle perhaps than these qualities which suggest that the subject is sub-human (animal-like) are others which depict her as non-human (monstrous). She is the embodiment of evil, a 'she-devil' who 'casts spells' and 'worships . . . black devils'. Incapable of acknowledging courage or intelligence in one who is 'but a female and a darky at that', he challenges both her humanity and femininity: 'Who would think a female so far gone in the breeding process capable of such treacherous conduct?' (p. 222) Yet, despite his attempts to defeminize and dehumanize Dessa, her femininity, for the reader, has been established in her reveries of Kaine and their lovemaking; her motherhood has been affirmed by her pregnancy; her courage has been demonstrated through her role in the slave revolt; and her intellect, as we shall see, is evidenced in the manipulation of her interrogator.

It is the narrator's representation of Dessa as Other which enables the reader to understand the complex and fragile psychic structure upon which he erects his self-identity. What is apparent is that the narrator's conception of 'otherness' serves to define, through a process of negative identification, his own self-concept. The narrator projects his irrational, submerged self onto the Other, defining himself in opposition to the projected image. Erik Erikson explains how this process of negative identification works:

> Identity formation normatively has its dark and negative side, which throughout life can remain an unruly part of the total identity. Every person and every group harbors a *negative identity* as the sum of all those identifications and identity fragments which the individual had to submerge in himself as undesirable or irreconcilable or which his group has taught him to perceive as the mark of fatal difference: in sex role or race, in class or religion.[36]

Thus we see that it is the narrator's effacement and degradation of Dessa which defines his own sense of self-superiority. It is her 'savagery' which confirms his 'civilization', her 'bestiality' which ensures his 'humanity', her 'evilness' which confirms his 'virtue'. Erikson's comments also illuminate the subjective source and destructive outcome of the moral outrage expressed by both Turner's and Dessa's interrogators. Such a response is motivated, Erikson suggests, by a threat of losing one's 'wholeness' – that is, one's sense of harmony and order – and can 'serve the efficient destructiveness of the machinery of oppression and war'.[37]

Williams structures her 'Meditations' around the struggle between Dessa and the narrator for control of the text. But this literary or rhetorical struggle is only the linguistic equivalent of the other struggles occurring in the text: racial struggle (black v. white), class struggle (slave v. master), and sex struggle (female v. male). Dessa seeks to avoid imprisonment in formal discourse as well as in society. Just as she rebels against her social bondage, so Dessa rebels against her metaphorical bondage within the text. She disrupts the text just as she disrupts the social system. Indeed, it is because she has threatened both social and literary structures – because she refuses to be confined in either the narrator's text or the social order imposed by whites – that she must be 'eradicated'.

The prologue as well as Dessa's interpositions into the narrator's journal are expressed in vernacular discourse. Contrasting his own more direct, linear, formal discourse with Dessa's allusive, discursive, oral discourse, the narrator observes, '[S]he answers questions in a random manner, a loquacious, roundabout fashion – if, indeed, she can be brought to answer them at all.' (p. 225) It is her dialect that masks Dessa's true intentions from the narrator, and, at the same time, allows the reader to gain what Williams elsewhere describes as 'limited access into the private and personal wishes of the slaves'.[38] It is precisely Williams's affirmation of the 'speech act' that links Dessa with what Houston Baker describes as 'the domain of experience constituted by the oral-aural community of the slave quarters', making Dessa an 'authentic voice' of the slave community.[39]

In 'Meditations', the meaning of the events resides in the nature of representation, determined largely by the perspective from which they are represented. As Dessa's story unfolds, the reader discovers that Kaine, whose name ironically suggests his biblical precursor, has been murdered by his master:

> . . . when Emmalina meet me that day, tell me Kaine don took a hoe at Mas and Mas don laid into him wid a shovel, bout bus' in his head, I jes run and when the hoe gits in my way, I let it fall, the dress in my way and I holds that up. Kaine jes layin there on usses pallet, head seepin blood, one eye closed, one bout gone. (p. 224)

The pregnant Dessa, falsely accused by her mistress of carrying the master's child, is subsequently sold to a slave trader, and becomes one of the leaders in an attempt to free her comrades. Along with her fellow slaves, Dessa manages to escape, but is recaptured and placed in confinement, where she awaits execution after the birth of her child. But Dessa refuses to be either killed in the text or 'killed into text', because to do so would be to surrender the control of her life to *an-other*.[40]

If the plot of the narrative revolves around an act of insurgency, its structure is shaped by what I call a kind of 'narrative insurgency'. The narrator's control over his journal is subverted by a series of 'interventionist' acts by Dessa which disrupt the narrator's account. Not only does Dessa refuse to give a full confession, but she circumvents the narrator's persistent attempts to extract information concerning other participants in the revolt. Unlike Turner, who enters into a kind of covenant with his interrogator, Dessa rejects such an implicit contract or consensual arrangement – which would limit the boundaries of her struggle. Despite the narrator's persistent attempts to loosen her 'reluctant tongue', Dessa chooses when she will speak, what she will say, and when she will remain silent. If she pre-empts the narrator's story in the prologue, she continues to employ strategies of narrative insurgency –

silence, non-acquiescence, evasion, and dissembling – throughout the narrative.

Repeatedly, the narrator expresses his frustration in attempting to elicit information from Dessa:

Oh, she may be sullen and stubbornly silent. (p. 211)

She refused on two occasions to speak with me. (p. 214)

My latest attempt to have speech with her was this morning . . . (p. 215)

We will try what a little pressure can accomplish with her reluctant tongue. (p. 216)

I do not make the mistake of putting her silence down to modesty or even fear but . . . stubbornness. (p. 216)

And she turned her head and would not speak with me anymore. (p. 225)

I grew more than a little impatient with the response – or lack thereof – which I have thus far elicited . . . (pp. 225-6)

I had phrased this question in various ways and been met with silence. (p. 226)

But aside from that offensive flicking of the eye, she would not respond. (p. 226)

I knew when she turned her head from me that for this day, anyway, I had gotten all from her that I could. (p. 238)

And when I called to her she would not respond. (p. 243)

At other times, Dessa hums and sings in order to avoid responding to the narrator's overtures:

I admit to being at a loss as to how to begin, but . . . was about to order her to cease her noise. (p. 215)

[S]he would hum, an absurd, monotonous little tune in a minor key, the melody of which she repeated over and over. (p. 226)

The humming became so annoying, I was forced to ask her to cease. (p. 235)

I asked quickly, perhaps too quickly . . . and . . . [t]he humming started again. (p. 238)

Dessa not only exercises control over the narrator's text through her silences and evasions, but emerges in her own voice through a series of 'recitals', refusing, as it were, to allow the narrator to inscribe her. The journal entries allow Dessa to emerge at several points in the narrative, displacing the formal discourse of the writer with her own vernacular voice. Her first words, in fact, are not at all in response to the narrator, but rather constitute a speech act of existential self-affirmation, which she delivers in a 'loud . . . even exultant note':

> I bes. I. And he [Kaine] in air on my tongue the sun in my face. The heat in my blood. I bes he; he me. And it can't end in this place, not this time. Not this. But if it do, if it do, it was and I bes. I bes. (pp. 215-16)

If the narrator is motivated by a desire to destroy, Dessa's initial response suggests a determination 'to be'.

The key to her identity, however, is not in her relationship to the narrator, but in her relationship to Kaine ('He chosed me. Mas ain't had nothing to do wid that. It Kaine what pick me out and say I be his woman' (p. 233).[41] Her love for him - and his death - prompts her rebellion. Dessa recalls that Kaine's final words are 'Nigga *can* do and my [Dessa's] name, my name and Nigga *can* do.' (Emphasis added.) Significantly, his words empower Dessa, who *responds* to his *call* to action: 'I kill that white man cause the same reason Mas kill Kaine. Cause I *can*' (p. 224). (Emphasis added.) With the death of Kaine, she senses herself as part of a network of purposeful - not arbitrary - power and struggle. The social and personal inform one another as Dessa gains knowledge of herself and access to larger social issues. Ultimately, it is through her own exercise of power and will to act that Dessa achieves the subversion of the system that oppresses her and her fellow slaves.

Similarly, it is the exercise of her rhetorical power to control her own voice and image which enables Dessa to subvert the narrator's text. She senses that formal discourse - which works for the narrator - works for her no better than the system does. She understands that part of the problem is language and representation - and, most importantly, who controls it. As a writer, the narrator has the power to control reality by controlling social imagery. It is because his language has the power to dispossess Dessa of humanity (just as the system has the power to dispossess her of freedom) that Dessa must challenge the narrator's representation. Her challenge to the narrator's historical record preserves between them an adversarial relationship and, at the same time, expresses Dessa's rejection of a formal discourse which excludes or misrepresents her. In the following exchange, significantly one of the few true dialogues taking place in the text ('She spoke to me of her own accord today, spoke to me, rather than the hot windless air, as had been her custom'), Dessa expresses her rejection of a language which can only perpetuate her imprisonment:

> [*Dessa*:] That writin what you put on that paper? . . . you be writin down what I say? . . . What you gon do wid it?
> [*Narrator*:] I told her cautiously that I would use it in a book I hoped to write.
> [*Dessa*:] Cause why?
> [*Narrator*:] Girl, what I put in this book cannot hurt you now. You've already been tried and judged.
> [*Dessa*:] Then for what you wanna do it?
> [*Narrator*:] I told her that I wrote what I did in the hope of helping others to be happy in the life that has been sent them to live . . .
> [*Dessa*:] You thank . . . you thank what I say now gon hep peoples be happy in the life they sent? If that be true . . . [w]hy I not be happy when I live it? I don't wanna talk no mo. [pp. 230, 231, 234]

Thus, we see that Dessa, who has physically already become a part of a collective struggle, achieves class consciousness in her personal identification with others. The physical autonomy toward which she struggles finds an equivalent expression in her protest against the transposition of her voice into the racist and patriarchal white male discourse which assigns to her and others 'their place' both in discourse and society.

As the story progresses, the narrator discovers himself increasingly haunted by Dessa. His journal entries begin to display an ambivalence, if not a change of attitude, toward his subject. After an earlier session in which he appears moved by Dessa's personal grief over the loss of her husband, the narrator comments, 'It is curious . . . how the negress, well, how she looks in the sun. For a moment today as I watched her I could almost imagine how Vaungham [her previous owner] allowed her to get close enough to stick a knife between his ribs' (p. 229). Hoping to cajole Dessa into disclosing more information by capitalizing upon her feelings, the narrator employs the strategy of 'fram[ing] all of his questions in such a way that Kaine can be referred to some manner'. Although acknowledging, finally, that 'her attachment to this Kaine appears quite sincere', he nevertheless attributes it to 'the basest of physical attraction'. (One suspects that he is, in fact, describing the basis of his own feelings rather than Dessa's.) The narrator, however, apparently begins to consider the humanity of his subject, and in doing so, is driven to rationalize his own actions:

> I cannot summon up all the same sense of contempt with which I first viewed this liaison. I must confess also that I feel some slight twinge - Not of guilt, rather of *compassion* in using her attachment to the young darky as a means of eliciting information from her. But the fact is that my stratagems - while not perhaps of the most noble *type* - are used in the service of a greater good and this consideration must sweep all else before it. (p. 237)

In their meeting of 27 June, the narrator '[looks] down at the pages of [his] notebook, blank save for the day's date, or at her [Dessa]' (p. 231). In juxtaposing the blank page and Dessa, the author symbolizes the futility of the narrator's effort to *capture* Dessa in his text. With perhaps ironic awareness, the narrator ruefully laments at 'how limited [his] vision had become'. Indeed, the limitations of his vision are nowhere more evident than later, during that same session, when he acknowledges the superficiality of his perceptions of Dessa:

> But now I know that the thick-lipped mouth, so savage in its sullen repose, can smile and even utter small jests, that lurking behind her all too often blank gaze is something more than the cunning stubborness which, alone, I first perceived, even noted that her skin, which appeared an ashen black in the light of the root cellar, is the color of strong tea and that even in the shade it is tinged with gold. (p. 239)

Not only does the 'girl' become the 'woman' in his notes, but the narrator, who has not referred to his charge by name throughout his story (suggesting his refusal to recognize her humanity), calls her by name not less than twenty-two times in his last four journal entries. (Significantly, Dessa drops the 'O' from her given name, Odessa, exercising the power not only, in the words of Mary Helen Washington, 'to name one's own experience'[42] in the telling of her own story, but also the power to name oneself, thus asserting her own identity in opposition to that imposed by the narrator.) Indeed, as the narrator leaves to join a posse in pursuit of a group of slave fugitives, he reflects, 'We have much to talk about, Odessa and I, when we resume our conversation.' (p. 244) Later, he continues to 'look forward to resuming my conversations with Odessa. She has a subtle presence, almost an influence which I have only become aware of in its absence.' (p. 244) Ultimately, rather than *possessing* his subject, the narrator himself becomes *possessed* by Dessa: ('[the sheriff] charged that I acted like one possessed').

It is finally with some irony that upon his return in the early morning of 4 July (a date the narrator notes with 'wearied surprise' in his journal), he discovers that Dessa is absent – vanished without any traceable clues to her route of escape. The narrator learns that Dessa's companions have not only eluded his posse, which has combed the countryside in vain pursuit of the fugitives, but that they have managed, moreover, to return and 'spirit away' Dessa. Thus, in the conclusion, Dessa is liberated from bondage as well as from the narrator's text.

The narrator's final representation of Dessa, more than anything else, threatens the system that the narrator seeks to preserve and defend in *The Work*. Gradual changes in the narrator's perceptions confirm that Dessa 'works roots' on the narrator, and in so doing, succeeds in reappropriating her voice and image in what is essentially an act of self-(re)possession. Dessa has escaped from *Roots* and the root cellar – leaving the narrator obsessed by her absence:

> She is gone. Even the smallest clue – but there was nothing, no broken twig to point the direction, no scent which the hound could hold for more than a short distance. Gone. *And I not even aware, not even suspecting, just – just gone.* (p. 248; emphasis added)

The last line suggests that meaning, for the narrator, has been determined exclusively by his own preconceptions. For this reason, he has been a misreader from the very beginning, and Dessa's actions only confirm his misreading. Her escape means freedom for Dessa and her unborn child and, with it, the failure of the narrator's effort. It creates a disruption in the system and a rupture in the preparation of the narrator's text. His sexist, racist, and classist presumptions have obscured for the narrator the character and motivations of his subject. Too late, the narrator realizes that he has underestimated his subject's will and intelligence: 'And to think that she - *she* was so deep as to give never an indication that they [her rescuers] were about.' (p. 246)

In fact, had the narrator been more attentive to Dessa's speaking (singing) text, he might have discovered some clues to her intentions. If Dessa refuses to communicate with the narrator, she does communicate with her fellow slaves in a language devised to mask her meaning. On the morning of her escape, Dessa converses with her emancipators through the lyrics of a spiritual:

> *Tell me sista, tell me, brotha how long will it be?*
> *Tell me, brotha tell me sista how long will it be?*
> *That a poor sinner got to suffer, suffer here?*
> *Tell me, sista tell me brotha when my soul be free?*
> *Tell me, oh, please tell me, when I be free?*
> *And the Lawd calla me home?* (p. 241)

Although the narrator recognizes Dessa's voice and is able to '[figure] out [the] words', he understands neither the meaning nor the motive of Dessa's song. Nor does he even suspect the significance of the response of her 'sistas and brothas':

> *Oh, it won't be long. Say it won't be long*
> *Poor sinner got to suffer here.*
> *Soul's goin to heav'n, soul's gon ride that heav'nly train.*
> *Cause the Lawd have called us home.* (p. 241)

In his failure to discern the secular significance of the spirituals, the narrator misreads them as 'only . . . quaint piece[s] of doggerel which the darkies cunningly adapt from the scraps of scripture they are taught' (p. 236). At best, he regards them simply as 'close harmonic part singing' which he finds 'rather interesting and pleasing to hear'. For Dessa and her interlocutors, however, the spirituals constitute a code necessary to disguise their communication from the whites. Dessa both represents and draws on an enabling tradition of black folk and vernacular discourse, epitomized in the spirituals. According to Geneva Smitherman, 'the oral tradition [in Black America] has served as a fundamental vehicle for gittin ovuh' - which she defines as spiritual and/or material survival. 'That tradition', continues Smitherman, 'preserves the Afro-American heritage and reflects the collective spirit of the race.' In other words, it is the oral tradition which has embodied the collective consciousness necessary to the struggle of the race. Historically, the consciousness and collectivity of the race, engendered by the potent oral tradition, have constituted the principal weapons by which blacks have been able to defend themselves against the technologically superior force of the media and arms controlled by the dominant class.

Significantly, both these concepts, collectivity and consciousness, are keys to understanding the function of the spirituals and the secular songs. The call-response dynamic that has shaped the black oral tradition is based on a process of mutuality which 'requires that one must give if one is to receive, and receiving is actively acknowledging another'.[43] As an 'interactive system', the call-response 'seeks to synthesize speakers and listeners in a unified movement' embodying 'group consciousness, co-operation, and the collective common good'.[44] Unlike the narrator, who uses written language as a means by which to define, control, and establish domination over others, Dessa uses spoken language as a means of interaction and struggle. It is through oral discourse that Dessa, with the help of her companions, plots a successful escape. In the third stanza, Dessa and her companions sing in unison, expressing a unified conscious-ness and affirming a unity of purpose:

> *Good news, Lawd, Lawd, good news.*
> *My brotha got a seat and I so glad.*
> *I hearda from Heav'n today.*
> *Good news, Lawdy, Lawd, Lawd, Good news.*
> *I don't mind what Satan say*
> *Cause I heard, yes I heard, well I heard from heav'n today.* (p. 243)

If formal discourse, for the narrator, separates and subjugates those who are different from the privileged, then oral discourse, for Dessa, creates a unifying bond of struggle and resistance among those defined as different in the dominant discourse. Thus, Dessa's accomplishment, as Williams tells the story, is to infiltrate formal discourse not only through inter-ventionist acts, but, indeed, through an *'out*cry' which draws on a wholly separate (oral and folk) tradition.

Language not only enables Dessa to obscure her intentions from the narrator, and oppose the system which he represents; it also functions more positively as a means of personal enrichment and empowerment. It is through Kaine's blues-like songs, which he would play 'sweet-soft' on his 'banger', that Dessa evokes memories recreating her life with him ('She knew the words; it was his voice that had been the music'):

> *Hey, sweet mamma, this Kaine Poppa*
> *Kaine Poppa callin his woman' name*
> *He can pop his poppa so good*
> *Make his sweet woman take to a cane.* (p. 208)

> *Lawd, gimme wings like Noah's dove*
> *Lawd give me wings like Noah's dove*
> *I'd fly cross these fields to the one I loves*
> *Say, hello darlin; say, how you be.* (p. 226)

The oral and folk tradition, then, provides for Dessa and the slave community (as it does for the author) not only a means of struggle and communication, but an imaginative resource, based on verbal, racial memory.

The unposed question, however, remains: what is to be done with the narrator's journal? Will it evolve from a pre-text into a text? Its initial status is that of a working paper or notebook for a longer, more authoritative public document. Yet the blindness of the recorder compromises the truth value of his journal, and thus, presumably, its usefulness as a blueprint for the anticipated work. If the narrator's journal were to be transposed into *The Work*, its authenticity would be subverted by his misreading of Dessa's character and motivation. The journal is not a reliable text because its author is not a competent reader; his discourse is produced by a false hermeneutic.

Williams's text is about the complex interplay of power, struggle, and discourse – literary and non-literary, oral and written (and to-be-written), public and private, individual and collective. It functions as a powerful critique of Styron, Gray, and other white scholars and writers who, through their historical domination of the print media, have controlled the images of black women. Williams's story not only renders to speech a powerful precedence over writing, but also calls into question the authenticity of white, male, formal discourse on blacks and women and, in the process, suggests to the reader the limitations of literary-historical discourse.

Her work, however, raises two issues which cannot be entirely resolved: (1) Has Williams produced what Stanley Fish calls a 'self-consuming artifact' in that she herself appropriates a form of discourse which her character (Dessa) implicitly and explicitly rejects?[45] Does the author, in other words, discredit the very form of discourse which makes it possible for her to deliver such a forceful critique? (2) Does Williams suggest in her relationship to Styron and in Dessa's relationship to the narrator that white males and black women cannot share a common language? Is she arguing, moreover, that whites do not know how to *read* black speech – and by extension, blacks and their experiences, making it impossible for the white writer to render an authentic portrayal of blacks?

Certainly there is an element of self-subversion in Williams's story in that the author does, in fact, problematize the very form of discourse which she herself replicates, that is, formal discourse and, more specifically, historical fiction. It would seem, however, that she replicates the form for the purpose of subverting a particular practice. While there may exist a paradox in demanding historical truth from a literary text, in which conventional meaning is regarded as immanent rather than referential, Williams's treatment acknowledges the elusiveness of her subject. In her characterization of Dessa, Williams represents an ambiguity and indeterminacy that suggest the essential 'otherness' of any subject, a quality which must ultimately elude any author who bases his or her fictional character on a historical model. It is the impossibility of *knowing* that quality of otherness, explored by the author in her characterization of Dessa, that distinguishes Williams's representation from Styron's.

Moreover, in her own intervention and *'out*cry' to an alternative tradition, Williams's strategy, in a sense, replicates that of her heroine. Williams's treatment, in effect, redefines what has been traditionally regarded as 'historical fiction'. Less a personal and imaginative reconstruction based on the 'official records' of what has happened, historical fiction as a genre, becomes, for Williams, a reconstruction based on other 'non-official' sources of past experience – the oral and folk tradition. It is a process which shifts emphasis from the authority of the written, and closed, solipsistic text (that is, the official record) to the oral, and open, collaborative text. In other words, the historical fiction *writer* enters into a dialogue with an *oral tradition* in a process that not only parallels the call-response pattern in Dessa's spirituals, but that redefines historical fiction itself as a kind of call-response operation. Interestingly, Ellison addresses this very issue in the context of a forum held at the thirty-fourth annual meeting of the Southern Historical Association in 1968:

> If you project in fiction your version of history, then you have an obligation to think about [the] other feed-ins from the common experience which are going to put to question your particular projection of history. I don't think that history is Truth. . . . Here in the United States we have had a political system which wouldn't allow me to tell my story officially. Much of it is not in the history books. Certain historians and untrained observers did their jobs, often very faithfully, but . . . the story they recorded was altered to justify racial attitudes and practices. But somehow, through our Negro American oral tradition . . . these reminders of the past as *Negroes* recalled it found existence and were passed along. Historical figures continued to live in stories or theories about the human and social dynamics of slavery, and the effects of political decisions rendered during Reconstruction. Assertions of freedom and revolts were recalled along with triumphs of labor in the fields and on the dance floor; feats of eating and drinking and of fornication, or religious conversion and physical endurance, and of artistic and athletic achievements. In brief, the broad ramifications of human life as Negroes have experienced it were marked and passed along. *This record exists in oral form and it constitutes the internal history of values by which my people lived even as they were being forced to accommodate themselves to those forces and arrangements of society that were sanctioned by official history. The result has imposed upon Negroes a high sensitivity to the ironies of historical writing and created a profound skepticism concerning the validity of most reports on what the past was like.*[46]

In response to the second issue, that is, whether or not whites can render a convincing and truthful representation of blacks, one can arguably conclude that Williams makes a case that whites will be able to decode neither black speech nor black life unless they first challenge the motives served by the dominant discourse. In one respect, the author provides a model of transformation by herself employing the (formal) discourse of domination in order to resist that same domination. In the process, she confronts the challenge faced by contemporary black writers who wish to preserve the strengths of vernacular discourse and the folk tradition within what has evolved into a formal, literate tradition. Like other modern black writers, Williams has inscribed the vernacular voice within a formal text, thereby transforming both the oral and formal traditions.

While Dessa's narrative interventions and subversions undermine some of the prevailing cultural myths and received notions about black women, Williams's 'Meditations' suggests that we must revise our expectations of white- and male-authored literary and non-literary texts about blacks and women; that we must learn, in the words of Adrienne Rich, '[to enter] an old text from a new critical direction'; and, furthermore, that the act of 'seeing' an old text 'with fresh eyes' is 'an act of survival'. As Rich puts it, 'We need to know the writing of the past, and know it differently than we have ever known it; not to pass on a tradition but to break its hold over us.' In the sense that Rich uses the term, then 're-vision' allows us to reclaim authentic historical and literary models, and in doing so, to liberate ourselves from old stereotypes.[47]

The major significance of Williams's text is that it draws the reader's attention to the representational and interpretative strategies of those who dominate formal discourse. It becomes a decoding device for reading texts by those who control social and literary structures. In this regard, Williams not only reveals the presumptions and pitfalls of racial- and gender-inflected cultural misreadings, but, perhaps more importantly she provides the reader with a model of how to read formal texts in which black and women's voices have been muted, suppressed, or misunderstood.

NOTES

I am grateful to Kathleen Diffley, William Caine, Peter Thornton, and Keneth Kinnamon for their helpful readings of earlier versions of this essay, and especially to Houston Baker for his detailed comments.

1 Sherley Anne Williams's recent novel, *Dessa Rose* (1986), an elaboration of 'Meditations on history', was published after this essay was substantially completed. I treat the novel in a forthcoming work.

2 Clearly, I have drawn on modern critical revisionist strategies. But revisionism, like metaphor, is a term which subsumes much - in this instance, a variety of literary-critical practices. While acknowledging my debt to Harold Bloom's (1973) notions of *misprision* and intertextuality, I prefer to describe my own methods more in terms of *re*reading than *mis*reading and *contra*textuality rather than *inter*textuality. His definition of revisionism notwithstanding, Bloom's strategies appear to emphasize the

generative or, perhaps more accurately, engendering aspects of the text as opposed to the corrective purposes of writing (and reading). My contratextual reading of Williams's novella is designed to demonstrate her deconstruction of the racist and sexist misreadings of an anterior text (regardless of intentionality) in order to reassert a prior (oral and biographical) text. As a corrective gesture, it cuts back through the detritus concealing the contours of the original in order to reclaim the primal experience from the deformation of race and gender-inflected historical-fictional misreadings. Although Williams writes within an intertextual tradition (that is, through textual antecedents), her purpose, in my reading, is to achieve a more accurate representation - or reconstruction - of the original experience. If the relationship between Styron and Turner can be described as creative misreading (*misprision*), I would describe that between Williams and Styron as one of corrective rereading. I am indebted to a conversation with my colleague, Keneth Kinnamon, for a clearer formulation of this strategy.

3 Styron 1967: 'Author's Note'; emphasis added.

4 Gates 1984: 294-6.

5 Styron 1967: 'Author's Note'; emphasis added.

6 See Clarke 1968.

7 Mike Thelwell writes: 'Is it possible . . . for a white southern gentleman to tune in on the impulses, beliefs, emotions, and thought-patterns of a black slave? This miracle of empathy entails an imaginative leap not only into history, but across cultures. It necessitates that writer divorcing himself from that vast mythic tradition about slavery, black people, and history which is so integral a part of his background. Then he has to devise a literary idiom through which to record, since the gentleman and the slave lack common language or experience.' 'Back with the Wind: Mr. Styron and the Reverend Turner', *ibid.*, 80.

8 Davis 1971: 10.

9 See Elkins 1959. Styron writes: 'One of the most striking aspects of the institution [of slavery] is the fact that in 250 years of its existence in America, it was singularly free of organized uprisings, plots, and rebellions. (It is curious that as recently as the late 1940s, scholarly insights were lagging, and I could only have suspected then what has since been made convincing by such historians as . . . Stanley Elkins: that American Negro slavery, unique in its psychological oppressiveness - the worst the world has ever known - was simply so despotic and emasculating as to render organized revolt next to impossible.' Styron, 'This quiet dust', in Duff and Mitchell 1971: 125-6.

10 See Aptheker 1969: 11. Notably, Aptheker contends that Styron's work contains substantial historical distortions: see Aptheker, 'A note on the history', in Duff and Mitchell 1971: 191-5.

11 See n. 2.

12 If Styron assumes the voice of a black slave speaking as Nat Turner himself in the first person, Williams's narrator presumes to speak for Dessa. (What is implicit in Styron - his appropriation of Turner's voice - is explicit in Williams's characterization.) Moreover, while Styron's character speaks standard, formal English in a style that critic Richard Gilman describes as 'novelistic', Williams's heroine preserves the idiom of the black vernacular. See Gates 1984: 286-96.

13 See, for example, Blassingame 1972 and 1977, and Levine 1977.

14 Commenting on the relationship between literary and historical discourse in his
    review of Styron's *Confessions*, Thelwell writes: 'Because the book is both "history"
    and a novel the public mind seems to have invested it with qualities it does not
    necessarily possess. The events and situations are assumed to be accurate because by
    being "historical" they must of necessity be "true". And as the "facts" of history are
    true, so, in a different sense, are the insights (read "symbolic truths") of the novel.'
    Thelwell, in Clarke 1968: 79.
15 Johnson 1980: 126.
16 Styron, in Duff and Mitchell 1971: 126-7.
17 Thomas R. Gray, 'To the Public', in *The Confessions of Nat Turner*, reprinted in the
    Appendix to Clarke 1968: 96.
18 *Ibid.*, 97.
19 Styron, in Duff and Mitchell 1971: 126.
20 Styron, 'Truth and Nat Turner: an exchange', in Duff and Mitchell 1971: 198.
    (Originally published in *The Nation*, 22 April 1968: 543-7.)
21 *Ibid.*, 198-9.
22 Eugene D. Genovese, 'The Nat Turner Case', in Duff and Mitchell 1971: 205.
    (Originally published in *The New York Review of Books*, 12 September 1968: 34-7.)
23 *Ibid.*
24 Quoted in Styron, 'Truth and Nat Turner', in Duff and Mitchell 1971: 199.
25 Thelwell in Clarke 1968: 91.
26 Ralph Ellison's position on the relation of history and literature points to some of the
    problems confronting the novelist: 'I'm all for the autonomy of fiction; that's why
    I say that novelists should leave history alone. But I would also remind us that the
    work of fiction finally comes alive through a collaboration between the reader and the
    writer. . . . If you move far enough into the historical past, you don't have that
    problem. . . . [When writing historical fiction] one, without hedging his bets, has to be
    aware that he does operate within an area dense with prior assumptions.' Ralph
    Ellison, William Styron, Robert Penn Warren, and C. Vann Woodward, 'The uses of
    history in fiction', in West 1985: 130, 131. (Originally published in the *Southern
    Literary Journal* 1 (Spring 1969): 57-90.)
27 Quoted from Davis 'Reflections on the black woman's role in the community of
    slaves' in Williams 1980: 200. All subsequent references are to the edition cited in
    the References. [Emphasis in original.]
28 *Ibid.*, 3.
29 *Ibid.*, 11. Davis bases her account on an event originally cited in Aptheker 1969:
    287-8.
30 See Stepto 1979 for a treatment of the significance of prefatory texts in black narrative
    writing.
31 Williams 1972: 35-6.
32 Critics Robert Stepto and Henry Louis Gates demonstrate the significance of literacy
    and formal discourse in gaining freedom and recognition for the slave. See Stepto
    1979 and Gates 1985: introductory essay. For a different perspective, somewhat
    closer to my own in its emphasis on 'the voice of the unwritten self', see Houston A.
    Baker's 'Autobiographical acts: the voice of the Southern slave' in Baker 1980:
    27-52.

33 Haley 1976.

34 This bit of riffing by Williams on the practice of conjuring (colloquially described as 'root work' in black vernacular discourse) was suggested as a result of my correspondence with Houston Baker.

35 Gabriel Prosser, along with Jack Bowler, planned a slave revolt in Henrico County, Virginia. On 30 August 1800, over 1000 slaves met 'armed with clubs, homemade bayonets, and a few guns'. Their attack on the city was thwarted, however, by a severe storm. Moreover, two slaves informed their master of the plot and Governor Monroe quickly mobilized the state militia. As a consequence, 35 blacks were hanged, 4 escaped, and 1 committed suicide. Gabriel himself was executed on 7 October 1800. Denmark Vesey was a free black carpenter (having purchased his own freedom in 1800) who lived in Charleston, South Carolina. Along with Peter Poyas, Mingo Harth, and others, Vesey made extensive preparations to revolt. Over a period of many months, slaves were recruited by appointed leaders and arms were stored, including 'two hundred and fifty pike heads and bayonets and over three hundred daggers'. Vesey had even written to Santo Domingo for assistance. The revolt was planned to take place on the second Sunday in July 1822, but was moved forward one month because of betrayal. Because many of his followers were miles outside of Charleston, however, Vesey was unable to communicate his change of plans. Ultimately, 139 blacks were arrested, and 49 sentenced to die. Thirty-seven of those condemned were hanged and the others were pardoned. Reportedly estimates of numbers involved range as high as 9000. Cited in Aptheker 1969: 219-26, 267-73.

36 Erikson 1975: 20. In the context of power relations, Michel Foucault defines 'the Other' as 'the one over whom power is exercised'. See Dreyfus and Rabinow 1982, 2nd edn, 1983: 220.

37 Erikson 1975: 20-1.

38 Williams 1972: 35.

39 Baker 1980: 43.

40 See Sandra M. Gilbert and Susan Gubar's discussion of this concept, based on Wolfgang Lederer's notion of woman's tendency to 'kill herself into art', in Gilbert and Gubar 1979: 14-15.

41 If Styron relates his protagonist's sexual ambiguities to the white slave mistress, Williams relates Dessa's sexuality to her slave husband.

42 In Washington 1980, Introduction, 'In pursuit of our own history': xiii.

43 Smitherman 1986: 108.

44 *Ibid.*: 109.

45 Fish 1974.

46 Ellison et al., in West 1985: 125-6; emphasis added.

47 Rich 1979: 35.

REFERENCES

Aptheker, Herbert 1969. *American Negro Slave Revolts*. New York: International Publishers. [Originally published 1943.]

Baker, Houston A., Jr 1980. *The Journey Back*. Chicago: University of Chicago Press.

Blassingame, John W. 1972. *The Slave Community*. New York: Oxford University Press.

Bloom, Harold 1973. *The Anxiety of Influence*. New York: Oxford University Press.

Bloom, Harold 1975. *A Map of Misreading*. New York: Oxford University Press.

Clarke, John Henrik 1968. *William Styron's NAT TURNER: Ten Writers Respond*. Boston: Beacon Press.

Davis, Angela 1971. 'Reflections on the black woman's role in the community of slaves', *The Black Scholar* (December): 13-15.

Dreyfus, Hubert L. and Rabinow, Paul 1982. *Michel Foucault: Beyond Structuralism and Hermeneutics*. Chicago: University of Chicago Press. 2nd ed. 1983. [This text by Foucault did not appear in print until published in this edition in English; the section from which the epigraph at the head of my chapter is quoted was translated by Leslie Sawyer, and appears on p. 255.]

Duff, John B. and Mitchell, Peter M. 1971. *The Nat Turner Rebellion: The Historical Event and the Modern Controversy*. New York: Harper and Row.

Elkins, Stanley M. 1959. *Slavery: A Problem in American Institutional and Intellectual Life*. Chicago: University of Chicago Press.

Erikson, Erik H. 1975. *Life History and the Historical Moment*. New York: W. W. Norton.

Fish, Stanley E. 1974. *Self-Consuming Artifacts*. Berkeley and Los Angeles: University of California Press.

Foucault, Michel: see Dreyfus and Rabinow 1982.

Gates, Henry Louis, Jr (ed.) 1985. ' "Race", writing and difference', *Critical Inquiry* 12: 1 (Autumn).

Gates, Henry Louis, Jr (ed.) 1984. *Black Literature and Literary Theory*. New York and London: Methuen.

Gilbert, Sandra M. and Gubar, Susan 1979. *The Madwoman in the Attic: The Woman Writer and the Nineteenth-Century Literary Imagination*. New Haven and London: Yale University Press.

Gray, Thomas R. 1968. *The Confessions of Nat Turner*, repr. in the Appendix to Clarke 1968. [Originally published in 1832 as *The Confessions of Nat Turner, the Leader of the Late Insurrection in Southampton, Va., As Fully and Voluntarily Made to Thomas R. Gray*. Richmond: Thomas R. Gray.]

Haley, Alex 1976. *Roots*. Garden City, NY: Doubleday.

Johnson, Barbara 1980. *The Critical Difference: Essays in the Contemporary Rhetoric of Reading*. Baltimore: Johns Hopkins University Press.

Levine, Lawrence W. 1977. *Black Culture and Black Consciousness: Afro-American Thought from Slavery to Freedom*. New York: Oxford University Press.

Neal, Larry 1985. *The Glorious Monster in the Bell of the Horn*, *Callaloo 23*, 8.1 (Winter): *Larry Neal: A Special Issue*, ed. Kimberley W. Benston.

Rich, Adrienne 1979. 'When We Dead Awaken: writing as re-vision', in *On Lies, Secrets and Silence: Selected Prose 1966-1978*. New York: W. W. Norton.

Smitherman, Geneva 1986. *Talkin and Testifyin*. Detroit: Wayne State University Press.

Stepto, Robert B. 1979. *From Behind the Veil: A Study of Afro-American Narrative*. Urbana: University of Illinois Press.

Styron, William 1967. *The Confessions of Nat Turner*. New York: Random House.

Washington, Mary Helen (ed.) 1980. *Midnight Birds: Stories by Contemporary Black Women Writers*. Garden City, NY: Anchor Books/Doubleday.

Williams, Sherley Anne 1972. *Give Birth to Brightness*. New York: Dial Press.

Williams, Sherley Anne 1980. 'Meditations on history', in *Midnight Birds: Stories by Contemporary Black Women Writers*, ed. Mary Helen Washington: Garden City, NY: Anchor Books/Doubleday.

Williams, Sherley Anne 1986. *Dessa Rose*. New York: William Morrow.

2

In No Man's Land: (W)Riting Gender and Race

George P. Cunningham

And the way we saw it, America ain't entered the question at all when it come to our land: Sapphira was African-born, Buscombe Wade was from Norway, and it was the 18 & 23'ing that went down between them two put deeds in our hands. And we wasn't even Americans when we got it - was slaves. And the laws about slaves not owning nothing in Georgia and South Carolina don't apply, 'cause the land wasn't then - and isn't now - in either of them places. When there was lots of cotton here, and we baled it up and sold it beyond the bridge, we paid our taxes to the U.S. of A. And we keeps account of all the fishing that's done and sold beyond the bridge, all the little truck farming. And later when we had to go over there to work or our children went, we paid taxes out of them earnings. We pays taxes on the telephone lines and Georgia and South Carolina ain't seeing the shine off a penny for our land, our homes, our roads, or our bridge.

Gloria Naylor, *Mama Day*

To put discourse into question is to reject the existing order. It is to renounce, in effect, the identity principle, the principles of unity and resemblance which allow for the constitution of phallocentric society. It means choosing marginality (with an emphasis on the *margins*) in order to designate one's difference, a difference no longer conceived of as an inverted image or as a double, but as alterity, multiplicity, heterogeneity. It means laying claim to an absolute difference, posited not within the norm but against and *outside* the norms.

Josette Féral, 'The powers of difference'

As a cultural construct deeply embedded in the American experience, the idea of the wilderness reveals fundamental national contests. This transformative journey from bondage to freedom - this self-privileging trope of both the settlers of New England and the enslaved blacks of the South - has recently been revised to describe the plurality of approaches of contemporary criticism. That white men, white women, and black men have already made expeditionary journeys into the wilderness, possessing it by mapping its terrain in starkly different ways, means that the black feminist critic, among 'others', writes her subject in an already sharply contested ground, a wilderness more aptly called by its alarming name: no man's land.[1] Sandra Gilbert and Susan Gubar, in their most recent study of women's writing, use this term as it is understood in the geography of twentieth-century warfare (and diplomacy) as the land between the cross-fire of rival armies: 'a vexed terrain – in which scattered armies of men and women all too often clash by day and by night'.[2] In the nineteenth century, it referred to a section of land bordering Texas but remaining outside of any effective legal jurisdiction; it was temporarily excused from manifest destiny for almost half a century. In this sense, no man's land is also the land beyond our material, discursive, and theoretical control: the land of the other, the untamed animal, the wild (mad) woman and wild man, the land that threatens as easily to feralize as to transform social organization and discourses.[3]

In framing my understanding of Mae Henderson's reading of Sherley Anne Williams's 'Meditations' within the territory of no man's land, I mean that zone of perceived otherness, transformation, and discursive struggle that locates the black feminist critic in relationship to a variety of historical and contemporary discourses that marginalize blacks and women. I also mean to reflect my understanding of Henderson's method-ological mode of address, a mode that problematizes those discourses. No man's land is a trope whose history still resonates strongly in consider-ations of gender and race. While the early white settlers *wrote* their trope into history, the slaves *sang* theirs, a difference which accounts for both Henderson's and my 'troubling' the notion of (w)riting in our titles. For black writers and critics, the oral tradition – that site of language beyond the text – identifies a zone of racial identity that informs, calls, and in-terrogates identities constituted through writing. As Williams notes, Afro-American literature is 'created within the framework of multiple relationships and the tension between the white literary and the black oral tradition'.[4] These multiple relations locate the black male and female writer and critic in an in-between zone where neither the oral nor the literary alone is seen as a completely adequate form of representation.

In mapping her own terrain, the black woman often locates herself discursively in a zone between white men, white women, and black men; she stands at a distance from black men, by virtue of gender, from white women, by virtue of race, and from white men by virtue of gender and race. As Henderson reads 'Meditations' as a discursive battleground, so I conceive of '(W)riting *The Work* and working the rites' as a strategy for reading that recovers the suppressed subjectivity of a black woman from contemporary discourses, including not only the white male discourse which marginalizes both blacks and women, but also discourses centered around blacks as men and women as white. As Barbara Omolade suggests:

> the question of black women's relationship to feminism has been raised primarily to discover why black women have not joined the women's movement in large numbers and have been generally hostile to feminism. In other words, it has been raised as a strategic and organizational issue by white feminists in order to develop better ways to recruit black women into their movement. The question rarely gets raised as a political or theoretical issue seeking greater clarity and understanding of black women and white women: their differences and similarities, their separate histories and possible common interests.[5]

What Omalode says about the relationship of black women to feminism, or what I would designate as the discourse of feminism, is also true about the relationship of black women to the discourse of race: in both cases her voice is perceived as a threat to the urgency of unity. To recast this concern in terms more theoretical, the voice of the black woman threatens the unity and the 'liberating' agendas of the discourse of race with the discourse of feminism, even as that voice threatens the unity and the 'liberating' agendas of the discourse of feminism with the discourse of race.

Henderson's reading is centered around concerns with 'power relations and discourse' - 'the struggle to dominate as well as to resist domination' - that are very similar to those Barbara Christian discusses in 'The race for theory'.[6] Christian argues that blacks have always engaged in theorizing, but in 'narrative forms, in the stories we create, in riddles and proverbs'. From the vantage point of what I am interpreting as the Afro-American oral tradition, Christian argues as well that the modes of conceptualization and the language of theory are formally 'alien', that recent critical theory is 'as hegemonic as the world which it attacks', and that the liberating strategies of various critical theories are themselves quests for power. She believes that literature possesses 'the possibilities of rendering the world as large and as complicated as I experienced it, as sensual as I knew it was. In literature I sensed the possibility of the integration of feeling/knowledge, rather than the split between the abstract and the emotional in which Western philosophy inevitably indulged' (p. 229). This integration, she argues, allows the black woman to 'pursue herself as subject'. In many ways, Henderson's reading of the hegemonic tendencies of critical theory is similar; yet, she seeks to establish the ground for a black female subjectivity *through*, rather than *against*, contemporary theory. Reading 'Meditations' as an embodiment of the battle of discourse and power, Henderson's method situates the black woman's text in an arena of struggle, rather than a zone of integration.

Henderson proposes to read that struggle in a text that centers on the multiple other of American society: the black woman slave, a figure who 'speaks' at once of race, gender, and class oppression and a subjectivity that inscribes her own journey from slavery to freedom. What is metaphor for the modern state of criticism – the journey from slavery to freedom – becomes a 'primal experience' for Henderson, a trope of origins that must be recovered from 'the deformation of race and gender-inflected historical-fictional misreadings'. Her approach to 'Meditations' is a sophisticated close reading informed by theoretical considerations that are in the background rather than the foreground of her essay. In order to talk about her method, I would like to bring her descriptive term for it – contratextualism – forward from her rather long second footnote. To recover a black female subjectivity, Henderson suggests that we should examine the strategies of revision black women writers employ. In exploring Williams's novella, Henderson explicates a range of nineteenth- and twentieth-century texts that include primary historical documents, spirituals, historical essays, and historical fiction. In her reading she emphasizes Williams's dialogic incorporation and subversion of modes of discourse that marginalize blacks and women. This revision through dialogic struggle is Henderson's contratextualism, a reading strategy that eschews the genealogical conception of the relationship between texts implied by the term intertextualism in favor of a conception of a conflictual relationship between texts. While I could disagree with certain details of her reading, I am more interested, in this context, in exploring her method and its implications for discussions of race and gender.

The horizontal planes of her first model of the interaction of discourses in 'Meditations' charts what can be read as three different relationships between orality and literacy in the novella. Derived from a reading of a work that self-consciously addresses issues of writing, subjectivity, and power, these planes should also be read as paradigms for the relationship of the other – the black, the woman, and the slave – to the text. The top plane, that of Nat Turner, Thomas Gray and William Styron, is the path of suppression that renders the oral slave an object in white male discourse. The middle plane, that of slave woman, Angela Davis and Sherley Anne Williams, is the path of revision that seeks to restore a lost oral subjectivity. The bottom plane, that of Dessa and the narrator, is the path of the dialogic struggle between oral subjectivity and literary hegemony. Henderson's reading draws our attention to the way in which the successful struggle of orality on the bottom plane critiques and deconstructs the successful domination by literacy on the top plane and enables Williams's revisionary strategy.

Henderson's further explication of these multifaceted relationships between and within these paradigms also indicate the complexity of the way gender and race interact in her essay. Her reading of 'Meditations' as a subversion of the relationships established among Turner, Gray, and Styron problematizes the neatness of the theoretical boundaries between oppression based on sex and oppression based on race. There exists already a tradition of reading the Turner and Styron relationship as modeling a specific racial oppression.[7] In rereading that relationship into the interaction between Dessa and the narrator, that model has crossed the border from a racial discourse to a discourse that focuses on the suppression of women. In doing so, Henderson foregrounds the way the white male narrator of 'Meditations' uses terms of biological (racial) difference to diminish Dessa's status as a person and a woman and the way William Styron uses terms of (biological) gender differences to diminish Nat Turner's status as a man. That the white male can apply both terms of gender and racial difference to black women and black men suggests the fluidity and the transmutability of the terms of these discourses. Throughout this essay, Henderson tends to conflate rather than distinguish between marginalization based on race, marginalization based on sex, and marginalization based on class. Perhaps in reading a narrative with a different focus, especially an intra-racial focus, these categories may interact in very different ways, but within the context of the narrator's relation to Dessa, a black woman slave, these categories of marginalization cannot be seen as separable. Henderson seems, here, less concerned with elaborating a theory of reading that privileges the categories of race and gender, than with developing a strategy of reading that is located in a place – that of the black woman – that allows her to explore the issues of language and power that prescribe and inscribe that place and the strategies of language and power that enable escape from those prescriptions and inscriptions.

The Afro-American oral tradition seems to me to provide that enabling center for Henderson's essay, a center that allows her to subsume issues of race, gender, and class oppression in terms of the interaction of discourses. I find her treatment of the oral tradition the most theoretically provocative part of her essay. That treatment differs markedly from traditional examinations of 'folklore in literature'.[8] This latter approach to reading focuses on the use by an author of forms, themes, and linguistic style from the oral tradition to give shape to a literary work. In doing so, the author's self-conscious mastery of form is emphasized, while varying degrees of continuity between a people's oral and literary traditions are proposed. As Gene Bluestein suggests, for Americans the study of folklore in literature provided 'a foundation for a national culture, . . . a legitimacy for American English (and vernacular diction) as well as the reaction against the subservience to European (and especially British) tradition'.[9] Henderson, however, treats the oral tradition as an independent discourse, and therefore emphasizes the discontinuity between the oral and the literary traditions. This approach to orality leads her to treat, in the case of 'Meditations', the forms, themes and language from the oral tradition as bringing into the constellation of the novella the vision of the Afro-American slave community. It becomes a place from which Dessa can speak as a whole person and fight discourses that attempt to marginalize her. It is a zone beyond the discursive control of white males that gives Dessa a strong sense of herself, a sense of relationship to a community, and a strategy for attaining her physical and textual freedom.

While it would be easy to argue that Henderson's notion of the role of the oral tradition is specific to Williams's text, I would like to make a case for the possibility of a broader application. To do so I suggest that Henderson's term 'contratextuality' not only provides a way of reading the relationship of texts to texts but can also profitably provide a way of understanding the oral tradition itself and the relationship of that tradition to texts. In this context, I am quibbling with Henderson's labeling of Dessa's discourse as a 'speaking (singing) *text*' [emphasis mine]. In fact the rest of Henderson's reading is based on the premise that the oral tradition is not governed by the same rules as the written tradition. It is just such a nontextuality or contratextuality that provides Dessa with a form of reasoning and a community that is beyond the narrator's white, male, and text-based imagination.

Rather than following contemporary criticism's expansion of the notion of texts to cover ever-increasing territory, I would follow Henderson's direction and expand the notion of contratextuality. As Henderson draws on the work of Geneva Smitherman and Houston Baker, I find Walter Ong's description of the fundamental differences between orality and literacy useful in charting the ways an oral discourse constitutes a way of understanding and describing the world that differs from a text-dominated vision. Ong describes literacy as a way of interpreting the world centered in vision, and orality as one centered in sound. In what he calls a 'sound-dominated verbal economy' there are no words outside of the act of speaking and therefore that economy does not make a distinction between words and acts, the word can not be closed off from the ongoing context of speaking and listening. Orality in this sense '*rites*', meaning the interweaving of the ordering of words with the ordering of deeds that usually describes a religious ceremony. It does not seek to look at words as ideas but rather as ordinary or extraordinary gestures in a day-to-day context. Ong further suggests that 'the fact that oral peoples commonly and in all likelihood universally consider words to have magical potency is clearly tied in, at least unconsciously, with their sense of the word as necessarily spoken, sounded, and hence power-driven.' Orality then is contratextual in its nature, in that its *riting* refuses the imaginative and social enclosures of *writing*.[10]

I would also suggest another use of the term 'contratextual' to talk about Henderson's strategy of reading orality. In this context, orality does not provide a repository of spoken texts that can be incorporated in the literary work; it does not provide a genealogical relationship between the oral and the literary but constantly points away from the literary – regardless of the author's intentions – to communities of speakers that are quite often marginalized by the words of texts. The use of the oral tradition by an author can be read, as Henderson does here, as situating the work contratextually in a struggle between the world of literacy and oral discourses. Further, to suggest that the oral tradition is a discourse, then, is equally to suggest its location in the social organization of a community of speakers. That orality sustains and organizes the distribution of local knowledge among these speakers. Since that oral tradition is located within a very specific community, it 'specifies' its societal history, and represents a collective and indeed political unconscious.[11] As such, it forms a discourse that may be dominated by the world of the written word, but is at the same time resistant to the power of literary authority.

Just as Dessa is able to escape the narrator's texts, Henderson's reading is suggestive of a way in which the presence of orality can be read to deconstruct models of literary authority and indeed the very notion of a singular literary authority. For one version of the Afro-American narrative, the move from orality (illiteracy) to literacy is ontological, is deeply embedded in the primal journey from slavery to freedom, and creates a meta-narrative of individual and racial uplift. In the nineteenth-century male slave narratives, there is strong tension between writing and orality with the path toward identity represented – in what Robert Stepto calls a 'narrative of ascent' – as the trajectory of literacy. That narrative 'launches an "enslaved" and semi-literate figure on a ritualized journey to a symbolic North; that journey is charted through spatial expressions of social structure, invariably systems of signs that the questing figure must read in order to be both increasingly literate and increasingly free.'[12] In this narrative, literacy is equated with freedom and illiteracy (orality) with bondage. Implicated, often self-consciously, however, in the journey toward literacy is an ascension to authority and to the privilege of authorship.[13] The narrative of ascension as a model for liberation becomes also the gesture in the Afro-American tradition that claims white male privileges for the black male. As Bell Hooks puts it, 'many black men who express the greatest hostility toward the white male power structure are often eager to gain access to that power. Their expressions of rage and anger are more a reaction against the fact that they have not been allowed full participation in the power game.'[14] Henderson's reading charts an alternate journey from slavery to freedom for Dessa. The slave woman's orality is no longer negative, the absence of literacy and the equivalent of bondage. Rather, the text represents bondage and orality is the zone of freedom. Orality viewed as a liberated and liberating zone makes 'Meditations' a commentary on and revision of the slave narrative; and Dessa's journey is ultimately a return to communal (self)-authorship rather than a flight into individualistic authority.

In a larger sense, Henderson's understanding of orality as a discourse demonstrates its centrality in understanding people who are marginalized in traditional written discourses and suggests the ways in which the absence of a notion of orality limits the power of contemporary theory to demonstrate a central aspect of the ordering power of language. A singular reference to Western texts and to *texts in general* circumscribes the flow of alterity, heterogeneity and difference contemporary criticism claims to liberate within the bounds of a Western, male and literate textual universe. If, as Fredric Jameson argues, the textual universe is merely the victorious side of a discursive struggle and texts 'cannot be properly assigned their relational place in a dialogic system without the restoration or artificial reconstruction of the voice to which they were initially opposed', then Henderson's contratextualism calls attention not only to the struggle for power within the textual universe but also to discursive struggles between the worlds of textual discourse and the oral worlds of women, blacks, and the working class.[15] She leaves us with the creatively 'troubled' word *(w)riting* which indicates a zone of interplay and struggle between texts and between oral and written discourses. These struggles create a free zone in which Henderson as a critic is bound neither by the singular focus on gender nor by a singular focus on race, and her subject, the black woman slave, is read as figuring her own journey from bondage in discourses to freedom.

NOTES

1 I have in mind here Geoffrey H. Hartman's *Criticism in the Wilderness* (1980); Elaine Showalter's 'Feminist criticism in the wilderness', in Showalter 1985: 243-70; and Henry Louis Gates's 'Criticism in de jungle', in Gates 1984: 1-24, as symbolic of that mapping.
2 Gilbert and Gubar 1987.
3 Flexner 1980: 411-12. My vision of the wild man, wild women, and the wilderness as the 'wild zone' is shaped by Hayden White's 'Forms of wildness: archaeology of an idea' in White 1978: 150-82, and by Dixon 1987.
4 Williams 1977: 542.
5 Omolade 1980: 247.
6 Christian 1989.
7 Henderson cites Clarke 1968.
8 For a complex discussion of the use of folklore by Zora Neale Hurston and Ralph Ellison, two Afro-American writers most familiar with and influenced by the oral tradition, see Robert Hemenway's 'Are you a flying lark or a setting dove?' and Robert O'Meally's 'Riffs and rituals: folklore in the work of Ralph Ellison', both in Fisher and Stepto 1979: 122-52, 153-69. Perhaps the most sophisticated treatment of the oral tradition in literature is Baker 1984.
9 Bluestein 1972: 15.
10 Ong 1982: 32, 73-4.

11 Susan Willis borrows the term from Zora Neale Hurston and suggests: ' "specifying" represents a form of narrative integrity. Historically, it speaks for a noncommodified relationship to language, a time when the slippage between words and meaning would not be tolerated.' Willis 1987: 16.

12 Stepto 1979: 167. Carby (1987) reminds us that in the nineteenth century women like Pauline Hopkins, Anna Julia Cooper and Frances E. W. Harper were equally committed to literacy as a means of 'racial uplift'.

13 Henry Louis Gates (1987a) gives a thorough discussion of the relationship between literacy and being for Afro-Americans in the nineteenth century.

14 Hooks 1981: 94.

15 Jameson 1981: 85. See also Walter J. Ong who suggests that most new critical theorists are exemplars of 'text-bound thinking': 1982: 160-74.

REFERENCES

Baker, Houston A., Jr 1980. *The Journey Back: Issues in Black Literature and Criticism*. Chicago: University of Chicago Press.

Baker, Houston A., Jr 1984. *Blues, Ideology and Afro-American Literature: A Vernacular Theory*. Chicago: University of Chicago Press.

Bluestein, Gene 1972. *The Voice of the Folk: Folklore and American Literary Theory*. Amherst: University of Massachusetts Press.

Carby, Hazel V. 1987. *Reconstructing Womanhood: The Emergence of the Afro-American Woman Novelist*. New York: Oxford University Press.

Christian, Barbara 1980. *Black Women Novelists: The Development of a Tradition*. Westport, CT: Greenwood Press.

Christian, Barbara 1989. 'The race for theory', in *Gender and Theory: Dialogues on Feminist Criticism*, ed. Linda Kauffman. Oxford and New York: Basil Blackwell.

Clarke, John Henrik 1968. *William Styron's NAT TURNER: Ten Writers Respond*. Boston: Beacon Press.

Cook, Michael G. 1984. *Afro-American Literature in the Twentieth Century: The Achievement of Intimacy*. New Haven: Yale University Press.

Dixon, Melvin 1987. *Ride Out the Wilderness: Geography and Identity in Afro-American Literature*. Urbana: University of Illinois Press.

Féral, Josette 1985. 'The powers of difference', in *The Future of Difference*, ed. Hester Eisenstein and Alice Jardine. New Brunswick: Rutgers University Press.

Fisher, Dexter and Stepto, Robert B. (eds) 1979. *Afro-American Literature: The Reconstruction of Instruction*. New York: Modern Language Association of America.

Flexner, Stuart Berg 1980. *I Hear America Talking*. New York: Touchstone Books.

Gates, Henry Louis, Jr (ed.) 1984. *Black Literature and Literary Theory*. New York: Methuen.

Gates, Henry Louis, Jr 1987a. *Figures in Black: Words, Signs, and the 'Racial' Self*. New York: Oxford University Press.

Gates, Henry Louis, Jr (ed.) 1987b. *'Race,' Writing and Difference*. Chicago: University of Chicago Press.

Gilbert, Sandra and Gubar, Susan 1987. *No Man's Land: The Place of the Woman Writer in the Twentieth Century Vol. I: The War of Words.* New Haven: Yale University Press.

Hartman, Geoffrey H. 1980. *Criticism in the Wilderness.* New Haven: Yale University Press.

Hooks, Bell 1981. *Ain't I A Woman: Black Women and Feminism.* Boston: South End Press.

Jameson, Fredric 1981. *The Political Unconscious: Narrative as a Socially Symbolic Act.* Ithaca: Cornell University Press.

Naylor, Gloria 1988. *Mama Day.* New York: Ticknor and Fields.

Omolade, Barbara 1980. 'Black women and feminism', in *The Future of Difference*, ed. Hester Eisenstein and Alice Jardine: New Brunswick: Rutgers University Press: 247-57.

Ong, Walter J. 1982. *Orality and Literacy: The Technologizing of the Word.* New York: Methuen.

Showalter, Elaine 1985. *The New Feminist Criticism: Essays on Women, Literature and Theory.* New York: Pantheon Books.

Smith, Sidonie 1974. *Where I'm Bound: Patterns of Slavery and Freedom in Black American Autobiography.* Westport, CT: Greenwood Press.

Stepto, Robert B. 1979. *From Behind the Veil: A Study of Afro-American Narrative.* Urbana: University of Illinois Press.

White, Hayden 1978. *Tropics of Discourse.* Baltimore: Johns Hopkins University Press.

Williams, Sherley Anne 1977. 'The blues roots of contemporary Afro-American poetry', *Massachusetts Review*, 18 (Autumn): 542-54.

Williams, Sherley Anne 1980. 'Meditations on history', in *Midnight Birds: Stories by Contemporary Black Women Writers*, ed. Mary Helen Washington. Garden City, NY: Anchor Books/Doubleday.

Willis, Susan 1987. *Specifying: Black Women Writing the American Experience.* Madison: University of Wisconsin Press.

3

A Mindless Man-driven Theory Machine: Intellectuality, Sexuality and the Institution of Criticism

James J. Sosnoski

A male perspective, assumed to be 'universal,' has dominated fields of knowledge.

Gayle Greene and Coppélia Kahn, *Making a Difference*

I should hope eventually for the erection of intelligent standards of criticism.

John Crowe Ransom, 'Criticism, Inc.'

To be signed with a woman's name doesn't necessarily make a piece of writing feminine. It could quite well be masculine writing, and conversely, the fact that a piece of writing is signed with a man's name does not in itself exclude femininity.

Hélène Cixous, 'Castration or decapitation?'

The male machine is a special kind of being, different from women, children, and men who don't measure up. He is functional, designed mainly for work. He is programmed to tackle jobs, override obstacles, attack problems, overcome difficulties, and always seize the offensive. He will take on any task that can be presented to him in a competitive framework, and his most important positive reinforcement is victory. . . . this ideology makes competition the guiding principle of moral and intellectual, as well as economic, life. It tells us that the general welfare is served by the self-interested clash of ambitions and ideas . . .

Marc Feigen Fasteau, *The Male Machine*

This is an essay about the tie between the institutional construction of intellectuality and the social construction of sexuality. Let me start with error.

Knowing that we do not know is knowledge. And further, knowing that what one thought one knew is no longer believable is the most significant form of knowing. Just as problems, in some sense, precede solutions and questions precede answers, so not-knowing, including not-knowing-one-does-not-know, precedes knowing. This is the precondition upon which an intellectual comes to know. She acknowledges that a problem remains a problem, that an answer does not answer. She acknowledges that she is in error. For her, paradoxically, being in error is not being wrong. Error, in this case, is heuristic. By contrast, the traditional critic, formed by a long anti-intellectual past, insists that what he already thinks will suffice. This is an essay about his willingness not to know.

Indeed, to err is human. We use many words for this contingency. Realizing the inevitability of changing our minds, we speak of making mistakes, being incorrect, finding ourselves wrong, and ridding ourselves of falsehoods. In each case, we offer reasons for changing what we believe, think and/or do. And what would the world be like if we didn't? Cultures change because persons attempt to alter unwelcome states of affairs, to transform errors into questions, to make right what was wrong, to rethink what is false. To be human is to err. Only fools believe they know more than they do not know. This is an essay about resisting change by restricting error.

Error is the state of believing what is untrue, wrong, incorrect, or mistaken. Living with error is not a simple state of affairs. Our use of the word encompasses and often combines a wide range of faults. 'Error' implies 'deviation from truth, accuracy, correctness, right'.[1] It is the broadest term in the following comparisons. On one side of the semantic spectrum, error is understood as 'a blunder, a slip, a *faux pas*, a boner'. These are 'mistakes'. The word 'mistake' suggests an error resulting from 'carelessness, inattention, misunderstanding'. It does not strongly imply wrong-doing. 'Incorrect' mostly means not correct. Since correctness refers to 'adherence to conventionality' (correct behavior), incorrect suggests little more than deviation from convention. It is a comment upon how accurate, precise or exact one is in performing some predesigned task. 'Wrong', on the other hand, in its primary sense, means 'not morally right or just; sinful; wicked; immoral' and, in a derived sense, 'not in accordance with an established standard, previous arrangement, given intention'. If you are wrong, it is because you 'oppress, persecute, aggrieve, or abuse someone'. Wrongs are offenses that should be punished. At the other end of the spectrum of error from a mistake is the word 'false', the most abstract and legal sense of error. 'False', whose root sense is

'deception', primarily means 'not true' (as in the phrase 'a false argument', *WNWD*). Falsehood refers to 'anything that is not in essence that
which it purports to be'. When deception is involved, the synonyms for
'false' are 'sham', 'counterfeit', 'bogus', and 'fake'. Given such contrasting ideas of error, it would seem that, when persons are incorrect, it is
not because they are sinful; that, when statements are false, it is not
because they are immoral. In the institution of criticism, however, these
terms appear to be conflated in judgments that incorrect statements are
wrong because they are false. This is an essay about a particular conflation
of error termed 'falsification'.

In this essay, I focus upon the institutional use of the word 'false' as a
term paired with 'true'. In particular, I focus upon the judgment that
critical arguments are 'false' as opposed to 'true'. The distinction between
an unsound and a sound argument is the only condition upon which
literary study as a discipline can be said to 'accumulate knowledge'.
Hence, 'falsification', 'falsifiability', 'verification', and 'verifiability' are
crucial theoretical concerns. Since, in practice, verification is the result of
falsification, I will focus upon the latter.[2] In literary studies, falsification is
a judgment that takes the general form of the utterance: 'Professor X is
"mistaken/incorrect/wrong" when he . . .' Correlatively, the falsifiability
of critical discourse is the condition of possibility for grades, ranks, publications.[3] These uses of the concept false depend upon a belief upon which,
in turn, the institution of criticism depends: that a claim about a text can
be proven false. Since this belief is an idealization of inquiry and therefore
an abstraction of it, I have coined the term 'falsificity' to identify the
particular conflation of errors upon which the institution of criticism is
based. In short, falsificity is the principle that it is logically wrong (and
therefore culpable and punishable) to mistake the incorrect for the correct.
I use the term 'wrong' in glossing 'falsificity' to emphasize that, in the
institution of criticism, critical arguments which are judged false are
judged so not on purely logical grounds but on the grounds that they are
'sham, counterfeit, bogus or fake' discourses and therefore punishable.
False arguments are construed as discourses 'not in essence what they
purport to be', that is, not logical. Since they are proffered as criticism,
they are instances of counterfeit discourses. According to the principle of
falsificity, to submit as criticism a discourse that is not logical is wrong
and hence to be punished – to be marked by an 'F', to be cast out of
editorial houses, to be denied an award. My critique of this principle is
that it encourages critics to disagree with each other in ways that do not

especially differ from familial quarreling wherein the keeper of the Logos is the Father who chastises his children. This is a paper about the construction of intellectuality as competitive quarreling.

In this essay, I shall not only try to show that, far from being an impersonal, detached, logical judgment, falsification is a rationalization of academic competition, but, more significantly, that it is a device for maintaining the patriarchal *status quo*. Ordinarily, the identification of error leads to useful changes. (Problems are resolved; thus, a negative state of affairs is changed.) But, paradoxically, changes in a 'system' can be prohibited by defining alternatives to it as errors. (It's wrong, so don't do it!) In the institution of criticism, for example, one is instructed to avoid false arguments, that is, to avoid illogic. This instruction seems thoroughly plausible until one recognizes that, in literary study, the identification of falsehood (illogic) reflects the social construction of the feminine as 'man's specular Other'[4] and thus maintains the patriarchal *status quo*. This is an essay about the oppression of women.

Error can be heuristic. But, falsificity makes error a punishable form of wrong-doing. When we consider that it is a central theoretical assumption in a patriarchal institution hierarchically structured by competition, it can be described as a 'mindless, man-driven theory machine' designed to stamp out alternatives to the system it regulates by regarding them as merely feminine.

The construction of intellectuality in the institution of criticism

The phrase 'traditional literary criticism' refers to a multitude of critics who differ widely among themselves. It is, nonetheless, a useful phrase because it designates a common form of argumentation. Nor is this an accident of history. The critics who have worked in the 'modern American university', which, Laurence Veysey argues in his *The Emergence of the American University*, took its shape shortly after the turn of the century, are trained in a common form of argumentation.[5] It is structured by an informal logic whose first articulator was Aristotle. In it, claims are supported by evidence and therefore can be verified. It is requisite in this tradition for critics to discriminate between correct and incorrect readings. For example, in *A Handbook to Literature*, the most widely used of its kind, we read of argumentation that 'its purpose is to convince a reader or hearer by establishing the truth or falsity of a proposition'.

Traditional argumentation has long-standing protocols. Most literary students trained in it, have been formed by its scholasticism. Dissertations, for example, follow a pattern reminiscent of the treatises of medieval theologians: 'Most rhetoricians recognized five parts for the usual argumentative discourse: *exordium*, *narratio*, *confirmatio* or *probatio*, *refutatio*, and *peroratio*.'[6] Before a traditional critic proves his own case ('confirmatio'), he gives the history of preceding arguments ('narratio') and afterward refutes the likely objections ('refutatio'). Traditional papers, if only in the first footnote, still begin with reviews of the scholarship, most of which is falsified in order to set the stage for the author's view. Footnotes – many of which, as Stephen Nimis points out, have no logical relationship to the argument they footnote[7] – are either formulaic gestures toward verification ('confirmatio') or falsification ('refutatio').

To our post-modern sensibilities, the theory of falsification that provides a basis for traditional criticism is recognizably 'modern'. As I implied above, in this essay the term 'modern' refers to the historical period characterized by the infusion of 'discipline' (in Foucault's sense) into the structure of Western society. By the late nineteenth century, an intellectualized conception of discipline led institutions of higher learning to reorganize along 'disciplinary' lines, which, in turn, led to a significant structural change that produced what is often called the modern or new American university. In Veysey's terms, the rise of the professions led to the development of disciplines of study which led to the creation of departments to house them. For the most part, the organization of a newly formed study as a discipline was modelled on the successful institutionalization of scientific research. Literary studies followed this pattern. Before the turn of the century philology gave literary study the disciplined appearance of a science of literature. Then, literary history did. New Criticism gives us a more recent legacy of attempts to reformulate literary studies as a discipline. The overt intention of New Critical theory, in classics like 'The Intentional *Fallacy*' (my emphasis) or *Theory of Literature*, was to make literary criticism objective, reliable, verifiable, and so on.

But, it is the fact that *men* endeavored to make criticism a discipline along scientific lines that most interests me here. Though women have argued for literary study as a science, the 'canonical' theoretical statements have been made by men. The unselfconscious 'maleness' of their insistence upon a science of criticism is notable. As Gayle Greene and

Coppélia Kahn remind us, 'a male perspective, assumed to be "universal,"
has dominated fields of knowledge'.[8] Literary criticism is no exception.
Consider the following remarks of I. A. Richards, John Crowe Ransom
and René Wellek.

Richards wished to put literary criticism on the solid footing of a
discipline. As Elmer Borklund points out, he began his career 'by virtually dismissing the entire critical tradition' prior to him.[9]

> A few conjectures, a supply of admonitions, many acute isolated
> observations, some brilliant guesses, much oratory and applied
> poetry, inexhaustible confusion, a sufficiency of dogma, no small
> stock of prejudices, whimsies and crochets, a profusion of mysticism,
> a little genuine speculation, sundry stray inspirations, pregnant
> hints and *aperçus*; of such as these, it may be said without exagger-
> ation, is extant critical theory composed.[10]

Simultaneously, in America, John Crowe Ransom took a similar view,
but couched it in business terms, unwittingly reflecting the extent to
which universities had become corporations.

> Professors of literature are learned but not critical men. . . . Never-
> theless, it is from the professors of literature, in this country the
> professors of English for the most part, that I should hope eventually
> for the erection of intelligent standards of criticism. It is their
> business.
>   Criticism must become more scientific, or precise and systematic,
> and this means that it must be developed by the collective and sus-
> tained effort of learned persons – which means that its proper seat is
> in the universities. . . . Rather than occasional criticism by amateurs,
> I should think the whole enterprise might be seriously taken in hand
> by professionals. Perhaps I use a distasteful figure, but I have the
> idea that what we need is Criticism, Inc., or Criticism, Ltd.[11]

Wellek believed that we were still recovering from 'a disaster'. For him,
literary criticism, which was 'taken over by politically oriented journalism' during the nineteenth century, became 'degraded to something
purely practical, serving temporal ends'. 'The critic', he laments,
'becomes a middleman, a secretary, even a servant, of the public'.[12] A

decade after the publication of *Theory of Literature*, he complained that literary scholars were too much on the defensive:

> Our whole society is based on the assumption that we know what is just, and our science on the assumption that we know what is true. Our teaching of literature is actually also based on aesthetic impera- tives, even if we feel less definitely bound by them and seem much more hesitant to bring these assumptions out into the open. The disaster of the 'humanities' as far as they are concerned with the arts and literature is due to their timidity in making the very same claims which are made in regard to law and truth. Actually we do make these claims when we teach *Hamlet* or *Paradise Lost* rather than Grace Metalious . . . But we do so shamefully, apologetically, hesi- tatingly. There is, contrary to frequent assertions, a very wide agree- ment on the great classics: the main canon of literature. There is an insuperable gulf between really great art and very bad art: between say 'Lycidas' and a poem on the leading page of the *New York Times*, between Tolstoy's *Master and Man* and a story in *True Confessions*. (pp. 17–18)

He goes on to defend the possibility not only of correct interpretations but also of correct evaluations. Pointing out that, though the complexity of art might make interpretation difficult,

> this does not mean that all interpretations are equally right, that there is no possibility of differentiating between them. There are utterly fantastic interpretations, partial, distorted interpretations. We may argue about Bradley's or Dover Wilson's or even Ernest Jones' interpretation of *Hamlet*: but we know that Hamlet was no woman in disguise. The concept of adequacy of interpretation leads clearly to the concept of the correctness of judgment. Evaluation grows out of understanding; correct evaluation out of correct under- standing. There is a hierarchy of viewpoints implied in the very concept of adequacy of interpretation. Just as there is correct inter- pretation, at least as an ideal, so there is correct judgment, good judgment. (p. 18)

For Wellek, the only factor that could keep literary criticism from being a 'secretary' to the public was falsification. That we could correctly understand that 'Hamlet was no woman in disguise' would allow us to make the 'good judgment' that *True Confessions* was degrading. For Wellek, the study of literature was *Literaturwissenschaft*, 'systematic knowledge'.

In retrospect, it is remarkable still that the main opponents to New Criticism in the 1960s did not question the view that literary criticism, even though it could not muster exacting objectivity, should be modelled on the sciences. They regarded New Criticism as not scientific enough. Northrop Frye, in his 'Polemical Introduction' to *Anatomy of Criticism*, outflanks the New Critics by arguing the case for a science of Literature rather than for a scientific method of interpretation. E. D. Hirsch's *Validity in Interpretation* critiques the theory of 'the intentional fallacy' by arguing that we can validly determine intention. In the 1960s, when anti-New Critical ferment began, system and method were, nonetheless, privileged terms. The most wide-scale attempt to make criticism into a science belonged to a movement that would have supplanted New Criticism by making its 'scientific' tendencies explicit, namely, structuralism. It is now an often-told tale how structuralism engendered post-structuralism.

To post-structuralist or post-modern critics, whose intellectual formation is deeply indebted to feminism,[13] traditional or modern theories of criticism are phallo/logocentric.

> Imagine someone (a kind of Monsieur Teste in reverse) who abolishes within himself all barriers, all classes, all exclusions, not by syncretism but by simple discard of that old specter: *logical contradiction*; who mixes every language, even those said to be incompatible; who silently accepts every charge of illogicality, of incongruity; who remains passive in the face of Socratic irony (leading the interlocutor to the supreme disgrace: *self-contradiction*) and legal terrorism (how much penal evidence is based on a psychology of consistency!) Such a man would be the mockery of our society: court, school, asylum, polite conversations would cast him out: who endures contradiction without shame? Now this anti-hero exists . . .[14]

For the most part, modern criticism is based on the notion that readings can be objective, impersonal and detached, that there is a discipline of literary criticism. Though traditional critics differ widely in their assumptions about interpretation, when contrasted with post-modern critics, they appear similar in their logocentrism. Working within this system, modern critics contend that their readings are demonstrable because textual or contextual evidence can show that rival readings are not logically supported. Since readings that are accepted as 'true' at an earlier moment in time can at a later date be shown to be 'false', the engine of this system is falsification. New readings supplant old readings. This is a familiar pattern to anyone studying literature. Most critics strive to come up with 'new' readings, and, in order to do so, have to clear their paths by falsifying the previously accepted ones.

In other words, what characterizes modern literary criticism is a principle of falsificity.

Intellectual sexuality in the institution of criticism

Literary criticism is a career. Burton Bledstein tells us in *The Culture of Professionalism* that the idea of a career emerged concomitantly with the rise of the professions in the nineteenth century in contrast to 'a random series of jobs, projects, or businesses providing a livelihood'.[15] It changed the lives of *men* because it articulated *their* aspirations as ambitions (emphasis mine). It involved 'a pre-established total pattern of organized professional activity, with upward movement through recognized preparatory stages, and advancement based on merit bearing honor'. Modern literary criticism was conceived during this period. Like professionals elsewhere, critics make their career patterns discernible in their *curriculum vitae* which require them to list chronologically 'preparatory stages', 'advancement' in employment, 'honors', and 'merit' – which, in their case, is signalled by increasing success in placing their work with prestigious publishers. What Bledstein calls a 'vertical' movement characterizes the careers of successful professional critics. For critics, an outstanding career is one in which they earn higher and higher salaries in a succession of jobs at increasingly prestigious institutions. Since the mid-nineteenth-century, professional success has been imaged as climbing a ladder of institutional status:

New expectations displayed themselves in a new style. In a social environment now offering vocational alternatives, young men could criticize, calculate, envision a ladder of advancement, and act with some measure of impunity toward their less flexible elders. Above

all, young men could begin thinking in vertical rather than horizontal imagery. They meant, very literally, to move up and away.
(p. 176)

Bledstein describes the shift in the sense of the purposefulness of a man's
life during the nineteenth century as a shift away from a belief in a
'calling' to a choice of a 'career', a shift easily discerned in the changing
ways ministers, lawyers, doctors and educators spoke about their professions. A 'calling' was not the choice of an individual, but a career most
certainly was. Bledstein's remark that a career was a choice for 'young
men' leaves unspoken that women were still 'called'.

The shift Bledstein describes was hierarchically and competitively configured not merely as a change in status and roles provoked by analogies
to ladders and races, but also as a change in the social construction of
masculinity provoked by images of gentlemen.

The inner intensity of the new life oriented toward a career stood in
contrast to that of the older learned professional life of the eighteenth
and early nineteenth centuries. In the earlier period such external
attributes of gentlemanly behavior as benevolence, duty, virtue, and
manners circumscribed the professional experience. Competence,
knowledge, and preparation were less important in evaluating the
skills of the professional than were dedication to the community,
sincerity, trust, permanence, honorable reputation, and righteous
behavior. The qualifying credentials of the learned professionals
were honesty, decency, and civility. (p. 173)

The career professional, by contrast, thought in terms of advancement.
The nineteenth-century gentleman gave way to the twentieth-century
businessman, who prospered in 'a competitive society in which unre-
strained individual self-determination undermined traditional life styles'
(p. 174). He is the prototype of the persona Marc Fasteau calls 'the male
machine'.

The male machine is a special kind of being, different from women,
children, and men who don't measure up. He is functional, designed
mainly for work. He is programmed to tackle jobs, override obstacles,
attack problems, overcome difficulties, and always seize the offensive. He will take on any task that can be presented to him in a

competitive framework, and his most important positive reinforcement is victory. . . . this ideology makes competition the guiding
principle of moral and intellectual, as well as economic, life. It tells
us that the general welfare is served by the self-interested clash of
ambitions and ideas . . .[16]

Bledstein remarks that in the development of nineteenth-century professionalism ambitious men were instrumental in 'structuring our discipline according to a distinct vision – the vertical one of career' (p. ix).
From this point of view, the development of literary study matches
Bledstein's delineation of the relationship between the growth of the
university and the rise of professionalism. To become a literary scholar is
to be professionalized, a social process involving the introjection of an
'intellectual competitiveness'. The 'masculine' qualities of exemplary
male professors were imitated and became the traits of an idealized career
profile. Exemplary male professors became 'role-models' for success
within the structure of the academy, a phenomenon which shaped the
field of literary study as we now know it.[17] We are the heirs of 'roles' that
are explicitly designed for the new gentleman, the businessman.

The history of literary study, for instance, can be understood as the
collective biography of exemplary *male* academic figures: George Marsh,
Francis March, Francis Child, Ulrich von Wilamowitz-Moellendorf,
Gustave Lanson, I. A. Richards, John Crowe Ransom, Cleanth Brooks,
and so on. The criss-crossing movement of their careers influenced the
newly developing field of literary study. Its historical development is, in
most respects, an account of these critical 'movements' which are usually
associated with key men who inspired schools of thought. Figures like
Child, Brooks and Lanson are historically significant because they became
exemplary figures. These men were 'exemplary' because in doing what
they believed ought to be done, they became examples for others. Modern
literary study developed as a profession to the extent that the manner in
which a particular man studied literature was widely imitated, to the
extent that a man's way of 'doing' criticism or scholarship became a trait
in the composite profile of the ideal professor of literature. Invariably, men
were the models underlying the ideal profile of the scholar/critic at specific
junctures in the development of literary studies. Over time, this idealized
career profile became a composite of masculine traits derived from the
superimposition of the portrayals of exemplary male scholars. Women
working in the academy, in order to succeed in their careers, had to

acquire these traits. As Hélène Cixous reminds us, a discourse 'signed with a woman's name doesn't necessarily make a piece of writing feminine. It could quite well be masculine writing'.[18]

Nowadays, to be a professional critic authorized by the institution of criticism still requires submission to an idealized career profile whose masculinity derives from male models. Since this profile is nowhere made explicit as such and *in toto*, I call it the 'Magister Implicatus' to personify and thus concretize the sum total of performances now demanded for accreditation as a professional critic.[19] He is the image we see when we look in the distorted mirror of our resumés. As we currently know him, the Magister Implicatus is a personification of an ideal male career. At present, he stands for the professionalization of the male scholar from the very first examination through various forms of discipline to the final authorization of his work. He is the unified personification of the ways professional critics are taught to portray themselves in official documents – *vitae*, grant applications, course descriptions and so on.

In his traditional and modern persona, the Magister's power enables or disables any member of the institution who introjects him. He punishes by making us believe we have failed, do not deserve tenure, have not published enough. He is the monster in the male machine, the instrument of self-discipline and self-abnegation. In his traditional guise, he is the personification of the patriarchal institution, the site for training, disciplining, schooling men. He professionalizes the amateur. He governs through our introjection of what the desired outcome of any performance must be if it is to be rewarded. It is his male interests that are served when critics serve their institutions by believing those beliefs that hold it together. An emotional bond to him is a bond to the patriarchal institution. In serving him, one serves it, often while believing he has one's best interests in mind.

The Magister Implicatus is the ghostly patriarchal figure who haunts our job descriptions, our textbooks, our examination committees, and other quarters of the institution of literary criticism. Not surprisingly, given the history of the institution of criticism, his profile is masculine. Because careers allow for professional advances along a ladder of institutional success (degrees, salaries, ranks and so on), the Magister through his exemplariness inspires critics to compete with one another for awards.

It is upon this one trait of the Magister Implicatus, his competitiveness, that I wish to focus your attention.

Falsificity is inextricably linked to competitiveness

In the present academy, competitiveness and falsificity are inextricably bound together. Critics are judged according to the extent to which they have successfully argued. The merit of their arguments is measured by the degree to which they have falsified their rival's claims and the degree to which their own arguments are deemed falsifiable. 'And merit is, of course, determined by competition. How else?'[20] The success of a critic is therefore inextricably linked with the extent to which he competes with rival critics.

Competition is usually defined as 'a striving for the same object, position, prize, etc., usually in accordance with certain fixed rules', (*WNWD*). Rule-governed striving is the generating principle of career success. Each juncture of the career path presents to the careerist a goal for which he must compete – a grade, a degree, a job, a promotion, a grant, and so on. In every case, the competitor is judged on the merit of his critical arguments. Hence, if we consider that arguments displace earlier arguments through falsification, then the successful competitor is the successful falsifier. Falsification and competitiveness are inextricable in this system.

As Helen E. Longino points out, 'Competition always involves a contest among individuals seeking the same thing when not all can obtain it'.[21] Some competitions, she argues, are based upon the availability of a single prize. As in a race, there is only one first 'prize'. As a consequence, the differences in abilities of the contestants is the salient factor. Such competitions are staged to establish who is 'the best' in a particular performance. There are many examples in literary criticism – competing for a job, a grant, an award. In other competitions the scarcity of the 'object' sought (the reward) creates a 'survival of the fittest' contest and the 'game' has to be played until winners are determined. In literary criticism, competing for publications, jobs, promotions, and salaries has the structure of a 'win/lose' (vs. 'prize') competition. In this type of competition the salient factor is not necessarily ability but perseverance, fortitude, endurance, doggedness, and so on.

When we look at literary criticism as an institution through the lens of competition, that is, when we study the ways in which critical argumentation has been institutionalized as a competition, a peculiar distortion of critical inquiry comes to light. In order to decide between winners and

losers in the various career games we all play, administrators, in choosing
to focus upon the success of critical arguments, force critics to reify their
understanding. Knowledge, as Pierre Bourdieu argues, becomes 'symbolic
capital'.[22] What we know has to be quantifiable, measurable and therefore
cumulative. We might say that insights have to be converted into information in order to be accumulated. In this system, the goal of criticism is
to 'accumulate knowledge', hence the critic who has accumulated the
most knowledge gets the most rewards. Central to this system is falsification.

Let's take a simple example. Jack believes that 'X' is the meaning of
poem '1'. He argues his case on the grounds of the beliefs 'A, B, and C'
which he takes to be factual. Jill believes that 'y' is the meaning of poem
'1'. She argues her case on the grounds of 'a, d, and q'. What are Jack's
options? Well, obviously, he could agree. He could say, 'I was mistaken
in believing B and C.' If he does so, he admits his reading is false and is
no longer eligible for an institutional reward. False arguments are not
rewarded. So, in order to maintain his reading, Jack has to say either that
d and q are irrelevant or that not-d and not-q are the facts. In other words,
to survive the competition among readers, he must maintain his beliefs,
otherwise he admits to error and loses status or merit.

In his *Psychology of Intelligence*, Jean Piaget terms the form of intellection I have just described 'assimilation', namely, the tendency to
assimilate all new experiences into the cognitive frameworks one already
possesses. He contrasts this mode of intellection to 'accommodation',
wherein inquirers allow new experiences to 'break down' the frameworks
they are accustomed to using.[23] It can be safely said that the institution of
criticism encourages assimilation. It does not help your career to go
around explaining how you are in error.

Considering that the institution of criticism encourages assimilation
and therefore falsification as the cognitive strategies best suited to the
accumulation of knowledge (information), we might, recalling Cixous's
use of 'the proper', term this cognitive style 'appropriation'.[24] Appropriation is the acquisition of knowledge understood as an entity (identities,
samenesses, that is, information); it is the assimilation of concepts into a
governing framework. Appropriation is an arrogation, confiscation, seizure
of concepts. Ideas can be owned and sold at will. They are proper-ties. A
contrasting mode of intellection, like intuition, a term I prefer to the term
'insight',[25] often involves the in-appropriate, the disconcerting, and so
on. Inappropriate because painful, humiliating; disconcerting in forcing

one to change one's beliefs. Moreover, intuitions are not appropriatable and thus nothing gets accumulated. Intuitions are unspecifiable.[26] Intuitions are multiple, diverse, *ad hoc*, diffuse, etc. Whereas logical problems have single solutions, intuited problems have plural solutions and often appear illogical.

For post-moderns, thankfully, the veracity of criticism is not a matter of logic. Thought is not single, unified, centered, present. Though I cannot rehearse post-modern critiques of logocentrism here, I believe that I am not alone in thinking that texts do not provide a factual ground to interpretive claims, that writers and readers are discursive subjects who cannot be codified, that distinctions between correct and incorrect are purely conventional, that truth is a signifier like all others. In short, in postmodern theorizing, the very possibility of falsification is thoroughly undermined as a worthwhile intellectual endeavor.

If falsification does not lead to knowledge, then why do we continue to accept it? Obviously, it serves some other purpose. In the case of traditional criticism, the purpose is to regulate competition. Competition always requires rules. Falsification is the governing rule. Thus, modern criticism is no more than a competition governed by an arbitrary rule interpreted by those institutionally empowered to do so. Falsificity is a mechanism of a disciplinary apparatus to regulate competition. In an academic context, 'regulation of competition' refers to the rules that govern the attribution of merit to critical performances. Every competition has to have fixed rules to ensure the result that someone will win. Falsification is a regulating mechanism in the sense that it is like tagging the person who is 'it'. Falsifying reminds one of the fiction boys use in childhood wargames – when an enemy is shot, the victor shouts, 'you're dead!', moving on to surprise the next opponent. Falsification is a similar device used by successful competitors to establish their progress (over the corpses of rival critics) along the way to winning. In critical games, though rationalized as a reward for possessing 'the best idea' among one's opponents, the competition is for a grade, a degree, a job, a publication, a promotion, a grant, an appointment. The awarding of these prizes in no way guarantees the value of the inquiry. Another irony in this system is that, whereas rules – like falsification – are designed to regulate, to keep under control the aggression involved, they have the effect of increasing it. Falsification, though construed as a regulator, functions only as a measurement of the logicality and frequency of successful counter-claims; hence, it has the effect of multiplying falsifications.

This system intensifies competition and leads to what I call intellectual machismo, the tendency toward an exaggerated expression of competition for the acquisition and appropriation of ideas. It is an exercise of power. In this sense, it is an instance of domination. The instigator, the person who picks the fight, confirms his sense that he is better than his rival often by creating a situation in which the rival, taken by surprise, is overwhelmed. In this scenario knowledge is power. Oddly, since it is an intellectually trivial pursuit, this wargame has the character of a parlor game. The machismic critic scores by knowing the most recent article, the exact date, the most stinging review, the precise reference, the received opinion, and so on. A side effect of these games is that it becomes impossible for the critic whose intellectual style is machismic to admit error. It is regarded as a fault, an embarrassment. This is a ridiculous posture. Ironically, the machismic intellectual, by telling what is obviously a kind of lie, places himself in a ludicrous position if he wishes finally to reach some understanding. Nevertheless, the machismic intellectual's discourse is permeated by utterances like 'Professor X is wrong.' Because, in the institution of criticism, falsification is bound up with the notion of 'wrong-doing', intellectual machismo has a Rambo effect. The heroic critic is obligated morally to rescue thinkers from the prisons of illogic, to stand up to illogic when no one else cares. He is armed to the teeth with falsifications. Nothing but his self-esteem is left in his wake. He is the supreme falsifier, appropriator, assimilator.

Assimilation, the hallmark of appropriation, mechanizes falsification. When undertaken aggressively, it becomes a machine that falsifies everything in its path. The machine is a simple idea-mower, a handy procrustean mechanism. The machismic intellectual already has a set of beliefs to encompass his world. When he encounters someone else's belief, one of two events occur. Either, the announced belief squares with his own and can be assimilated as a confirmation of what he already believes, in which case verification occurs as a kind of negative falsification (we're right, so they're wrong). Or, as is more often the case, the announced belief does not square with his and is assimilated into his belief system as an error. In the latter instance, the Ramboist (this is, after all, a school of thought that needs a name) finds counter-evidence in his stock of beliefs, or identifies a lapse in logic, or invokes an authority (someone who believes what he believes). In short, since he cannot assimilate a belief that is inconsistent with his belief system, it enters his framework as a false belief. In his Ramboistic wargames, critical arguments are not distinguishable from quarrels. Quarreling is 'a dispute or disagreement, especially one marked by anger and deep resentment' and 'implies heated verbal strife' that 'often suggests continued hostility as a result' (*WNWD*).

Though arguments are said to be logical, dispassionate, detached, impersonal, objective and so on, and in this sense, can be regarded culturally as 'masculine', looked at closely, especially in the light of a critique of falsification, they are difficult to distinguish from quarrels. Oddly, the more one examines arguments (intellectual masculinity), the more one finds quarrels (intellectual effeminateness). Similarly, the more one looks at intuition and the confession of error, etc. (intellectual femininity), the more it looks like a strong, incisive, powerful mode of knowing (intellectual virility).

Intellectual compassion, commitment, collaboration, concurrence, and community

Literary criticism is intellectual work. Unlike work-for-profit, the success of which can be enhanced by competition, intellectual work requires compassion, commitment, collaboration, concurrence, and community. I list these as alternatives to the components of traditional criticism I have critiqued. In this section, I try to articulate my intuitions about them. I admit at the outset that not all of them are obvious alternatives to a competitive system. Collaboration is clearly an alternative to competition, compassion to machismo, intellectual community to scholarly individualism. Once I supply the phrase for which the term stands, it becomes clear that commitment-to-the-public-welfare is an alternative aspiration to self-interested-careerism. Concurrence, however, is not the obvious alternative to appropriation. Consequently, in what follows I write about concurrence inchoately, hoping to stir further discussion.

Let me begin with the need for intellectual compassion. Compassion is ordinarily understood as 'sorrow for the sufferings or troubles of another' (*WNWD*) and can be related to the kind of empathy that is necessary for a commitment to collaborative concurrence about painful problems relevant to a community.[27] I contrast it with intellectual machismo. Intellectual compassion allows one intellectual to enter imaginatively into the problems of another. Collaboration depends upon the ability of one intellectual to enter into the pain or suffering that another is attempting to resolve.

This contrasts to the kind of intellectual antagonism that competition spawns, which interferes with the resolution of problems.

Problems are not equivalent to puzzles. A problem is frustrating, painful, and difficult; it calls for the articulation of many questions. Each question differs, and therefore questioning requires the breaking down of preconceived frameworks because of the difficulty of formulating the problem in a way that does not simply appropriate it. Collaborative inquiry is not an instance of differing perspectives ultimately coming together in a unified framework. Instead, it seeks intellectual concurrence (rather than appropriation). Concurrence, by which I mean an agreement to join intellectual forces to get something done, is a plausible alternative to appropriation only on the condition that the differences among the researchers are allowed free play. In this form of collaboration, researchers are invited into the group not because they represent the same point of view but because they represent different and even incompatible points of view. Since getting-at-'my'-truth no longer governs the inquiry, quarrels are abandoned while concurrence is sought because any idea that helps solve the problem helps. Removing contradictions or inconsistencies from one's discourse is less important than resolving the cultural conflicts we call racism, elitism or sexism. Concurrence of this sort is desirable in literary research.[28]

Literary criticism calls for intellectual collaboration. The form of critical collaboration I have been advocating converges upon the apprehension of a problem and the critics involved band together to seek solutions to it. This form of collaboration in literary criticism occurs when a group of differing intellectuals, bound together by the acknowledgment of a textual/cultural problem, concur about a possible reading of it. By concurring, they do not seek conformity; they seek the coincidences among their differences. In this collaboration, concurrences about the problem and the solution are transpersonal. This does not necessarily imply a common ideal or telos holding the group together. Intellectual compassion and care hold the group together. In this form of collaboration, intellectual subject positions are not configured competitively. Differences are crucial. Reading is not an appropriation by an individual; it is the political concurrence of a group.

Inescapably, collaboration is the heart of the practice of literary study, despite the patriarch's insistence upon individualistic readings. How do we therefore explain that we rarely acknowledge it? Maria C. Lugones and Elizabeth V. Spelman note that:

The desire to excel, the desire to avoid obscurity, and the desire for distinction become definitive of a competitive attitude in a context of opposition and they come, in their turn, to be shaped by this context. For at the heart of the desire to excel in the context of opposition, is the desire to excel not merely in some non-comparative sense, but to excel over others, to better them. . . . The overriding preoccupation is with standing out against the performances of others. . . .

A competitor qua competitor sustains quite a different conception of herself and others than she would if she were engaged in activities in which it is appropriate to think about other humans as needy or as collaborators.[29]

As they remind us, competition is 'essentially self-centered' (p. 237). It makes 'one's own success and well-being . . . impossible without someone else's failure and/or misery' (p. 241). But, they argue, there is an alternative to the politics of competition – communal excelling.[30]

Collaboration takes place within the polis, the aggregate of communities. An intellectual community is a concurrence of intellectuals. Intellectual communities engender different and sometimes competing collaborations. As Lugones and Spelman write,

There are contexts in which the desire to avoid obscurity and the desire for excellence are not only compatible with but necessary ingredients of projects that are properly communal. In those cases these desires are incompatible with an individualistic conception of excellence and of the participants in the project. (p. 238)

Though the word 'community' includes the word 'unity', communities are not unities. Obviously, a notion of community can be deconstructed by pointing out that it implies an essential, central, unity, that it implies the 'presence' of some entity.[31] My concern here is not so much with the aberrations of a metaphysics of presence but with the naive assumption that communities are in fact unities. I do not mean to suggest by privileging the word 'community' that every individual in a community communes, that is, moves through the understanding of common goals and ideals toward identity, sameness. Though the word unfortunately suggests some kind of entity that is unified, it is possible to think of a community as a theatre in which intellectual 'play' is dramatized. In this play, the dramatis personae, each with distinct characteristics uniquely performed, act together toward a resolution of a problem. This is a play of differences that concurrently respond to a problem differentially perceived.[32] In this play, critics enjoy differing subject positions and their characters change, that is, they exchange subject positions. The bond of an intellectual community is intellectual compassion, the imaginative entry into another's problem.

In the terms now under discussion, critical inquiry is the compassionate accommodation of difference. Such inquiries are, by this definition, collaborative. But, to be housed in universities, collaborative inquirers (research groups) must, in some sense, *share* problems with communities. And, ultimately, communities of intellectuals can only legitimize themselves in the institution of criticism to the extent that they inquire into problems characterizing the various public spheres that make up our cultural formation.[33] These are not individualizing possibilities and considering them brings us circuitously back to a consideration of 'theory' (but not a man-driven one). Although falsification cannot and should not be recuperated by post-modern critics, in the context of communal inquiry, it seems foolish, if not impossible, to try to do without the heuristic value of error since problems are related to errors, and to inquire requires error and the breaking apart of preconceptions. Inquiries are written (or, in a grammatological sense, inscribed) as questions. Just as texts are intertexts that encompass myriad cultural formations, so inquiries are texts. Knowing this is theorizing.

Theorizing is not necessarily making theories. Theory-making is patriarchal. Theory is often used as a weapon. Theory is an effective instrument of falsification. And so on. But systematic theories that feed into competitive schemes are only the husk of theorizing. It is in the understanding of a problem through differing intuitions of it that theorizing occurs. Out of these intuitions arises a more general view of critical performance than is available to the solitary scholar. Competition obscures this phenomenon. In a competition among critics, theories become machines of falsification. They are used to refute the assumptions of rival critics. But in a communal inquiry, theorizing is informed by intellectual compassion and arises out of the urgency to end the pain associated with a specific problem. In that endeavor, performances must be made as effective as possible. Theorizing helps.

The precondition of possibility for intellectual compassion, commitment, collaboration, concurrence, and community is the de-masculinization of the Magister Implicatus. Why quarrel?

NOTES

I would like to thank my colleagues Ann Ardis, Dale Bauer, Art Casciato, Susan Jarratt, Kristina Straub, Andy Lakritz of Miami University and Patricia Harkin of Akron University for their intellectual compassion. Because of the intellectual community their concurrence occasions, what I have written is, in most respects, collaborative.

1 All of the quotes in this paragraph are references to *Webster's New World Dictionary*, hereafter cited as *WNWD*. I have used this dictionary simply because it compares semantically related terms.

2 Though this theorem comes from the philosophy of science (Popper 1968: 40), it applies to literary criticism whose disciplinary orientation mimics the institutional-ization of scientific research.

3 To give the grade 'F' presupposes that the discourse so assigned is false. The same principle pertains to any grade below 'A +'. This system of 'grading' also pertains to ranking and the unqualified or qualified acceptance or rejection of papers submitted for publication.

4 This is an extension of Luce Irigaray's thematic in Irigaray 1985.

5 Veysey 1965. In this essay, I conflate the terms 'traditional' and 'modern' in a sense that combines Foucault's (1977) delineation of the period of our history dominated by 'discipline' and Lyotard's (1984) suggestion that we are 'post-modern' because the conditions of knowledge production have radically changed. In this context, the reliance on various kinds of warranting in informal logic which Toulmin (1972) sees as the defining characteristic of university studies called disciplines fits well into the notion of 'modern' as the logocentric world-view under critique by 'post-moderns'.

6 Corbett 1971: 303.

7 His essay, which is written in English, is ironically entitled, 'Das Fussnoten: das Fundament der Wissenschaft'. It is ironic that a classicist should write this article, since his is among the most heavily footnoted of all fields.

8 Greene and Kahn 1985: 1-2.

9 Borklund 1977: 440.

10 Richards 1925: 6.

11 Ransom 1968: 328-9.

12 Wellek 1967: 3.

13 While deconstruction seems to reign in the news of our profession, post-modern feminism is far more vital. Indeed, post-modern criticism is inconceivable without feminism. Far more important than the deconstruction of literary texts is the politiciz-ation of literary study, a project in which feminists have led the way.

14 Barthes 1975: 3.

15 Bledstein 1976: 172.

16 Fasteau 1975: 1.

17 In this section I take an admittedly general look at some aspects of our collective past that can be understood as the historical conditions of the career profile of the literary scholar/critic. Most of my remarks are based on research conducted by the Group for Research into the Institutionalization and Professionalization of Literary Studies (GRIP). Many of the papers published in *The GRIP Report* involve brief historical

accounts of exemplary academic figures: George Marsh, Francis March, Francis Child, Ulrich von Wilamowitz-Moellendorf, Gustave Lanson, Cleanth Brooks, and so on. The GRIP collaboration is sponsored by the Society for Critical Exchange, a national organization dedicated to collaborative work in literary theory.

18 Cixous 1981: 52.

19 This paragraph summarizes an essay entitled 'The Magister Implicatus: a configuration of orthodoxy', originally published in *The GRIP Report*, a revised version of which is included in a volume of GRIP essays under consideration for publication.

20 Longino, 'The ideology of competition', in Miner and Longino 1987: 253. For detailed discussions of competition and women, see Miner and Longino 1987.

21 Ibid.: 250.

22 Bourdieu 1979: 171-83.

23 Piaget 1963: 8.

24 I draw on Cixous's distinction between the 'proper' and the 'gift' because it succinctly captures the relationship between knowledge and social institutions.

25 I earlier used the term 'insight' in place of the term 'intuition' for rhetorical reasons. Also, for reasons that will become apparent later, I define intuition not in the traditional way as 'the immediate knowing of something without the conscious use of reasoning' (*WNWD*), but as the instantaneous accommodation of unspecifiable differences.

26 I use 'intuition' in roughly Michael Polanyi's sense of 'insight' (Polanyi 1958: 90-1). In his account of intelligence, he focuses upon 'tacit knowledge' which is so complex that it cannot be articulated because the particulars are unspecifiable. Unlike Polanyi, however, I regard the 'unspecifiability' of insight as owing to the relationship between our short- and long-term memories.

27 See Lugones and Spelman 1987 for a detailed discussion of compassion. My use of the term, suggested to me by their essay, differs from theirs.

28 Unlike scientific theories, literary theories are not paradigms for research. Whereas in paradigmatic research theories govern the formulation of questions in the search for sameness, in literary research groups many, even contradictory, theorems can be used in search of differences that might precipitate concurrences. See David Shumway and James Sosnoski, 'Critical protocols', *The GRIP Report*, vol. 2 (Research in Progress Circulated by the Society for Critical Exchange, 1984).

29 Lugones and Spelman 1987: 236-7.

30 I agree with Lugones and Spelman that competition has its political usefulness and support their contention that groups competing collectively for the welfare of the public can be beneficial. As they point out, while competition is akin to excelling, communal excelling is not destructive in the way that an individual's competing in self-interested ways is. For them, the crucial difference is that in communal excelling, self-interest is regulated by the interests of the group.

31 I am thinking here of Jean-Luc Nancy's work on community in his *La Communauté Désoeuvrée* (1986).

32 One of the topics in Laclau and Mouffe 1985 is the possibility of differences in political action.

33 Without a strong relationship to public spheres, 'intellectuals' are vulnerable to elitism. This is as true of an intellectual who works in a university as it is of any other.

REFERENCES

Barthes, Roland 1975. *The Pleasure of the Text*. Trans. Richard Miller. New York: Hill and Wang.

Belsey, Catherine 1980. *Critical Practice*. London and New York: Methuen.

Bledstein, Burton J. 1976. *The Culture of Professionalism*. New York: W. W. Norton.

Borklund, Elmer 1977. *Contemporary Literary Critics*. New York: St Martin's Press.

Bourdieu, Pierre 1979. *Outline of a Theory of Practice*. Ed. Jack Goody, trans. Richard Nice. Cambridge: Cambridge University Press.

Cixous, Hélène 1981. 'Castration or decapitation?' Trans. Annette Kuhn. *Signs: Journal of Women in Culture and Society* 7.1 (Autumn): 41-55.

Corbett, Edward P. J. 1971. *Classical Rhetoric for the Modern Student*. New York: Oxford University Press.

Fasteau, Marc Feigen 1975. *The Male Machine*. New York: Dell Publishing Co.

Foucault, Michel 1977. *Discipline and Punish: The Birth of the Prison*. Trans. Alan Sheridan. New York: Vintage.

Frye, Northrup 1957. *Anatomy of Criticism: Four Essays*. Princeton: Princeton University Press.

Greene, Gayle and Kahn, Coppélia 1985. *Making a Difference: Feminist Literary Criticism*. London and New York: Methuen.

Hirsch, Jr, E. D. 1967. *Validity in Interpretation*. New Haven: Yale University Press.

Irigaray, Luce 1985. *Speculum of the Other Woman*. Trans. Gillian G. Gill. Ithaca: Cornell University Press.

Jardine, Alice and Smith, Paul (eds) 1987. *Men in Feminism*. London and New York: Methuen.

Laclau, Ernesto and Mouffe, Chantal 1985. *Hegemony and Socialist Strategy*. London: Verso.

Lugones, Maria C. and Spelman, Elizabeth V. 1987. 'Competition, compassion and community: models for a feminist ethos', in Miner and Longino 1987.

Lyotard, Jean-François 1984. *The Postmodern Condition: A Report on Knowledge*. Trans. Geoff Bennington and Brian Massumi. Minneapolis: University of Minnesota Press.

Miner, Valerie and Longino, Helen E. 1987. *Competition: A Feminist Taboo*. New York: The Feminist Press at The City University of New York.

Moi, Toril 1985. *Sexual/Textual Politics: Feminist Literary Theory*. London and New York: Methuen.

Nancy, Jean-Luc 1986. *La Communauté Desoeuvrée*. Paris: Christian Bougois.

Nimis, Stephen 1984. 'Fussnoten: das Fundament der Wissenschaft', *Arethusa*, 17.2 (Fall): 105-34.

Piaget, Jean 1963. *The Psychology of Intelligence*. Paterson, New Jersey: Littlefield, Adams.

Polanyi, Michael 1958. *Personal Knowledge*. Chicago: University of Chicago Press.

Popper, Karl R. 1968. *The Logic of Scientific Discovery*. New York: Harper and Row.

Ransom, John Crowe 1968. 'Criticism, Inc.', in *The World's Body*. Baton Rouge: Louisiana State University.

Richards, I. A. 1925. *Principles of Literary Criticism*. New York: Harcourt, Brace and World.

Toulmin, Stephen 1972. *Human Understanding: The Collective Use and Evolution of Concepts*. Princeton: Princeton University Press.

Veysey, Laurence R. 1965. *The Emergence of the American University*. Chicago: University of Chicago Press.

Wellek, René 1967. *Concepts of Criticism*. New Haven: Yale University Press.

Wellek, René and Warren, Austin 1956. *Theory of Literature*. New York: Harcourt, Brace and World.

4

The Uses of Quarreling

Gayle Greene

James Sosnoski concludes his paper with the question, 'why quarrel?' And what feminist would want to quarrel with his critique of 'the construction of intellectuality as competitive quarreling' or with the ideals of 'compassion', 'collaboration', 'concurrence', 'community' that he proposes as alternatives? 'Falsificity', as he terms it, the identification of error, the belief that 'a claim about a text can be proven false', is the basis of literary studies and is inextricably linked with competition: 'Most critics strive to come up with "new" readings, and, in order to do so, have to clear their paths by falsifying the previously accepted ones' (p. 63). 'This is an essay about the oppression of women', Sosnoski says, since the 'intellectual machismo' he describes, 'knowledge as the acquisition and appropriation of ideas', is part of the same system that oppresses women, a system based on 'power' and 'domination'.

Sosnoski traces this mode of intellection back to Aristotle, through scholasticism, and through the rise of the professions which led to the formation of the disciplines in the late nineteenth century and to the definition of criticism as a scientific study. '*Men* endeavored to make criticism a discipline along scientific lines'; and his use of the word 'men' is deliberate, since ' "canonical" theoretical statements have been made by men' (p. 59) and the historical development of literary studies is 'an account of these critical "movements" which are usually associated with key men who inspired schools of thought' (p. 65). With the rise of professions literary criticism became a career; the literary critic became a 'professional', became 'professionalized' – 'a social process involving the introjection of an "intellectual competitiveness" '. The model of success was male and women in the academy had to imitate it in order to succeed (p. 65).

New Criticism was part of an effort to claim scientific status for literature, and even challenges to New Criticism (such as structuralism) still assumed that criticism was a science and did not challenge the logocentric

assumption that 'their readings are demonstrable because textual or contextual evidence can show that rival readings are not logically supported'
(p. 63). Sosnoski suggests that we reverse our customary views and
proposes 'intuition' (which is multiple, diverse, diffuse, and plural) as a
better mode than 'falsificity': 'Oddly, the more one examines arguments
(intellectual masculinity), the more one finds quarrels (intellectual
effeminateness). Similarly, the more one looks at intuition and the confession of error, etc. (intellectual femininity), the more it looks like a strong,
incisive, powerful mode of knowing (intellectual virility)' (p. 71). As
alternatives to the components of the traditional approach he critiques, he
suggests collaboration (rather than competition), compassion (rather than
machismo), intellectual community (rather than scholarly individualism).

So why quarrel? How could a feminist critic quarrel with this analysis
when it was the very discontents Sosnoski is articulating that motivated
us to critique the masculinist assumptions of literature and criticism and
to develop alternative modes of critical inquiry? It was just such uneasi-
ness with intellection as 'acquisition . . . arrogation, confiscation, seizure'
(p. 68) that inspired the development of feminist criticism. So why does
this essay make me want to reach for my gun?

It's partly a sense of *déjà vu*, finding familiar ideas coming back across
the years, repackaged as new, under male signature. Sosnoski writes as
though the women's movement hadn't happened, with its critique of the
patriarchal values he critiques; he writes as though the 1960s hadn't
happened, with their experiments abolishing grades and devising educational incentives besides competition. He seems not to see that change –
whether we envision it in terms of reform or of revolution – requires that
we take stands, requires that we know (or think we know) truth from
error; and he seems not to understand the uses of anger in such efforts.
Being a feminist begins in outrage at injustice (which we think we know
from justice) and requires an energy which is often best fuelled by anger.

The question of how change occurs is of vital concern not only to
feminists but to anyone interested in progress. Sosnoski argues that
'falsificity' works against change because, while seeming to clear space in
a way that allows for change, it actually maintains the *status quo* by
perpetuating patriarchal values such as logocentrism, competition, rivalry,
power, domination. It is perhaps useful to be reminded how difficult it is
to forge genuine challenges to the intellectual and cultural paradigms we
inherit, how difficult to extricate our forms of resistance from the system
we oppose, though feminist scholars have known this for some time.[1]

This question – can we fight the oppressor by using the oppressor's weapons? – has informed feminist scholarship from the beginning and it recurs in various ways. Can we, in Audre Lorde's terms, use the master's tools to dismantle the master's house? Can women writers adapt genres and conventions that have been developed to express male experience to express female experience? Can we use language to oppose patriarchal ideology when that ideology is itself reinscribed within language? (Abel, Jacobus, Gauthier). Can feminist critics use traditional literary critical methods and approaches to challenge the 'dominant male intellectual traditions', or are we, when borrowing, always 'borrowing troubles', as Ellen Messer-Davidow suggests; and if so, what sorts of tools do we invent in their place?[2] Since there is no place outside culture, no 'Archimedean standpoint outside of social life' (in Jameson's term[3]), no place beyond ideology, beyond language, how can we devise a theory and practice which are genuinely oppositional? It is disagreement on these issues that is currently dividing feminist scholarship in the form of the debate between Anglo-American and French feminist critics.

Sosnoski's analysis of falsificity as a competitive mode which is the 'engine' of 'the system' is illuminating. But the competitive values Sosnoski deplores are more profoundly – and more politically – ingrained in intellectual inquiry than he suggests. He claims that the institutionalization of 'critical argumentation' as 'competition' is a 'peculiar distortion' (p. 67), when, far from being a distortion, it comes with the territory, is inherent in and even identical with the process of intellection, of critical inquiry, as it occurs in our culture. Evaluating, distinguishing, discriminating, discerning the 'true' from the 'false', is knowing as we know it.

Invidious comparison (for that is what it comes down to) is the basis of western epistemology. As Jacques Derrida has demonstrated, the binary oppositions on which western philosophical thought is constructed dictate a conception of truth as single and non-equivocal and imply the subordination of the second element to the first. Womanhood is relegated to the place of non-truth and man occupies the position of sovereign subject and origin of meaning.[4] To reverse the order of the pairing – as Sosnoski does when he proposes the traditionally 'feminine' attribute of 'intuition' in place of the traditionally 'masculine' attribute of logic – is only to reduplicate the hierarchical system. To suggest that what looks like masculinity is actually femininity and that what looks like intellectual effeminateness is actually intellectual virility, far from challenging the system which is the source of the problem, simply perpetuates the old stereotypes. An oppositional mode would require that we re-envision such terms rather than simply reverse them.

Falsificity determines not only our methods but our subjects. Discrimination, the notion of 'the best that has been thought and said,' built the literary canon: 'literature, as a concept and a practice, is a particular selection and organization of texts ("rightly sifted and rightly studied")'.[5] Even those of us who reject the authority of the canon are inevitably involved, in our teaching and writing, in making choices according to some principle of invidious comparison. In choosing which works to teach and write on, we select some texts and omit others. Interpretation itself is a matter of making distinctions, discriminations, since in interpreting we sort out the various elements of a text according to principles of order or hierarchy.

Moreover, 'discrimination' has a political dimension. Western epistemology is grounded in western culture and the hierarchical structure of knowledge has its basis in power, in the subordination, colonization – the exclusion, omission, silencing – of the 'other' or 'others'. Sosnoski implies that intellection is something which occurs in ideal space when he contrasts 'intellectual work' with 'work-for-profit', suggesting that literary criticism is 'intellectual work', which, 'unlike work-for-profit, the success of which can be enhanced by competition . . . requires compassion, commitment, collaboration, concurrence, and community' (p. 71). But intellectual work cannot be so neatly distinguished from work-for-profit, since it is similarly motivated. Grades, degrees, grants, salaries may not bring the financial returns of market-place transactions, but they are the currency of higher learning in America. Indeed, Sosnoski's own terms suggest an economic dimension when he cites Pierre Bourdieu's description of knowledge as 'symbolic capital'; it is this conception of knowledge as 'quantifiable, measurable, and therefore cumulative' that allows 'the critic who has accumulated the most knowledge [to get] the most rewards' (p. 68). It is difficult to avoid associating this view of knowledge with capitalism.

No thought can be free of or uncontaminated by the material conditions that support it. The intellectual activity Sosnoski is describing takes place within the university, an institution deeply implicated in a socio-economic system whose law is competition. One might even argue that the university and the learning it supports are Ideological State Apparatuses, apparatuses which 'assure reproduction of the submission of labour power to the rules of the established order'.[6] In England and Europe there seems to be a clearer understanding of the educational system as an instrument of social regulation, of the curriculum as a tool of colonization, than in America.[7] In America, though the sexist and political assumptions of many particular educational practices are understood, critiques of education tend to be aimed less at understanding the way the system functions within society and more at specific problems within the system.

Insofar as the society which supports the university is competitive, so too is what goes on in the university. Academia is a meritocracy where the stakes are small and the battles are fierce; in fact the battles are fierce *because* the stakes are small, in a ratio that seems perverse until we realize that scarcity is the driving principle – and resources have been scarce in recent years, especially in the Humanities. As Evelyn Fox Keller and Helene Moglen suggest, 'as universities are presently constituted, influence and power are by definition in limited supply; in accordance with larger social assumptions the whole motivational structure is seen as organized around these limitations'.[8]

How would we go about implementing Sosnoski's suggestions? What exactly would we do? Stop competing, since by competing we only perpetuate the system we seek to change. Stop being feminist critics, since, if a feminist is someone who believes in cooperation and a critic is someone engaged in competition, then to be a 'feminist critic' is a contradiction in terms.[9] But to stop is to lose the game (if it is only a game) when we've barely begun. Sosnoski's description of the grades, degrees, jobs, publications that academics pursue as trivial pursuits or parlor games (pp. 69, 70) is a drastic misreading, itself a trivialization, of what is at stake. Jobs are only trivial pursuits to someone who has had one so long s/he's forgotten what it's like not to have one; to anyone who needs one, they are matters of survival – if not of life or death (since presumably people who don't get tenure don't starve in this society), they are matters of life or death within the profession. We need jobs in the profession in order to have any effect on the profession. As to whether we can fight the oppressor with the oppressor's weapons, we have no choice. We have no others. I realize that I am avoiding the complicated question of the relation of means and ends, a question so complex as to be finally insoluble. But we would be mad to defer action until we have settled such points.

What if we stop competing and nobody else does? Nobody else will, unless there is a revolution in the whole system of values and rewards that motivates behavior. Competition is so engraved in our hearts and minds, ingrained in every aspect of our lives – intellectual, emotional, professional – that exhortations to avoid it will not do. It is as deep in our lives as the Protestant ethic and the spirit of capitalism and is inextricably linked with both. The idea that we can change this by an exercise of individual moral will is testimony to how successfully capitalism makes itself invisible as a form of motivation and makes problems seem susceptible to solution by individual efforts. It buys into a belief in individualism which is the real engine of the system, the real driving force behind competition, an engine of which 'falsificity' is a mere piston.

It's a jungle out there and feminists are an endangered species. This is why militaristic terms and metaphors have characterized our enterprise from the start. Viragos and Amazons represent us; we dance through minefields, storm toolsheds, dismantle houses, steal the language, wrest the alphabet; we 'resist', commit 'treason', reappropriate and redirect the 'canons' that have been turned against us; and the word 'strategy' has entered the literary critical vocabulary with unprecedented vigor (Kolodny, Marcus, Lorde, Ostriker, Fetterley, Robinson, DuPlessis). Recall the beginning of *A Room of One's Own*, when Woolf, tracking the subject of women writers, is asked to leave Oxbridge and is kicked off the lawn. Feminist criticism has always been an effort of seizing occupied territory, storming an arsenal or bastion which excludes and is alien to us. This is not to say that we cannot work together, or should not, wherever possible in our interactions with colleagues and students, exercise compassion and concern. Of course we should. Most of us could not have survived without the help and encouragement of other women, individually and collectively (though competition has also been known to exist among feminists). But there are enemies out there – in a system which is inimical to what we stand for, in the forces of reaction that marshal themselves against us in a post-feminist era. Actually, feminists have been working together for many years. Sosnoski argues for collaborative work as though this were a new idea, when it has been at the heart of feminist scholarship from the beginning. Anthologies, often compiled by two or more editors and including the work of a dozen or more scholars, played a vital role in defining and developing feminist criticism (for example, Diamond and Edwards; Brown and Olsen; Eisenstein and Jardine; Hull, Scott, and Smith; Abel, Hirsch, and Langland; Lenz, Greene, and Neely; Greene and Kahn; Newton and Rosenfelt). Some feminist critics have been involved in the even more difficult enterprise of co-authorship: Gilbert and Gubar; DuBois, Kelly, Kennedy, Korsmeyer, and Robinson, to name only a few. In England, such groups as the Feminist English Group, the Women's Studies Group Centre of Contemporary Culture, the Birmingham Centre for Contemporary Cultural Studies, have been carrying on the work of cultural criticism: *Rewriting English* [10], which offers a fascinating analysis of reading and writing as 'cultural apparatuses', came out of the Birmingham Centre. These collaborative efforts, however, are signed by more than one person – whereas though Sosnoski refers to his essay as 'in most respects, collaborative', it bears only one signature. But there is nothing mystically different about collaborative criticism: it too is engaged in coming up with new readings that supplant old readings.

What most of us do is work out some terms, some compromise mode between competition and cooperation in our interactions with others and with the institutions that support us. I continue to submit papers for publication, seek grants in order to acquire time to write more such papers, evaluate the papers others have submitted for publication, assign grades – all of which participates in the value system which my writing and teaching oppose. My students graduate and take jobs in businesses, banks, advertising firms; they become cogs in a system I deplore. There is no way out of this bind, no way to avoid being employed by an educational system which is bound to a social system which transforms our best efforts of subversion into support, whatever we tell ourselves. We live amidst contradiction. And I'll bet that I have a keener sense of this than Sosnoski can have. As a woman, my behavior and appearance are more strictly regulated than his are, dictated by codes I repudiate yet conform to. My sense of contradiction begins when I get dressed each day; I walk a fine line in my interactions with colleagues, trying not to threaten while also salvaging some self-respect. I perform complex negotiations in order to maintain my footing in an academic hierarchy I deplore, in order to achieve power within that hierarchy, in order perhaps to exert some slight influence in changing that hierarchy. Each day is a minefield through which I pick my way in sensible but not unbecoming shoes. But I do not kid myself that this can be wished or willed away.

We teeter precariously along fine lines. We pick our stands, decide which positions we can best defend, what battles we have a chance of winning, and fight them compassionately (if that is possible). And perhaps even to think of this as 'contradiction' is itself to be caught in the hold of a binary opposition. As Keller and Moglen suggest:

> Given the fact that neither competition nor cooperation alone can adequately describe real interaction between people in a real world . . . how many of our difficulties are exacerbated by the acceptance of a bifurcation between these two modes of interaction? All of us, it seems, would be aided by an entirely new perspective . . . that posits an *a priori* dialectical relation between competition and cooperation that might differently shape our development . . . the recognition of a fundamental interconnection that is essential to dialogic engagement.[11]

Perhaps it would liberate us to think not in terms of contradiction, but of dialectical relation. To acknowledge this interaction of competition and cooperation in our behavior might unlock the hold of an either-or category and allow us to envision new possibilities.

Though it is probably not apparent from what I have just said, I actually welcome the participation of men in feminism – though I suspect they can never be more than fellow travellers. But I find Sosnoski's position, however well-intentioned, obfuscating to the point of being disempowering. We need to cut through the mystification that obscures the nature of the work we do. Sosnoski's argument resembles other positions prevalent in academia, where things get talked about in a never-never land of bourgeois idealism removed from the realities of people's lives or of the profession. This is why academics don't have labor unions, better salaries, protection for part-time employees. We need to see things for what they are, to call them by their proper names, before we can change them.

Change is hard. Anyone who has tried to change or even thought about it or who has seriously engaged in teaching anyone anything, knows this. To change oneself or someone else, to learn something new or to teach something new, requires that someone give something up, whether political power or a cherished illusion; and people don't willingly let go of what they have. This is why change often requires violent means. But short of this, it requires power. Anyone involved in efforts of change needs power; educators, critics, feminists, reformers, need power; women especially need power because men have more to give up than women do. To underestimate the difficulties of this is simply to lose. To lose is to remain in the positions of marginality where we have always been. This is my quarrel with Sosnoski.

NOTES

1 We emphasized this problem in the Introduction to *Making a Difference*: 'Feminist scholarship and the social construction of woman'. Greene and Kahn 1985: 1-36.

2 See Ellen Messer-Davidow's discussion of 'ways of reconstituting knowledge' for a brilliant analysis of this issue: Messer-Davidow 1987: 66.

3 Jameson 1981: 65.

4 Derrida 1979; Furman 1975: 75.

5 Batsleer et al. 1985: 26; see also Belsey's discussion of F. R. Leavis's *The Great Tradition* in terms of the 'production of discrimination' and 'the making of hierarchies through judgments of relative human value, not just in literature but in life': Belsey 1982: 129.

6 Althusser 1971: 143-5, 132; Althusser describes 'the educational' as having replaced the church as 'the dominant' cultural apparatus (p. 157).

7 See, for example, Batsleer et al. 1985; Longhurst 1982; Sinfield 1985 and the numerous studies referred to by Sinfield.

8 Keller and Moglen 1987: 22.

9 Keller and Moglen (1987) also note that 'the morality of the women's movement, with its emphasis upon mutuality, concern, and support, seems tremendously difficult to implement in the real-world situations of the current academic marketplace.' As feminist scholarship moves into 'the conventional reward system', collectivity comes to seem like 'a myth that seems ever more remote from our actual experience' (pp. 29-30). The anthology in which this essay appears, *Competition: A Feminist Taboo*, offers fascinating discussions of this and numerous other contradictions that beset feminists (Miner and Longino 1987).

10 Batsleer et al. 1985.

11 Keller and Moglen 1987: 36-7.

REFERENCES

Abel, Elizabeth, Hirsch, Marianne and Langland, Elizabeth (eds) 1983. *The Voyage In: Fictions of Female Development*. Hanover, NH: University Press of New England.

Althusser, Louis 1971. 'Ideology and ideological state apparatuses (notes towards an investigation)', in *Lenin and Philosophy and Other Essays*, trans. Ben Brewster. New York and London: Monthly Review Press: 127-86.

Batsleer, Janet, Davies, Tony, O'Rourke, Rebecca and Weedon, Chris 1985. *Rewriting English: Cultural Politics of Gender and Class*. London and New York: Methuen.

Belsey, Catherine 1982. 'Re-reading the Great Tradition', in Widdowson 1982: 121-35.

Brown, Cheryl L. and Olsen, Karen (eds) 1978. *Feminist Criticism: Essays on Theory, Poetry, and Prose*. Metuchen, NJ: Scarecrow Press.

Derrida, Jacques 1979. *Spurs: Nietzsche's Style*. Trans. Barbara Harlow. Chicago: University of Chicago Press.

Diamond, Arlyn and Edwards, Lee R. (eds) 1977. *The Authority of Experience: Essays in Feminist Criticism*. Amherst: University of Massachusetts Press.

DuBois, Ellen Carol, Kelly, Gail Paradise, Kennedy, Elizabeth Lapovsky, Korsmeyer, Carolyn W. and Robinson, Lillian S. 1985. *Feminist Scholarship: Kindling in the Groves of Academe*. Urbana: University of Illinois Press.

DuPlessis, Rachel Blau 1985. *Writing Beyond the Ending: Narrative Strategies of Twentieth-Century Women Writers*. Bloomington: Indiana University Press.

Eisenstein, Hester and Jardine, Alice (eds) 1980. *The Future of Difference: The Scholar and the Feminist*. Boston: G. K. Hall.

Fetterley, Judith 1978. *The Resisting Reader: A Feminist Approach to American Fiction*. Bloomington: Indiana University Press.

Furman, Nelly. 'The politics of language', in Greene and Kahn 1985: 69-79.

Gauthier, Xaviere 1980. 'Is there such a thing as women's writing?', in *New French Feminisms*, ed. Elaine Marks and Isabelle de Courtivron. Amherst: University of Massachusetts Press: 161-4.

Gilbert, Sandra M. and Gubar, Susan 1979. *The Madwoman in the Attic: The Woman Writer and the Nineteenth-Century Literary Imagination*. New Haven: Yale University Press.

Gilbert, Sandra M. and Gubar, Susan 1987. *No Man's Land: The Place of the Woman Writer in the Twentieth Century*. New Haven: Yale University Press.

Greene, Gayle and Kahn, Coppélia 1985. *Making a Difference: Feminist Literary Criticism*. London and New York: Methuen.

Hull, Gloria T., Scott, Patricia Bell and Smith, Barbara (eds) 1982. *All the Women are White, All the Blacks are Men, But Some of Us are Brave*. Old Westbury, NY: Feminist Press.

Jacobus, Mary 1979. 'The difference of view', in *Women Writing and Writing About Women*, ed. M. Jacobus. New York: Barnes and Noble: 10-21.

Jameson, Fredric 1981. *The Political Unconscious: Narrative as a Socially Symbolic Act*. Ithaca: Cornell University Press.

Keller, Evelyn Fox and Moglen, Helene 1987. 'Competition: a problem for academic women', in Miner and Longino 1987: 21-37.

Kolodny, Annette 1980. 'Dancing through the minefield: some observations on the theory, practice and politics of a feminist literary criticism', *Feminist Studies*, 6.1 (Spring): 1-25.

Lenz, Carolyn Ruth Swift, Greene, Gayle and Neely, Carol (eds) 1980. *The Woman's Part: Feminist Criticism of Shakespeare*. Champaign: University of Illinois Press.

Longhurst, Derek 1982. ' "Not for all time, but for an Age": an approach to Shakespeare studies', in Widdowson 1982: 150-63.

Lorde, Audre 1981. 'The master's tools will never dismantle the master's house', in *This Bridge Called my Back: Writings by Radical Women of Color*, ed. Cherrie Moraga and Gloria Anzaldua. Watertown, Mass.: Persephone Press: 98-101.

Marcus, Jane 1982. 'Storming the toolshed', *Signs: Journal of Women in Culture and Society*, 7. 3: 622-40.

Marcus, Jane 1984. 'Still practice, a/wrested alphabet: toward a feminist aesthetic', *Tulsa Studies in Women's Literature*, 3. 1/2 (Spring/Fall): 79-97.

Messer-Davidow, Ellen 1987. 'The philosophical bases of feminist literary criticisms',

New Literary History, 19. 1 (Autumn): 65-103. Repr. in *Gender and Theory: Dialogues on Feminist Criticism*. ed. Linda Kauffman. Oxford and New York: Basil Blackwell, 1989.

Miner, Valerie and Longino, Helen E. (eds) 1987. *Competition: A Feminist Taboo?*. New York: Feminist Press.

Newton, Judith and Rosenfelt, Deborah (eds) 1985. *Feminist Criticism and Social Change: Sex, Class and Race in Literature and Culture*. New York: Methuen.

Ostriker, Alicia Suskin 1986. *Stealing the Language: The Emergence of Women's Poetry in America*. Boston: Beacon Press.

Robinson, Lillian S. 1984. 'Treason our text: feminist challenges to the literary canon', *Tulsa Studies in Women's Literature*, 3.1/2 (Spring/Fall): 83-98.

Robinson, Lillian S. 1985. 'Their canon, our arsenal', No. 21 in the Working Papers Series of the Stanford University Institution for Research on Women and Gender. Stanford, CA: 1-20.

Robinson, Lillian S. 1987. 'Canon fathers and myth universe', *New Literary History* 20 (Autumn): 23-35.

Sinfield, Alan 1985. 'Give an account of Shakespeare and Education, showing why you think they are effective and what you have appreciated about them. Support your comments with precise references', in *Political Shakespeare: New Essays in Cultural Materialism*, ed. Jonathan Dolimore and Alan Sinfield. Ithaca and London: Cornell University Press: 134-57.

Widdowson, Peter 1982. *Re-Reading English*. London: Methuen.

5

Treating Me Like an Object: Reading Catharine MacKinnon's Feminism

William Beatty Warner

Man fucks woman; subject verb object.

> Catharine MacKinnon,
> 'Feminism, marxism, method, and the state'

Men are strangely positioned in relation to feminism. Most feminist writing is written by women, addressed to other women; it enters and constitutes the circle of women's common concerns. Feminist discourse is not shaped for men's reception; they are the silenced problem in this situation. If they listen, they listen as eavesdroppers. When one has not been clearly and directly addressed, there are peculiar risks to speaking: one may be judged an obtuse and intrusive boor, who ventures where he is not invited, and speaks out of turn. In fact it is not clear that feminist discourse promises men a turn. Men may have always already had theirs. A turn for men to speak on the questions of feminism, without speaking out of turn, may be what the play space of *Feminism and Institutions* is all about. But if men are excluded in advance from speaking in the space of feminist discourse, this turn may be false or forced in some fundamental way, and then the play structure of this collection will not really change this fundamental fact.

However, there are reasons to believe that feminism's exclusion of men is not complete. That men are addressed by feminism, not directly, as partners in dialogue, but indirectly, may be opined from the fact that many feminists covertly expect men to 'get the message'. Only in this way could feminism redraw the social charter, by restructuring everything from housework to pleasure. Silenced in advance by a discourse which discusses social arrangements in which they have a vital interest, men are positioned to *overhear* language to which they are not invited to respond. Viewed from the standpoint of a democratic ideology of the 'free' transmission of ideas, this collective silencing of men (whatever the difference of their politics) may seem unfair. But given the history of gender relations, it is strangely apposite. For men have been positioned in relation to feminist discourse in a fashion which seems to echo the way feminism has demonstrated women to have been positioned by masculinist discourse: they find themselves compelled to overhear in silence a language not addressed to them, but which is supposed to guide or change their behavior. The embarrassment which men may feel operates as a repetition of what men have made women feel many times before.

Offered the opportunity for a critical engagement with feminism, I find myself immediately distrusting two of the most readily available modes of response. The objective critical analysis presents itself as that which can be seen by any observer dispassionate enough to look. Such an analysis would stand apart from what feminism is trying to do at the many levels of its operation and work, so as to describe its value, and the limits of its value. This form of address assumes that I am speaking neither as a male nor a female, but as a rational being, an epistemological stance beneath which feminism finds a covert male bias under its overt neutrality. The drawbacks of an objective criticism of feminism should be all too evident. Such a way of writing obscures the several ways in which I find myself already thrown into a personal, social, and political relationship to feminism: the anger of feminist critique of the subordination of women to man in this culture is not just another 'idea' out there for me to consider, but is a critical discourse aimed at men in general, and all persons, whatever their/our differences, who have learned to be men, including me. This social and critical agon is already operating to shape my approach to feminism, throwing me into a hermeneutic relation to feminism which is prior to an abstract relation based on the claims of truth. The very cultural object with which I would begin dialogue – feminism – has itself put in question the possibility of anything like the 'dispassionate' neutrality and objectivity that traditional codes of academic analysis have idealized.

There is another pathway for engaging feminism which seems just as problematic as the methods of objective knowledge: the earnest sympathetic dialogue. Here I would begin by defining myself as self-present to an experience labeled in advance as 'male', so, from that 'male position' I might respond to what I understand feminism to be saying. Perhaps adopting an engagingly personal voice, I could begin by affirming my broad solidarity with feminism; this would entitle me to describe my unease with various particular positions of feminism. A sincere tone would be requisite. The sympathy with which I would describe my understanding of struggles not my own might be paired with an acknowledgment of differences of gender viewpoint which could never be completely effaced. To legitimize such a mode of address, I could refer, in imitation of the personal mode familiar within feminism, to the contingencies of history which might make me less resistant to feminist criticism than many men. My earliest experience predisposed me to know women as equals. In growing up, I was closest to my twin sister. She and I were raised by a mother who was a successful writer, whose mother was in her turn a famous opera singer.

What makes such a mode of address impossible is its presumption. It presumes upon a shared social agenda which may no longer exist – or may never have existed. It assumes that the difference between men and women is of a fixed nature, and can be defined; that across such a distance, subjects self-present to each other in speech can engage in a dialogue, where men and women could, with good will and the right openness to each other, talk their way to some collective understanding and social truth. The feminist critique of our culture and society may be so fundamental and pervasive that it has thrown the agents, ground-rules and agenda of that social dialogue into question. After feminism, it appears less clear what women or men are or want, and if they were to know, how their differences and commonalities might be construed. Initiating a dialogue in such a situation would require that one understands one's desire in relation to feminism, and can name it without all the ruses of social masquerade; and that within the vertiginous whirl of the war now going on between masculinist and feminist positions, and within the various feminisms, one could assume the role of that diplomat in gender relations who could define the conditions for a peace settlement binding within the new heterosexual commonweal.

To respond to feminism personally and as a male would merely implicate this essay in what I take to be one of the abiding limitations of too much of current argumentation in and about feminism – speaking from the standpoint of one's gender. If it has become too facile to declare – as Plato, Freud, and Woolf in very different ways have done – that everyone is bisexual, then of late it has surely become too comforting to suppose that one's gender offers a pure and absolute place from which to speak. Instead, it may just lead to a charade in control of the subject, where the speaker assumes not only that she/he knows their diacritical difference from the opposite sex, but that they comprehend, in the secure, chummy and unreflective way in which one might belong to a club, team, or party, what their own sex is, and/or 'has in common'. Speaking from the standpoint of gender has become a way not of investigating, but of erasing the necessity or full complexity of one's position, whatever the sources of that position are.

Feminism confronts its reader with the problem which has always challenged its own discursive formations: how to name, hear, or describe an other (in this instance, 'woman') so that that other does not, through the work of one's writing and thought, become a version of the same ('man' for example, or what 'man' has always known 'woman' to be). A dialogic response to feminism needs to come to terms with what Simone de Beauvoir emphasizes in the introduction to *The Second Sex*: the non-symmetrical, non-complementary aspect of woman's position as 'other', opposite man. The objective and personal responses to feminism seek to occlude the challenge of this other in two different ways: first through the absorption of the other into a comprehending scientific subject; and second through a settling of this otherness into a knowable difference-between-the-sexes. There is a third way to annul otherness, all the more subtle for the way it seems to be doing just the opposite: by staging a melodramatic encounter of man and woman, where the male speaker postulates as his interlocutor a romantically enigmatic Other. This myth of woman-as-sphinx turns out to be familiar and comforting enough; *she* quickly becomes a site for oedipal heroism. Thus my problem becomes, how can one begin an exchange in language with feminism where the otherness of the other would not be reduced by the form of the exchange, so that the variety and ambiguity of the differences between men and women, reader and text, myself and feminism, would not, as part of the game, have to be declared in advance in a clear and explicit way, but would be allowed to work themselves out over the course of that response?

That the question of men's relationship with feminism has become a timely issue for our intellectual culture is suggested by the publication, during the final revisions of this essay, of the collection *Men in Feminism*.[1] There male and female critics develop varied and subtle theoretical reflections on the same topic which I am exploring: what is the position of those men who have read and endorsed a good deal of the feminist critique of masculinist culture? The collection is compelling for the way each analysis of this question documents the cultural problem it would explore. If in psychoanalysis, dream analysis becomes a second secondary revision of the dream, then in cultural analysis, the secondary revision of *Men in Feminism* offers a strangely new yet strangely familiar transposition of the social text of feminism. By describing my reservations about this collection, I can offer a clearer sense of my chosen point of departure for a critical engagement with feminism. *Men in Feminism* intentionally provokes us to think about those men who are or wish to be 'in' feminism. They might be 'in' feminism conceptually, through their endorsement of feminism's political positions, but they also may be, more problematically, 'in' feminism in another way: they desire to enter (violate, enjoy, experience) feminism in a fashion which is analogous with the way a male (lover?, seducer?, rapist?) might seek to enter woman. This analogy forces us to confront the necessity of a sexual element in men's relation to feminism. The metaphorics of sexuality may write itself into every phrase of that relation. But just as feminism critiques the recurrent sexualizing of women by masculinist culture, the effort to analogize feminism with women can displace and attenuate the critical force of feminism. Because feminism is a discursive formation which develops a comprehensive critique of culture, it becomes limiting and partial to take feminism as a figure of women, and to reduce men's engagement with feminism to a sexual exchange, whether personal or collective, real or fantasmatic.

In this essay, I diverge from the implied ground rules of *Men in Feminism*. In order to debate the problem of men in feminism, a number of the essays in that volume assume or define a politically correct feminism for men. In the volume's exchanges, the issue of a prescriptive 'political correctness' becomes a matter for explicit debate.[2] It is this implied consensus, however tenuous and plural, which allows the critical gaze to pass over, through, and beyond the many issues raised by feminism. This sense of terrain already traveled allows that reflexive gesture by which men and women can join to debate men's proper (or improper) relation to feminism. Though the resulting articulation of positions is fascinating, it risks traveling too fast. By contrast, I would like to retrace several steps on this implied itinerary, so as to understand and even contest what I take to be some of the fundamental conceptual problems of feminism, as they express themselves in that specific form of feminism which Catharine MacKinnon develops. Thus, to re-engage the metaphorics of *Men in Feminism*, my own critical engagement with feminism is neither launched from within feminism, nor from some hostile or antagonistic position outside feminism, but from the region of feminism's border with other discursive formations. This boundary position does not involve me in claims to any special objectivity about feminism. Instead it suggests my sense that the critical issues raised by feminism are not yet resolved. By staying behind to read some of feminism's initial positions, I hope to be able to come to terms with the political rhetoric and cultural work of feminism.

It is the gambit of this essay that a critical exchange with feminism may best be attempted through a detailed reading of particular feminist texts. I have chosen selected writings of Catharine MacKinnon because her work brings the political task of feminism into the foreground of feminist intellectual work. But while MacKinnon's essays have been influential, and they attempt to summarize and reconcile many of the central concepts of feminism, her final positions are neither typical nor 'mainstream'. Her positions, and the assumptions about social relations out of which they emerge, are at odds with liberal humanist feminism, and with French feminism, which she explicitly criticizes. A brief description of MacKinnon's work will suggest why it offers a valuable test case of an effort to do theoretical criticism which is also politically engaged. In the early 1980s Catharine MacKinnon published a two-part essay in *Signs* entitled 'Feminism, marxism, method, and the state', which sought to bring together a broad range of feminist critical work of the 1960s and 1970s into a internally consistent synthesis. To do this MacKinnon carries out a strong reading of Marxism[3] so that the resources of its critique of social and political domination can be put to work for feminism. She does not offer a theory about feminism, but about feminist theory – theory which aims to advance feminist goals. Thus Part I of her essay, subtitled 'An agenda for theory', is explicitly paired with the more practical sequel, subtitled 'Toward feminist jurisprudence'; and both these essays need to be read against the practice her theory is intended to explain, justify and advance. In her book, *Sexual Harassment of Working Women*, MacKinnon sought to define the legal context for interpreting sexual harassment as a form of sex discrimination. In 1985 she worked with city officials of Indianapolis to draft an ordinance against pornography, many of the terms of which were later endorsed in 1986 by the Attorney General's Commission on Pornography.

Though MacKinnon's final views – on everything from rape and pornography to civil liberties and the state – are not typical, the systematic radicality of MacKinnon's writing offers special advantages for my reading. MacKinnon often takes to their logical limit ideas which other feminists invoke in a more guarded and tentative way. Thus, when it comes to the use of a fundamental idea of feminism – like the idea that

masculinist culture makes woman the manipulated object of male subjectivity – MacKinnon's work allows us to read the metaphysical presuppositions, full tendency, and practical effects of this idea. But what is the value
of my resorting to *close reading* of political texts? For MacKinnon's work
has the tone of a manifesto, carrying the urgent intention that its ideas be
understood 'as they are written'. The bold directness and chiseled concision of MacKinnon's style are indices of her clear purpose, polemical
decision, and fixed determination. To take account of the pragmatic
political tendency of MacKinnon's work it is essential not simply to
bracket, but to make a detailed accounting of the theme, content, and
intent of her feminism. But we must do more. Because this is a 'reading',
in the sense used in literary studies, it will take seriously, and seek to
interpret, the language-bound rhetorical turns of MacKinnon's text,
everything from the *way* she frames her argument, to the *tone and coloring* of her language, and the *details* of her text. I assume that these are
crucial aspects of what allows this text to do its political and conceptual
work. To use modes of reading developed in the areas of literary analysis
and psychoanalysis to analyze the latent logic of MacKinnon's essay,
from within the language of its own argument, will be indispensable if we
are to release some of the unconscious tendencies of MacKinnon's feminist
writing. My reading will seek to overcome the separation between logic
and rhetoric, content and form, concept and style through which the conventional discourses of social analysis occult their authority. Only then
can we hope to come to terms with the divergence between what feminism
says, states, sees, and what it expresses dialogically and performs discursively. This divergence within feminism's language, while often
obscured or denied, is a constitutive part of what allows feminism to
change the value of women in culture.[4]

The dialectical emergence of the feminist subject

MacKinnon's first *Signs* essay describes and enacts an event of central
importance to feminism: the emergence of a feminist subject who can
assume a newly empowered place on the stage of history. This event is
presented indirectly through another story or scenario: an encounter
between feminism and Marxism, whereby feminism becomes the revealed
truth of the Marxist critique of domination, and through the feminist
'method' of 'consciousness raising', the instrument of a revolutionary

encounter with state power. MacKinnon first describes how feminist theory is weakened when it is not fortified by the encounter with Marxism she advocates. Too often feminism has been assumed to be nothing more than 'a loose collection of factors, complaints, and issues which, taken together, describe rather than explain the misfortunes of the female sex'.[5] By contrast MacKinnon states the ambitious goal for feminist theory her article is to set the agenda for reaching: 'The challenge is to demonstrate that feminism systematically converges upon a central explanation of sex inequality through an approach distinctive to its subject yet applicable to the whole of social life, including class' (p. 14). By this argument, feminism is not to be a self-contained alternative to Marxism, simply another theory one chooses because, for example, one is a woman. Feminism, by MacKinnon's account, must encompass and complete, go through and beyond what Marxism does by explaining what Marxism can't explain (sex discrimination) as well as explaining what it does try to explain. Thus it is a global project, with explanatory power over the whole social field. Feminism, MacKinnon implies, is not just the next step in social theory; it is the next step in history. What are the conceptual and narrative means by which MacKinnon makes this surpassing of Marxism by feminism seem possible or likely?

MacKinnon takes the speculative dialectic first formalized by Hegel, and adopted for revolutionary social theory and practice by Marx, and makes it the instrument, engine, and plotting device of her own narrative of feminism's victory over Marxism. MacKinnon's use of a dialectic allows her to do several things: to take the critique of class domination developed by Marx and extend it to a feminist critique of the subordination of woman; and to describe, summarize, and critique the great variety of feminist work, with its divergent premises, so they become contributing moments in a newly unified and conceptually coherent feminism; finally, the dialectical form of her essay makes the progress from social transformation led by Marxism to that mounted by a radical feminism, seem logically, rhetorically, and historically inevitable. How is the dialectic able to serve MacKinnon in all these ways? While the word 'challenge' in the phrase 'the challenge is to demonstrate' may suggest the effort, whether individual or collective, necessary to launching a feminist theory, the conceptual and rhetorical appeal of the dialectic comes from the autonomy of motion it implies. Like a game, intense rivalry or a chemical reaction, once antagonists or agents or ideas are drawn into the ordered oppositional encounter of the dialectic, some sort of forward movement and metamorphosis to a higher form appears inevitable. It is like a perpetual motion machine, whose movement is periodic, but spirally advancing and forever new. Moments of transformation and overturning approach when there is a specular reciprocity between the terms which encounter one another, then, suddenly, a determinate negation of the differences between terms in preparation for a movement to a higher level. These changes of state are presumed to be efficient: everything that existed at the earlier stage is broken down (undergoes destruction), but then is raised up (to new forms and uses). The wonderful magic of the dialectic consists in its apparent autonomy: there is no manipulation of this sequence of change from outside the dialectic, and yet change is neither random, nor without direction: it unfolds in a logical direction through the unhindered encounter of the terms/antagonists of the dialectical narrative.[6]

MacKinnon begins the dialectical encounter of feminism and Marxism with an extended analogy, and develops it through a (mock) dialogue or debate. The first sentence of 'Feminism, marxism, method, and the state: an agenda for theory' defines the initial structuring analogy of the essay: 'Sexuality is to feminism what work is to marxism: that which is most one's own, yet most taken away' (p. 1). In the paragraphs which follow, MacKinnon aligns each basic term of the Marxist critique of capitalism with a term of feminism: sexuality is analogous with work, because both are made of mind and matter, both are expropriated for the use of others, and both are socially constructed and constructing. In a similar way desire is analogized with value, heterosexuality with class, gender and family with capital, reproduction with production. For both feminism and Marxism, control is declared to be the central political issue. This set of analogies serves to set Marxism and feminism opposite one another, so that, 'confronted on equal terms, these theories pose fundamental questions for each other' (p. 3).

MacKinnon next stages a dialogue, which will explore differences as well as similarities. In reading this fictional 'dialogue' one soon notices that the reference of the terms 'feminism' and 'marxism' is overdetermined. They are not just rival systems for choreographing social liberation; they also figure two gender positions - 'marxism' for men, and 'feminism' for women. MacKinnon rehearses the struggle between these two. Acting as fair-minded referee, she describes how Marxism and feminism have usually tried to reduce, accuse, subsume the other. The Marxist critique of feminism is rehearsed: analysis of society in terms of sex ignores class, divides the proletariat, is too often carried on in the name of liberal and individualistic values, on behalf of privileged middle-class women. Feminism criticizes Marxism as a system which is male-defined, obscures woman's distinctive social experience and unity, and seeks a change in class relations that would leave women's inequality to men unchanged. Thus, MacKinnon finds that each accuses the other of reform, 'where (again in each one's terms) a fundamental overthrow is required' (p. 4).

MacKinnon assumes that women are not defined by any intrinsic factor like biology, but are a social construction produced by and for male power. This leads to the particularly extreme negation of woman which other feminists have noted in MacKinnon:

> A woman is a being who identifies and is identified as one whose sexuality exists for someone else, who is socially male. . . . If . . . female sexuality cannot be lived or spoken or felt or even somatically sensed apart from its enforced definition, so that it is its own lack, then there is no such thing as a woman as such, there are only walking embodiments of men's projected needs. (pp. 19-20)

Donna Haraway remarks on the irony which besets this definition: 'MacKinnon's radical theory is totalizing in the extreme . . . producing what Western patriarchy itself never succeeded in doing - feminists' consciousness of the non-existence of women, except as products of men's desire.'[7] MacKinnon's characterization of woman as a blank screen, given her only visible definition by male power, is not just historically descriptive; by the formal rules of the dialectic, a determinate negation of 'woman' will be essential for her emergence as a newly empowered subject, the woman (of the future) her essay heralds.

Woman can begin to exist in a new way through a process or method called 'consciousness raising', a pathway of inquiry grounded in what MacKinnon calls the 'feminist concept of the personal as political'. Consciousness raising has a special role to play in this dialectical progression: as 'a concept', in a more technical sense of the Hegelian *Begriff*, it functions as a hook to carry a term (in this case woman) in a movement which combines destruction, saving, and raising up (called 'sublation', or *aufheben*) on to a higher level of the dialectic. In this way woman goes from being the shattered and negated victim of male power to being someone who lays claim to a newly formed and raised consciousness. MacKinnon's account turns feminist 'consciousness raising' into a pun

on the Hegelian dialectic. The superiority to Marxism MacKinnon claims
for this method on behalf of feminism is based upon its ability to allow
women to confront the way domination operates both inside and outside
the victim. The personal interiorizing tendency of this 'method' allows
feminism to take the way man has objectified woman, and interiorize that
'woman' as part of a dialectical movement beyond masculinist cultural
formations. Both inside and outside 'male paradigms', woman's subjectivity has grown more comprehensive than man's.

The emergence of the female subject of feminism is made possible by
her overcoming of the status she has been given by masculinist culture –
that of an object. This apparently happens dialectically, but if we look
more closely at MacKinnon's analysis we shall find something else. Let's
locate the precise steps by which MacKinnon argues for the possibility of
woman's moving beyond subjection as object to male subjectivity, to
becoming a Subject in her own right. According to MacKinnon, the male
'objectification' of woman is not just an attitudinal or ideological matter,
but that which shapes sexuality into 'a material reality of women's lives'
(p. 25). Borrowing from the Marxist analysis of the commodity fetish,
MacKinnon describes the way woman is constructed and valued as a
fetish object by the social relations tailored to male interest: 'Like the
value of a commodity, women's sexual desirability is fetishized: it is made
to appear a quality of the object itself, spontaneous and inherent, independent of the social relation which creates it, uncontrolled by the force that
requires it' (p. 26). This leads, according to MacKinnon, to certain
degraded kinds of sexual practice: 'it helps if the object cooperates: hence,
the vaginal orgasm; hence faked orgasms altogether. Women's sexual-
ness, like male prowess, is no less real for being mythic. It is embodied'
(pp. 26-7). According to MacKinnon these objectifications of woman's
sexuality are the 'primary process of the subjection of women' (p. 27). A
couple of paragraphs later, MacKinnon will stage the decisive overcoming
of woman's subjection. But before this can happen, and as part of this
article's sustained analogical relationship with Marxism (and the relationship with man figured indirectly though Marxism), a crucial argument is
launched: MacKinnon distinguishes feminism from Marxism on the issue
of objectification and alienation. This apparently abstruse theoretical
debate is the place where MacKinnon plots woman's victory over the
object:

Objectification in marxist materialism is thought to be the foundation of human freedom, the work process whereby a subject becomes embodied in products and relationships. Alienation is the socially contingent distortion of that process, a reification of products and relations which prevents them from being, and being seen as, dependent on human agency. But from the point of view of the object, objectification *is* alienation. For women, there is no distinction between objectification and alienation because women have not authored objectifications, we have been them. Women have been the nature, the matter, the acted upon, to be subdued by the acting subject seeking to embody himself in the social world. (pp. 27-8)

From within the narrative of the master/slave episode in Hegel, part of the slave's hidden power comes from his greater proximity to the object world through work; within Marx's translation of that story, the worker's power comes from the union of the revolutionary consciousness of his own alienation with the power which accrues to the workers because of their greater proximity to the material conditions of life. In this passage of MacKinnon's text, the crucial juncture in her argument comes when, after she has distinguished the Marxist concepts of 'objectification' and 'alienation', she then asserts the woman's point of view as not that of the slave/worker, that is the subject who is inferior to another subject (the master/the capitalist/man), but as 'the point of view of the object'. Woman *is* the object. Not only does this intensify woman's subjection to man, as placed below even the worker, who at least can work upon the objects of the world. It takes woman completely out of the world of subjects. This is important, for this also takes woman out of the pathway of mediations, by which she could, like the slave in Hegel's speculative dialectic, or the worker in Marx's materialist dialectic, ascend through the social world of subjects. Instead within MacKinnon's account, subject and object become two terms in a trope of antithesis, here coded to become a pure moral opposition. This moral condemnation of the object, and the position of the object, prepares not for a complex and imperfect dialectical progression, but rather for the reversal by which the woman ascends to a position of pure subjectivity (as Woman). This abolition of the object is most crucial, because without some un-sublated notion of the object and the material, MacKinnon has inadvertently given her argument over to a radical idealism. Below we shall try to gauge some of the effects of this idealism.

In the course of MacKinnon's account the meaning of the terms 'subject' and 'object' have undergone significant change. They no longer seem to have the positional and relational status which allows subjects and objects in a sentence to reverse places, or one human subject to take another as its object, who is in *its* turn then capable, as a second human subject, of taking the first as its object. This is the sort of morally neutral usage which Freud draws upon when he describes the infant's relation to the mother's body as 'object-relations theory'. Instead, MacKinnon's analysis draws upon the semantic resources of the word 'object' as found in the phrase 'treating me like an object'. This, as we have seen, is what MacKinnon says masculinist culture has done to women since its beginnings. But MacKinnon radicalizes this accusation by moving from the term denoting a simile or comparison – male subjects have treated women subjects 'like', in the same unfeeling and inhuman way, one might treat an object – to a condition of being: within the system of male power woman *is* an object.

The counter-movement MacKinnon's essay describes – woman's oscillation from the abject position of object to being a subject – is justified by the assertion of what might be called a philosophic or interpretive voluntarism. Through MacKinnon's account, the opposition subject/object is no longer a fundamental distinction of philosophy or grammar, but instead becomes a notion which is dispensable by fiat. She writes: 'Having been objectified as sexual beings while stigmatized as ruled by subjective passions, women reject the distinction between knowing subject and known object – the division between subject and objective postures – as the means to comprehend social life. . . . woman's interest lies in overthrowing the distinction itself' (p. 22). Notice that in these sentences the opposition passes from being the agent and object of knowledge to being two 'postures' a single subject might assume, to finally being a distinction which can be 'overthrown'. One sees what is problematic about this gesture, if one asks: what is it that in this sentence calls, from the authority of their experience as sufferers, for the 'overthrowing' of the distinction between subject and object? It can't be anything but a subject. There is no way for the subject or *cogito* (a person defined as subject by her practice of self-consciousness) to stand outside her being as subject, simply because she wishes to do so. It seems to be this two-sidedness claimed for consciousness raising – 'it is at once common sense expression and critical articulation of concepts' (p. 22) which allows MacKinnon to think feminism has gone beyond what she labels disapprovingly as the 'subject/object split'. But this does not mean that MacKinnon's *own* ways of thinking and writing have gone beyond such an opposition. Thus right up to the last sentence of her essay, Marxism and man still lie outside the compass of woman's subjectivity, and are made the objects of her analysis. The positional and oppositional status of subject and object has reasserted itself beneath the voluntaristic interdiction against their use.

If one were to state the plot of MacKinnon's 'agenda for theory' in one sentence it would have the pure oppositional rhythm of a revenge fiction: woman goes from being the object of male power to being a subject in her own right. By becoming heir to the subjectivity once reserved for the male subject, the raising of woman's consciousness would be the story of woman's ascension from victim to victor, from object to subjecthood. Directed by a rational analysis of power, and enabled by the morally justified abolition of objects, MacKinnon's projection of woman toward the condition of pure subject is readable in two ways. First, MacKinnon concludes Part One of her essay with this climactic image of reversal:

Compared with marxism, the place of thought and things in method and reality are reversed in a seizure of power that penetrates subject with object and theory with practice. In a dual motion, feminism turns marxism inside out and on its head. . . . feminism revolution-izes politics. (p. 30)

Revolution happens through reversal. Feminism can take charge from her inferior brother, Marxism, and turn him 'inside out and on [his] head' because of the claim that she has overcome the split between subject and object, theory and practice. This superiority as method allows feminism to carry out another kind of reversal: the 'seizure of power' by which power can be taken out of male hands. Thus part two of this article characterizes the state as male, and begins to frame the 'feminist jurisprudence' which can work to open the power traditionally focused in the state to manipu-lation by feminism. MacKinnon's adoption of this strategy in framing her ordinance against pornography in Indianapolis necessitated forming alliances with the Right. In debate with feminists at a conference on 'Feminist discourse, moral values and the law', sponsored by the Buffalo Law School, on 19 October 1984, MacKinnon defends this strategy. The language she uses offers an example of the masterful female subject, making calculations of advantage to women from the position of a rational transparency of conceptual operations:

We are looking to empower women. We have the audacity to think that we might be able to use the state to help do it. It is either going to do something real for us or it is not. We can decide that the state is not an arena to use; we can also decide that it is not an arena to use in this case.[8]

Feminism's newly empowered position in relation to Marxism suggests what has been the deeper rhetorical tendency of MacKinnon's analysis. The ascension of the Woman to the position of Subject is presented as a dialectical progress; but beneath the dialectic MacKinnon explicitly invokes, her text is determined by the trope of antithesis, no longer understood as a single moment in a dialectical progression, but rather as an operation which takes two terms and (as implied by the etymology from the Greek) 'place[s] [them] against' one another, as opposing terms. This means there is to be nothing of subject in object, object in subject, man in woman, woman in man. Antithesis is the trope which facilitates the chiasmic turn by which purely oppositional terms undergo a pure reversal of priority. The woman/object (of masculinist discourse) becomes subject; the man/subject becomes object (of a feminist discourse). Objects had only apparently been abolished, for this argument does not move us into a purely rational domain of spirit or absolute knowledge. Instead the new objects are Marxism - 'turned upside down and inside out' - and 'man', now objectified as the Objectifier of woman - rapist, pornographer, and wielder of victimizing, illegitimate forms of state power. There is an irony about the 'audacious' feminist manipulation of state power MacKinnon advocates: such a manipulation seems to confer upon the feminist subject those qualities of mastery which seemed the properties of the male subject from the perspective of woman-as-object.

MacKinnon's narrative of the encounter of Marxism and feminism, man and woman, issues, four paragraphs from the end of her essay, in a description of the climactic overturning of the masculinist system as we know it. In this culmination of the reading-lesson this essay has been, MacKinnon describes what her ideal reader will have learned to do to the powerful structures of male domination which have encircled her - a demystification of the 'reality'-effect of male power as it has constructed woman as nothing:

Male power is real; it is just not what it claims to be, namely, the only reality. Male power is myth that makes itself true. What it is to raise consciousness is to confront male power in this duality: as total on one side and a delusion on the other. In consciousness raising, women learn they have *learned* that men are everything, women their negation, but that the sexes are equal. The content of the message is revealed true and false at the same time; in fact, each part reflects the other transvalued. If 'men are all, women their negation' is taken as social criticism rather than simple description, it becomes clear for the first time that women *are* men's equals, everywhere in chains. (p. 28)

This moment *sounds* dialectical: we have the moment of contradiction (woman negated, but actually equal), then the revolution of terms which enables the overthrow of a prior system. In the process a chain of opposing terms (male power, woman; the real, myth; total, a delusion; everything, their negation) reflect and negate one another, as different levels of knowledge collide and conflict, so there can emerge a radically new self-consciousness for Woman. But that this account is non-dialectical is suggested by the way nothing is extracted from the secondary term 'man' by and for the elevated term 'woman.' MacKinnon's essay began with a quite overt, partially dialectical encounter between feminism and Marxism, which enabled MacKinnon to take a good deal from Marxism for feminism: a critique of domination, the idea of commodity fetish, the revolutionary consciousness of the oppressed, a critique of an insidious system of cultural oppression, and a scenario of liberation. But here, by essay's end, the oscillation between antithetical terms of this set of Manichaean oppositions issues in an epiphany about the mythic and delusional quality of what has been taken as real (male power, woman's negation). The stark polarities of this argument seem justified, at an affective and rhetorical level of the argument, by the all too real abuses of women by empowered men. But the conceptual career of this argument, with its realignment of men and women in terms of abstract and idealized categories (like myth and reality), helps guide MacKinnon toward antithetical representations of sex – as falsely controlling woman or conceptually void – and feminism – as either authentically unmodified or fatally compromised.

In following MacKinnon's staging of the emergence of the feminist subject, we have found MacKinnon's writing sustaining a strangely contradictory relation to the dialectic as developed by Marxism. On the one hand her argument depends upon that dialectic – its naturalness, the way it allows a borrowing from Marxism, its general evocation of the progressive movement of history, the way it allows her to narrate a summary totalization of the feminist position. But, on the other hand, MacKinnon's writing is non-dialectical in the way it depends upon the tropes of anti-thesis and analogy, and becomes Manichaean in its bifurcation of subject and object. This diverges from the terms of both Marx's and Hegel's use of the dialectic, where the 'object' will be crucial and valued, not demol-ished. I do not call attention to these tendencies of MacKinnon's writing so as to call her back to a correctly dialectical thought. In the light of the work of Foucault, Derrida, de Man, and Deleuze, and the whole turn from Hegel toward Nietzsche their work has fostered, the critique of the total-izing and homogenizing tendencies of dialectical thinking has become widely appreciated.[9]

MacKinnon's revisionary use of the dialectic in conjunction with the tropes of analogy and antithesis is an essential aspect of her political rhetoric, and of the polemical force it achieves. But what may seem like a minor and abstruse matter – the *way* in which the feminist subject emerges to subject the object to itself as the prevailing subject – ends up having decisive conceptual consequences in the design of MacKinnon's program-matic position. The remainder of my essay will explore two effects of this pattern of thought: the difficulty of imagining sex on the grounds of her argument, and the particularly radical separation of her strain of feminism from its 'others' – not just men, but black women, black men, and other feminists. It will be my claim that in both these ways MacKinnon reduces the plurality and heterogeneity of the social and cultural terrain.

The central analogy of feminist discourse

The idea that in masculinist culture woman is positioned as the object of man's subjectivity is one of the central, perhaps the most ubiquitous, themes of feminist cultural criticism. We find this idea receiving varied but compatible development in feminist writing from Simone de Beauvoir to Laura Mulvey. Consider this passage from *The Second Sex*: 'with penis, hands, mouth, with his whole body, a man reaches out toward his partner, but he himself remains at the center of this activity, being, on the whole, the *subject* as opposed to *objects* that he perceives and *instruments* that he manipulates; . . . the feminine flesh is for him a prey, and through it he gains access to the qualities he desires, as with any object.'[10] By contrast with the behavior of this primitive male, we are told that '[w]oman's eroticism is much more complex, and it reflects the complexity of the feminine situation.'[11] The most influential studies of the bifurcation of subject and object by gender have focused upon film and advertising, and the way these media train the male gaze to objectify women. In *Ways of Seeing*, John Berger illustrates how woman is composed as having internalized a desire to receive the male gaze she invites. In her enormously influential essay on Hollywood cinema, 'Visual pleasure and narrative cinema', Laura Mulvey shows how the female film star is given a 'to-be-looked-at-ness' which makes her available to several modalities of a gaze coded as male: that of the male protagonist, the camera, and the film spectator.[12] Both these analyses expose the gender dissymmetry in the media representations they analyze. But the ethos which orients each critique suggests an extreme position which is, strictly speaking, impossible: that one can imagine social life without humans being the objects of the gaze of others. Even the most radical cultural forms for controlling the gaze – the monastery, the harem, and purdah – restructure rather than annul the relation of gazing subject and gazed-at object. Let's analyze MacKinnon's particularly rich development of this familiar feminist topos.

Man is to woman as subject is to object. MacKinnon's essay makes this idea, condensed into the six-word sentence – 'Man fucks woman; subject verb object' (p. 27) – a description, an accusation, and, as we have seen above in following the course of her dialectical narrative, that which prepares the pure reversal by which man becomes the object of an emergent feminist subject. MacKinnon's vivid six-word rendering of the bifurcation of subject and object by gender allows us to see the way this idea is founded upon an analogy. Here, the parallel construction of the two clauses establishes an analogy between sex and grammar, between the relation between man and woman fucking and the subject and object joined by a transitive verb. From the context within which the sentence appears, it is apparent that both these ways of relating are in turn aligned with the insidious epistemological system ordained by male power – 'objectivity: the ostensibly noninvolved stance . . . [knowing] from no particular perspective, apparently transparent to reality' (pp. 23-4). Woman, according to MacKinnon, becomes the matter and medium of man's knowing: 'Woman through male eyes is sex object, that by which man knows himself at once as man and as subject' (p. 24). This relation between two modes of knowing is expressed through another analogy: 'Objectivity is the methodological stance of which objectification is the social process' (p. 27). Finally sex, grammar, and epistemology are linked to politics by the initial analogy of this essay – that between Marxism and feminism: '[Marxism and feminism] exist to argue, respectively, that the relations in which many work and few gain, in which some fuck and others get fucked, are the prime moment of politics' (p. 3). It will be useful for us to consider the term 'analogy', because the basic interpretive work and social analysis of MacKinnon's essays rest upon a chain of analogies between the antithetical relation of subject and object in sex, politics, knowledge, and language.

What is an analogy? An analogy establishes a relation, correspondence, or resemblance between two terms, spheres, objects. Often, as with a metaphor, the force of the analogy depends not upon the proximity of the two terms, and thus the exactness of the analogy, but upon the difference between the two terms which this analogical yoking holds together. The difference between two terms that the analogy would mendaciously elide establishes the resistance to the current of meaning passing through the analogy. If two phenomena are simply the same, there is no interest or purpose in likening them through analogy; it does not allow you to see either term in a new way. This is why the dictionary defines an analogy as a 'correspondence in some respects, especially in function or position, between things otherwise dissimilar'.[13] What is correspondent in MacKinnon's chain of analogized terms is the drastic non-reciprocity and power imbalance between two fixed positions: the (male) subject who fucks, objectifies, knows, and the (female) object that gets known, objectified, and fucked. By aligning, through analogy, the personal sphere (of sex) with the political sphere (of work), the culture's official way of knowing (objectivity) with its way of subordinating women (objectification), the power imbalance this chain of analogies works to establish is made to seem as ironclad as the grammatical one between the subject which predicates and the object predicated. If antithesis is MacKinnon's trope for expressing difference, analogy is the trope she uses to express convergence. Since an analogy allows two to be seen as one, it helps orchestrate the convergence of a series of antithetically opposed terms into a narrative of feminist unity. Both are at work in the sentence 'Man fucks woman; subject verb object.'

The use of the word 'fucks' is part of a carefully calculated strategy to critique male uses of power. The vulgarity of her usage disrupts academic decorum by parodying in her analysis what men have commonly done to women – used a vulgar language of sex and power to shock women into silenced subordination. Only here this gesture is repeated in reverse, so the object of MacKinnon's critical analysis (violence, power) gets repeated and reinscribed in her own use of language. But there is another more important reason why MacKinnon describes gendered social exchanges in terms of sexuality. According to her, one of the chief failures of Marxism arises from the weakness of its analysis of sexuality. To develop the idea of the centrality of sexuality for a radical feminism, MacKinnon relies upon the premises of a determinist sociological explanation of the origin of gender roles. Sexuality becomes an insidious means by which a woman 'becomes a woman' in the double sense of identifying with the stereotype and having sex with a man: 'Sex as gender and sex as sexuality are thus defined in terms of each other . . . what women learn in order to "have sex," in order to "become women" - woman as gender - comes through the experience of, and is a condition for, "having sex" - woman as sexual object for man, the use of women's sexuality by men' (p. 17). Here 'having sex' means being sexed (gendered), means being subordinated. Like so much of MacKinnon's analysis of the social, we get an encircling wall of reciprocally supporting processes.

By MacKinnon's account, sex (at least heterosexual sex) becomes the original and continuing sin, which determines woman's social construction as subordinate to male power. From here it is a short step to characterizing most of the forms of lived heterosexuality as essentially analogous with rape. Thus in the second part of the essay MacKinnon disputes Susan Brownmiller's attempt to separate sexuality and rape, and then demonstrates the way the many forms of heterosexual practice (from violent rape to apparently complicit desire) may be analogized through the most crucial fact about these practices - woman's loss of control. But by making 'sexuality' the main instrument of men's domination of women, what she calls the very 'linchpin of gender inequality', sexuality as a general phenomenon of human and animal life remains untheorized in this feminist 'agenda for theory'. Sexuality becomes abstract because the seven specific social forms through which sex dominates woman - rape, incest, sexual harassment, pornography, contraception/abortion, prostitution, and lesbianism - are said to take their shape from the exercise of male power. The force of male power does not modify or displace female sexuality; it invents those forms of sexuality she calls her reader to join in abolishing. What sex 'is' aside from these false practices becomes a blank cipher in MacKinnon's text. Sex is not a forceful locus of legitimate experience which subsists, in the past or present, beneath its appropriation by male power in some sort of disturbed but ongoing relationship to pleasure or reproduction, or that ambivalent social bonding called love. Instead, MacKinnon makes sex the functional equivalent to those cranial implants used in some science fiction movies by aliens from outer space (here Man) to turn humans (here Woman) into robots under their control. Operating with magical efficacy within the subjectivity of the victim, sex makes 'woman', her body and inner self, a function of male power.

Sex Minus Zero

Although MacKinnon has much to say about what sex should *not* be, she does not suggest any positive theory of sexuality, whether framed by a man or a woman, which she could accept, in however revised a form. In fact she works to defend her own treatment of sexuality from incursions from male theorists like Freud, Lacan and Foucault.[14] Freud and Lacan do not frame their work upon sexuality so that one can grapple conceptually or politically with social practices like rape and pornography. So let's pose this question: what would two male theorists of sexuality, Freud and Lacan, say on the question MacKinnon presses us to consider – the matter of sexuality and control? I am not here imposing psychoanalysis as the only way to conceptualize sexuality; instead it is an influential model of sexuality which offers a counterpoint to a political analysis like MacKinnon's which divests sexuality of any conceptual content.

In psychoanalysis, sex is precisely that which one does not control, have, or possess as a subject, in the mode of conscious mastery. There are many reasons for this. For Freud, the mind is an energy system, constantly negotiating its relationship to other energy systems, moved by drives which seek a pleasurable release of energy, structured by a complex set of conscious and unconscious intra-psychic traces of memory and fantasy, which shape the particular ways a given person lives his or her desire. Within this psychology, sexuality is not something one merely does; it is a pervasive factor, which will not submit to the rule of some presiding conscious subject. Lacan translates Freud's interpretation of psychic life so as to emphasize the way language 'insists' in the unconscious, thereby structuring human desire in alienating and unexpected fashions. For Lacan, the detours of desire are errant, perverse, and witty. Thus within a psychoanalytic frame, human sexuality is always going out beyond itself, is itself a kind of lack, hole, or need, which points toward the other in the mode of wishing. There seems to be no acknowledging, in MacKinnon's discourse, of this dispersed and lost quality of a desire and sexuality which both is and is not one's own.[15]

Sexuality in the psychoanalytic frame is not theorized as an exchange between statically conceived subjects and objects, or polemicized around the issue of who *controls* sexuality.[16] The zero-sum game, where one wins and the other loses, a social pattern which is deeply ingrained in contemporary capitalism, and which MacKinnon sees everywhere in the social exchange between the sexes, may be antipathetical to the way psychoanalysis imagines sexuality. If MacKinnon's work construes sexuality as a problem for woman (her domination by male power), to which she can then postulate a rather simple solution (control for woman), then to complicate her representation of sexuality would depend upon reintroducing terms she has subordinated to the imperatives of the emergent feminist subject – pleasure, the object, and language.

To come to terms with that which is uncontrollable, excessive and fundamental about sexuality in human culture, one would need to conceptualize sexuality as a non-idealist exchange between two positions – persons who can participate as both a subject which never gains a total and abstract control of the exchange, and an object of the subjectivity of the other and themselves, an object not anathematized or abolished on moral grounds as anti-human.[17] Then the sexuality which could pass between and among the positions of subject and object would depend upon mobilizing these concepts for an interpretation of this encounter:

1 An understanding of the *centrality of pleasure*, as part of the interior experience of the subject, that which motivates sex, and is one of its issues. Pleasure can be conceived on a physiological or physical model (as for example Freud's definition of it as the movement of a living system from greater to lesser entropy and 'unpleasure'), or in terms of a personal psychology which can inscribe it into a life narrative. Because pleasure involves an energy relation, the pleasure of the subject disrupts the idealist impulse in Western thought; it disturbs the effort to conceptualize sex as a social form (marriage), an ideal (love), the law of biology (reproduction), or the nexus of personal value (in relationships). What this active role for pleasure in sexuality would suppose is . . .

2 . . . the *persistence of a role for the object* in sexuality. There is no way to think sexuality apart from the object, for sex and its pleasures are experienced by the subject through an object – the subject's sensate body. The object is not just the medium, it is also the focal point of sexual

pleasure. Lovers - to know each other erotically, to feel desire for each other's bodies - probably need to objectify the other, perhaps as beautiful, or as possessor of this or that part or quality. Within a psychoanalysis of sexuality, the concept of the fetish suggests the instability of the opposition between subject and object: the fetish is not a dead object, and fetishizing is not a perverse behavior one could do without (nor is it morally equivalent to 'treating a person like an object'). Instead, the fetish is a constitutive aspect of human desire, and does not respect the neat subject/object oppositions of traditional epistemology and ethics.[18] We need a more patient, and ethically dispassionate, understanding of how objects - whether a flag, a face, or a tune - become endowed by a desiring subject with energy and allure. By what process do they cease to be mere things, instead becoming (with art, and like art) the bearers of pleasure, value, and culture? As such, objects would then be seen as participating in . . .

3 . . . the *constitutive role of language* in the formations of human sexuality. Because the subject must operate in the world through the objectifying medium of language, and we only know the object through the subjectifying medium of language, language becomes the term which blurs the relation between the subject and object. Thus exchange in the social sphere - as in hiring, marriage, sex, gossip, etc. - is predicated upon knowing persons through those material aspects of the person which can circulate, and in doing so become more than insensate objects, become the immaterial signs of some intended [or mistaken] social meaning. Subjects know others through vows, gifts and stories; the sight of nakedness, and the exchange of body fluids - saliva, sperm, vaginal fluid, blood. These sign/things of persons become media of exchange which are susceptible to all the usual lapses and detours of language. We do not control, with our original intention, the way a sign we produce will be read.

Decapitalizing m(M)arxism; capitalizing B(b)lacks

Through its summary analysis and critical condensation of other feminist work, MacKinnon's essay enacts the emergence of a feminist subject who writes, reads, and interprets in order to invent a new kind of discourse - radical feminism. If we look more closely at MacKinnon's essay, especially in the footnotes where she often swerves from passive constructions and third-person narrative to make direct first-person comments to her reader about her own writing practice, we can trace the means by which the writing subject works in the political subject. There, a 'value positing I' operates behind the apparently impersonal narrative with which MacKinnon describes the emergence of the feminist subject of feminism. Since her diagnosis of the social makes *taking control* (of woman's life and sex from men) her most urgent task, all her writing labors to empower the feminist subject as the favored term of an ethically charged antithesis. This is achieved through a series of inclusions and exclusions, a defining of boundaries, and an assertion of hierarchical valuations, which total-ize the terrain of culture through a series of conceptual operations: MacKinnon construes every term as impeding or advancing the forward movement of feminism, negates all that stands in its way (like old styles of sex), thereby reducing much of what is plural, different, and heterogen-eous in the social and cultural terrain. The value-positing which motivates these efforts is readable through the textual practices by which she decapi-talizes M(m)arxism, capitalizes b(B)lacks, and subordinates other femin-isms to the advance of her own. By following these compositional efforts, we can take note of the ironies which attend her project. MacKinnon gives the term 'feminist' a rigorous, proper and 'unmodified' meaning which would begin to build community by being intolerant of difference. Her manner of debating Marxists and other feminists offers a version of exchange about what the social is which is anti-social.

As a precondition for narrating their (apparently) dialectical transfor-mation, Marxism and feminism must be presented so that there is a balanced and specular relation between them. But this requires a prior, at least proximate, *equality* between the two terms of the dialectic. Indeed a *making equal* will be crucial not only in the dialectical narrative between male theory (marxism) and female theory (feminism), but to the explicit content of most feminisms. Sometimes making equal requires contraven-ing convention, and an exercise of the most direct kind of authorial asser-tion. There is a symptomatic instance of this kind of writerly assertion in the headnote to the article, where MacKinnon explains and justifies her de-capitalization of the 'M' in Marxism:

> I have rendered 'marxism' in lower case and 'Black' in upper case and have been asked by the publisher to explain these choices. It is conventional to capitalize terms that derive from a proper name. Since I wish to place marxism and feminism in equipoise, the dis-parate typography would weigh against my analytic structure. Capi-talizing both would germanize the text. I also hope feminism, a

politics authored by those it works in the name of, is never named after an individual. (p. 2)

The conventions for capitalizing English are tied to more than the proper name; capitalization also becomes a very graphic and typographical index of importance, as when we capitalize the first letters of God, Queen Elizabeth, President Reagan. The question of importance and equality seem to weigh upon MacKinnon when she designs her 'analytic structure' – the structure of the dialectic – so that it has the 'equipoise' to take her to the proper destination, where a strong feminist theory emerges on the other side of its encounter with Marxism. By decapitalizing the 'M' in Marxism, MacKinnon decreases the importance and prestige of that system of thought: shifts (intellectual) capital from M(m)arxism to feminism, and decapitates Marxism. This small change in typographical usage becomes a telling sign of the interpretive force operating, behind the apparent autonomy and 'naturalness' of its dialectic narrative, to change what might be called the ratio of value between Marxism and feminism, man and woman.

In the dialectical narrative which MacKinnon constructs, and we have summarized, a good deal of the social persuasiveness of the analysis will come from the degree to which MacKinnon seems to succeed in representing and incorporating the different positions of the social sphere into her narrative. Since one of the most important differences in contemporary American culture is that between white and black, and since that difference of race cuts across difference of gender, her way of handling the difference white/black is one of the symptomatic stress points of her narrative. Blacks, both male and female, become the non-recuperable other of her dialectical narrative. In the same headnote where MacKinnon explains her decapitalization of Marxism, she justifies her decision to capitalize the 'B' in blacks. Let's gauge the meaning of this gesture.

Black is conventionally (I am told) regarded as a color rather than a racial or national designation, hence is not usually capitalized. I do not regard Black as merely a color of skin pigmentation, but as a heritage, an experience, a cultural and personal identity, the meaning of which becomes specifically stigmatic, and/or glorious and/or ordinary under specific social conditions. It is as much socially created as, and at least in the American context no less specifically meaningful or definitive than, any linguistic, tribal, or religious ethnicity, all of which are conventionally recognized by capitalization. (p. 2)

This passage suggests the reasons blacks have a special importance in MacKinnon's essay. As inheritors of the effects of slavery, no group is more obviously the victim of a social system which constructs them as subordinate. Also, and perhaps more importantly for MacKinnon, the racism of this culture makes blacks appear a group which, in spite of their manifold differences, is essentially one. Thus blacks become a kind of model for the sort of unity MacKinnon wishes to establish for women. But blacks are also a problem for this feminist analysis. Because blacks cut across the gender line, they threaten the integrity of the terms 'woman' and 'man' in MacKinnon's text. Blacks must be kept apart, an apartness which, as the laudatory tone of MacKinnon's headnote implies, is a privilege: this special apartness is expressed by the 'recognition' by 'capitalization' MacKinnon confirms on them. But that this apartness could become a dubious advantage is suggested at a formal level of the essay, for the black with the special (capitalized) position above and apart will be kept outside of the (lower-case) dialectic between M(m)arxism and feminism, which brings advantageous social transformation. This double imperative for the use of blacks – to be brought into the story, but be kept outside the story as a special case – means MacKinnon must carefully control the way blacks enter her story. There are two readable instances of the discrete and privileged marginality conferred upon blacks in MacKinnon's narrative.

When MacKinnon is describing what can divide women of different social level and status, she acknowledges that the sort of gender oppression discovered by middle-class women can seem comparatively abstract to those who are less advantaged:

But the pain, isolation, and thingification of women who have been pampered and pacified into nonpersonhood – women 'grown ugly and dangerous from being nobody for so long' (note 7) – is difficult for the materially deprived to see as a form of oppression, particularly for women whom no man has ever put on a pedestal. (p. 6)

A reader of this sentence might assume that the interpolated quotation – 'grown ugly and dangerous . . .' – was written by one of these middle-class women who have lived and critiqued the process by which they have been pampered into 'nonpersonhood'. But, as note 7 explains, the quote is from a quite different social and literary context: 'Toni Cade (now Bambara) thus describes a desperate Black woman who has too many children and too little means to care for them or herself.' By the transfer of meaning through citation into a new context, the language written to describe 'a desperate Black woman' can speak to and for the 'pampered' white woman. This use of citation is shaped to enable the term 'women' to go through a dialectical augmentation so that it can stand for 'all women'. MacKinnon explains the logic behind her strategy:

> By using her phrase in altered context, I do not want to distort her meaning but to extend it. Throughout this essay, I have tried to see if women's condition is shared, even when contexts or magnitudes differ. (Thus, it is very different to be 'nobody' as a Black woman than as a white lady, but neither is 'somebody' by male standards.) This is the approach to race and ethnicity attempted throughout. I aspire to include all women in the term 'women' in some way, without violating the particularity of any woman's experience. Whenever this fails, the statement is simply wrong and will have to qualified or the aspiration (or the theory) abandoned. (p. 6 n. 7)

What is most remarkable about this passage is the special sensitivity MacKinnon extends to black women on a problem which she does not acknowledge at those other moments in her dialectical narrative when she incorporates the perspective, knowledge, or experience of a particular author or group into the progress of her dialectic. The problem as stated by her is how to include 'all women' in the term 'women', 'without violating the particularity of any woman's experience'. Here, she makes the sincerity of that aspiration convincing by speaking in a mode which confesses her most genuine authorial desire ('I do not want to distort . . . I aspire to include . . .'); describes her writing as a tentative effort ('I have tried to see if . . . Whenever this fails, the statement is simply wrong . . .'); and shows sensitivity to the offensiveness this kind of merging of two very different social experiences – those of 'desperate' Black and 'pampered' white – even to the extent of promising to abandon her own 'aspiration' or 'theory' if the effort fails. In writing this remarkable (and very uncharacteristic) qualification to her theory, for and to black women, MacKinnon indirectly acknowledges the violence of the dialectical effort to overcome (destroy, conserve, and raise up) the difference of the other, here the difference between women and races. But, ironically enough, after the scrupulousness demonstrated here, MacKinnon seems all the more justified in negating, through a totalizing dialectic, the particularity of other terms negated, for example feminists of different persuasions, or black men, or white men.

What finally justifies the occlusion of the difference between black and white woman is their common subordinate position opposite man: 'neither is "somebody" by male standards.' But at the very point in her argument when MacKinnon is giving a definition of that male power which defines woman's commonality, the black as the marginal but essential supplemental term in her analysis returns again, again in a footnote. Here is MacKinnon's definition of the 'closed system' of 'male power': *'Power to create the world from one's point of view is power in its male form'* (p. 23 n. 54; MacKinnon's emphasis). Since power to create reality from one's point of view is not described as contingent, but is in its very 'form' essentially tied to the 'male' gender, this act of definition raises the question of the black men. Few have accused *them* of having much power. So MacKinnon adds a note which protects her definition of power as male from contamination by this special instance:

> This does not mean all men *have* male power equally. American Black men, for instance, have substantially less of it. But to the extent that they cannot create the world from their point of view, they find themselves unmanned, castrated, literally or figuratively. This supports rather than qualifies the sex specificity of the argument. (p. 23 n. 54)

Note the efficacy here of the circular definition: since women equal victims lacking power; and men equal power; if black men have no power, then, to that extent, they become like women. This argument is not designed to deal with vexing pragmatic social questions, such as the extent to which black men might be both powerless in relation to white men, and dominating and exploitative toward women in general, or toward one group of women in particular - black women. Rather, this aside overlooks these problems because of the special (capital) position given to blacks apart. Instead, MacKinnon's note works to use black men to protect the original definition (women = victims lacking power; men = power), in a particular way - through a circular definition of black men which metaphorizes gender. Black men, placed opposite white male power, and 'unmanned,' and therefore not-men, but ones who (in the terms of masculinist psychology) are 'castrated', and thus like 'women'. The use of this circular definition of black-man-as-woman to 'defend' black men produces its own ironic effects. Black men's particularity and difference (from white men, from black women, from white women) is reduced, at the very moment, and with the very conceptual terms (the idea of their lack of power), mobilized to protect that difference (from white men). Though black men are not favored by MacKinnon with a promise in the form of a direct address extended to black women, both serve the forward movement of the overcoming of (white) male power by women.

Feminism unmodified

Nowhere does the problem of how to incorporate difference and otherness into the advance of her argument become more vexing than in MacKinnon's relationship to those other feminists who have thought through a different feminist practice. One of the central compositional strategies of Part I of the essay consisted in writing a synthetic 'agenda for theory' which would include generous reference to an extraordinary range of the major feminist writing of the last two decades so as to help unify feminism for political action. MacKinnon writes footnotes which develop wonderfully concise critical responses to that work. MacKinnon's essay then can function as an annotated bibliography which values the variety and difference of other feminisms, at the same time that MacKinnon incorporates and moves beyond that work. The relegation of most reference to other feminist work to the footnotes allows it to be given a decidedly supporting role in the unfolding of the unifying dialectical design only her own essay will grasp and figure.

Perhaps because of debates and resistances occasioned by the publishing of Part I in the Spring of 1982, the question of the differences within feminism becomes an explicitly thematized problem in Part II of the essay, a year and a quarter later. In two long footnotes near the beginning of Part II, MacKinnon explores the correct conceptual and political response by feminism to the failure of 'all women' to develop the consensus that 'life as we have known it . . . is not all, not enough, not ours, not just' (II, p. 637). While she expresses sympathy with 'the unwillingness, central to feminism, to dismiss some women as simply deluded while granting other women the ability to see the truth', MacKinnon is dismissive when she distinguishes her own critical articulation between the radical feminism she advocates and all other feminisms. Here is how she institutes a hierarchy among feminisms:

> But just as socialist feminism has often amounted to marxism applied to women, liberal feminism has often amounted to liberalism applied to women. Radical feminism is feminism. Radical feminism – after this, feminism unmodified – is methodologically post-marxist. (II, p. 439 n. 8)

Part of the task of MacKinnon's writing is to take those feminisms whose indebtedness to something extrinsic to feminism is marked by their modifier, and subdue them to a form of feminism which has the conceptual power to unify women and feminism in their differences. Since only radical feminism has shed its earlier conceptual debts (by becoming 'methodologically post-marxist'), only it can become a feminism which is unmodified, uncompromised, and unalloyed.[19] MacKinnon's willingness to develop criticism of other feminisms shows an iconoclasm before what might be called the easy pluralism of American academic thought, especially as that pluralism manifests itself as feminist celebrations of its own variety. But there is something more than vigorous criticism in MacKinnon's reading of other feminisms. There is a refusal to let the position of the other stand, as the locus of an otherness which is non-recuperable, and may entail a history or way of knowing which must be given a separate authority, to which she might relate dialogically.

In the same footnote where others fall short of true feminism, the work of Andrea Dworkin and Adrienne Rich is singled out for their deep affiliation with MacKinnon's own project. In the language which describes the project of (radical) feminism, we can trace the sources of MacKinnon's intolerance. Dworkin and Rich (and MacKinnon):

> exemplify feminism as a methodological departure. This feminism seeks to define and pursue women's interest as the fate of all women bound together. It seeks to extract the truth of women's commonalities out of the lie that all women are the same. . . . This politics is struggling for a practice of unity that does not depend upon sameness without dissolving into empty tolerance, including tolerance of

all it exists to change whenever that appears embodied in one of us.
A new community begins here. (pp. 639-40 n. 8)

Here McKinnon presents the vanguard position that every other
feminism should follow. Her refusal to tolerate other feminisms is not
merely a matter of tone, style, or personal disposition; it is a structural
and conceptual result of her project: forging a feminism which can bind
women who are not the 'same' within the single unified body of (radical)
feminism. To accomplish this end, other feminisms must be demolished
as 'other' so their set of terms and pathways of investigation are extracted
and incorporated into the larger movement MacKinnon's writing would
guide.

What MacKinnon's language implies but can never clearly acknowledge is the presence of that censorious juridical critical eye/I which has
the power to scan the body of feminism, decide upon that 'all it exists to
change', and repudiate any form of anti-feminism, even when it appears
'embodied in one of us'. Here, as in our discussion of MacKinnon's
revisionary use of the dialectic, we can see that beneath and inside an
apparently dialectical critical process, MacKinnon breaks the terms of
her analysis into a pure atemporal antithesis: in this case, between the
authentic 'unmodified' body of feminism, and those opposing elements
within feminism which challenge its advance and must be opposed.[20]

In the construction of her essays, MacKinnon's indignation and intolerance are carefully controlled by the structure of the argument; they can
even seem like 'the highest kind of love'. But in an open debate, like the
one sponsored by the Buffalo Law School, the antagonistic quality of her
thought becomes socially readable. Thus in responding to Carol Gilligan's
work, MacKinnon praises the 'strong and elegant sensitivity in the
work', and the 'deeply feminist' 'impulse to listen to women', to hear the
'different voice' with which women have learned to speak. But she then
announces her 'political infuriation' with Gilligan's refusal to see that
this 'different voice' Gilligan so values (what MacKinnon describes as its
'relatedness, responsibility, and care virtues') embodies the virtues of
women victimized by their subordination to male power. MacKinnon is
also 'troubled' that Gilligan's analysis may even get women 'identifying
with what is a positively valued feminine stereotype'. MacKinnon would
turn this analysis toward the more fundamental question of power. When
MacKinnon and Gilligan break into open debate on the issue of the
contaminating effects of power, the crucial issue – what constitutes the

authentic voice of women – pivots on the question of whether one should accept the voices of existing women as what woman's voice should be.

Gilligan: Your definition of power is his definition.

MacKinnon: That is because the society *is* that way, it operates on his definition, and I am trying to change it.

Gilligan: To have her definition come in?

MacKinnon: That would be part of it, but more to have a definition that she would articulate that she cannot now, because his foot is on her.

Gilligan: She's saying it.

MacKinnon: I know, but she is articulating the feminine. And you are calling it hers. That's what I find infuriating.

Gilligan: No, I am saying she is articulating a set of values which are very positive.

Dunlap: I am speaking out of turn.[21]

This dialogue/debate develops into an impasse because MacKinnon's message – woman *is* the effect of male power – renders hollow in advance the tone of any living woman's voice, including those Gilligan studies and values. Such studies are 'infuriating' and intolerable because they threaten to arrest feminism in an absorption in woman's present condition, instead of striving to blaze a pathway toward an as yet unrealized 'world'. MacKinnon's project, like other feminist or non-feminist radical projects, operates according to the Enlightenment assumption (which goes back to Rousseau) that the present social order is in some very fundamental sense false, corrupt, and unjust. By this argument, the ultimate authority of feminism arises from its claim to articulate a 'woman's perspective' which does not yet exist: 'The claim that a sexual politics exists and is socially fundamental is grounded in the claim of feminism *to* women's perspective, not from it' (p. 22). This future-oriented axiom of MacKinnon's feminism explains why Part I of MacKinnon's essay is not presented as feminist theory, but as an 'agenda' for one. Rather than being a sign of the intellectual modesty of this project, it is a sign of its ambition. To set the agenda always implies one assumes the authority to speak for a group by defining, out of the whole range of possibilities, what will be the topics, terms and goals which will shape the collective discussion. Thus, in diplomacy, as in this exchange between MacKinnon and Gilligan, the most tenacious battles will unfold around setting the agenda.

There is a final irony about this exchange between MacKinnon and Gilligan: this debate performs what it thematizes, the impossibility of finding a (single) authentic voice, not so much for women, but for the women's movement called feminism. MacKinnon would make her feminism the form and forum for a new feminist unity - 'A new community begins here.' But the absoluteness of the categories embodied in her feminism, and her intolerance for feminisms spoken in 'a different voice', has meant that her work has become a catalyst for the expression of a plurality within feminism which resists any totalizing unity. But I do not think we should measure MacKinnon's feminism against the consensus it seeks. To construe sex as essentially equivalent to rape, to further the bifurcation of subject and object by gender, and to assume the whole anti-pathetical stance of an 'unmodified' and uncompromising feminism opposite its 'others' - all these positions open her writing to the criticism I have offered it in this essay. But it may be precisely these positions - however problematic their conceptual content - which carry the greatest efficacy in changing social practice. Elsewhere I have sought to show that it is the very extremity of MacKinnon's analysis, and the hyperbole of her political rhetoric which bear the force that helps change the value of women in culture.

It is no easy matter for MacKinnon, or her reader, to gauge the contexts for calculating the effects of this intellectual and political practice. Thus from the vantage point of Foucault's analysis of sexuality, both MacKinnon and her theoretical antagonists (like psychoanalysis) are too uncritical in accepting the idea that sexuality is the person's central defining essence. By this Foucauldian analysis, MacKinnon's efforts to limit pornography, redefine sexual harassment, and align sex with rape, involve less a radical break with the social discourses on sexuality she would control than a new feminist episode in the modern deployment of sexuality.[22] The changes MacKinnon's feminism helps to initiate may be different than those intended; her feminism is probably operating within unsuspected cultural economies, helping to move us toward destinations quite unforeseen.

NOTES

Many thanks go to Ellen Dubois for a helpful early conversation about this piece, and her generosity in making a valuable file of materials available to me. Thanks also to Charles Bernheimer, Larysa Mykyta, Claire Kahane, Naomi Shor, Neil Hertz, and Jill Robbins for invaluable advice during revision.

1   Jardine and Smith 1987.

2   See Alice Jardine, 'Men in feminism: *odor di uomo or compagnons de route?*', and Andrew Ross, 'No question of silence', both in Jardine and Smith 1987.

3   MacKinnon 1982; 1983. The use in this chapter of a capital M for Marxism is further discussed on pp. 112-15.

4   This latter idea is the focal theme of another as yet unpublished essay entitled: 'Force, value and feminism: a reading of Catharine Anne MacKinnon.' There I use the concept of cultural value developed by Nietzsche and Heidegger to read the political rhetoric of MacKinnon's writing.

5   MacKinnon 1982: 14. Citations in parentheses to MacKinnon's essay are to Part I, except where a roman numeral II, followed by the page number, indicates a citation to Part II.

6   Dialectical thinking, whether speculative and conceptual or materialist and historical, is one of the most influential and pervasive kinds of thought developed by the Western tradition. It is at work when a country or people tell its story, in the Bildungsroman and the confessional; and it does not turn out to be so easy to elude as some of the avant-garde would have us think. Paul de Man and Jacques Derrida never tire of telling us that it is not so easy to elude dialectical thinking as many assume. But MacKinnon's essay makes use of a particularly pure concept of this way of thinking, brought to the service of theorizing feminism, and I hope to show that this has far-reaching and sometimes rather unexpected consequences for MacKinnon's argument in particular, and for other feminisms as well.

7   Haraway 1985: 78.

8   *Buffalo Law Review*, 34: 72.

9   See Foucault 1977; Derrida 1978; de Man 1979; Deleuze 1983. Derrida has developed a criticism of feminism for its programmatic reliance upon that dialectical conception of history which homogenizes the 'flow' of history, and the use of a speculative dialectic which may inadvertently end up making 'woman' the same as 'man'. See Derrida 1982.

10 de Beauvoir: 414-15.

11 Ibid.: 415.

12 Berger 1972; Mulvey 1975.

13 *The American Heritage Dictionary*, ed. William Morris. New York: American Heritage Publishing Co., 1969.

14 MacKinnon writes that Foucault does 'not systematically comprehend the specificity of gender - women's and men's relation to these factors - as a primary category for comprehending them . . . Lacan notwithstanding, none of these theorists grasps sexuality (including desire itself) as social, nor the content of its determination as a sexist social order that eroticizes potency (as male) and victimization (as female).' (p. 22 n. 12)

15 MacKinnon's discourse is, in the best Anglo-American fashion, profoundly anti-psychoanalytic in all of its impulses. This is so at several different levels: at the level of her asserted positions, her writing does not allow us to envision any positive collective social practice of sexuality; at a more personal level, there is an embarrassed reticence about any inscription of her own life into some sexuality. By contrast, one branch of contemporary feminism, by contesting psychoanalytic ways of theorizing, and

refusing to theorize gender, has developed psychoanalytic theory into a powerful instrument for feminist readings of everything from film and popular culture to philosophy and literature. Here I am thinking of the work of feminist critics as various as Laura Mulvey, Juliet Mitchell, Kaja Silverman, Naomi Shor, Luce Irigaray, and Jane Gallop.

16 This is not to say however that other social goals of feminism, such as equality, may not be a fundamental aspect of a valuable sexuality. This is an idea explored in Roy Roussel's readings of the 'conversation of the sexes' in literary texts: Roussel 1982.

17 I do not, of course, offer this as a fully grounded theory of sexuality, but rather as the sketch of an alternative to MacKinnon, which allows me to bring into relief those aspects of sexuality which her text puts out of play. It is intended as a polemical antidote to the anti-sexual tendency of an analysis of all relations between men and women under the sign of power.

18 Although Freud theorized the fetish as an aspect of male desire, feminist theorists have begun to contest that specification by gender. See Schor 1985.

19 In note 8 to this passage MacKinnon uses this simple typology to rank feminist writing under radical feminism. Mary Daly's *Gyn/Ecology* 'is formally liberal no matter how extreme or insightful'; since Shulamith Firestone's analysis 'rests on a naturalist definition of gender . . . her radicalism, hence her feminism, is qualified'; a work by Susan Griffin is 'classically liberal in all formal respects.' Sometimes MacKinnon's criticisms of other feminists are more nuanced. She borrows what she takes to be the strongest insight of Millett's *Sexual Politics* - that 'it is sexuality that determines gender, not the other way around' - but then qualifies this attribution in a note, where she acknowledges that Millett's 'explicit discussion, however, vacillates between clear glimpses of that argument and statements nearly to the contrary.' (p. 17 n. 37)

20 Again an analogy with Marxism seems apt: MacKinnon seems Leninist in the way she would purge those 'counter-revolutionary elements' that threaten the revolution.

21 *Buffalo Law Review*, 34 (1985): 74-5.

22 MacKinnon's emphasis upon the way sex is the means for men to subordinate and violate women is sometimes heard by other feminists as foreclosing possibilities to make sex a positive factor in the woman's movement. A speaker from the floor after one lecture questioned her on why issues of gender hierarchy should be 'narrowed' to 'issues of sex': 'It seems to me that sexuality is and are of both power for, as well as victimization of, women.' (*Buffalo Law Review*, 34 (1985): 11-87.)

REFERENCES

Berger, John 1972. *Ways of Seeing*. Harmondsworth: Penguin.

de Beauvoir, Simone 1953; repr. 1974. *The Second Sex*. Trans. H. M. Parshley. New York: Vintage.

Deleuze, Gilles 1983. *Nietzsche and Philosophy*. New York: Columbia University Press.

de Man, Paul 1979. 'Genesis and genealogy', in *Allegories of Reading*. New Haven and London: Yale University Press.

Derrida, Jacques 1978. 'From a restricted to a general economy: a Hegelianism without reserve', in *Writing and Difference*. Trans. Alan Bass. Chicago: University of Chicago Press.

Derrida, Jacques 1982. 'Choreographies': interview by Christie V. McDonald, *Diacritics*, 12 (Summer): 66-76.

Foucault, Michel 1977. 'Nietzsche, genealogy, history', in *Language, Counter-Memory, Practice*. Ed. and trans. Donald Bouchard. Ithaca: Cornell University Press: 139-64.

Haraway, Donna 1985. 'A manifesto for cyborgs: science, technology, and socialist feminism in the 1980s', *Socialist Review* 15.2 (March/April): 65-107.

Jardine, Alice and Smith, Paul 1987. *Men in Feminism*. New York and London: Methuen.

MacKinnon, Catharine 1979. *Sexual Harassment of Working Women*. New Haven and London: Yale University Press.

MacKinnon, Catharine 1982. 'Feminism, marxism, method, and the state: an agenda for theory', *Signs: Journal of Women in Culture and Society*, 7.3 (Spring): 515-44. Repr. in *Feminist Theory: A Critique of Ideology*, ed. Nannerl O. Keohane, Michelle Rosaldo, and Barbara C. Gelpi. Chicago: University of Chicago Press, 1981/2.

MacKinnon, Catharine 1983. 'Feminism, marxism, method and the state: toward feminist jurisprudence', *Signs: Journal of Women in Culture and Society*, 8.4 (Summer): 635-58.

Mulvey, Laura 1975. 'Visual pleasure and narrative cinema', *Screen*, 16.3 (Autumn): 6-18.

Roussel, Roy 1982. *The Conversation of the Sexes: Seduction and Equality in Selected 17th and 18th Century Texts*. New York: Oxford University Press.

Shor, Naomi 1985. 'Female fetishism: the case of George Sand', *Poetics Today*, 6.1-2.

6
Treating Him Like an Object:
William Beatty Warner's 'Di(va)lution'

Donna Landry

William Beatty Warner wishes to 'release' (p. 96) some of the unconscious tendencies of Catharine MacKinnon's writing: he would liberate
the Iron MacMaiden from her tower of feminist certainty, from her
fortress within a 'feminism unmodified',[1] by revealing that, deconstructively speaking, she can never fully control her own discourse, that it does
some of its work without her will or desire. The walled city of an unmodified feminism, unthreatened by men's hostility or scorn, must be shown
as fissured from within. A white man attempts to release a white woman
from fixed principles, lest she remain symbolically, as Jane Gallop might
put it, 'a rigid virgin - phallicized'.[2] At various points in his essay,
Warner attempts to rescue from MacKinnon's tyranny, from her willful
abuse of discursive power, at least five classes of prisoner: dialectical
thinking, (hetero)sexuality, 'm(M)arxism', 'B(b)lack' men, and finally
feminism itself. Warner wishes to imply that MacKinnon's authoritative
tone and sense of feminism as 'radical feminism' purely, uncoupled from
any master discourse, renders her theory authoritarian and exclusionist as
well as, in its failure to articulate any possibility for feminist (hetero)sexual
pleasure, joyless and puritanical:

> 'Sex as gender and sex as sexuality are thus defined in terms of each
> other . . . what women learn in order to "have sex," in order to
> "become women" - woman as gender - comes through the experi-
> ence of, and is a condition for, "having sex" - woman as sexual
> object for man, the use of women's sexuality by men' (p. 17). Here
> 'having sex' means being sexed (gendered), means being subordi-
> nated. Like so much of MacKinnon's analysis of the social, we get
> an encircling wall of reciprocally supporting processes. (p. 109)

And that encircling wall is what Warner finds so maddening; he must find ways of breaking it down or overcoming it, climbing in through the sorority's windows, trying to get at feminism without being 'in' it, without participating in any of the tense encounters that mark *Men in Feminism*.[3]

Turning one of the most problematical moments in that collection into a paradigm for its presentation of men's relation to feminism generally – Paul Smith's 'desperate irony' about men attempting to 'penetrate' feminism, 'a more or less illegal act of breaking and entering, entering and breaking, for which these men must finally be held to account'[4] – Warner tries to distance his approach to feminism from 'their' playfully rapacious one:

> But just as feminism critiques the recurrent sexualizing of women by masculinist culture, the effort to analogize feminism with women can displace and attenuate the critical force of feminism. Because feminism is a discursive formation which develops a comprehensive critique of culture, it becomes limiting and partial to take feminism as a figure of women, and to reduce men's engagement with feminism to a sexual exchange, whether personal or collective, real or fantasmatic. (p. 94)

For a man who has himself made a career out of the sexual tropology of various discourses, and the ways in which women are both 'responsible' for rape and incapable of understanding it, this may seem a curious agenda – much more curious than Warner's other quarrel with *Men in Feminism*, that these male feminists move ahead too quickly, too eager to be 'correctly' feminist. In *Reading Clarissa: The Struggles of Interpretation*,[5] Warner struggles to establish a strategy of reading by which Clarissa ought to be *grateful* for her rape by Lovelace because it gives her something exciting to write about: 'For since something genuinely arresting has happened to Clarissa, a skillful presentation of her drugging and rape allows her to dominate Lovelace and his allies in the pen-knife scene. Clarissa finds the story of her whole life has taken on new vividness and form. The magnitude of her fall imbues all the details of her past with new interest' (p. 94). With new interest, that is, for the playfully rapacious discourse of the deconstructive critic insensitive to sexual politics, who finds that Lovelace's 'way of operating engenders something shared and mutual', while by contrast, 'Clarissa seems irreducibly self-centred, and her friendship with Anna Howe chill and uninteresting' (pp. 38-9). In

responding to books on *Clarissa* by Terry Castle and `Terry Eagleton,
Warner releases a trace of his own interests as a critic by seeming to
resent that Clarissa's narrative and Castle's book work in feminist ways
'so as to increase [Clarissa's] value'.[6]

Fascinated but fearful, Warner claims to have chosen to write about
MacKinnon precisely because 'the very extremity' of her analysis and
'the hyperbole of her political rhetoric . . . bear the force that helps
change the value of women in culture' (p. 122), a project about which
he would seem to be ambivalent at best. Writing as a female feminist
respondent to Warner, I am not 'free' to 'choose' my tactics without
taking certain considerations into account, if I wish to respond responsibly;
rather, I am compelled to do at least two things: to defend MacKinnon
against what in Warner's critique might constitute a contribution to the
anti-feminist backlash many of us have been experiencing within as well
as outside the academy, and, where necessary, to distinguish my position
from hers. For I know that from the beginning of my encounter with
MacKinnon, and with Warner's rewriting of MacKinnon, what I might
object to in MacKinnon's 'unmodification' of feminism – her desire for
purity and homogeneity within a post-marxist feminist practice – is not
really the same as what makes Warner uncomfortable. Even where Warner
and I might appear to draw upon the same intellectual lineages, our
investment is different. As a female feminist, one has reason to be
suspicious of Warner; his reputation precedes him.

'*Odor di uomo or compagnons de route?*' Alice Jardine has asked
regarding men in feminism.[7] Perhaps there is an '*odor di femminismo*', a
hint of bad faith in my turning on Warner something resembling his own
diagnostic gaze. In that case perhaps my own text will not be immediately
recuperable as either 'ladylike',[8] moralist, totalist, or liberal-pluralist. At
least one male reader of an earlier version of this response has found my
attitude towards Warner's attempt to engage with feminism self-defeat-
ingly severe, with the consequence that said reader emerged feeling 'oddly
and self-protectively complacent', claiming that 'if the choice is between
attempting an inevitably failing feminist fellow-traveling and a confessed
sexism, I'll take the latter.' I can only hope that other male readers will
reach very different conclusions.

While making certain ostensibly post-psychoanalytic, deconstructive
objections to MacKinnon's position, Warner fails to read his own text
deconstructively, to subject his own analysis to the same politico-theo-
retical scrutiny he turns upon (MacKinnon's) feminism. And by failing to

do so, he lands himself, tropologically speaking, back in that same 'melodramatic encounter of man and woman' he wishes to avoid, that romantic scenario of male postulator and enigmatic female Other, which he characterizes as the third unacceptable approach available to men engaging with feminism, along with 'objective critical analysis' (p. 91) and 'earnest sympathetic dialogue' (p. 91):

> There is a third way to annul otherness, all the more subtle for the way it seems to be doing just the opposite: by staging a melodramatic encounter of man and woman, where the male speaker postulates as his interlocutor a romantically enigmatic Other. This myth of woman-as-sphinx turns out to be familiar and comforting enough; *she* quickly becomes a site for oedipal heroism. (p. 93)

At the level of tropes, this banished scenario re-emerges within his own discourse, disrupting and rhetorically undermining his ostensible arguments in a devolutionary way, intractably devolving from them and undercutting their persuasiveness. These arguments, his critique of MacKinnon's homogenizing impulses and totalizing view of ideology, her prematurely willed subsumption of marxist dialectics within feminism, her effacement of sexual pleasure, her problematical enlistment of black people as mere counters in her analysis, and her undialogical intolerance regarding other feminisms, remain arguments which, I think, many feminists might otherwise feel inclined to accept. 'Otherwise' because Warner's tropes to a damaging degree betray another agenda from the comradely criticism for which he would appear to be toiling. It is not a matter of expecting a text, however self-critically 'conscious', to dispel its unconscious subtexts, figurations, and symptomatic stress-points. Rather, with Pierre Macherey, we might wish to argue that a text's gaps and contradictions signify 'the unconscious which is history, the play of history beyond its edges, encroaching on those edges' and that 'this is why it is possible to trace the path which leads from the haunted work to that which haunts it'.[9] Nevertheless, Warner's silence on the tropology of his own discourse indicates an absence of that self-reflection which both feminists and men in feminism should be accustomed to practising in a moment when we can no longer ignore the lessons of the marxist critique of ideology or the deconstructive recognition of the subject's irreducible complicity with its objects of investigation.

Though Warner specifically repudiates the spurious use of an engagement with feminism as a site for 'oedipal heroism', his reading of MacKinnon-as-ArchFeminist is rooted in oedipal struggle. As a Derridian commenting on feminism, Warner writes in the wake of Derrida's interview, 'Choreographies'.[10] In the first two versions of his essay,[11] this relation to Derrida's pronouncements on feminism was explicit, with Warner drawing upon the father's astute criticisms of contemporary feminism yet reproving him for failing to 'practice . . . the arduous double task he suggests for a deconstructive feminist politics' (II, p. 7). Ironically, Warner finds Derrida subject to 'Oedipal anxieties' (II, p. 6), at the very moment when he, Warner, reveals his own in trying to distinguish his project from Derrida's, to supersede it, to be more lovable than his father, his methodological maker and master. The implicit question in Derrida's interview – Now, after feminism, will she love me? – haunts Warner's reading of MacKinnon as well. If Derrida puts himself in the position of what Warner calls 'a paternal choreographer of the (feminist) dance', while insisting on its spontaneity (II, p. 6), Warner plays impresario to a (feminist) diva, while pointing out that the aria she sings is painfully forceful, violent, ambitious, demeaning to men, exclusionist regarding black men and other feminisms, insufficiently dialectical, and only partly aware of its relation to representation and value – in other words, nothing much to do with *him* really, though he has arranged the performance. Warner tries to efface himself from the stage of his reading of MacKinnon just as surely as Derrida would disappear into the feminist dance, that 'history of absolutely heterogeneous pockets, irreducible particularities, of unheard of and incalculable sexual differences'.[12] In both cases, the dance and the diva function erotically and spectacularly for their male producers.

Like a Lovelace in Parisian clothing, or the Paul Smith given to desperate ironies, Warner operates a metaphorics of rapacious desire in relation to Woman/Feminism. The first such metaphor emerges in a passage playfully legitimating, through a mock-naive autobiographism, Warner's status as a feminist fellow-traveler. Warner cites as 'the contingencies of history' which might make him less resistant to feminist criticism than many men the fact that this earliest experience predisposed him to know women as equals. These crucial women are a twin sister, a mother who was a 'successful writer', and a maternal grandmother who was a 'famous opera singer' (p. 92). The move from merely 'successful' to 'famous' is significant: Warner's essay is haunted by a phantom Diva of Feminism to whose siren song he wishes to harken in order to be rapt, disarmed, transfigured. But the fame that such a powerful figure would acquire is also threatening to the professionally-minded academic, whose modicum of 'fame' is always in jeopardy, always imperiled by the latest critical fashion, and not least by feminism, with its potential to change cultural values and to disable even male feminist fellow-travelers from speaking out or talking back as freely as they might wish.

The diva is one of those rare figures of power in Anglo-European culture with a female body, whose voice commands the center of the operatic action, whose presence on stage elicits and orchestrates the diffuse libidinal energies of the audience. As Jean-Jacques Beineix's film *Diva* obsessively insists, the diva's fans are compelled to fetishize her, hoping to steal her voice, her dress, in acts of homage that she can only perceive as rape, and that feed all too easily into the circuitry of commercial recording which a 'true' diva, who thrives on live audiences, will abhor. In performance the diva holds her audience in thrall through the sheer erotic power of herself as spectacle, her voice as instrument of theatrical self-presentation. In *Diva*, the performance which the young fan illicitly records and which 'becomes' the diva throughout the film, is a performance of Catalani's 'La Wally' in which the heroine sings that she will go far, far away and be seen no more. The young fan, rapt by the erotic power of the diva's song of willed absence and abstinence, of eternal deferral, of a passion that can never be consummated, says in response simply: 'It's tragic. In the end she throws herself into a gorge.' The end of so much female erotic force so theatrically displayed must be a tragic ending, according to the operatic script. In the film, the fan wins the diva's affections, an almost unthinkable victory for the young postal worker, by giving her the tape he has made without her knowledge in defiance of her public pronouncements on illicit recording. (By giving her the tape he also contravenes the plans of two sinister stereotypes from the multinational recording business who have threatened the diva with marketing a pirated version of the tape.) What has been taken from her against her will can now be restored by the male fan in a blaze of generosity. What once constituted 'rape' can now be seen as 'true' homage/hommage:[13] the young fan becomes a man in relation to the diva by returning his fetish-objects (her dress, her voice) to her one by one. The diva only sings about suicide as an historical fiction; in the cinematic 'real' she accepts her 'symbolic' rapist as a 'true' lover.

Warner's characterization of MacKinnon as ArchFeminist turns on her partial appropriation of the diva's role. She is, and is not, the voice of a feminism he can (re)produce as powerful and be rapt by, spectatorily. For MacKinnon is also the Iron Maiden of feminism: refusing homage/

hommage; distrusting, as culturally prefabricated and subversive of feminist ends, the 'Woman's Voice' celebrated by Carol Gilligan; using argumentative force, not erotic suasion, to change cultural values; refusing to throw herself into any of the available gorges of nihilism, defeatism, or polite compromise.

A kind of stylistic transference emerges in Warner's essay: how often he refers to MacKinnon's analytical voice as if she were an operatic performer, while relying on musical metaphors in the production of his own discourse: 'the *tone and coloring* of her language' [original emphasis] (p. 96); 'The relegation of most reference to other feminist work to the footnotes allows it to be given a decidedly supporting role' (p. 118); 'orchestrate' (p. 108); 'We need a more patient, and ethically dispassionate, understanding of how objects – whether a flag, a face, or a tune – become endowed by a desiring subject with energy and allure' (p. 112).

Warner claims that he has chosen MacKinnon to sing the feminist aria because her work 'takes to its logical limit ideas which other feminists invoke in a more guarded and tentative way' (p. 95). Thus her 'extremism' is made to seem both representative of and superior to feminism as a whole. Warner finds MacKinnon especially admirable because she breaks up that threatening collectivity of militant women who celebrate their own variety through their solidarity against men:

> MacKinnon's willingness to develop criticism of other feminisms shows an iconoclasm before what might be called the easy pluralism of American academic thought, especially as that pluralism manifests itself as feminist celebrations of its own variety. (p. 119)

The critique of 'easy pluralism' in American academia is potentially productive, but in this context it seems misplaced. The praise of 'gutsy' (II, p. 28) iconoclasm here smacks of the 'woman I'd hire' trope – the trope of power as selection and possession, with the feminine object of exchange desirable precisely because she too is powerful and has a distinctive voice, not a 'collective' one: *my* diva. Not like all those other girls. And – to my relief – she doesn't like all those other girls. She only likes some of them passionately, the committed ones, a possibility that Warner refuses to address responsibly, with the result that his continual return to the problem of *hetero*sexuality reads like homophobic occlusion, a distorting bias which suggests that MacKinnon's radical feminist analysis, and its logical extension into a lesbian if not a separatist praxis, have failed fully to communicate themselves over and above Warner's prejudices. Not to address lesbianism more directly, since MacKinnon herself does not in these essays, may be a sign of 'discretion' on Warner's part, but there is no excuse for his banishing of all sexual possibilities except heterosexuality from his analysis.[14]

Throughout his essay, Warner keeps coming back to the fascination exerted upon him by female fame, by individuality of voice, but he also appears to be threatened by it. So long as we remain safely within the exchange of women by men, a trope most prominently displayed in the concatenation of 'exchange in the social sphere – as in hiring, marriage, sex, gossip, etc.' (p. 112), Warner is not threatened. But when it becomes a matter of 'successful', even 'famous' professional academic women displacing him and his right to speak – and exchange (women, ideas) – then a plaintive tone emerges. The diva will not be won over after all.[15]

Embattled thus as an arbiter of the new whose purchase on cultural innovation has been limited by feminism, Warner must also use MacKinnon's operatic power against her, and implicitly against 'feminism', since MacKinnon as ArchFeminist has come to stand for the cultural work done by feminism as a whole. MacKinnon's refreshing iconoclasm is also totalizing intolerance. By means of analogy, her work makes the present non-reciprocity and power imbalance between men and women seem 'ironclad' (p. 108); with 'systematic radicality' she carries out a 'strong' reading of marxism (p. 95); 'The bold directness and chiseled concision of MacKinnon's style are indices of her clear purpose, polemical decision, and fixed determination' (p. 96); MacKinnon's proposing of an agenda for feminism is 'Rather than being a sign of the intellectual modesty of this project . . . a sign of its ambition' (p. 121). Ostensibly, this is not dispraise on Warner's part, merely another form of admiration. Yet MacKinnon's rigor becomes antagonistic intolerance in Warner's reading of the Buffalo debate between MacKinnon and Carol Gilligan, in which MacKinnon annihilates the grounds for any future authentic feminist diva-ism by rendering 'hollow in advance the tone of any living woman's voice' (p. 121). Tropologically, 'MacKinnon' takes on a bifurcated role easily recuperable by anti-feminist traditionalism: caught between the seductive, sexually powerful Diva and the rigorous, uncompromising Iron Maiden, where are the voices and bodies of the heterogeneous, unreified, but not 'easy pluralist' feminists – dauntingly promiscuous feminists? – whom Warner endorses to perform their culturally iconoclastic work?

As is apparent from his prose as well as his schema for an alternative to MacKinnon's treatment of sexuality as a 'zero-sum game' (p. 111), Warner values 'dispense', spending, Bataillean transgression. In his eagerness to 'save' sex as 'uncontrollable, excessive and fundamental' (p. 111), Warner overstates his case and underestimates the microtechnologies of power that produce our knowledge of sexuality, rendering it not totally 'controllable', perhaps, but certainly 'manipulable' within the circuits of capital and exploitable commercially and politically. Warner's rigid adherence to the uncontrollable excessiveness and fundamentality of 'sex' is at odds with his brief invocation of the Foucault of *The History of Sexuality*, for whom 'sexuality' is neither transgressive, knowable outside the discursive inscription of it in particular cultures and historical moments, nor possessable as 'one's own', as MacKinnon would have it, a means to truth.

Warner uses Foucault's argument to undermine MacKinnon's claim that sexuality is the 'linchpin of gender inequality' (p. 109), but silently abandons Foucault for psychoanalysis when (hetero)sexuality needs to be rescued. To do otherwise would be to jeopardize that 'new heterosexual commonweal' (p. 92) that Warner insists upon positing as his vision of a utopian future, substituting for Derrida's 'unheard of and incalculable sexual differences' a vision of a re-vamped heterosexuality. There is a reason for Warner's slippage in and out of a Foucauldian problematic, for his defensiveness regarding (hetero)sexuality. Something has happened, historically, to jeopardize his argumentative, discursive, Bataillean-transgressive flow.

MacKinnon, intent upon empowering women, those who have been cast historically as 'objects' *par excellence*, has attempted to go beyond the 'subject/object split' (p. 102) characteristic of male metaphysics, thus 'inadvertently' risking 'a radical idealism' (p. 101). Apparently more terrifyingly for Warner, she has failed to 'abolish' the object in fact, for the coming into being of women as subjects seems to involve the objectification of *men*, 'now objectified as the Objectifier of woman – rapist, pornographer, and wielder of victimizing, illegitimate forms of state power' (p. 104). One might think that Warner ought to find this dialectical process of reversal and transformation, this sublation of men's previously unchallenged power in women's newfound mastery, this subjection of men to women's objectifying gaze, both inevitable and defensible. He even insists on the 'crucial and valued' (p. 106) and necessary and 'pleasurable' (p. 110) status of the 'object' within dialectics and the psychoanalytical schema of desire. But in Warner's analysis these objects are never men. Somehow, the pleasures of the object vanish when the objectification of men is brought into play; Warner remains hostile to feminism's invest-ment in women's struggle towards subjectivity: 'If one were to state the plot of MacKinnon's "agenda for theory" in one sentence it would have the pure oppositional rhythm of a revenge fiction: woman goes from being the object of male power to being a subject in her own right' (p. 103). *Revenge fiction?* Warner would apparently deny the political efficacy of women's struggling for self-determination and the consequently radical reconstruction of subjectivity, gender, and sexuality that political struggle entails. His satirical swipe at MacKinnon for protesting the male invest-ment in objectification – They're treating me like an object! – becomes his own implicit shriek at the thought of MacKinnon's 'audacious' (p. 104) female seizure of power. What, then, has Warner to do with feminism, we may well ask. Perhaps there was more to his determination to stay behind (p. 95) reading MacKinnon rather than fellow-traveling 'too fast' with *Men in Feminism* (p. 92) than met the eye.

Warner's essay may not be 'totalizingly' antifeminist, but it remains more than a little hostile to feminism and more than a little rapt by the spectacle of its own textual production, its own self-regarding discursive prowess that can be called upon to 'release' the MacMaiden's discursive unconscious. This forcing of feminist (and female) 'issues' *once again* by a rapacious male critic preoccupied with the threatened increase of 'the value of women in culture' suggests that Warner has not reflected suf-ficiently upon his own subject position nor upon the historically specifiable connections between male violence, (hetero)sexuality, and women's oppression in all cultural spheres, so brutally epitomized by rape.[16] Apparently unable to imagine materially a gendered perspective different from his own, and the oppressive and exploitable consequences of this privileged unknowing, Warner sees in the women who have been subject to him not so much those women, their desires and disfigurations, but rather yet another image of his *own* subjection, to the repressively disci-plinary culture of late capitalism, a culture which he is writing to resist.

His resistance would be more thoroughgoing, and of more use to feminism, if he would subject his own extremely problematical desires to a feminist political critique and reject the playful rapacity to which men no longer have any theoretically or politically defensible right in the present moment, and for the moment. Perhaps such moves might be envisageable if Warner were to work against his exploitatively spectatorial, antagonistically rapt relation to feminism. He could think again about that 'earnest sympathetic dialogue' which his anti-humanist training has led him to reject prematurely and cavalierly – if only he weren't so 'musical'.

NOTES

1 Warner makes much of this formula, which is also the title of MacKinnon's new book, *Feminism Unmodified: Discourses on Life and Law* (Cambridge, MA: Harvard University Press, 1987). His playing on the phrase, while neglecting to mention the book's existence, strikes me as capricious to say the least.
2 This is what Gallop says of Luce Irigaray's relation to Lacan: 'Irigaray is afraid of being trapped by her debt, but in her militant refusal she becomes a rigid virgin – phallicized. She believes there must be a way out of the Freudian/Lacanian Oedipal closed circuit, but revolt against the Father is no way out': Gallop 1982: 91.
3 Jardine and Smith 1987.
4 See Paul Smith, 'Men in feminism: men and feminist theory', in Jardine and Smith 1987: 33; and Cary Nelson's reporting of Smith's own description of this strategy as 'desperate irony' in Nelson's useful essay, 'Men, feminism: the materiality of discourse', ibid.: 171.
5 Warner 1979.
6 Warner 1983: 20.
7 '*Odor di uomo or compagnons de route?*' in Jardine and Smith 1987: 54–61.
8 I am troping here on Nancy Armstrong's review of Poovey 1984. Armstrong writes: '*The Proper Lady* cannot critique the discourse of sexuality since it observes the proprieties of traditional criticism. Thus today's literary institution places us in something of a double-bind situation which makes it virtually impossible to speak politically and also politely.' Armstrong 1984: 1257.
9 Macherey 1978: 94.
10 Derrida 1982.
11 I will refer hereafter to the two earlier versions of Warner's essay as 'I' and 'II', respectively.
12 Derrida 1982: 68.
13 See Gallop 1982: 91, for this turn upon the term.
14 In the first two versions of his essay, Warner had merely banished them to the margins (and the footnotes) of his text – when he was not explicitly dismissing them, as in 'although her radical feminist positions often seem impossible (to imagine living)' (II, p. 9). He also explicitly marginalizes specific practices like lesbianism in such dismissive allusions as 'right-wing women or lesbian sadomasachistics [*sic*]' (II, p. 27).
15 In the first and second versions of his essay, a note of nostalgia emerged more clearly as Warner assessed some of the cultural contradictions that the feminist aria has produced: 'The competitiveness endemic to most "male" professions is criticized, but the achievement of women in these same professions is often celebrated' (II, p. 54);

'Woman can be revalued by making her the one who is read because she counts as one who is carrying something new into culture' (II, p. 55). Not, one might add, the something new that 'women' have always 'carried' into culture – in the shape of the next generation.

16   In this respect, Warner's blindness to his blindness on the subject of rape and its gender specificity parallels Foucault's own, as illuminated so effectively by Monique Plaza. Plaza reminds Foucault of how his sweepingly theoretical pronouncements on rape effectively contradict his earlier theorization in *The History of Sexuality* of the need for a politics of heterogeneous local interventions and situationally specific forms of resistance (1981: 34; the quotations are from p. 96 of Foucault 1978):

> Michel Foucault, you have not clearly analyzed the place of the 'enunciative modality,' which you adopt when you talk about rape. If you had, when the Magistrates' Association asked you to give your opinion about rape, you would not have launched right away into a completely preemptive 'theoretical' explanation. You would have first 'turned toward the women' who are currently struggling. And you would not at any time have tried to convince us that *we* are mistaken. You would not have lost a certain political memory, and you would have remembered that insofar as we are exposed in the front lines in the strategic field of patriarchal power relations, we are in the best position to structure 'resistances, each of them a special case: . . . possible, necessary, improbable; . . . spontaneous, savage, solitary, concerted, rampant, . . . violent,' [irreconcilable] . . .

REFERENCES

Armstrong, Nancy 1984. *Modern Language Notes*, 99.5 (1984): 1252-7.

Derrida, Jacques 1982. 'Choreographies': interview by Christie V. McDonald, *Diacritics*, 12 (Summer): 66-76.

Foucault, Michel 1978. *The History of Sexuality, Vol. I: An Introduction*. Trans. Robert Hurley. New York: Pantheon.

Gallop, Jane 1982. *The Daughter's Seduction: Feminism and Psychoanalysis*. Ithaca: Cornell University Press.

Jardine, Alice and Smith, Paul (eds) 1987. *Men in Feminism*. New York and London: Methuen.

Macherey, Pierre 1978. *A Theory of Literary Production*. Trans. Geoffrey Wall. London: Routledge and Kegan Paul.

MacKinnon, Catharine A. 1987. *Feminism Unmodified: Discourses on Life and Law*. Cambridge, MA: Harvard University Press.

Plaza, Monique 1981. 'Our damages and their compensation. Rape: the will not to know of Michel Foucault', *Feminist Issues*, 1.3: 25-35 originally published in *Questions féministes*, 3 (1978).

Poovey, Mary 1984. *The Proper Lady and the Woman Writer: Ideology as Style in the Works of Mary Wollstonecraft, Mary Shelley, and Jane Austen*. Chicago and London: University of Chicago Press.

Warner, William Beatty 1979. *Reading Clarissa: The Struggles of Interpretation*. New
    Haven and London: Yale University Press.
Warner, William Beatty 1983. 'Reading rape: marxist-feminist figurations of the literal',
    Diacritics, 13: 12-32.

Part II

Gendering Post-modernism
and Post-structuralism

These essays interrogate post-modernism as a cultural movement and a socio-historical period. They discuss different methodological approaches to historiography, and offer starkly different assessments of post-modernism's relation to feminism. The essayists evaluate recent work on the intersections of post-modernism, feminism and deconstruction. Some suggest new methods for relating post-modernism to cultural politics; others posit a politics of subjectivity as a way out of the present impasse between feminism and deconstruction.

Linda Hutcheon's 'The Post-modern Ex-centric: The Center that Will Not Hold' celebrates multiple manifestations of ex-centricity in post-modern literature and culture. Hutcheon relates the debates about the term 'post-modernism' to critical theory, showing how the post-modern novel attacks liberal humanism and challenges the grounds upon which we have traditionally established judgments of order, coherence, and certainty. Tracing the roots of these developments to the 1960s, she analyzes the subsequent emergence of black men's and black women's voices in literature and criticism, and discusses the emerging voices of other ethnic groups. Post-modernism is a transitional stage, a first step towards radical change in aesthetics and politics.

In 'Writing Cultural History: The Case of Post-modernism', Vincent B. Leitch critiques Hutcheon's traditional historiographical methods, methods which are devoted to integrating and thematizing epochs, rather than exposing the cruelty of economic interests, political forces, and ideologies in these epochs. We are thus left with vague oppositions between humanism and 'difference', a vagueness which is also a disservice to radical feminism. The politics of post-modernism as rendered by literary historians is emptied of relation to nationalism, totalitarianism, imperialism, and neo-colonialism. How would our understanding of post-modernism be altered, Leitch asks, if it stemmed not from literary history but from institutional history?

Bernard Duyfhuizen's 'Deconstruction and Feminist Literary Theory II' provides an overview of criticism in the 1980s, ranging from marxism and deconstruction to semiotics and reader-response criticism. He examines the reciprocal influences of critical theory and feminist theory, reproaching male compilers of anthologies who ignore feminist contributions to literary theory. Duyfhuizen sees the work of Gayatri Spivak and Alice Jardine as models of new directions for further research on feminism and deconstruction.

Bella Brodzki and Celeste Schenck's 'Criticus Interruptus: Uncoupling Feminism and Deconstruction' challenges the heterosexual coupling of feminism and deconstruction, arguing that the dialectic has reached an impasse. They offer alternative directions in theory and criticism which point the way out: new emphases on the politics of theory, the politics of subjectivity, and global politics in general. They are interested in theorizing new modes of subjectivity, modes which do not repeat the mistakes of feminism's early essentializing formulations. Their analyses of three stories by Jamaica Kincaid are a vivid demonstration of their theory's relevance.

7

The Post-modern Ex-centric: The Center That Will Not Hold

Linda Hutcheon

No one says a novel has to be one thing. It can be anything it wants to be, a vaudeville show, the six o'clock news, the mumblings of wild men saddled by demons.

> Loop Garoo, black cowboy, in Ishmael Reed's *Yellow Back Radio Broke-Down*

Anyone writing a novel . . . must have a clear and firm idea as to what is good and bad in life.

> John Bayley, *Tolstoy and the Novel*

Like much contemporary literary theory, the post-modernist novel[1] puts into question a whole series of interconnected concepts that have come to be generally associated with what we conveniently label as liberal humanism: autonomy, transcendence, certainty, authority, unity, totalization, system, universalization, center, continuity, teleology, closure, hierarchy, homogeneity, uniqueness, origin. To put these concepts into question is not to deny them - only to interrogate their relation to experience, without the kind of foreclosing assurance that the second epigraph suggests. The process by which this is done is a process of installing and then withdrawing (or of using and abusing) those very contested notions.

This is the post-modern: the fundamentally contradictory, resolutely historical, inescapably political critique (both theoretical and aesthetic) of contemporary culture that got its name from its paradigm: the post-modern architecture of Charles Moore, Paolo Portoghesi, Riccardo Bofill, Robert Stern, and many others. Criticism does not necessarily imply destruction, and post-modern critique, in particular, is a paradoxical and questioning beast. Charles Newman has stated, rather polemically, that 'Post-Modernism reflects not a radical uncertainty so much as an unconsidered suspension of judgment',[2] but in being so very categorical, he misses the point of the post-modern enterprise: it is neither uncertain nor suspending of judgment. What it does is question the very bases of any certainty (history, subjectivity, reference) and of any standards of judgment: who sets them? when? where? why? Post-modernism marks less a negative 'disintegration' of or 'decline' in order and coherence,[3] than a challenging of the very concepts upon which we judge order and coherence.

No doubt, this interrogative stance, this contesting of authority, is partly, at least, a result of the decentralized revolt, the 'molecular politics',[4] of the 1960s. I think it would be hard to argue that this challenge to models of unity and order is directly caused by life today being more fragmented and chaotic than in previous times; yet many have done so, claiming that our fiction is bizarre (and even outdated and irrelevant) because life itself is more bizarre than art.[5] This view has been called simplistic and even 'lunatic'[6] in the light of history – both literary and social. But whatever the cause, there have been serious interrogations of those once accepted certainties of liberal humanism.

These challenges have now become the truisms of much contemporary theoretical discourse. One of the major ones – one that has come from both theory and aesthetic practice – has been to the notion of center, in all its forms. In Chris Scott's post-modern historiographic metafiction *Antichthon*, the historical character, Giordano Bruno, lives out the dramatic consequences of the Copernican displacing of the world and of humankind. From a de-centered perspective, as the novel's title suggests, if one world exists, then all possible worlds exist: historical plurality replaces atemporal eternal essence. In post-modern psychoanalytic, philosophical and literary theory, the further decentering of the subject and its pursuit of individuality and authenticity has had significant repercussions on everything from our concept of rationality to our view of the possibilities of genre.[7]

If the center will not hold, then, as one of the Merry Pranksters (in Tom Wolfe's *The Electric Kool-Aid Acid Test*) put it, 'Hail to the Edges!' The move to rethink margins and borders is clearly a move away from centralization with its associated concerns of origin, oneness and monumentality that work to link the concept of center to those of the eternal and universal. The ex-centric, the local, the regional, the non-totalizing, are reasserted as the centre becomes a fiction – necessary, desirable, but a fiction nonetheless.

Much of the debate over the definition of the term post-modernism has revolved around what some see as a loss of faith in this centralizing and totalizing impulse of humanist thought.[8] Offered as alternatives to system-building are theories which privilege the dialogized or hybrid[9] or which contextualize the urge to totalize as only a momentary aspiration in the history of philosophy.[10] Both Marxism and Freudian psychoanalysis have been attacked as totalizing 'meta-narratives', yet one could argue that they have been fruitful in analyses of post-modernism precisely because their 'split' model (class struggle or conscious/unconscious) allows a very post-modern – that is, contradictory – anti-totalizing kind of totalization. And, while much of the actual criticism of post-modern fiction is still premised on a humanist belief in the universal human urge to generate systems that will order experience,[11] the fiction itself challenges such critical assumptions. Pynchon's *Gravity's Rainbow* inscribes and then undercuts – in a typically post-modern way – the certainties of the ordering impulse of positivistic science as well as of humanist history and literature by its over-totalization, by its parodies of systematization.

When the centre starts to give way to the margins, when totalizing universalization begins to self-deconstruct, cultural homogenization too reveals its fissures, but the heterogeneity that is asserted in the face of that totalizing (yet pluralizing) culture does not take the form of many fixed individual subjects,[12] but instead is conceived of as a flux of contextualized identities: contextualized by gender, class, race, ethnicity, sexual preference, education, social role, etc. As we shall see shortly, this assertion of identity through difference and specificity is a constant in post-modern thought.

To move from difference and heterogeneity to discontinuity is a link that at least the *rhetoric* of rupture has readily made in the light of the contradictions and challenges of post-modernism. Narrative continuity is perhaps most obviously threatened; that is, it is both used and abused. The nineteenth-century structures of narrative closure (death, marriage) are undermined by those post-modern epilogues that foreground how, as writers and readers, we *make* closure: Fowles's *A Maggot*, Thomas's *The White Hotel*, Atwood's *The Handmaid's Tale*. John Banville's *Doctor Copernicus* ends with 'DC' – both the protagonist's initials and the (initiating and reiterating) 'da capo' which refuses closure. Similarly the modernist tradition of the more 'open' ending is both used and abused by post-modern self-consciously multiple endings (Fowles's *The French Lieutenant's Woman*) or resolutely arbitrary closure (Rushdie's

Midnight's Children). From the point of view of theory, Derrida has argued that closure is not just not desirable, but not even possible, and he has done so through his language of supplement, margin, and deferral. But the particularly paradoxical post-modern aspect of what may appear radical here is underlined by Richard Rorty when he points out the paradoxical *reliance* of deconstruction (like realism) upon a historically determined concept of metaphysics that it wants to deny: the one that attempts to create 'unique, total, closed vocabularies'.[13]

This contradiction is typical of post-modern theory. The decentering of our categories of thought always relies on the centers it contests for its very definition (and frequently its verbal form). The adjectives may vary: hybrid, heterogeneous, discontinuous, anti-totalizing, uncertain. So may the metaphors: the image of the labyrinth without center or periphery might replace the conventionally ordered notion we usually have of a library, for instance (in Eco's *The Name of the Rose*), or the spreading rhizome might be a less repressively structuring concept than the hierarchical tree.[14] But the power of these new expressions is always paradoxically derived from that which they challenge. It may indeed be true, as Craig Owens argues, that '[w]hen the postmodernist work speaks of itself, it is no longer to proclaim its autonomy, its self-sufficiency, its transcendence; rather, it is to narrate its own contingency, insufficiency, a lack of transcendence'.[15] But it is also clear that this definition relies on its inverting of a set of values which it contests.

The contradictory nature of post-modernism involves its offering of multiple, provisional, contextualized alternatives to traditional, fixed, ahistorical, unitary concepts, in full knowledge of (and even exploiting) the continuing appeal of those very concepts. Post-modern architecture, for example, does not reject the technological and material advances of High Modernism of the International Style: it cannot. But it can subvert its uniformity, its ahistoricity, its ideological and social aims (and consequences). As architect/theorist Paolo Portoghesi writes: 'In place of faith in the great centered designs, and the anxious pursuits of salvation, the postmodern condition is gradually substituting the concreteness of small circumstantiated struggles with its precise objectives capable of having a great effect because they change systems of relations.'[16] This is not a claim to homogenization or totalization, but rather to heterogeneity and provisionality that goes well beyond any simply formal play with types of non-selection, verbal or architectural,[17] to suggest political and social intent.

The center may not hold, but it is still an attractive fiction of order and unity, one that post-modern art and theory continue to exploit, while still subverting it. That fiction takes many forms in the institutions of culture and, in many of them, its limitations are becoming the focus of attention. The very walls of the traditional museum and the very definition of a work of art come under fire in the performances of Albert Vidal, for instance. His 'The Urban Man' is a kind of anthropological performance ritual in which Vidal spends five hours a day in a major public place in a city (for example, at Miami's Metro Zoo or the Place d'Youville in Quebec City) offering to passers-by an 'exhibit' of post-modern man going about his daily business – eating, telephoning, dozing. Similarly, the notion of the physical book is challenged in formally hybrid 'intermedia',[18] and, of course, the categories of genre within literature are regularly challenged these days. Fiction looks like biography (Banville's *Kepler*), autobiography (Ondaatje's *Running in the Family*), history (Rushdie's *Shame*). Theoretical discourse joins forces with autobiographical memoir and Proustian reminiscence in Barthes's *Camera Lucida*, where a theory of photography grows out of personal emotion with no pretense to objectivity, finality, or authority.

The ex-centric, the off-center: ineluctably identified with the center it is denied. This is the paradox of the post-modern and its images are often as deviant as this language of decentering suggests: for example, the freak as it appears in films like *Carney* or novels like E. L. Doctorow's *Loon Lake*, Carter's *Nights at the Circus*, and Quarrington's *Home Game*. The multi-ringed circus becomes the pluralized paradoxical metaphor for a decentered world where there is only ex-centricity.

Another form of this same move off center is to be found in the contesting of centralization of culture through the valuing of the local and peripheral: not New York or London or Toronto, but William Kennedy's Albany, Graham Swift's fens country, David Adams Richards's Maritimes. Post-modern architects similarly look to the local idiom and ethos for their forms. And post-modern painters, sculptors, video artists, novelists, poets, and film-makers join with these architects in collapsing the high/low art hierarchy of earlier times, in an attack on high art centralization of academic interest on the one hand, and, on the other, on the homogeneity of consumer culture which adapts, includes, and makes all seem accessible by neutralizing and popularizing. To collapse hierarchies is not to collapse distinctions, however. Post-modernism retains, and indeed celebrates, differences against what has been called the 'racist logic of the exclusive'.[19] The modernist concept of alienated otherness is challenged by the post-modern questioning of binaries that conceal hierarchies (self/other). When Edward Said calls for theory today to have an 'awareness of the differences between situations' in its 'critical consciousness' of its position in the world,[20] he is going beyond the early Foucauldian definition of modernity in terms of otherness alone. Difference suggests multiplicity, heterogeneity, plurality, rather than binary opposition and exclusion.

It is again to the 1960s that we must turn to see the roots of this change, for it is those years that saw the inscribing into history[21] of previously 'silent' groups defined by differences of race, gender, sexual preference, ethnicity, native status, class. The 1970s and 1980s have seen the increasingly rapid and complete inscribing of these same ex-centrics into both theoretical discourse and artistic practice as andro-(phallo-), hetero-, Euro-, and ethno-centrisms have been vigorously challenged. Think of Doctorow's novel, *Ragtime*, with its three paralleled families: the Anglo-American establishment one and the marginal immigrant European and American black ones. The novel's action disperses the center of the first and moves the margins into the multiple 'centers' of the narrative, in a formal allegory of the social demographics of urban America. In addition, there is an extended critique of American democratic ideals through the presentation of class conflict rooted in capitalist property and moneyed power. The black Coalhouse, the white Houdini, the immigrant Tateh are all working-class, and because of this – not in spite of it – all can therefore work to create new aesthetic forms (ragtime, vaudeville, movies).

To assert the cultural importance of the 1960s civil rights movement in the United States is not to deny its political significance. Indeed the rise of militant black protest in literature in the 1960s had direct political consequences. Since then, black literature has also forced a reconsideration of cultural specificity, the canon, and methods of analysis that have had repercussions beyond the borders of America, for it is possible to argue that it literally enabled feminist and other forms of protest. What Henry Louis Gates, Jr calls a 'signifying black difference'[22] challenged the ethnocentrism that made the black into a figure of negation or absence – just as androcentrism absented women. What is important to recall, however, is that difference operates *within* each of these challenging cultures, as well as against the dominant. Blacks and feminists, ethnics and gays, native and 'Third World' cultures, are not monolithic movements, but consist of a multiplicity of responses to a commonly perceived situation of marginality and ex-centricity. And there have been liberating effects of moving from the language of alienation (otherness) to that of decentering (difference), because the center used to function as the pivot between binary opposites which always privileged one half: black/white, male/female, self/other, intellect/body, West/East, objectivity/subjectivity – the list is now well known. But if the center is seen as a construct, a fiction, not a fixed and unchangeable reality, the 'old either-or begins to break down', as Susan Griffin put it,[23] and the and-also of multiplicity and difference opens up new possibilities.

The autobiographical novels of black American men in the 1960s have given way to a more structurally and ideologically complex form of narrative in the years since, probably partly because of the new voice of black women writers. There is post-modern desire to 'make and unmake meaning, effect a simultaneous creative surge and destructive will'.[24] But black women have been aided in their particular 'voicing' by the rise of the women's movement. There seems to be a general agreement that – not unlike the black civil rights and the Québécois separatist movements and the French intellectual left activists of May 1968 – the American left was both largely male and sexist.[25] The reaction of women against this took a very 'sixties' form: a challenging of authority (male, institutional), an acknowledgment of power as the basis of sexual politics, a belief in the role of socio-cultural context in the production and reception of art. All of these contestations would contribute to forming the basis of the paradoxes of post-modernism in the immediate future, as feminists and others recognized that, in Ellen Willis's words, 'sexism, heterosexism, racism, capitalism and imperialism intersect in complex, often contradictory ways.'[26]

Black women brought to this ex-centric re-ordering of culture not just a very precise sense of the social context and community in which they work, but what Barbara Christian has called an awareness of their own personal and historical past as the 'foundation for a genuine revolutionary process'.[27] As women in a black (as well as white), male-dominated, heterosexual society, writers like Alice Walker and Toni Morrison have offered alternatives to the alienated other, the individual subject of late capitalism that has been the subject of bourgeois fiction:[28] collective history and a newly problematized sense of female community. The black male world of Morrison's *Song of Solomon* is literally a 'Dead' world that denies life to the women who take on its name (Ruth); the ex-centric community of Pilate, Hagar and Reba is outside normal society (white or black), outside the town, and infinitely attractive because of its position.

Women operate differently from men here, even in the forms of their revenge. Male revenge - Guitar's - is both as abstract and totalizing ('White people are unnatural. As a race they are unnatural' [p. 157]) as that which it avenges in white culture. On the other hand, female revenge - Circe's - is concrete and specific: it is wreaked on the white family she served and outlived. Her personal historical context validates her vengeance against their property and their heritage. The issue of class joins that of race and gender in the juxtaposing of middle-class bourgeois Ruth and the ex-centric Pilate who is beyond materialism, beyond the structures and strictures of society. In this way she is almost beyond class, and even beyond gender: her wisdom comes from the paternal line, her name is male, yet she does not live up to its male connotations of washing her hands of responsibility. Her subversions of these gendered associations are partly because she is really her own construction. In the face of society's marginalization of her (she is demonic, unnatural, with no navel), 'she threw away every assumption she had learned and began at zero' (p. 149), setting her own values and goals. What is important is that her ex-centric position gives her an 'alien's compassion for troubled people' (p. 150) that allows her to give up 'all interest in table manners or hygiene' in exchange for 'a deep concern for and about human relationships' (p. 150). The powerful conflating of class, gender, and racial issues can be seen if we compare Pilate to the novel's other masculine-named woman - the white poet Michael-Mary Graham. Heavy irony points to this *parody* of the ex-centric: 'Marriage, children - all had been sacrificed to the Great Agony and her home was a tribute to the fastidiousness of her dedication (and the generosity of her father's will)' (p. 192).

This kind of exposition of the complicitous dovetailing of race, class, gender, and ideology has had its impact beyond just women writers or blacks or even Americans in general. To offer just one example of the post-modern self-consciousness about the complex interconnection of the various -centrisms: in John Fowles's *A Maggot*, the major confrontation of the novel (set in the eighteenth century) is between a male, middle-class lawyer, Ayscough, and a female, lower-class whore-turned-prophet, Rebecca Lee: 'these two were set apart from each other not only by countless barriers of age, sex, class, education, native province and the rest, but by something far deeper still: by belonging to two very different halves of the human spirit' (p. 425). Rebecca's image for Ayscough's inability to understand her is that they have different alphabets and what she says will not fit his (pp. 313, 379). Fowles puts gender at the heart of difference here, as Rebecca chides her inquisitor about unearned male power over women – social, physical, and moral. It is a power and authority that blame woman for the sins of man in order to maintain the fiction of 'man's superior status vis-à-vis womankind' (p. 318). She rejects his constant attempts to make her a 'mirror of thy sex' (pp. 357, 422), that is, a sinful image projected from himself onto her. Rebecca's heretical religious beliefs in Holy Mother Wisdom (and her divine female trinity) and in the likelihood of Christ being a woman are blasphemy to Ayscough. Not content to accept her 'natural place as help-meet to man, in house and home alone' (p. 436), she has other plans: 'Most of this world is unjust by act of man, not of Our Lord Jesus Christ. Change that is my purpose' (p. 424). In this she joins with the absent male 'hero', known as His Lordship (and Our Lord – the connection is made textually [p. 418]), who 'would doubt all: birth, society, government, justice' (p. 441) in disobeying the laws of man and God (the Father) as incarnated in his own father. The challenges to patriarchy – Christian, familial, societal – are directly linked with the protests of class and gender, and here they come from men as well as women, but it is woman who is given the voice in this novel.

Fowles does not really address the issue of race, but almost every other kind of centered structure is called into question. In the introduction to the special issue of *Critical Inquiry* called ' "Race," Writing, and Difference', Gates calls race 'the ultimate trope of difference' (p. 5). From a male black perspective, that may seem the case. Of course, for feminists, gender has taken on that metaphoric role. In both cases, however, it is difference that defines; it is difference that is valued in and for itself. Most theoretical discussions of difference owe much to the work on the differential system of language and its signifying processes by Saussure, Derrida, Lacan and others. The single and unitary concept of 'otherness' has associations of binarity, hierarchy, and supplementarity that postmodern theory and practice seem to want to reject in favor of a more plural and depriveging concept of difference and the ex-centric. Postmodernist discourses – either those by women, Afro-Americans, natives, ethnics, gays, and so on or those provoked by their stands – try to avoid the trap of reversing and valorizing the other, of making the margin into a center, a move that many have seen as a danger for deconstruction's privileging of writing and absence over speech and presence or for some feminisms' gynocentralizing of a monolithic concept of Woman as other than Man. Post-modern difference is always plural and provisional. It is always, to borrow Barbara Johnson's phrase, a 'critical difference'.

It has frequently been pointed out that post-modernist theory and practice, despite what I have just asserted, have been resolutely white male phenomena, that even feminism has been influenced largely by male models of thought: Mill, Engels, Heidegger, Nietzsche, Marx, Baudrillard, Lyotard, Foucault, Barthes, Derrida, Lacan.[29] There are a number of ways of explaining – or recuperating – this fact. One could, as does Alice Jardine, admit the maleness, but categorically state that its reconceptualization of difference 'will be gendered as female'.[30] The potential essentialism of her assertion of 'supplementary jouissance' as defining Woman is as problematic as its (unproved) assertion itself. The credibility of such a view is undermined considerably by her conflation of the female with modernity (male modernity) in the mode of Kristeva, Irigaray, and Montrelay. Another way of dealing with the maleness of post-modern models like that of deterritorialization[31] is to argue that, were we to accept that male/female are merely illusions within a system of power, we could deploy the model without fear of its maleness interfering with feminist analysis.[32] But post-modern thought rejects the glossing over of both the differences among the 'minoritarian' groups' members and the difference in relation to the dominant culture. In Derrida's terms: 'Masculine and feminine are not even the adverse and possibly contracting parts, but rather the parts of a pseudo-whole',[33] a pseudo-whole which post-modernism contests through its rethinking of the value of the ex-centric and its implication of difference as what Mary Jacobus has called 'a multiplicity, joyousness, and heterogeneity which is that of textuality itself'.[34]

The multiple, the heterogeneous, the different: this is the pluralizing rhetoric of post-modernism that rejects both the abstract category of single otherness created by 'coercive separation and unequal privileges'[35] as well as by the more concrete relegation of the other to the role of 'object for enthusiastic information-retrieval'.[36] The pluralized language of margins and borders marks a position of paradox: both inside and outside. Given this position, it is not surprising that the textual form that heterogeneity and difference often take in post-modern art is that of parody – the intertextual mode that is paradoxically an authorized transgression: its ironic difference is set at the very heart of similarity.[37] Feminist artists like Silvia Kolbowski and Barbara Kruger use ads and commercial fashion plates in new parodic contexts in order to attack the capitalist production of homogeneous images of women. In Kolbowski's 'Model Pleasure', for instance, she parodically works to appropriate both these images and the pleasure they produce for both male and female viewers.[38] Black writers – both male and female – parody or repeat with differences the many traditions within which they work: European, American, black, white, oral, written, standard language, black vernacular. The figure of repetition has been claimed as a tradition in black culture,[39] and the particularly post-modern variant of this repetition may well be parody: Morrison's utopian three-women household in *Song of Solomon* inverting and challenging the dystopic one in Faulkner's *Absalom, Absalom!*[40]

Parodic double-voicing or heterogeneity is not just a device which allows contesting assertions of difference. It also paradoxically offers a textual model of collectivity and community of discourses. The text, but even the title alone, of Yolande Villemaire's *La Vie en prose* points both to the parodic contesting of the clichéd romantic vision of 'la vie en rose' and also to the name of an important women's journal in Quebec, *La Vie en rose*. Such assertion – both intertextual and ideological – of community is never, however, intended as a move towards homogenization. Post-modern art is always aware of difference, difference *within* any grouping too, difference defined by contextualization or positioning in relation to plural others. This is one of the lessons of its ex-centric forebears, as Barbara Johnson has shown in her discussion of Zora Neale Hurston's 'way of dealing with multiple agendas and heterogeneous implied readers'.[41] Post-modern art inherits this concern for context and for the enunciative situation of discourse: that is, the contextualized production and reception of the text. The ironic strategy of black 'signifying'[42] shares this concern to contextualize, not to deny or reduce, difference.

To be ex-centric, on the border or margin, inside yet outside, is to have a different perspective, one that Virginia Woolf once called 'alien and critical', one that is 'always altering its focus',[43] since it has no centering force. Joan Jonas has described her video performance piece *Organic Honey's Visual Telepathy/Vertical Roll* (1972) in similar terms: 'I developed different identities as states of being translated into images appeared in the work. For a time, *Organic Honey* was my alter ego: the woman merged with the dog and *Organic Honey* dissolved in a howl. Narcissism was consciously explored in relation to the mirror and the video. Indoors, using masks and disguises, I played my image for what it was worth: fragmenting parts, seeing double, triple, halves, all in close-up. Outside, my persona abstracted itself: I kept a physical distance from the audience. And that distance became for me something one can shape and inflect something very physical.'[44]

This same shifting of perspective, this same concern for respecting difference, can also be seen within post-modern theoretical discourse today. Feminist theory offers perhaps the clearest example of the importance of an awareness of the diversity of history and culture of women: their differences of race, ethnic group, class, sexual preference.[45] It would be more accurate, of course, to speak of feminisms, in the plural, for there are many different orientations that are subsumed under the general label of feminism: images of women criticism; canon-challenging and women's literary history; separatist or women-centered gynocriticism; feminist 'critique' of patriarchal ideology in male texts; psychoanalytic studies of female subjectivity; theories of *écriture féminine* or *parler femme*; lesbian attacks on heterosexism; marxist-socialist contextualizing; deconstructive interrogations of cultural constructs; women's perspectives on Afro-American, 'Third World', native, and colonial experience and identity. And the list could go on. These different feminisms range from liberal humanist to radical post-structuralist in orientation. They consider women as both writers and readers.[46] Like black theory, these kinds of feminism all integrate theory and practice (or experience) in a way that has had a profound effect on the nature of post-modernism, where theoretical and artistic discourses can no longer be neatly separated.

When Gloria Hull polemically stated that 'Black women poets are not "Shakespeare's sisters"' in response to writing for a volume with that title,[47] she forcefully illustrated the position of the ex-centric towards one particular and dominant center - liberal humanist discourse. Women, blacks, Asians, natives, the working class, and gays have all contested the humanist assumption that subjectivity is produced by or based in eternal values and/or material causes, arguing instead, with Teresa de Lauretis, that subjectivity is constituted by 'one's personal, subjective, engagement in the practices, discourses, and institutions that lend significance (value, meaning, and affect) to the events of the world'.[48] Unlike the male, white, Eurocentered post-structuralist discourse that has most forcefully challenged humanism's whole, integrated ideal of subjectivity, however, these more ex-centric positionalities know that they cannot reject the subject wholesale, largely because they have never really been allowed it.[49] Their

ex-centricity and difference have denied them access to Cartesian rationality and relegated them to the realms of the irrational, the mad, or, at
best, the alien. They participate in two contradictory discourses: the
liberal humanist one of freedom, self-determination, rationality, and also
one of submission, relative inadequacy, and irrational intuition.[50]

In this light, Toni Morrison's *Tar Baby* parodically inverts the feminist
centrism that privileges an essentialized 'female', making Son the
creature of sexual not rational power, of fluid identity, of unclear origins
(despite his generic name). Jadine, on the other hand, chooses to accept
the model and roles of white, European, male culture that, as a black
woman, she might question: 'she chooses in effect to be a creation rather
than a creator, an art historian rather than artist, a model rather than
designer, a wife rather than woman.'[51] This novel self-consciously evades
the danger that post-modern discourse constantly must attempt to skirt:
that it will essentialize its ex-centricity or render itself complicit in the
liberal humanist notions of the universal (speaking for all women, all
blacks, etc.) and the eternal (forever).

Post-modernism does not move the marginal to the center. It does not
invert the valuing of centers into that of peripheries and borders, as much
as it uses that paradoxical doubled positioning to critique the inside from
both the outside and the inside. Just as Padma, the listening, textualized
female reader of Rushdie's *Midnight's Children*, pushes the narration in
directions its male narrator had no intention of taking, so the ex-centrics
have not only overlapped in their concerns with post-modernism, but
have pushed it in new directions. For instance, the perspective of these
inside-outsiders added race, ethnicity, sexual orientation, and gender to
the class analysis of ideology of Althusserian marxists. The never fully
articulated, but always present, system of preconceptions which govern a
society includes these differences; differences that challenge from within
the possibility of mastery, objectivity, impersonality; differences that do
not allow us to forget the role of power, of those 'social arrangements of
patterned disparity'.[52] They have not allowed theory or criticism or art to
pose as apolitical.[53] This kind of political motivation within post-modern
theory and practice owes much to specifically feminist and marxist challenges to the relations both with modes of representation and with expectations in consumption.[54]

Edward Said has urged theory to base itself in experience:'Criticism
cannot assume that its province is merely the text, not even the great
literary text. It must see itself, with other discourse, inhabiting a much

contested cultural space.'[55] He seems not to have noticed that feminism, along with other ex-centrics, has been doing just this for some time now - taking a position within the historical and political world outside the ivory tower. Terry Eagleton, however, has noticed: 'It is in the nature of feminist politics that signs and images, written and dramatized experience, should be of especial significance. Discourse in all its forms is an obvious concern for feminists, either as places where women's oppression can be deciphered, or as places where it can be challenged. In any politics which puts identity and relationship centrally at stake, renewing attention to lived experience and the discourse of the body, culture does not need to argue its way to political relevance.'[56]

Indeed there are many who have claimed the radical political potential of feminism, especially in conjunction with marxism and/or deconstruction.[57] The thematization of writing and difference as anti-patriarchal subversions of oppression is also clear in women's writing, from Audrey Thomas's *Intertidal Life* to Alice Walker's *The Color Purple*. The political power of the creative process has been claimed not only by women but by black male writers such as Ishmael Reed and Leon Forrest. The right of expression - however unavoidably implicated in liberal humanist assumptions - is not something that can be taken for granted by the ex-centric. But the *problematizing* of expression - through contextualization in the enunciative situation - is what makes the ex-centric into the post-modern. Many theorists have argued that the major modes of feminist thought are contextual - social, historical, cultural.[58] Post-Saussurian or post-structuralist theory has been one of the strongest forces in moving the emphasis from linguistic and textual system to discursive process, to semiosis or the mutual overdetermination of meaning, perception and experience in the act of signifying.[59] And this is the theory most often associated with post-modernism. The reasons for the association are fairly obvious. Both share a concern for power - its manifestations, its appropriations, its positioning, its consequences, its language. So too do some forms of feminism, of course. All work to challenge our traditional essentialized anchors in God, father, state, and Man through acknowledgment of the particular and the different.

From the margins, from the borders of conventional art forms, come the performance-based sculptures or installations of artists like Angelika Hofmann, Helga Mohrke and Heike Ponwitz and the commentaries of Lyotard on Ruth Francken.[60] Laurie Anderson's multimedia image-spectacles use the high art-historical and low pop-cultural clichés against themselves in order to move the masculine subject of representation off-center, to problematize traditional cultural meaning-making.[61] Ex-centric post-modern art like this shares the radical skepticism and concern for silenced contradictions that characterize so much of post-modern theoretical discourse today – from marxism to deconstruction to feminism. All aim to be self-conscious and self-critical, turning their skepticism also against themselves, as Margaret Atwood turns her critical eye to the excesses of separatist feminist utopias in her novel, *The Handmaid's Tale*.

In this kind of post-modern fiction, such self-reflexivity cannot be separated from the notion of difference. In her fiction (or autobiography or biography), *The Woman Warrior*, Maxine Hong Kingston links the post-modern metafictional concerns of narration and language directly to her race and her gender:'story-talking' (the Chinese expression for narrating) is what women do. (As the next book, *China Men*, shows, the men are powerful, however, in their silence.) Language is inescapably gendered for the Chinese: 'There is a Chinese word for the female *I* – which is "slave". Break the women with their own tongues!' (p. 47). And it is in terms of language that the young Chinese-American girl attempts to construct her subjectivity: 'I could not understand "I." The Chinese "I" has seven strokes, intricacies. How could the American "I" . . . have only three strokes . . .?' (p. 166). Like her mother, the female narrator story-talks, twisting tales 'into designs' (p. 163), and trying to unite the Chinese and 'barbarian' tongues like her model, the Chinese woman poet, Ts'ai Yen (p. 209). To story-talk is to avenge wrongs (her patriarchally unspeakable aunt, dead by suicide). The mythic woman warrior of the title is literally marked by her parents' vengeance: they write their wrongs on her back. The writing narrator shares her fate: 'What we have in common are the words at our backs. The ideographs for *revenge* are "report a crime" and "report to five families." The reporting is the vengeance – not the beheading, not the gutting, but the words. And I have so many words – "chink" words and "gook" words too – that they do not fit on my skin' (p. 53).

Her rethinking of personal, familial, and racial history is similar to that of feminist historians in its study of the exclusions that inevitably result from attempts to form totalizing unities or neat evolutions.[62] The same is true in literary history, of course, as the ex-centric challenge the canon. And we have witnessed a similar contesting of the conventions and institutions of art, with their protective boundaries that prevent art's contaminating affiliation with other cultural practices. In protest, Jenny Holzer's feminist critiques of male representation often appear as public posters on New York City walls or on T-shirts. And the closure of narrative (in literature, film, video, dance) is contested in the name of various ex-centric counter-forces: contingency, repetition, interruption/rupture.

I would not argue a relationship of identity between post-modern theory and practice, but there is little doubt as to the commonality of their concerns. Thanks to the ex-centric, both have managed to break down the barrier between academic theoretical discourse and contemporary art – which is usually marginalized, not to say ignored, in the academy. Even more than black theory, perhaps, it has been feminism that has shown the impossibility of separating the theoretical and the aesthetic, the political and the epistemological. As Stephen Heath has proclaimed: 'Any discourse which fails to take account of the problem of sexual difference in its own enunciation and address will be, within a patriarchal order, precisely indifferent, a reflection of male domination.'[63]

What has been added most recently to this list of 'enabling' differences is that of ethnicity. The ethnic revival of the 1960s in America has been well documented.[64] Studies like Sollors's *Beyond Ethnicity* are made possible by post-modern rethinking of difference in the face of modern, urban, industrial society that was expected to efface ethnicity. Instead, ethnic identity has changed from being a 'heathenish liability' to being a 'sacred asset' (p. 33) through a very post-modern, contradictory divided allegiance: what Sollors calls consent and descent. Outside of North America too there are texts which overtly challenge cultural notions of the centrality of the metropolis: both France and England are former colonial empires, with strong centralized cultures that are now being upset by their own history, as Arab, African, West Indian voices demand to be heard. In their post-modern forms these voices are particularly contradictory and contesting. Salman Rushdie's novels are not just about India or Pakistan. The very form of the texts themselves constantly remind the reader of his/her own ethnocentric biases, for these are encoded in the very words being read. In *Midnight's Children*, Saleem tells us that he speaks in Urdu; yet we had assumed he spoke English, since we read his words in our own language. In *Shame*, Omar Khayam wants to learn to read English, but the Shakil sisters feel that 'Angrey double-dutch' will drive him mad. And all this, including the sisters' dialogue, we read in English and, in our unconscious and deeply embedded ethnocentrism, assume to be spoken in English – at least until passages like this trip us up.

It is the post-modern contradictions of works like those of Gayl Jones (*Corregidora*) or Joy Kogawa (*Obasan*) that point to the paradoxical kind of differences that are entailed in being Afro-American or Japanese-Canadian women. Often this is also a class issue, as in Ishmael Reed's attacks on Europeanized American high-brow culture in the name of multi-ethnic lower-middle-class American culture – a culture we find acceptably quaint or colorful in Gabriel García Márquez's Macondo, but less intellectually acceptable often in our own. In all these cases, it is specific and local differences that are affirmed in opposition to the modernist cosmopolitanism of an Eliot or a Pound. Perhaps the interest displayed in the protagonist of D. M. Thomas's *The White Hotel* has something to do, not just with the historical and sado-masochistic violence of her fate, but with the fact that she is not a modernist cosmopolitan so much as the archetypal post-modern ex-centric victim: a woman, half-Jew, half-Catholic, half-Polish, half-Ukrainian.

This multiple inside-outside position is clearly also the situation of the Chinese-American woman writer we have already seen in Maxine Hong Kingston's work. In *The Woman Warrior*, the young American-born Chinese girl lives in a world that is doubly split: 'Normal Chinese women's voices are strong and bossy. We American-Chinese girls had to whisper to make ourselves American-feminine' (p. 172). Not allowed to be fully Chinese (and not wanting to be), yet never fully Americanized, she also grows up in a Chinese patriarchal ethos which does not welcome daughters, which has an oft-repeated saying: 'It is more profitable to raise geese than daughters', which leaves women behind in villages in China while men remarry in the new world and never return. In response to her mother's statement that '[a] husband may kill a wife who disobeys him. Confucius said that', the narrator adds bitterly 'Confucius, the rational man' (p. 195), putting the ironic emphasis on gender as well as reason. In *China Men*, the intersection of feminine and national identity is even more powerfully revealed. As a child, hearing her father's Chinese obscenities and curses against women, the narrator tries to come to terms with what she sees as his hatred of her: 'What I want from you is for you to tell me that those curses are only common Chinese sayings. That you did not mean to make me sicken at being female' (p. 9).

In such post-modern historiographic metafiction as this, language – nationalist, sexist, racist – is the basis of the narrator's search to define her different (female, Chinese, American) subjectivity. And language is also the basis on which the exclusive center rejects: her father was labeled as illiterate by American immigration officials because he could not read English, but only Chinese. It is through language that the status of difference as ex-centricity is thematized. In his laundry, the girl's father marks all the items to be cleaned with 'Center' and thus provokes her to ask 'how we landed in a country where we are eccentric people' (p. 9). While it is always a fact that the ex-centric relies on the center for its definition, that all forms of radical thought cannot help but be 'mortgaged to the very historical categories they seek to transcend',[65] this very post-modern paradox should not lead to despair or complacency. The theory and practice of post-modern art has shown ways of making the different, the off-center, into the vehicle for aesthetic and even political consciousness-raising – perhaps the first and necessary step to any radical change. I do not think that post-modernism is that change, but it may presage it. It may be an enabling first stage in its enacting of the contradictions inherent in any transitional moment: inside yet outside, inscribing yet contesting, complicitous yet critical. 'Hail to the Edges!'

NOTES

1 By post-modernist fiction I mean not all metafiction (much of which is modernist in its autotelic self-isolation), but rather what I would like to call 'historiographic meta-fiction', a popular form today which is like post-modern architecture in being paradoxically self-reflexively parodic and yet laying claim to actual historical characters or events: Rushdie's *Midnight's Children*, Eco's *The Name of the Rose*, Findley's *Famous Last Words*, for instance. See Hutcheon 1983 and 1985.

2 Newman 1985: 201.

3 Kahler 1968.

4 Sayres et al. 1984: 4.

5 Zavarzadeh 1976: 9; Federman 1981: 6.

6 Newman 1985: 57.

7 Derrida 1972; Hoffman 1986: 186.

8 Lyotard 1984.

9 Bakhtin 1981.

10 Richard Rorty, according to Schaffer 1985: xiv-xv.

11 For example, McCaffery 1982; Kawin 1982.

12 Cf. Russell 1985: 239.

13 Rorty 1984: 19.

14 Deleuze and Guattari 1980.

15 Owens 1980: 80.

16 Portoghesi 1983: 12.

17 Lodge 1977.
18 Caramello 1983: 4.
19 Bois 1981: 45.
20 Said 1983: 242.
21 Gutman 1981: 554.
22 Gates 1984c: 3.
23 Griffin 1981/2: 291.
24 Clarke 1980: 206.
25 Aronowitz 1984: 38; Morgan 1970; Moi 1985a: 22, 95.
26 Willis E. 1984: 116.
27 Christian 1985: 116.
28 Willis S. 1985.
29 Suleiman 1986: 268 n. 12; Jardine 1982: 55; Ruthven 1984: ii.
30 Jardine 1982: 60.
31 Deleuze and Guattari 1980.
32 Massumi 1985: 17-20.
33 Derrida 1984: 89.
34 Jacobus 1979b: 12.
35 Said 1985: 43.
36 Spivak 1985: 245.
37 Hutcheon 1985.
38 Smith P. 1985: 192.
39 Snead 1984.
40 Willis S. 1984: 278-9.
41 Johnson 1985: 278.
42 Mitchell-Kiernan 1973; Gates 1984c: 285-32.
43 Woolf 1945: 96.
44 Jones and Krause [*sic*] 1975: 17.
45 See Haynes 1985 for the need for male gays to theorize beyond feminism to a 'homoaesthetic'.
46 A very limited bibliography would include the following. (Where there have been too many even to begin to list, I have given a representative text.) Images of women: Cornillon 1972. Literary history and canon-formation: Showalter 1977. Gyno-criticism: Spacks 1976. Feminist critique: Showalter 1979; Ellmann 1968; Munich 1985. Psychoanalytic feminism: Mitchell 1974; Gallop 1982; Silverman 1983; de Lauretis 1984. French feminism: Jones 1985; Marks and de Courtivron 1980. Lesbian feminism: Zimmerman 1985; Kennard 1986. Marxist/socialist: Newton 1981; Moi 1985a; Kaplan 1985; MacKinnon 1981/2; Marxist-Feminist Literature Collective 1978. Deconstruction: Spivak 1978; Kamuf 1982; Belsey 1980. Black: Willis S. 1985; Christian 1980, 1985; Pullin 1980; Smith B. 1979. Third World/native: Spivak 1985; Alloula 1986. For an overview based on a theory of waves of feminisms, see Eisenstein 1983. Much of this work has been on women as writers. For women as readers, see Flynn and Schweickart 1986; Culler 1982; Batsleer et al. 1985.
47 Hull in Gilbert and Gubar 1979.
48 de Lauretis 1984: 159.

49 Miller N. K. 1982. There is also, of course, a strong strain of feminism that is liberal humanist in its assumption of a unified self and integrated consciousness as the goal for women. For opposing views, see Moi 1985a: 70-88, and Kaplan 1985. On a similar humanist impulse in black theory see Miller R. B. 1981.
50 Belsey 1980: 65.
51 Byerman 1985: 213.
52 MacKinnon 1981/2: 2.
53 Fetterley 1978: xi; Moi 1985a: 175n. v. Ruthven 1984; Moi 1985b: 95 v. Foucault 1980.
54 Mulvey 1979: 179.
55 Said 1983: 225.
56 Eagleton 1983: 215.
57 Culler 1982: 63; Belsey 1980: 129.
58 Gilligan 1982; Dubois 1983; Donovan 1984.
59 de Lauretis 1984: 184.
60 Lyotard and Francken 1983.
61 Foster 1985: 132.
62 Carroll 1976; Lerner 1979.
63 Heath 1978: 53.
64 Greer 1984; Boelhower 1984; Sukenick 1985: 51-2, 64-5.
65 Moi 1985: 88.

REFERENCES

Alloula, Malek 1986. *The Colonial Harem*. Trans. Myrna and Wlad Godzich. Minneapolis: University of Minnesota Press.
Aronowitz, Stanley 1984. 'When the New Left was new', in Sayres et al. 1984: 11-43.
Bakhtin, Mikhail 1981. *The Dialogic Imagination: Four Essays by M. M. Bakhtin*. Trans. Michael Holquist and Caryl Emerson. Austin and London: University of Texas Press.
Banville, John 1976. *Doctor Copernicus*. New York: W. W. Norton.
Barthes, Roland 1981. *Camera Lucida: Reflections on Photography*. Trans. Richard Howard. New York: Hill and Wang.
Batsleer, Janet, Davies, Tony, O'Rourke, Rebecca and Weedon, Chris 1985. *Rewriting English: Cultural Politics of Gender and Class*. London and New York: Methuen.
Belsey, Catherine 1980. *Critical Practice*. London: Methuen.
Boelhower, William 1984. *Through a Glass Darkly: Ethnic Semiosis in American Literature*. Venice: Helvetia.
Bois, Yve-Alain 1981. 'The sculptural opaque', *Sub-stance*, 31: 23-48.
Bowles, Gloria and Klein, Renate Duelli (eds) 1983. *Theories of Women's Studies*. London: Routledge and Kegan Paul.
Byerman, Keith E. 1985. *Fingering the Jagged Grain: Tradition and Form in Recent Black Fiction*. Athens and London: University of Georgia Press.
Caramello, Charles 1983. *Silverless Mirrors: Book, Self and Postmodern American Fiction*. Tallahassee: University Presses of Florida.

Carroll, Bernice A. (ed.) 1976. *Liberating Women's History: Theoretical and Critical Essays*. Urbana: University of Illinois Press.

Christian, Barbara 1980. *Black Women Novelists: The Development of a Tradition 1892-1976*. Westport, CT and London: Greenwood.

Christian, Barbara 1985. *Black Feminist Criticism: Perspectives on Black Women Writers*. New York: Pergamon.

Clarke, Graham 1980. 'Beyond realism: recent black fiction and the language of "The Real Thing" ', in Lee 1980: 204-21.

Cornillon, Susan Koppelman (ed.) 1972. *Images of Women in Fiction: Feminist Perspectives*. Bowling Green, Ohio: Bowling Green University Popular Press.

Culler, Jonathan 1982. *On Deconstruction: Theory and Criticism after Structuralism*. Ithaca, NY: Cornell University Press.

de Lauretis, Teresa 1984. *Alice Doesn't: Feminism, Semiotics, Cinema*. Bloomington: Indiana University Press.

Deleuze, Gilles and Guattari, Félix 1980. *Mille Plateaux*. Paris: Minuit.

Derrida, Jacques 1972. 'Structure, sign, and play in the discourse of the human sciences', in Macksey and Donato 1972: 247-65.

Derrida, Jacques 1984. 'Voice ii', *boundary 2*, 12. 2: 76-93.

Donovan, Josephine 1984. 'Toward a women's poetics', *Tulsa Studies in Women's Literature*, 3. 1-2: 98-110.

Dubois, Barbara 1983. 'Passionate scholarship: notes on values, knowing and method in feminist social science', in Bowles and Klein 1983: 105-16.

Dundes, Alan (ed.) 1973. *Mother Wit from the Laughing Barrel: Readings in the Interpretation of Afro-American Folklore*. Englewood Cliffs: Prentice-Hall.

Eagleton, Terry 1983. *Literary Theory: An Introduction*. Oxford: Blackwell.

Eisenstein, Hester 1983. *Contemporary Feminist Thought*. Boston: Hall.

Ellmann, Mary 1968. *Thinking About Women*. New York: Harcourt.

Federman, Raymond (ed.) 1981a. *Surfiction: Fiction Now . . . and Tomorrow*. 2nd edn, Chicago: Swallow Press.

Federman, Raymond 1981b. 'Surfiction: four propositions in form of an introduction', in Federman 1981a: 5-15.

Fetterley, Judith 1978. *The Resisting Reader: A Feminist Approach to American Fiction*. Bloomington and London: Indiana University Press.

Flynn, Elizabeth A. and Schweickart, Patrocinio (eds) 1986. *Gender and Reading: Essays on Readers, Texts, and Contexts*. Baltimore and London: Johns Hopkins University Press.

Fokkema, Douwe and Bertens, Hans (eds) 1986. *Approaching Postmodernism*. Amsterdam and Philadelphia: John Benjamins.

Foster, Hal 1985. *Recodings: Art, Spectacle, Cultural Politics*. Port Townsend, WA: Bay.

Foucault, Michel 1980. *The History of Sexuality. Vol. I: An Introduction*. Trans. Robert Hurley. New York: Vintage.

Fowles, John 1985. *A Maggot*. Toronto: Collins.

Gallop, Jane 1982. *Feminism and Psychoanalysis: The Daughter's Seduction*. Ithaca, NY: Cornell University Press.

Gates, Henry Louis Jr (ed.) 1984a. *Black Literature and Literary Theory*. London and New York: Methuen.

Gates, Henry Louis Jr 1984b. 'Criticism in the jungle', in Gates 1984a: 1-24.

Gates, Henry Louis Jr 1984c. 'The blackness of blackness: a critique of the sign and the Signifying Monkey', in Gates 1984a: 285-321.

Gates, Henry Louis Jr (ed.) 1985. ' "Race," writing and difference', *Critical Inquiry*, 12.1.

Gilbert, Sandra M. and Gubar, Susan 1979. *Shakespeare's Sisters*. Bloomington: Indiana University Press.

Gilligan, Carol 1982. *In a Different Voice: Psychological Theory and Woman's Development*. Cambridge, MA: Harvard University Press.

Greene, Gayle and Kahn, Coppélia (eds) 1985. *Making a Difference: Feminist Literary Criticism*. London and New York: Methuen.

Greer, Colin. 'The ethnic question', in Sayres et al. 1984: 119-36.

Griffin, Susan 1981/2. 'The way of all ideology', in Keohane et al. 1981/2: 273-92.

Gutman, Herbert G. 1981. 'Whatever happened to history?', *The Nation*, 21 November: 521, 553-4.

Haynes, Todd 1985. 'Homoaesthetics and *Querelle*', *Subjects/Objects*: 71-99.

Heath, Stephen 1978. 'Difference', *Screen*, 19. 3: 51-112.

Hoffmann, Gerhard 1986. 'The Absurd and its forms of reduction in postmodern American fiction', in Fokkema and Bertens 1986: 185-210.

Hutcheon, Linda 1983. 'A poetics of postmodernism?', *Diacritics*, 13. 4: 33-42.

Hutcheon, Linda 1985. *A Theory of Parody: The Teachings of Twentieth-Century Art Forms*. London and New York: Methuen.

Hutcheon, Linda 1987. 'Theorizing postmodernism', *Textual Practice*, 1.1: 10-31.

Jacobus, Mary (ed.) 1979a. *Women Writing and Writing About Women*. London: Croom Helm.

Jacobus, Mary 1979b. 'The Difference of View', in Jacobus 1979a: 10-21.

Jardine, Alice 1982. 'Gynesis', *Diacritics*, 12: 54-65.

Johnson, Barbara 1980. *The Critical Difference*. Baltimore: Johns Hopkins University Press.

Johnson, Barbara 1985. 'Thresholds of difference: structures of address in Zora Neale Hurston', *Critical Inquiry*, 12.1: 278-89.

Jonas, Joan and Krause, Rosalind [*sic*] 1975. 'Seven years', *Drama Review*, 19. 1: 13-17.

Jones, Ann Rosalind 1985. 'Inscribing femininity: French theories of the feminine', in Greene and Kahn 1985: 80-112.

Kahler, Erich 1968. *The Disintegration of Form in the Arts*. New York: Braziller.

Kamuf, Penny 1982. 'Replacing feminist criticism', *Diacritics*, 12: 42-7.

Kaplan, Cora 1985. 'Pandora's box: subjectivity, class and sexuality in socialist feminist criticism', in Greene and Kahn 1985: 146-76.

Kawin, Bruce F. 1982. *The Mind of the Novel: Reflexive Fiction and the Ineffable*. Princeton: Princeton University Press.

Kennard, Jean E. 1986. 'Ourself behind ourself: a theory for lesbian readers', in Flynn and Schweickart 1986: 63-80.

Keohane, Nannerl O., Rosaldo, Michelle Z. and Gelpi, Barbara C. (eds) 1981/2. *Feminist Theory: A Critique of Ideology*. Chicago: University of Chicago Press.

Kingston, Maxine Hong 1976. *The Woman Warrior: Memoirs of a Girlhood Among Ghosts*. New York: Knopf.

Kingston, Maxine Hong 1981. *China Men*. New York: Ballantine.

Lee, A. Robert (ed.) 1980. *Black Fiction: New Studies in the Afro-American Novel Since 1945*. London: Vision.

Lerner, Gerda 1979. *The Majority Finds Its Past: Placing Women in History*. London: Oxford University Press.

Lodge, David 1977. *The Modes of Modern Writing: Metaphor, Metonymy, and the Typology of Modern Literature*. London: Edward Arnold.

Lyotard, Jean-François 1984. *The Postmodern Condition: A Report on Knowledge*. Trans. Geoff Bennington and Brian Massumi. Minneapolis: University of Minnesota Press.

Lyotard, Jean-François and Francken, Ruth 1983. *L'Histoire de Ruth*. Paris: Le Castor Astral.

McCaffery, Larry 1982. *The Metafictional Muse*. Pittsburgh: University of Pittsburgh Press.

MacKinnon, Catharine A. 'Feminism, marxism, method, and the state: an agenda for theory', in Keohane et al. 1981/2: 1-30.

Macksey, Richard and Donato, Eugenio (eds) 1972. *The Structuralist Controversy: The Languages of Criticism and the Sciences of Man*. Baltimore: Johns Hopkins University Press.

Marks, Elaine and de Courtivron, Isabelle (eds) 1980. *New French Feminisms*. Amherst, MA: University of Massachusetts Press.

Marxist-Feminist Literature Collective 1978. 'Women writing: *Jane Eyre, Shirley, Villete, Aurora Leigh*', *Ideology and Consciousness*, 1. 3: 27-48.

Massumi, Brian 1985. 'The power of the particular', *Subjects/Objects*: 6-23.

Miller, Nancy K. 1982. 'The text's heroine: a feminist critic and her fictions', *Diacritics*, 12: 48-53.

Miller, R. Baxter (ed.) 1981. *Black American Literature and Humanism*. Lexington: University Press of Kentucky.

Mitchell, Juliet 1974. *Psychoanalysis and Feminism*. Harmondsworth: Penguin.

Mitchell-Kernan, Claudia 1973. 'Signifying', in Dundes 1973: 310-28.

Moi, Toril 1985a. *Sexual/Textual Politics: Feminist Literary Theory*. London and New York: Methuen.

Moi, Toril 1985b. 'Power, sex and subjectivity: feminist reflections on Foucault', *Paragraph*, 5: 95-102.

Morgan, Robin (ed.) 1970. *Sisterhood is Powerful: An Anthology of Writings from the Women's Liberation Movement*. New York: Vintage.

Morrison, Toni 1977. *Song of Solomon*. New York: Signet.

Morrison, Toni 1981. *Tar Baby*. New York: New American Library.

Mulvey, Laura 1979. 'Feminism, film and the *Avant-Garde*', in Jacobus 1979a: 177-95.

Munich, Adrienne 1985. 'Notorious signs, feminist criticism and literary tradition', in Greene and Kahn 1985: 238-59.

Newman, Charles 1985. *The Post-Modern Aura: The Act of Fiction in an Age of Inflation*. Evanston, IL: Northwestern University Press.

Newton, Judith Lowder 1981. *Women, Power, and Subversion: Social Strategies in British Fiction 1778-1860*. Athens, GA: University of Georgia Press.

Owens, Craig 1980. 'The allegorical impulse: toward a theory of postmodernism, part 2', *October*, 13: 59-80.

Portoghesi, Paolo 1983. *Postmodern: The Architecture of the Postindustrial Society*. New York: Rizzoli.

Pullin, Faith 1980. 'Landscapes of reality: the fiction of contemporary Afro-American women', in Lee 1980: 173-203.

Rorty, Richard 1984. 'Deconstruction and circumvention', *Critical Inquiry*, 11.1: 1-23.

Rushdie, Salman 1982. *Midnight's Children*. London: Picador.

Rushdie, Salman 1983. *Shame*. London: Picador.

Russell, Charles 1985. *Poets, Prophets, and Revolutionaries: The Literary Avant-garde from Rimbaud through Postmodernism*. New York and Oxford: Oxford University Press.

Ruthven, K. K. 1984. *Feminist Literary Studies: An Introduction*. Cambridge: Cambridge University Press.

Said, Edward W. 1983. *The World, the Text and the Critic*. Cambridge: Harvard University Press.

Said, Edward W. 1985. 'An ideology of difference', *Critical Inquiry*, 12. 1: 38-58.

Sayres, Sohnya, Stephanson, Anders, Aronowitz, Stanley and Jameson, Fredric (eds) 1984. *The 60s Without Apology*. Minneapolis: University of Minnesota Press.

Schaffer, E. S. 1985. 'Editor's introduction: changing the boundaries of literature, theory, and criticism', *Comparative Criticism*, 7: xi-xxiv.

Scott, Chris 1982. *Antichthon*. Montreal: Quadrant.

Showalter, Elaine 1977. *A Literature of Their Own: British Women Novelists from Brontë to Lessing*. Princeton: Princeton University Press.

Showalter, Elaine 1979. 'Toward a feminist poetics', in Jacobus 1979a: 22-41.

Silverman, Kaja 1983. *The Subject of Semiotics*. New York: Oxford University Press.

Smith, Barbara 1979. 'Toward a black feminist criticism', *Women's Studies International Quarterly*, 2: 183-94.

Smith, Paul 1985. 'Difference in America', *Art in America*, 73.4: 190-9.

Snead, James A. 1984. 'Repetition as a figure of black culture', in Gates 1984a: 59-79.

Sollors, Werner 1986. *Beyond Ethnicity: Consent and Descent in American Culture*. New York and Oxford: Oxford University Press.

Spacks, Patricia Meyer 1976. *The Female Imagination: A Literary and Psychological Investigation of Women's Writing*. London: Allen & Unwin.

Spivak, Gayatri 1978. 'Feminism and critical theory', *Women's Studies International Quarterly*, 1. 3: 241-6.

Spivak, Gayatri 1985. 'Three women's texts and a critique of imperialism', *Critical Inquiry*, 12.1: 243-61.

Sukenick, Ronald 1985. *In Form: Digressions on the Act of Fiction*. Carbondale and Edwardsville: Southern Illinois University Press.

Suleiman, Susan Rubin 1986. 'Naming and difference: reflections on "Modernism *versus* Postmodernism" in literature', in Fokkema and Bertens 1986: 255-70.

Willis, Ellen 1984. 'Radical feminism and feminist radicalism', in Sayres et al. 1984: 91-118.

Willis, Susan 1984. 'Eruptions of funk: historicizing Toni Morrison', in Gates 1984a: 263-83.

Willis, Susan 1985. 'Black women writers: taking a critical perspective', in Greene and Kahn 1985: 211-37.

Woolf, Virginia 1945. *A Room of One's Own*. Harmondsworth: Penguin.

Zavarzadeh, Mas'ud 1976. *The Mythopoeic Reality: The Postwar American Nonfiction Novel*. Urbana: University of Illinois Press.

Zimmerman, Bonnie 1985. 'What has never been: an overview of lesbian feminist criticism', in Greene and Kahn 1985: 177-210.

8

Writing Cultural History:
The Case of Post-modernism

Vincent B. Leitch

Starting in the early 1970s, literary intellectuals in America took to constructing historical accounts and surveys of the development of twentieth-century Euro-American culture in which the favorite outline or sketch that emerged portrayed a genteel era superseded by a modernist upheaval followed by a post-modernist revolt. Characteristic of both modernism and post-modernism was a complex network of connections and disconnections with preceding eras. On the whole, intellectuals who rendered early accounts of post-modernism labored to isolate, explain, and concatenate continuities and discontinuities between modernism and post-modernism. Since the terrain of modernism was itself unstable and contested, the emergent topographies of post-modernism seemed most notable for their heterogeneity. In the 1970s and 1980s, for example, literary intellectuals couldn't agree whether Ezra Pound was the archetypal modernist or the leading proto-post-modernist, nor could they concur on how to handle the decade or so following the Second World War. If modernism effectively ended in the late 1940s and post-modernism commenced in the late 1950s, then the immediate post-war decade remained unsituated. Many literary artists who matured in this period – for instance, W. H. Auden, Saul Bellow, Arthur Miller, Theodore Roethke, Richard Wright – seemed neither modernist nor post-modernist. Not surprisingly, one job that preoccupied the first historians of post-modernism entailed the rigorous articulation of the relations between the old and the new eras so as to ensure a place for troublesome or marginal figures and phenomena. The model for the project of historicizing the modernist-post-modernist shift was invariably rooted in both a binary mode of thinking and a totalizing conception of history. In this model, an ideal account of post-modernism would aspire to be not only differentiated, but encyclopedic and definitive. As a result, contesting such a history required that inconsistencies, omissions, and errors should be pointed out.

However new or radical post-modernism was, the favorite historiographical methods used to construct accounts of the post-modern period were derived from traditional practices. To be specific, historical treatments of the post-modern world view (or ethos) depended on the old notion of *Weltanschauung* developed by Dilthey and his followers and/or on the procedures of *Geistesgeschichte* employed by Spengler and his epigones. In other words, the philosophy of history frequently pressed into service presupposed, first, that the arts of an age expressed the spirit of the time or reflected its world view, and, second, that this particular historical modality (*Geist* or *Weltanschauung*) could be portrayed. Interestingly, various influential versions of American post-modernism argued that the emergence of the marginal figure – for example, the non-white, the non-Anglo, the non-male, and/or the non-middle-class – characterized the post-modern era. Put more abstractly, this version of post-modernism pictured the 'eruption of difference' or the 'flowering of the eccentric' as the predominant cultural fact or force of the times. From a historiographical perspective, such a thematic operation meant that the new centrality of oddity not only rendered post-modernism different from modernism, but constituted the essence of the post-modern ethos. One might say that 'difference' came to signify sameness or that 'eccentricity' signalled centrality. Whatever specific picture emerged, it was this normalizing of the abnormal which not only typified post-modernism but also manifested the methodology of traditional historiography with its commitment to integrating and thematizing the arts of an era.

What was quite often missing from accounts of post-modernism was a sense of the rhetorical or discursive grounds of historiography. For example, the activities of thematizing, of rendering portraits, and of concatenating data typically received little, if any, reflection. Nor was there much consideration given to the interests explicitly and implicitly served in fabricating works about contemporary paradigm shifts or changes in world views. The political import of history writing frequently went unreflected upon, as did the pedagogical force or message inherent in creating historical discourse. Concomitantly, criticism of destructive elements characteristic of the modern and post-modern eras rarely occurred. That the post-modern might represent decline or disintegration seemed out of the question.

In 'The post-modern ex-centric: the center that will not hold', to take one example, Linda Hutcheon has offered as a schematic history of post-modernism a comprehensive and often unreflective survey of avant-garde culture between the 1960s and 1980s. This text is nicely representative in its omissions and in its lack of self-reflection. What is obviously missing is any specificity concerning developments in economics and politics. In addition, many well-known conservative and radical critics of post-modern literary culture do not appear: there is no mention of M. H. Abrams, Walter Jackson Bate, and Denis Donoghue, nor of Gerald Graff, Ihab Hassan, and Frank Lentricchia. By design or default, Hutcheon has occupied a truncated terrain in spite of her evident comprehensiveness and her ample bibliography. The radical critique of the post-modern avant-garde for its complicity with consumer capitalism has gone unexamined in her celebration of the new. Nor has she found anything particularly dangerous in post-modernism. Moreover, the possibility that the institution of literary studies might benefit or profit from the rise of so-called post-modernist literature and/or criticism seems foreign to her thought. Ultimately, this specific account of post-modernism was cast in the mode of an allegorical romance: a happy discourse about an adventurous and circus-like world and time largely free of fatal cruelty, all of which thankfully superseded the oppressive era of humanism. Needless to say, such an inflation of post-modernism, typical of histories of post-modernism, approaches apologetics, not to say boosterism.

Accounts of post-modernism have generally accorded some consideration to the emergence of feminism in the 1960s and thereafter. In this regard, Hutcheon's text is characteristic. Again, however, she minimizes radical and conservative positions – in this case the extreme wings of the feminist movement. Where some radical feminists, in particular, 'replaced' the marxist notion of 'class' with the idea of 'gender', Hutcheon substitutes for 'gender' the post-structuralist concept of 'difference', which allows her to cast feminists as one more marginal or eccentric group representative of *difference* – a *difference* which is now the central and defining feature of post-modernism, the spirit of the age. By metaphorically substituting 'difference' for 'gender', Hutcheon has displaced the emphasis on social, psychological, and cultural constructs which the very concept of 'gender' was meant to foreground. In this way, the age-old patriarchal ideology of biological difference has lost specificity, becoming structurally and metaphorically equivalent to all humanistic 'centrisms'. What was gained in philosophical and historiographical sweep has been lost in critical point and political pertinence.

To reiterate, historians of post-modernism regularly engaged in allego-
rizing and in apologetics. In the struggle between post-modernism and
modernism, the post-modern half of the binary pair represented the
desirable, the new, the vital, the liberating. Hutcheon's special version
pits 'humanism' against 'difference'. As *the* 'unit idea' or paradigmatic
metaphor structuring the post-modern period, 'difference' manifested
itself variously as triumphant paradox, eccentricity, marginality, provisionality, perspectivism, multiplicity, heterogeneity, plurality, skepticism, discontinuity, contextuality, and so on, in a liberating network of
linked concepts opposed to humanism's oppressive unity, homogeneity,
totalization, universalism, centrality, and so forth, in a chain of self-
evidently negative concepts. Furthermore, Hutcheon's choice of *'liberal*
humanism' as the specific target of post-modernism has the dual effect of
elevating the emergence of post-modernism into an epochal event and of
importing an implicit utopian politics into the argument. Without saying
so, Hutcheon favors anarchy, meaning here a non-hierarchical *socius* of
separate communities possessing no control or power over one another.
Given her implicit leftist perspective and her positive view of post-
modernism, Hutcheon's anti-humanist and anti-Leninist critique of
central authority prompts, as her final gesture, an upbeat restatement of
a 1960s merry prankster: 'Hail to the Edges!'

As is wont to happen, the literary genre, rhetorical mode, and political
theory deployed in an historical account constitute an underlying reticu-
lated structure to the discourse. Romance, metaphor, and anarchy (all
featured in Hutcheon's text) are of a piece, as Hayden White illustrated in
Metahistory.[1] Like many other historians of post-modernism, Hutcheon
reveals scant awareness of the status of her own discourse, which purports
to be straightforward, unproblematic literary journalism. By adopting the
discursive stance of empathetic chronicler, Hutcheon frees herself from
engaging in causal analysis, which enables her to move swiftly and sympathetically through the vast spectacle of contemporary culture and to
sketch a broad and colorful canvas. Evidently, Hutcheon's text is itself
cast in a pre-post-modern vein free from parody, self-conscious problematizing, and difference – key textual hallmarks of post-modernity.

Unexpectedly, Hutcheon concludes her text by distancing herself from
post-modernism, portraying this cultural phenomenon as a possible
'transitional moment' or 'first stage' to epochal 'radical change'. This
final surprising vision of a post-post-modernity (or of an end to the post-
modern era) expresses the fervent wish of a committed romancer and

anarchist enamoured of the metaphorical language of 'stages' and 'transitions' dear to the old measures of traditional historiography.

Let's speculate. Perhaps the best way for an historian of an era to construe history is to imagine or project himself/herself above and beyond the events in question. A certain 'aftering' is unquestionably helpful, if not essential: not only does it set up a plot that ends in satisfying closure (however provisional), but it creates conditions favorable for a project of survey and recapitulation. One way to escape such a traditional transcendental position and to refuse the ambitious role of historian is to adopt the vocation of reporter or chronicler caught up in the flow of events. A crucial effect of this tactical stance is to import a humbling partiality into the project. The chronicle or field report presents itself as an historical genre of limited means and abbreviated aspirations. Perhaps the key feature of such writing is the absence of both overt interpretation and its occasions for misreading events. Unlike the overreaching historian of an age, the chronicler minimizes innumerable risks, including those involved in defending argumentative or evaluative positions. Structurally speaking, the historian is an outsider belatedly writing his/her way inside whereas the chronicler is an insider sending contemporaneous records to the outside. To confute the classic historiographical structure of 'outside and after' with 'inside and during' would require occupying a special spatio-temporal boundary located at or near the end. In addition, this project would cast its originator in the role of (post-modern) trickster, who mixes apologetics with disinterest while inmixing 'during' with 'after' and the 'inside' with the 'outside'. Such hesitation or stuttering, which describes Hutcheon's historiographical stance as it does Hassan's, for example, seems at once timid and shrewd. However much it solicits an enervating caution and intimacy, it does tactfully sap grand aspirations toward thoroughgoing objectivity and totalization. As such, it constitutes something of an unspoken critique of the Faustian bravura associated with traditional historiography's search for discrete world views and time-spirits. Hutcheon deserves credit for occupying this eccentric terrain.

During the Space Age new modes of historiography flowered in opposition to older practices. Among such innovations were the history of mentalities pioneered by the members of the *Annales* school, the archaeology/genealogy propounded by Michel Foucault[2] and his admirers, the cliometrics first widely promoted by Robert Fogel and Stanley Engerman,[3] and the institutional history derived from Talcott Parsons[4] and various neo-marxists. As later employed by literary intellectuals like

Richard Ohmann in *English in America* (1976), Grant Webster in *The Republic of Letters* (1979), Peter Hohendahl in *The Institution of Criticism* (1982), and Gerald Graff in *Professing Literature* (1987), institutional history took into consideration in its accounts of contemporary cultural history the roles played by professional journals, university presses, academic conferences, special-interest associations, and funding agencies. In short, institutional historians examined aspects of the professionalization and commodification of the arts so typical of modern and 'postmodern' Western societies. One beneficial outcome of such an emphasis was a view of history as a loose conglomeration of contending groups rather than as an integrated constellation of objects and events expressing a unified spirit or reflecting a dominant world view. Another salutary outcome was that economic interests and forces came in for conscious consideration and careful scrutiny. In addition, hermeneutic labor resulted because the linkages between cultural works, economic interests, and professional programs required disclosure.

One wonders what understanding of post-modernism we would have if it stemmed from institutional history? Since too few historians of post-modernism have taken into account institutional groups, values, goals, agencies, and struggles, the phenomenon of post-modernism has usually seemed ethereal, airy, disembodied. The platitudinous opposition of epochal 'difference' and 'humanism' offers a representative case in point. While the demonstration of personal mastery gained over post-modernism by such old style fabrications does possess the virtue of foregrounding the fictionality or discursivity of history writing, it blocks the emergence or eruption of a 'post-modern' historiography, just as it fails to chronicle important developments in such an historiography.

The reigning image or projection of post-modernism is encapsulated in various models of plural discourse – models having serious political implications not only for the enterprise of post-modernism but for its historiography. In place of the old monaural record player is the multi-track stereo with its dozens of overlaid voices. Dialogue or, better yet, polylogue replaces monologue. In this triumphant vision of post-modernism, no voices are subjected to authoritarian subordination, consensus, or unification. Quite obviously, the politics of such a post-modernism is out of step with present-day forces of nationalism, totalitarianism, imperialism, and neo-colonialism. So too the economics of multinational corporations and world banks run counter to the post-modern project. In essence, every kind of political, economic, and cultural centralization or unification constitutes an anti-post-modern formation. Speaking ideologically, this configuration renders post-modernism in relation to current forms of political and economic organization not only critical and antinomian, but radically anti-establishmentarian and utopian. It is this frequently unthematized political thrust of post-modernism that is often omitted in historical accounts of the post-modern era. Also, too often missing is an analysis of the evident capitulation of the post-modern project to existing central agencies of economic funding and political control. The clear preference in post-modern doctrine for local or regional, (semi)autonomous micropolitical effort leaves largely undisturbed the wider area of national and international politics. As a consequence, chance alone rather than organization must dictate the future possibilities of mass politics. Should the many voices of post-modern protest ever harmonize, it would presumably be by accident. Post-modern polylogue explicitly disdains macropolitics. Accordingly, a comprehensive historical account of post-modernism that is unaware of such political implications, in international as well as institutional contexts, bears witness to a deficient historiography – an historiography that overlooks socio-economic and political forces in focusing on disembodied cultural milieux.

NOTES

1   White 1973.
2   Foucault 1972.
3   Fogel and Engerman 1974.
4   Parsons 1982.

REFERENCES

Abrams, M. H. 1979. 'How to do things with texts', *Partisan Review*, 46: 566-88.
Bate, W. Jackson 1982. 'The crisis in English Studies', *Harvard Magazine* (September-October): 46-53.
Donoghue, Denis 1981. *Ferocious Alphabets*. Boston: Little Brown.
Fogel, Robert William and Engerman, Stanley L. 1974. *Time on the Cross: The Economics of American Negro Slavery*. Boston: Little Brown.
Foucault, Michel 1972. *The Archaeology of Knowledge*. Trans. A. M. Sheridan Smith. New York: Harper and Row.
Foucault, Michel 1977. *Discipline and Punish: The Birth of the Prison*. Trans. Alan Sheridan. New York: Vintage.

Graff, Gerald 1979. *Literature Against Itself: Literary Ideas in Modern Society*. Chicago: University of Chicago Press.

Graff, Gerald 1987. *Professing Literature: An Institutional History*. Chicago: University of Chicago Press.

Hassan, Ihab 1971. *The Dismemberment of Orpheus: Toward a Postmodern Literature*. New York: Oxford University Press.

Hohendahl, Peter Uwe 1982. *The Institution of Criticism*. Ithaca, NY: Cornell University Press.

Lentricchia, Frank 1980. *After the New Criticism*. Chicago: University of Chicago Press.

Ohmann, Richard 1976. *English in America: A Radical View of the Profession*. New York: Oxford University Press.

Parsons, Talcott 1951. *The Social System*. Glencoe, IL: The Free Press.

Parsons, Talcott 1982. *On Institutions and Social Evolution: Selected Writings*. Ed. Leon H. Mayhew. Chicago: University of Chicago Press.

Webster, Grant 1979. *The Republic of Letters: A History of Postwar American Literary Opinion*. Baltimore: Johns Hopkins University Press.

White, Hayden 1973. *Metahistory: The Historical Imagination in Nineteenth-Century Europe*. Baltimore: Johns Hopkins University Press.

9
Deconstruction and Feminist Literary Theory II

Bernard Duyfhuizen

Deconstruction and feminism have probably been the most debated issues in literary theory during the 1980s. These two critical movements share an interdisciplinary emphasis and an interest in texts that have both directed and misdirected much of traditional Western thought. Many recent critical studies demonstrate how well feminist and deconstructive theories join to reveal why significant texts by women have been excluded from the traditional canon of literary studies; to produce powerful and unsettling readings of canonical works; and to raise vital questions about basic unstated assumptions that underscore traditional critical practice. As a result, both have, for the purposes of critical inquiry, displaced restrictive conventions and ideas that implicitly or explicitly exclude concepts threatening conventional logocentric truths and androcentric epistemologies.

Feminists have turned to deconstruction, however, more often than deconstructionists have turned to feminism. Indeed, the deconstruction most prevalent in America is 'conventionally' associated with the 'Yale School' - a designation referring to five male professors who were together at Yale from the 1970s to the mid-1980s (Harold Bloom, the late Paul de Man, Geoffrey Hartman, and J. Hillis Miller; and Jacques Derrida, their frequent French visitor). Derrida himself has not been immune to feminist influence, although as Michael Ryan observes,

> Derrida's 'feminist' vocabulary - 'hymen,' 'invagination,' and the like - is in many ways problematic from the feminist perspective. But in that it is designed to trouble the metaphysical assumptions that inform a . . . phallocratic, univocal style of thinking and writing (itself merely a symptom), it can point the way toward another style,

one that is less repressively erect, more attuned to complexity and difference, less given to the closure of absolute truth because more capable of trusting the apparent danger of an open question.[1]

The question of Derrida's commitment will be explored more fully when we turn to Robert Scholes's comments on the 'misguided' attempts to align deconstruction and feminism and to the work of Alice Jardine, whose theory of gynesis confronts directly the place of the feminine within or around post-modern theories such as deconstruction. The Yale School, however, has been reproached for instituting a new old-boy system of deconstructive inquiry by concentrating most of their attention on the traditional male-dominated canon, so that it may be recanonized as self-deconstructing texts.[2]

Even though feminist deconstruction deserves, indeed demands, equal attention, most of the metacritical accounts of deconstruction tend either to overlook female contributions or to relegate such contributions to the textual margins of notes and bibliographies.[3] Three cases in point are Christopher Norris's *Deconstruction: Theory and Practice* (1982), Vincent B. Leitch's *Deconstructive Criticism: An Advanced Introduction* (1983), and Jonathan Arac, Wlad Godzich, and Wallace Martin's collection of essays (all by men) *The Yale Critics: Deconstruction in America* (1983). In Norris's volume only 5 female critics are cited in an index that contains around 120 proper names (not all are critics, but George Eliot is the only other non-male representative); in Leitch's, only 12 of the 139 names listed belong to women; and in *The Yale Critics* only 5 of the 154 listed are women. This last text includes Jonathan Arac's nod to feminist critics inspired by the Yale School:

> For reasons that need further study, women have made notable use of the Yale Critics. . . . Not only are the important books of younger critics associated with the Yale Critics largely by women: Frances Ferguson, *Wordsworth: Language as Counter-Spirit*; Patricia Parker, *Inescapable Romance*; Margaret Homans, *Women Writers and Poetic Identity*; Barbara Johnson, *The Critical Difference*; Margaret Ferguson, *Trials of Desire: Renaissance Defenses of Poetry*. But also in *The Madwoman in the Attic*, which culminates a decade's work of feminist critical revisionism that many have shared, Sandra Gilbert and Susan Gubar assert that they 'based' their method upon Bloom's influence-studies.[4]

For reasons that are hard to account for, only Barbara Johnson of this group (disciples?) makes it into the index (but not for this mention in the text). This paltry acknowledgment is made worse by the fact that in every case (with the exception of Norris's criticism of Cynthia Chase's deconstructive narratology [pp. 133–4]) the in-text citations are little more than name-dropping.

Leitch, for example, only mentions Barbara Johnson once in his text proper (in two notes he briefly discusses her work): 'We find this effort [to take up psychoanalysis] on occasion in Miller and Riddel, but rarely in de Man. Bloom, Hartman, Johnson, Mehlman, and others are more fully steeped in and committed to psychoanalytic theorizing' (pp. 101–2). Of the seven critics listed here, the first five receive extensive attention in *Deconstructive Criticism*, so their names are or become extremely familiar to the reader, and Jeffrey Mehlman had been cited twelve pages earlier in the chapter. But [Barbara] Johnson's first name has been bracketed out of Leitch's text. By such an act Leitch excludes 'Barbara' Johnson's feminine name and grants her limited presence in the deconstructors' club with her patronymic last name. This allegory of naming rehearses the patriarchy's conventional control over the marks of identity – the proper name – which assure the social and legal privileging of the male.

Barbara Johnson, herself, recognizes the problem of her (non)association with the Yale School. In her 1984 talk at the University of Oklahoma (where she was replacing Paul de Man at a conference on deconstruction at Yale), 'Gender theory and the Yale School', Johnson writes of her former colleagues at Yale and of the image of the feminine that appears in their work. What she discovers is the figuration of woman in metaphors that seek to avoid a frank confrontation with the questions of gender difference. These images of highly delimited women may have served interpretive ends, but there was no inquiry into what 'woman' means. Johnson then turns to look at herself as 'a Yale daughter' and reveals (discovers?, admits?) that 'no book produced by the Yale School seems to have excluded women as effectively as *The Critical Difference*.' Although she is unwilling to concede that her text is entirely devoid of questions important to feminist thought, she clearly sees that at this early stage in her writing she had been unable 'to resist the naturalness of female effacement in the subtly male pseudo-genderlessness of language'.[5] Crucially for Johnson comes the awareness that it is not enough to be a deconstructor who is female; instead, a more fully articulated and political interplay of gender and theory is necessary to overcome criticism's habitual exclusion and effacement of women.

Leitch's exclusion and effacement of female critics is not only lamentable but seemingly symptomatic of an anti-feminist stance, which comes through most clearly in the odd way he uses undefined personal pronouns. Studies of sexist language have shown us that the most prevalent form of sexism in our language is the conventional use of 'he' as the mark for an undefined referent: 'As the reader confronts the text, he . . .'. Leitch's text predominantly follows this convention, but it also betrays an occasional use of *feminine* pronouns that appear calculated to insult any reader. 'Deconstructors,' Leitch tells us, 'whether moderate or extremist, whether Hartman or Derrida, characteristically and continuously emphasize the signifier over the signified, and rarely, if ever, mention the lost and forgotten referent. Only the opponent of deconstruction thinks to name the referent. Put bluntly, if someone wants to discuss the referent, you may presume *she is hostile to deconstruction*' (pp. 117-18; emphasis added). Leitch may claim that I have fallen into the trap by seeking to mention the 'referent', but in this passage and throughout his text we can see that Leitch has a set of referents in mind when he uses the signifier 'deconstructors'. Moreover, the most persistent 'opponent[s] of deconstruction' have been male: M. H. Abrams, Gerald Graff, and Denis Donoghue, to name a few; surely there are women who oppose deconstruction, but there are also many who find it liberating. Even when Leitch casts the role of the deconstructor as feminine, the conjunction of signifiers produces a fantastic signified:

> Foucault's visionary project offers a 'deconstructive' mode of reading that breaks open the spaces of interpretation and liberates the coded signifier. At this scene of the edge critical writing and reading become heterogeneous, parodic, and carnivalesque. Ideologically motivated, the critic, a dispersed subject, playing the clown and idiot, champions error so as to undermine the rules of the culture, which assign her a fixed role in the controlled exchanges of knowledge and power. (p. 248)

We can see that Leitch's overall point in the passage addresses the feminist issue of fixed societal roles, and in that light the use of 'her' could be justified; however, the characterization of 'the critic' as 'clown and idiot' trivializes the activity into sound and fury signifying nothing.

Although Leitch's text will irritate feminists seeking to learn from this 'Advanced Introduction', Norris articulates the 'strangeness' of Derrida's inquiry (via Nietzsche) into feminine style, which Derrida equates with his conception of 'writing' as a deconstruction of the logocentric belief that puts speech always before writing. Thus, feminine style seeks a break with the rigidly rational, objective, and referential style that has been privileged by the 'fathers' of rhetoric as the only discourse for the communication of truth.[6] As Norris observes:

> Derrida can quote very much to the point from a text like *Ecce Homo* which indeed seems to equate the multiplicity of styles in Nietzsche's writing with his intimate knowledge of women. . . . His point, however, is not to document the character of Nietzsche's erotic sensibility but to trace those *textual* feints and suggestions that elude any normative logic of sense. Of course there is nothing self-evident about Derrida's curious equation between woman, sexuality and the swerve from logic into figurative language. What he is out to convey is the effect of a reading which 'perversely' cuts across the normal conventions of relevance and hermeneutic tact. (p. 72)

Norris takes the question of Derrida's 'equation' no further, although this is a perfect occasion to examine the work of feminist critics exploring the question of a distinct 'feminine style' or *l'écriture féminine*. What Norris leaves us with are the dismissive modifiers 'curious' and ' "perversely" ', which characterize such ideas as aberrations best left to criticism's side show.

Fortunately, other studies by men do seriously consider how post-structuralist theory, especially deconstruction, relates to feminist criticism. Although not about deconstruction, two established male critics have explored feminist criticism's alignment with other post-structuralist criticisms. Robert Scholes in *Semiotics and Interpretation* (1982) uses a semiotic (with some unstated deconstructive moves) approach to explore the cultural coding of the female genitalia, particularly the clitoris, in language and in three selected texts (Cleland's *Fanny Hill*, Freud's *Three Essays on the Theory of Sexuality*, and Lawrence's *Lady Chatterley's Lover*). What he finds is a linguistic, cultural, and literary tendency to eliminate the clitoris entirely or at least to restrict and condemn its function in female sexuality.[7] I will turn to Scholes's more recent views on feminism and deconstruction shortly.

Wayne C. Booth's essay 'Freedom of interpretation: Bakhtin and the challenge of feminist criticism' (1982) speculates on Mikhail Bakhtin's neglect of the influence of sexual difference in formulating his concept of 'heteroglossia' (the polyphony of voices embedded in an individual's knowledge and usage of language). To show the effect of this omission, Booth examines the characterization of women in Rabelais and shows how critics have handled it, particularly Bakhtin, who views the scatological laughter at a female character's expense as symptomatic of a regenerative, politically progressive, laughter. Yet the laughter is that of men rather than women; the texts by and about Rabelais are written by men for men: 'The truth is that nowhere in Rabelais does one find any hint of an effort to imagine any woman's point of view or to incorporate women into the dialogue. And nowhere in Bakhtin does one discover any suggestion that he sees the importance of this kind of monologue, not even when he discusses Rabelais' attitude toward women.' Booth discovers that to read from the ideological perspective of feminism markedly changes his experience, 'vexing me out of laughter and into thought'.[8] Yet problematic in both Booth and Scholes is that they come to their insights reading male texts but not also exploring these issues in female texts.

Michael Ryan's study *Marxism and Deconstruction* (1982) is not strictly devoted to literary criticism – although Ryan does provide provocative readings of some marxist texts. Instead, Ryan explores the particular alignments that can be made between marxist epistemologies and deconstructive philosophy, particularly with relation to how deconstruction can be used to read certain marxist texts in a way that uncovers Marx's own version of 'undecidability'. Crucial to Ryan's inquiry is the distinction between scientific marxism and critical marxism. For the former, marxism is reduced to a series of determinate axioms that resist (suppress) any change, thereby establishing a communist *status quo* that seeks control over knowledge so that it may preserve its hold on power. For the latter, marxism is seen as a continuing revolution of thought, open to change and shifts in power. Thus for Ryan, clearly a critical marxist,

> deconstruction is the development in philosophy which most closely parallels such events in recent critical marxism as solidarity, autonomy, and socialist feminism. It marks a critical opening, a reexamination of the conceptual infrastructure which informs institutions and practices, a reexamination which is necessary if the other openings

are to be given a theoretical basis and a justification against the
mobilization of reactive, hierarcho-absolutist concepts of 'socialism'
against them. To affirm the abyss deconstruction opens in the domain
of knowledge is politically to affirm the permanent possibility of
social change. Deconstruction both opens the possibility of an infinite
analytical regress in the determination of final, absolute truths and
implicitly promotes an infinite progress in socially reconstructive
action. It opens the possibility of further social, political-economic,
sexual-political, and cultural revolutions, as opposed to closing them
off in the aprioristic monumentality of a formal scheme, or in the
generality of a universally inclusive institution, or through the
coercive power of a norm of transcendental 'science' conceived as
absolute knowledge. (p. 8)

As this passage makes clear, Ryan's scope is obviously larger than
literature or literary criticism. Ryan sees deconstruction within the
context of social action and political change. The significance for literary
criticism of aligning marxism, feminism, and deconstruction rests in the
potential for radical intertextual and extratextual critical readings that will
break down the insular enclaves of many university departments of literature. The process of deconstructive reading, with its rigorous attention to
unsettling metaphysical oppositions (speech/writing, presence/absence,
serious/non-serious) that grant privilege to the first term, provides feminist
readers with a means for examining the metaphysical opposition of male/
female which has been clearly hierarchized within the tradition of Western
thought. Similarly, marxism allows for the study of the opposition in the
context of economic production, where again a hierarchy of value for
labor has operated to the detriment of women.

For feminist literary criticism the deconstructive reading of the terms
male/female extends to a dismantling of the established literary canon to
allow for previously excluded texts by women to be studied both for their
literary merit and for their significance in reconstructing our cultural
sensibility along non-sexist lines. When applied, for instance, to modes of
literary production in the last two centuries, this critique reveals that the
books that were popular and widely read were often by women. Yet the
establishment through a long tradition of critical statements by men,
about men, and for men of a different (patriarchal and elitist) set of aesthetic norms relegated these texts to the bibliographic backwaters as social
curiosities despite their obvious role in influencing socio-cultural norms

and values. It must be stressed that the critical activity of recovering neglected writers is not merely a neutral reclamation project. Instead, this activity engages in a political struggle to open restrictive and repressive critical ideologies to the play of 'sexual difference' which has been long either excluded from the study of literature or repressed by a 'masculine' mode of reading that was considered the established norm. Socialist feminism, Ryan tells us, offers women a political and social alternative to masculine forms of domination; socialist feminism becomes for Ryan a paradigm of critical marxism's potential to begin effecting change. The alignment with deconstruction is built out of a shared necessity to inquire critically and to rewrite the texts that govern our lives.

But programs for rewriting texts depend on projects for reading, a subject Jonathan Culler examines in his book *On Deconstruction: Theory and Criticism after Structuralism* (1982). Culler pays particular attention to the history of feminist reading practices and their relation to deconstruction, and he attempts to show how feminist criticism, 'which began with something quite different in mind', is 'brought up against the questions that deconstruction addresses' (p. 83). Culler's first task is to dissociate feminism from the pejorative category of post-structuralism; then he can concentrate on the 'stories of reading' produced by feminist criticism.

The idea of 'literary competence' based on past reading experience, extracted from Culler's earlier *Structuralist Poetics*,[9] established Culler as a reader-response critic. In *On Deconstruction* he shifts from generalized literary competence to the issue of gender experience, and in particular to the question: 'What difference does it make if the reader is a woman?' (p. 42). This question leads Culler to explore the stories of 'reading as a woman' that have been appearing with increasing frequency in critical journals and books. Culler traces three 'moments' in feminist criticism. First, there is the feminist 'conviction that their experience as women is a source of authority for their responses as readers', and this has 'encouraged feminist critics in their revaluation of celebrated and neglected works'. Such a criticism 'takes considerable interest in the situations and psychology of female characters, investigating attitudes to women or the "images of women" in the works of an author, a genre, or a period' (p. 46). 'In its second moment, feminist criticism undertakes, through the postulate of a woman reader, to bring about a new experience of reading and to make readers – men and women – question the literary and political assumptions on which their reading has been based' (p. 51). 'Feminist criticism of the second moment works to prove itself more rational, serious, and reflective than male readings that omit and distort. But there is a third moment in which, instead of contesting the association of the male with the rational, feminist theory investigates the way our notions of the rational are tied to or in complicity with the interests of the male' (p. 58). I quote Culler at length here because his particular formulations of this series of moments (history? 'his-story' of feminist criticism?) show Culler to be walking a fine line between feminism and deconstruction.[10]

These three moments represent a shift in focus from specific texts and reading experiences, to a broader theory of reading based on sexual difference, to a concern with the metaphysical concepts that direct and restrict interpretive force within an established set of conventional norms. But it is precisely to the notion of conventional norms that deconstruction pays its greatest attention, since 'what is the norm' always implies 'something that is not the norm', something that threatens the established mode of operations. Later in *On Deconstruction* Culler turns directly to the question of a feminist deconstructive criticism:

> The deconstruction of [the man/woman] opposition requires investigation of the ways in which various discourses - psychoanalytical, philosophical, literary, historical - have constituted a notion of man by characterizing the feminine in terms that permit it to be set aside. The analyst seeks to locate points at which these discourses undo themselves, revealing the interested, ideological nature of their hierarchical imposition and subverting the basis of the hierarchy they wish to establish. Derridian deconstruction might assist these investigations since many of the operations identified, for example, in Derrida's study of the treatment of writing also appear in discussions of woman. Like writing, woman is treated as a supplement: discussions of 'man' can proceed without mention of woman because she is deemed to be automatically included as a special case; male pronouns exclude her without calling attention to her exclusion; and if she is considered separately she will still be defined in terms of man, as his other. (p. 166)

Culler's prime example of this exclusion and supplementation of 'woman' in discourse is psychoanalysis - a discourse that is both concerned with sexuality and is emblematic, particularly in the texts of Freud and Lacan, of a phallogocentrism that places the penis as the central 'point of reference: its presence is the norm, and the feminine is a deviation, an accident or negative complication that has befallen the positive norm' (p. 167). Citing the work of Luce Irigaray, Sarah Kofman, Juliet Mitchell, Shoshana Felman, Hélène Cixous, and Julia Kristeva,[11] Culler shows the power and variety of feminist readings of Freud's suppression of female sexuality in theories of penis envy, derivativeness, and inferiority of woman as sexual being. Culler observes that this deconstructive reading of Freud 'reveals that woman is not marginal but central and that the account of her "incomplete sexuality" is an attempt to construct a male plenitude by setting aside a complexity that proves to be a condition of sexuality in general' (p. 171).

To this point, I have been concerned with accounts and non-accounts of deconstruction and feminism written almost exclusively by men. In Vincent Leitch, Christopher Norris, and the writers included in *The Yale Critics* we find a blindness to feminist issues in deconstruction; in Michael Ryan socialist feminism serves as a paradigm for a promising deconstructive marxism; and in Jonathan Culler stories of reading as a woman mark a clearly feminist territory in the larger project of deconstruction. The last clause, however, is troubling, since given a shift in focus we could also mark a clearly deconstructive territory in the larger project of feminism. Despite Culler's obvious sympathy with feminist criticism, he ultimately sees it as secondary to deconstruction. As Elaine Showalter observes: 'Culler's deconstructionist priorities lead him to overstate the essentialist dilemma of defining the *woman* reader, when in most cases what is implied and intended is a *feminist* reader'.[12] There are two crucial distinctions Showalter makes here: first, her italicized terms mark out two categories. The former requires that the male critic engage in 'cross-dressing' or female impersonation; the latter marks out an epistemological set of concepts the male critic can learn to better account for the role of gender in reading. Second, she asks if Culler's formulation of 'reading as a woman' is different for male and female readers?

Patrocinio Schweickart, in her fine essay 'Reading ourselves: toward a feminist theory of reading' (1986), sees Culler's theory as taking him to a privileging of the 'impossibility of reading': the deconstructive plot always finds the text in a condition of undecidability that leaves unresolved questions of author, text, and the reading subject. For Schweickart this movement away from an 'optimistic' reading based on a dialectical theory of text/reader interaction has nothing to offer the 'feminist' reader because it resituates itself in a continuing play of deferral – a condition women have too long been forced to accept.[13] Robert Scholes, likewise, finds Culler's attempt 'to locate feminism within deconstruction' troublesome if not outright 'misguided'. In his essay 'Reading like a man' (1987), Scholes questions whether the whole attempt to align deconstruction and feminism is misguided although illuminating.

Scholes bases his dissent first on the recognition that deconstruction, as a critical paradigm, is a matter of choice and practice within established institutional systems; whereas feminism, as a critical paradigm, is also a matter of choice and practice, but is additionally tied to the biological determinism of gender. (Scholes uses the term 'class' instead of 'biological determinism', but this feint at the conceptual system of political struggle underscores the humanistic basis of his comments.) This biological determinism has, through time, been loaded with cultural and social systems that have been at the center of feminist politics and that inform most feminist criticism. Since men represent a different determinism, Scholes believes, the male critic 'may work within the feminist paradigm but never be a full-fledged member of the class of feminists' (p. 207). Deconstruction, however, has as its goal the dismantling of such deterministic notions; therefore, Scholes finds feminism and deconstruction to be 'founded upon antithetical principles', and that 'is why attempts to reconcile them should provoke the horrified fascination of an acrobat attempting an impossible feat' (p. 208).

The performer to whom Scholes directs our gaze is none other than Jonathan Culler as he attempts the daring feat of reading as a woman. Scholes sees Culler as basing his theory on the key concept of the reader's experience – experience as a woman – as a constitutive element in interpretation. But to then make this 'experience' available to himself and other male critics, Culler must conceptualize 'experience' by seeing it always already as an essence or construct, which can then be a subject of deconstruction. Scholes reads this move as just another form of phallogocentrism, a reinstitution of power and control over the processes of reading both texts and the feminine. Scholes demonstrates his point by anachronistically bringing a text of Derrida's to bear on Culler's claims:

By collapsing the problem of feminine experience into the question of feminine essence, Derrida achieves mastery over feminism. He insists that feminism is in fact a form of phallogocentrism: '. . . for me deconstruction is certainly not feminist. At least as I have tried to practise it, I believe it naturally supposes a radical deconstruction of phallogocentrism, and certainly an absolutely other and new interest in women's questions. But if there is one thing that it must not come to, it's feminism. So I would say that deconstruction is a deconstruction of feminism, from the start, insofar as feminism is a form – no doubt necessary at a certain moment – but a form of phallogocentrism among many others.' (p. 212)[14]

Coming from the high priest of deconstruction, this statement seems to sign either a non-alignment pact with or a declaration of war against feminism; or does it? The opening clause seems so disarmingly straightforward that one would hardly recognize Derrida in such an ontologically clear expression. But the next sentences play with an ambiguous 'it' that calls back into question the labels of deconstruction and feminism Derrida uses. If deconstruction can be deconstructed then so can feminism, particularly if one defines feminism as a new system revealing a 'truth', a 'logos', about reality. There is nothing new in this tautology. What is significant is that Derrida and Scholes (although possibly for different purposes) seem to be warning us that the issue of how feminism and deconstruction come into alignment is much more vexed than we might have previously thought. Indeed, if I take the lessons in feminist reading given by Culler, I could conceivably go to any text and mimic 'his' procedures for unmasking the phallocentric presuppositions controlling the discourse. My own consideration of Leitch's phallocentric exclusions and appropriations of woman is a gesture toward 'reading as a woman'. Though at the same time, I would in no way claim that I have taken this reading as far as it might go, and in the light of Scholes, Schweickart, and Showalter I wonder whether what I have done is especially feminist.

Instead, I am drawn to see my concerns here as a form of what Showalter calls 'critical cross-dressing'. In that position, I find that beyond the obvious finding of fault with those deconstructors who ignore feminist issues, I am hard put to discover moments of blindness in Ryan, Culler, Booth, or Scholes. Yet I come away from these accounts of feminism (by men, for men?) with a sense of surface understanding that makes feminist reading a usable strategy in my critical bag of tricks. But there is also the nagging sense that there is more to it. This present collection, in which you are reading this re-vision and extension of a review essay that first appeared in *Tulsa Studies in Women's Literature* (1984), and the collection *Men in Feminism* edited by Alice Jardine and Paul Smith (1987), focus our inquiry on the vexed questions of gender in criticism, on questions of critical understanding, of appropriation or mutual growth, of rights and privileges to write about the other gender. What inevitable 'lacks' is each critic forced to operate under? Are there ways to bridge the gaps through a dialogue on theory? Or, is such a project of bridging fraught with a utopian idealism that could actually reinstate a tyranny of critical blindness at precisely the moment it claims insight? Clearly even to approach these questions we cannot leave the story of deconstruction and feminist literary theory only half told; therefore, I will turn now to two texts by noted feminists who are clearly identified with deconstruction: Gayatri Spivak and Alice Jardine.[15] My discussion of Spivak appeared in the first version of this essay; Jardine's work marks a significant movement since the time of that first version in understanding deconstruction and its relation to the feminine.

I was drawn to Spivak by a desire to understand Derrida's earlier feminist moves – his critique of phallocentrism through the notion of a feminine style. Spivak provides such an account and more in her essay 'Displacement and the discourse of woman' (1983), although she has been conspicuously associated with deconstruction ever since the publication of her translation of Derrida's *Of Grammatology*.[16] In her essay Spivak is less concerned with writing by women or reading as a woman; instead, she concentrates on the practice of phallocentric discourses to organize particular sets of ideas around a symbolic representation of 'woman': 'The discourse of man is in the metaphor of woman' (p. 169). Thus within the tradition of, for example, philosophic discourse, 'woman' becomes the representative of such ideas as Truth, Justice, Virtue, and Poetry. Spivak observes, however, that this representation is always of a generalized 'woman' rather than a particular woman, and that the act of generalization is in fact always a constructed fiction of a masculine image of particular masculine ideas. 'Woman' is, therefore, always displaced from women, just as women have been, in various periods including the present, excluded by the social text from speaking truth, participating in the law, exercising self-virtue, or writing literary or philosophical texts.

'Can Derrida's critique [of logocentrism, phallogocentrism, and phallocentrism] provide us a network of concept-metaphors that does not appropriate or displace the figure of woman?' (p.170). Apparently not, according to Spivak, because rather than merely righting [writing?] a wrong, deconstruction displaces 'woman' again, by marking the originary moment of generalization in an impersonation: the faked orgasm. Spivak writes:

The deconstructive structure of how woman 'is' is contained in a well-known Nietzschean sentence: 'Finally – if one loved them . . . what comes of it inevitably? that they "give themselves," even when they – give themselves. The female is so artistic.' [*The Gay Science*] Or: women impersonate themselves as having an orgasm even at the time of orgasm. Within the historical understanding of women as incapable of orgasm, Nietzsche is arguing that imperson-ation is woman's only sexual pleasure. At the time of the greatest self-possession-cum-ecstasy, the woman is self-possessed enough to organize a self-(re)presentation without an actual presence (of sexual pleasure) to re-present. This is an originary displacement. (p. 170)

It is exactly this kind of approach that Christopher Norris dismisses in the passage quoted earlier. What Spivak finds, however, is that the model 'woman' in deconstructive discourse of a female style in a 'Writing' = 'Woman' equation is always already doubly displaced: 'But perhaps the point is that the deconstructive discourse of man (like the phallocentric one) can declare its own displacement (as the phallocentric its placing) by taking the woman as object or figure' (p. 173).

In deconstruction's objectification of 'woman' Spivak finds an inter-pretive hinge with which she seeks to deconstruct Derrida's ability to 'problematize but not fully disown his status as subject' (p. 173). And although she admires Derrida's efforts, and is quick to point out that he has few male followers in this direction of his thought (Spivak does cite Ryan's and Culler's work as exceptions), the fact is that 'real' women have never been 'the heroes of philosophy'. The male philosopher's move is always to appropriate a generalized conception of 'woman' that is always already displaced by an impersonation. But where then are women to go to become subjects producing their own discourse?

About two-thirds of the way through her essay, Spivak takes stock:

My attitude toward deconstruction can now be summarized: first, deconstruction is illuminating as a critique of phallocentrism; second, it is convincing as an argument against the founding of a hysterocentric to counter a phallocentric discourse; third, as a 'feminist' practice itself, it is caught on the other side of sexual difference. At whatever remove of 'différance' (difference/deferment from/of any decidable statement of the concept of an identity or

difference) *sexual difference is thought*, sexual *differential* between
'man' and 'woman' remains irreducible. (p. 184)

At this point, Spivak's marxist affinities begin to show through as she
makes some suggestions about the role of deconstruction in feminist
criticism:

> The collective project of our feminist critic must always be to
> rewrite the *social* text so that the historical and sexual differentials
> are operated together. Part of it is to notice that the argument based
> on the 'power' of the faked orgasm, of being-fetish, and hymen, is,
> all deconstructive cautions taken, 'determined' by that very political
> and social history that is inseparably co-extensive with phallocentric
> discourse and, in her case, either unrecorded in accessible ways, or
> recorded in terms of man. Since she has, indeed, learned the lesson
> of deconstruction, this rewriting of the social text of motherhood
> cannot be an establishment of new meanings. It can only be to work
> away at concept-metaphors that deliberately establish and cast wide a
> different system of 'meanings'. (p. 185)

Significantly, for my own critical efforts, Spivak presents a program that
cannot be easily adopted by just anyone who happens to read her text. As
she observes toward the end of her essay, 'even the strongest personal
goodwill on Derrida's part cannot turn him quite free of the massive
enclosure of the male appropriation of woman's voice' (p. 190). Men
writing on and working in deconstruction have much to learn from
Spivak's essay. The primordial irreducibility of sexual difference produces
a space across which much critical activity can be shared. Our project,
then, women and men, should be a writing of criticism attuned to the
forces of sexual difference that are latent not only in established ideas,
epistemologies, and discourses, but also in contemporary theories that
seek ways out of the logocentric patterns of Western culture. Gayatri
Spivak's essay marks a significant new directive for feminists and deconstructors alike, a directive that brings me to the work of Alice Jardine.

In *Gynesis: Configurations of Woman and Modernity* (1985), Jardine
engages the inquiry that Norris and Leitch omit and that Culler has over-
simplified. Like Scholes, Jardine is interested in the negotiation of feminist
thought with theories of 'modernity' (what Anglo-Americans call 'post-

modernism'). Deconstruction is clearly one of the theories of modernity, although Jardine, by and large, avoids delimiting labels; indeed, a major part of her project is to distinguish how narrow definitions of Anglo-American feminism have created a theoretical cul-de-sac that French theorists have moved beyond. Scholes's use of the passage from Derrida, quoted earlier, is a case in which Jardine might say that Scholes has defined the term 'feminist' (as in 'deconstruction is certainly not feminist') in the empirical, pragmatic tradition of Anglo-American feminism. In so doing, he easily comes to the conclusion that Derrida is hostile to feminism, and therefore deconstruction and feminism are antithetical. But if 'feminism' is restricted to only a formalized set of concepts, then no one should be surprised to see it as open to deconstruction. On the other hand, if we begin to see, as Jardine does, the slippage surrounding terms like 'feminist', 'feminism', 'women', 'Woman', and 'feminine' in critical discourse, then we begin to see as well the power of gynesis to unsettle the conceptualization of the feminine within the master narratives of the late twentieth century – whether they are traditional, deconstructive, or feminist.

Where Scholes seeks to separate feminism and deconstruction, Jardine seeks to intersect the two: '*gynesis*: the putting into discourse of "woman" [as a verb 'at the interior of those narratives that are today experiencing a crisis in legitimation'] as that *process* diagnosed in France as intrinsic to the condition of modernity' (p. 25). The difference between these two views is somewhat paradoxical in that the kind of feminism Scholes implies (the political and critical feminism of America) is antithetical to many French theorists. As Jardine observes:

> The major new directions in French theory over the past two decades – those articulated by both men and women – have, by and large, posited themselves as profoundly, that is to say conceptually and in *praxis*, anti- and/or post-feminist. Feminism, as a concept, as inherited from the humanist and rationalist eighteenth century, is traditionally about a group of human beings in history whose identity is defined by that history's representation of sexual decidability. And every term of that definition has been put into question by contemporary French thought. (pp. 20-1)

What we have are procedures – modernity (deconstruction) and feminism – that share certain activities such as the unsettling of established patriarchal conventions, yet which differ in their narrative organization: feminism seeks a certain closure around a newly revealed truth; while modernity avoids closure because if closed it would merely repeat or parallel the master narratives (religion, philosophy, history) it has sought to delegitimize.

The avoidance of closure is a crucial aspect of Jardine's text, which marks its own avoidance by its interrogative style. By showing the extent and the range of questions theory confronts, Jardine maps out a territory to be explored. But significantly, she confronts the time/space opposition to imply that this territory, the territory of 'Woman', is not only a space, a body. Instead, the opposition's gender identifications are intersected in the intersection of theory and praxis that marks the 'woman as process' in the writing of modernity. The result is a calling into question of the writing subject, the status of textual systems of signification, and the reading-effect. 'Of course, it is causality itself that is in question here: a disbelief in origins, heredity, legitimations, intentionality, progress' (p. 90). One might add a disbelief in destinations, in the postal sense of the misdirected, purloined, dead letter. Jardine believes that we must move beyond the androcentric fictions of origin and destination, and into 'Fiction' – the play of textuality that demands no absolute context in 'truth' – into the configuration of Woman produced by gynesis.

Along similar lines as Spivak's discussion of displacement, Jardine draws a distinction between women and the 'Woman' of theoretical discourse, raising first the question of what one has to do with the other: Must theoretical writing about/through/inside Woman necessarily speak to the specific condition of women? Second, there is the question of how 'Woman' moves from the exploited status as a symbolic object in patriarchal discourse to a subversive and vital force in contemporary theory. If this shift is the case, then clearly there is a dichotomy between deconstruction practised by many male critics and feminist literary theory, but the question then becomes whether we are talking about an unbridgeable gap (Scholes) or a developing dialogue and intersection (Jardine). This question is compounded further by questions of gender and genre that infiltrate both the content and enunciation of contemporary critical theory. However, the more fully we explore the contexts of our literary, cultural, social, and political institutions through theories that are likewise contextually aware of their relation to those institutions, the closer we will come to understanding the processes that make, unmake, and remake the world we engage – both empirically and conceptually –

each day. Significantly, this understanding cannot be neutral in a world that still systematizes oppression.

As I look back on the process of this inquiry, I see that what started as an empirical exercise of cataloging the neglect of feminist deconstruction by male, Anglo-American deconstructors has made me aware of issues shaping the future of critical discourse. With the idea of gynesis we can begin to see a powerful and productive intersection in literary theory. Deconstruction and feminist literary theory can dialogically come together in a multi-dimensional criticism that is aware of both its practices and its biases. I am not talking about some sort of utopian pluralism; instead, I am suggesting a theory, process, and practice that can be passionately self-critical in an age when certainty is a symptom of a nostalgia for a past that will not come again.

NOTES

1 Ryan 1982: 195. Subsequent references to Ryan and the following works will be cited in text: Culler 1982; Jardine 1985; Leitch 1983; Norris 1982; Scholes 1987; Spivak 1983.
2 See Spivak 1980; and Johnson 1985.
3 In addition to the works examined here, two other well-known studies of contemporary criticism neglect feminist theory: Graff 1977; and Lentricchia 1980.
4 Afterword, in Arac et al. 1983: 187.
5 Johnson 1985: 110, 112; in Davis and Schleifer 1985, 3 of the 10 contributors are women – of the 197 names listed in the index, only 20 are women.
6 This discourse was long protected by the denial of education to women. If rational discourse allowed one access to the seats of power, it was deemed necessary by the male hierarchy to exclude women from this means of advancement. As is being shown in such work as Perry 1980, women were forced to develop their writing along lines very different from that of men; hence the genres and subjects open to a woman's pen were severely limited and were often excluded from the established canon of literary study. A vital element in feminist studies is the recovery of these texts hitherto considered marginal, and by deconstructing the phallocentrism of the literary canon, these rediscovered texts by women can take a significant place in a liberated literary canon.
7 Scholes 1982: ch. 8.
8 Booth 1982: 65-6, 68.
9 Culler 1975: 113-30. A superb example of Culler's principles applied to feminist concerns is Annette Kolodny's widely anthologized essay 'A map for rereading: or, gender and the interpretation of literary texts' (Kolodny 1980), which also seeks to deconstruct Harold Bloom's patriarchal vision of the anxiety of influence.

10 One could compare Culler's history with that proposed by Elaine Showalter in her essays 'Toward a feminist poetics' (1979) and 'Feminist criticism in the wilderness' (1981); both reprinted in Showalter 1985a.

11 As compared to Norris and Leitch, Culler lists 37 women among the 185 names in his index. More to the point, Culler directly discusses not only feminist critics and their issues, but female critics doing other kinds of deconstruction. See, for example, pp. 235-42, where he discusses Barbara Johnson's deconstructive reading of Melville's *Billy Budd* (Johnson 1980).

12 Showalter 1983.

13 Schweickart 1986.

14 Scholes provides the following reference for Derrida's statement: *Critical Exchange*, 17 (Winter 1985). It should be noted that in some feminist circles deconstruction is also not feminist. Showalter, in 'Toward a feminist poetics', suggests that women working in deconstruction and other 'scientific' rather than 'humanistic' criticisms 'risk being allotted the symbolic ghettos of the special issue or the back of the book for their essays' (p. 140). Showalter made her prophecy come true in *The New Feminist Criticism* when Nancy K. Miller's contribution appeared in the back of the book.

15 I am forced to bypass much work I admire and many critics who have also been concerned with issues of this essay; it is certainly time for a full assessment of female critics who also work in deconstruction.

16 For Spivak's early views on deconstruction, see her Translator's Preface to Derrida 1976: ix-lxxxvii.

REFERENCES

Arac, Jonathan. Afterword, in Arac et al. 1983: 176-99.

Arac, Jonathan, Godzich, Wlad and Martin, Wallace (eds) 1983. *The Yale Critics: Deconstruction in America*. Minneapolis: University of Minnesota Press.

Booth, Wayne C. 1982. 'Freedom of interpretation: Bakhtin and the challenge of feminist criticism', *Critical Inquiry*, 9: 45-76.

Culler, Jonathan 1975. *Structuralist Poetics: Structuralism, Linguistics and the Study of Literature*. Ithaca: Cornell University Press.

Culler, Jonathan 1982. *On Deconstruction: Theory and Criticism after Structuralism*. Ithaca: Cornell University Press.

Davis, Robert Con and Schleifer, Ronald (eds) 1985. *Rhetoric and Form: Deconstruction at Yale*. Norman: University of Oklahoma Press.

Derrida, Jacques 1976. *Of Grammatology*. Trans. Gayatri Chakravorty Spivak. Baltimore: Johns Hopkins University Press.

Duyfhuizen, Bernard 1984. 'Deconstruction and feminist literary theory', *Tulsa Studies in Women's Literature*, 3: 159-69.

Graff, Gerald 1977. *Literature Against Itself: Literary Ideas in a Modern Society*. Chicago: University of Chicago Press.

Jardine, Alice 1985. *Gynesis: Configurations of Woman and Modernity*. Ithaca: Cornell University Press.

Jardine, Alice and Smith, Paul (eds) 1987. *Men in Feminism*. New York and London: Methuen.

Johnson, Barbara 1980. 'Melville's fist: the execution of *Billy Budd*', in *The Critical Difference: Essays in the Contemporary Rhetoric of Reading*. Baltimore: Johns Hopkins University Press.

Johnson, Barbara 1985. 'Gender theory and the Yale School', in Davis and Schleifer 1985: 101-12.

Kolodny, Annette 1980. 'A map for rereading: or, gender and the interpretation of literary texts', *New Literary History*, 11: 451-67.

Leitch, Vincent B. 1983. *Deconstructive Criticism: An Advanced Introduction*. New York: Columbia University Press.

Lentricchia, Frank 1980. *After the New Criticism*. Chicago: University of Chicago Press.

Miller, Nancy K. 1985. 'Emphasis added: plots and plausibilities in women's fiction', in Showalter 1985: 339-60.

Norris, Christopher 1982. *Deconstruction: Theory and Practice*. New York: Methuen.

Perry, Ruth 1980. *Women, Letters, and the Novel*. New York: AMS.

Ryan, Michael 1982. *Marxism and Deconstruction: A Critical Articulation*. Baltimore: Johns Hopkins University Press.

Scholes, Robert 1982. *Semiotics and Interpretation*. New Haven: Yale University Press.

Scholes, Robert 1987. 'Reading like a man', in Jardine and Smith 1987: 204-18.

Schweickart, Patrocinio P. 1986. 'Reading ourselves: toward a feminist theory of reading', in *Gender and Reading: Essays on Readers, Texts, and Contexts*, ed. Elizabeth A. Flynn and Patrocinio P. Schweickart. Baltimore: Johns Hopkins University Press: 31-62.

Showalter, Elaine 1983. 'Critical cross-dressing: male feminists and the woman of the year', *Raritan*, 3.2: 142-3.

Showalter, Elaine (ed.) 1985a. *The New Feminist Criticism: Essays on Women, Literature, and Theory*. New York: Pantheon.

Showalter, Elaine 1985b. 'Feminist criticism in the wilderness', in Showalter 1985a: 243-70.

Showalter, Elaine 1985c. 'Toward a feminist poetics', in Showalter 1985a: 125-43.

Spivak, Gayatri Chakravorty 1980. 'Finding feminist readings: Dante-Yeats', *Social Text* (Fall): 73-87.

Spivak, Gayatri Chakravorty 1983. 'Displacement and the discourse of woman', in *Displacement: Derrida and After*, ed. Mark Krupnick. Bloomington: Indiana University Press: 169-95.

10
Criticus Interruptus: Uncoupling Feminism and Deconstruction

Bella Brodzki and Celeste Schenck

Besides assessment of Bernard Duyfhuizen's claim that an alliance between feminism and deconstruction has much to offer the literary critic, response to his essay requires first a sense of the identity of the speaker, then a determination of why and for whom he is speaking, and finally some acknowledgment of what is at stake in who does the speaking. Our reaction to his essay, then, will take the form of a fourfold, hopefully integrated, reading which will range rather farther than we first anticipated. The first section will examine the gendering of the marriage Duyfhuizen advocates, as well as the genders (and their implications for this discussion) of the critics involved in the debate. The second looks more closely at the text Duyfhuizen lets speak for him, analyzing the reasons why he might assent to this act of critical ventriloquism. The third part of our response disrupts the opposition of feminism and deconstruction by introducing a third term, politics, which forces the terms of the debate on to new ground: the politics of theory itself, and the even more presently compelling politics of the subject. The last section is an experimental reading of two stories from Jamaica Kincaid's *At the Bottom of the River* which aims at mapping intersections beyond the reach of either feminism or deconstruction, as well as the prescribed complicity between them.

The gendering of theory

Critical testimony to the difficulty of the alliance notwithstanding, feminism and deconstruction, as the title of Duyfhuizen's essay 'Deconstruction and feminist literary theory II' suggests, is an already established albeit tempestuous marriage. To the extent that they can (each) be monolithically represented, feminism and deconstruction have been set up within American critical discourse as a couple, and a heterosexual couple and privileged couple at that. There is something inherently gendered (or is it sexy?) in the pairing of schools so readily identifiable with women and men, female and male practitioners. That is, Duyfhuizen's title, and the division within his essay between male and female critics, like Alice Jardine's configurations of woman and modernity, assume the sexual difference of the couple: deconstructionists, or theorists, are male, and feminists, who take responsibility for gender, properly female. Clearly, as the spate of new books on the dialogue between the sexes suggests (Jardine and Smith's collection *Men in Feminism*, Jardine's own work-in-progress on writing couples, and even *Gender and Theory: Dialogues on Feminist Criticism*), after a period of marked, deliberate critical separatism, hetero-sexual marriage, even in critical discourse, is back in style: feminism and deconstruction, gender and theory, woman and modernity – the cozy, familiar, nuclear ménage of hers and his.[1]

If feminism and deconstruction as an irresistibly binary formulation presents too married a face to the world, in fact this critical coupling has been anything but easy. Robert Scholes finds the partners to be represen-tative of 'antithetical principles', locked in a kind of marriage of heaven and hell which must be acknowledged as 'misguided' if illuminating, while Patrocinio Schweickart finds the alliance of feminism with decon-structive reading strategies to be at the very least politically problematic, perpetuating the 'play of deferral', that 'condition women have too long been forced to accept', as Duyfhuizen phrases it (pp. 183-4). But even speaking from among those willing to entertain the pair, Duyfhuizen himself points out that the relationship has been far from mutual: 'Femin-ists have turned to deconstruction . . . more often than deconstructionists have turned to feminism' (p. 174). And taking male deconstructors to task for inadequately recognizing the theoretical contributions of femi-nism to a rethinking of our cultural inheritances forms the first part of Duyfhuizen's exegetical project. Feminists, by contrast, have done all the work of the relationship, interrogating deconstruction's use of woman as a category, adapting its methodologies to the feminist task of revising the canon, questioning periodization and genre, drawing attention to the oppositional strategies they have in common. Frances Bartkowski's dis-cussion of that 'union forever deferred' in an early issue of *Enclitic*, the Peggy Kamuf and Nancy Miller debate and Christie McDonald's 'Choreo-graphies' in the 1982 'Cherchez la femme' issue of *Diacritics*, Gayatri

Spivak's early translation of and commentaries on Derrida, Barbara Johnson's theorizing of sexual difference as a critical difference, Mary Jacobus's deft restoration of the woman in the text, and Alice Jardine's positioning of gynesis are the most prominent American feminist dialogues with deconstruction.[2] But feminism has also, as the near silence of male theorists on feminism attests, had more to gain from the alliance. In fact, feminist critics who have allied themselves with deconstruction, either to adapt its insights or to critique it from the position of knowing it thoroughly, may have profited institutionally, like the generation of American male critics who first imported the continental 'philosophy' of Derrida, by their association with the legitimizing influence of French theory. The marriage (or is it a no-less-erotic oedipal arrangement?) clearly has served some of *her* purposes, although the exchange has been far from bilateral.

The reasons for the omission of feminist theory from the annals of American deconstruction – now duly institutionalized, as Duyfhuizen's history of their histories attests – are complex and do not rest merely with the relative inconsequentiality of feminism to the hierarchies of discursive power. The binary opposition that is, inevitably, feminism and deconstruction has in this case favored the second term, for in some circles deconstruction has had critical cachet and institutional prestige that some feminists have found irresistible. But feminism has nonetheless complicated the picture decidedly in ways revealed by the tonal undertext and anxious authorial interruptions of Duyfhuizen's well-intentioned review. Feminism may remain more changed by deconstruction than *that* theory by feminism, because of the power structures that inhere in critical discourse, but also because the biological determinism of gender precludes, or at the very least problematizes, the appropriation of feminism, the right to speak as a feminist, by male critics. The question used to be whether there could be a feminist man; now the question is whether there can legitimately be a male feminist critic, or as Elaine Showalter puts it, mimicking Jonathan Culler (who is in turn echoing Mary Jacobus), 'whether a male feminist is in fact a man reading as a woman reading as a woman'.[3] As Joseph Boone formulates the problem in another essay, the male feminist's task remains the 'finding [of]a position *from which* to speak'.[4]

Even within an essay that does not address these issues, Duyfhuizen reveals anxiety about his own positioning in a self-conscious discussion of his critical processes. His unmasking in male critical texts of 'phallocentric exclusions and appropriations of woman is [his] gesture toward "reading as a woman" ' (p. 185), but not having 'taken this reading as far as it might go', he wonders whether 'what I have done is especially feminist' (p. 185). In fact, Duyfhuizen questions the limits of his own feminist critical insight – 'beyond the obvious finding of fault with those deconstructors who ignore feminist issues, I am hard put to discover moments of blindness in Ryan, Culler, Booth, or Scholes' (p. 185) – and yet he also worries that somehow accounts of feminism in male texts (including, admittedly, his own) amount to no more than 'a sense of surface understanding that makes feminist reading a usable strategy in my critical bag of tricks' (p. 185). Male critics, after Showalter's scathing review article on the topic, are especially sensitive to charges of 'cross-dressing' – Boone, in fact, sets out to 'redress' the issue altogether – yet Duyfhuizen himself 'is drawn to see my concerns here as a form of what Showalter calls "critical cross-dressing" ' (p. 185). (But even strategic critical cross-dressing brings with it its own anxieties for male critics, as Duyfhuizen's slip of anatomical 'penis' for the signifying 'phallus' betrays [p. 182]. No feminist reader could fail to note this slip, nor would she make it, not having the same stake in the mistake as a man.) Duyfhuizen is a fellow traveller by virtue of his willingness to *épater* fellow deconstructors for their failure to address feminism appropriately; however, he can only comfortably speak for the marriage his title champions ventriloquistically, by paraphrasing the text of a female feminist critic whose agenda he wishes to adopt. If the readers of Duyfhuizen's review find themselves wondering, by the close, where exactly he stands on the topic of feminism and deconstruction, the problem is precisely that he cannot stand where he would like to speak.

Feminist theory is optimistically bound to deconstruction by means of the democratic conjunction 'and' in his title, but more tellingly, Duyfhuizen allies himself with Alice Jardine, who speaks what he cannot overtly say, in the almost transcendent registers of the essay's close. The deferential tone with which Duyfhuizen describes Jardine's project captures a moment of reversal in which only a female feminist critic can speak about the compatibility of feminism and deconstruction, that 'developing dialogue and intersection' (p. 190) in which Duyfhuizen, like his text's heroine, is so invested.[5] Duyfhuizen uncritically credits Jardine's discovery of gynesis with all 'the power to unsettle the conceptualization of the feminine within the master narratives of the late twentieth century – whether they are traditional, deconstructive, or feminist' (p. 189). By the end, Duyfhuizen seems to have experienced something of an epiphany, playing pilgrim Dante to Jardine's leading Beatrice. Reading her, he moves by his own report from 'an empirical exercise of cataloguing the neglect of feminist deconstruction by male, Anglo-American deconstructors' to the awareness 'of issues shaping the future of critical discourse'. By the close, his rhetoric becomes decidedly climactic as feminism and deconstruction 'dialogically come together' in 'passionately self-critical' practice (p. 191).

What matter who is speaking?

Duyfhuizen's 1984 essay 'Deconstruction and feminist literary theory' in *Tulsa Studies in Women's Literature* ended with a sober acceptance of Gayatri Spivak's astringent reminder in her essay, 'Displacement and the discourse of woman',[6] that the primordiality of sexual difference is the non-negotiable condition of any collaboration between feminism and deconstruction. In the revised and updated essay, Duyfhuizen seems particularly relieved to find a new voice on the scene, one for whom there are no irreducible differences, only interventions. He even sets up a kind of natural progression from Spivak to Jardine, as if both conceptually and politically Jardine's inclination toward intersections represents a higher stage of consciousness than Spivak's wary resistance to the project at hand. While Duyfhuizen cites Spivak's admiration for Derrida's 'feminist moves' - his critique of phallocentrism through the notion of a feminine style - he has some difficulty with Spivak's unequivocal assertion that even deconstruction is not immune from philosophy's temptation to 'appropriate or displace' the figure of 'woman' for its own discursive ends (quoted in *Tulsa Studies*, p. 166). Duyfhuizen's response to Spivak's caveat is that her program 'cannot be easily adopted by just anyone who happens to read her text' (p. 167). Not able to meet gender requirements for entrance into that problematic but exciting critical space he envisions where women and men can both speak, he betrays his own realization that in this instance he will be the one left standing silenced at the threshold. Precisely because Duyfhuizen's sustained hopes for an alliance between feminism and deconstruction eventually merge with Jardine's critical project, indeed become indistinguishable from it, any response to his essay necessarily includes address of *Gynesis: Configurations of Woman and Modernity* (1985).

Jardine identifies a space within modernity coded (by the master narratives) as feminine, then retheorizes and occupies that space herself. To that extent, she locates a point of substantial contact between feminism and deconstruction, which may amount to having the last word on them. Although deconstruction figures largely in the cultural response to loss which she defines as modernity, it is not the only critical discourse to exploit the discursive power of 'woman', as other, absence, lack. Moreover, and as she would have it significantly for feminism, Jardine wants to theorize that it is possible to occupy that space as a woman for whom experience has political texture and importance. And her strategy of recounting and reclaiming the 'putting into discourse of "woman"' (p. 25), or gynesis, is canny, continually questioning its own categories and hypotheses, shifting the boundaries between the areas she seeks to intersect, seeking to avoid the reified polarities of continental philosophy and American pragmatism, French feminist theory and American feminist praxis. Jardine's theoretical goal, to the extent that she has one, is to 'open a space for women to write in' within the symbolic discourse of the continental fathers. And her rhetoric, suggesting the stakes of this oedipal stake-out, is fully military, even technological: 'interference', 'borderline disputes', 'crisis', 'strategy', 'vigilance', 'interfacing', 'neutralization', 'intervention', 'mapping', 'intersubjective warfare'.

But the problem with this configuration of woman and modernity, as some critics have noted, is that it remains limitingly oedipal, situating itself in the (preferred) French space between masters and disciples. The preoccupation of *Gynesis* with legitimation, with rightful inheritance, with what Sharon Willis calls the 'family metaphorics of legacy',[7] may have transferential implications as well: may gynesis be another form of the daughter's seduction, both a willed restoration of relationship with the father (of whom old-style seduction is no longer possible) and a replacement of the mother? The more broadly cultural 'loss of the paternal fiction' which fuels modernity for Jardine, and which weakens and dilutes the American scene for her, may be just as much a personal crisis in legitimation for a transatlantic feminist. Jardine's story, for all her attentiveness to exploding binary oppositions, remains a tale of two countries, France and America, and primarily a narrative of heterosexual exchange between fathers and daughters. She has, in short, rewritten the romance, more genealogical than laterally heterosexual, that Duyfhuizen so ardently invests in. And what this romantic paradigm occludes, as Sharon Willis formulates it, are 'other differences, those of power distributions across race and class' – for example, 'the scene of "warring sisters," that is, the conflicting tendencies within American [not to mention French] feminist alliances' (p. 39).[8]

What a male feminist critic like Duyfhuizen would find welcoming in Jardine's theory of gynesis is that it can be practised by anyone of either gender (not so ironically it has been historically appropriated by men) – that is, that the 'woman-in-effect' is a rhetorical space within language which is only semiotically gendered, that 'the signifier "woman" does not necessarily mean the biological female in history' (p. 42). In point of fact, Jardine remains faithful to Derrida's suspicion of fixed (even gendered) identity and Kristeva's ambivalence about sexing the dissident category of woman in her own ambivalent pronouncement that 'the assurance of any given subject's sexual identity may have become the wrong question for modernity. There seems to be no question . . . that the space of alterity to be explored always already must connote the female' (p. 114). This restriction of 'woman' and 'the feminine' to 'processes that disrupt symbolic structures in the West' (p. 42) is the very aspect of her theory which remains problematic for female feminist critics for whom it matters, increasingly, who is speaking. Thus to us it is not merely a question of who occupies the space coded (overdeterminedly) as feminine, but who finally is the speaking subject.

The politics of subjectivity

Where Jardine sees interventions and Duyfhuizen hopes for intersections, we read an impasse. Feminism and deconstruction, in their compellingly heterosexual arrangement, is in our determination presently a moot issue: the dialectic has played itself out. Obsession with what we have called a nuclear model has, in fact, also limited the terms of debate to continual restitution of a seemingly stable opposition, or worse, reduced the dynamic to an infinite and unproductive regress. We aim instead at disrupting the couple, at breaking up the 'natural' pairing of feminism and deconstruction, by the introduction of at least a third term which has recently challenged each of the principals to clarify his/her position. In short, as we answer collaboratively Duyfhuizen's solid, summarizing, single voice with our own two disjunctive and often antithetical ones (the ur-text of our response has sometimes been that of Willis's ' "warring sisters" ': argument and more argument), we inevitably change the configuration. The sexiness of that binary alliance, feminism and deconstruction, no longer compels the same interest, particularly as they have been increasingly criticized for some of the same failures of vision. Current critical debate has moved beyond the terms that contain Duyfhuizen's essay. In short, there are more chairs than two at the table.

The current critical situation – the turn to and preoccupation with the politics of theory, the politics of subjectivity, and global politics more generally – may be sensed in several recent responses of feminists and deconstructionists to new theoretical questions. Feminist and deconstructionist methodologies co-exist productively in some of these inquiries, and in others they are mobilized against one another. But the force of critical energy is directed elsewhere: *against* the privileging of interiority and *toward* the complex political constitution of whatever we still think of as identity. As feminism and deconstruction have both increasingly been called upon to define their politics, feminism has begun to remove the blinkers that preoccupation with gender alone imposes, and deconstruction has recently asserted what it claims has been an 'always already there' commitment to praxis.[9] Derrida himself, for example, has been compelled to address both racism and feminism, and the consequences for debate have been surprising. More moral outrage than analysis, Derrida's uncharacteristically essentializing reading of the word apartheid ('the most racist of racisms'[10]) for the catalog of *Art contre/against Apartheid*, 'Racism's last word', comes in for some corrective re-historicizing in the Anne McClintock and Rob Nixon response in the same volume of *'Race,' Writing and Difference* in which Derrida's piece is reprinted.[11] Gayatri Spivak's exposure of the imperialist text within the feminist text of Brontë's *Jane Eyre*, that darling of women's studies courses, is aimed at first-world, liberal humanist feminism. Spivak's deconstruction reveals that the same character, Jane Eyre, who from a purely feminist perspective may be celebrated for her self-possession, her agency in the world, her inalienable English right to self-determination, does so, when the lens is shifted, across the backs of dark madwomen, obscured colonial subjects, unacknowledged others.[12] Naomi Schor's 'This essentialism which is not one: coming to grips with Irigaray' is framed by a discussion of the politics of women's studies, in response to Derrida's 'Women in the Beehive' seminar, the transcription of which appears in *Men in Feminism*. Schor maintains that women's studies is not just another cell in the academic beehive. First she defuses the use of the word essentialism as the latest form of 'intellectual terrorism', and then she re-tropes exemplary essentialisms which might save women's studies from institutional recuperation. Biddy Martin's disruption of the singular boundedness of lesbian autobiography includes black, Hispanic, and Southern lesbian autobiographical writing in an essay on autobiographical identity, such that 'lesbianism comes to figure as something other than a totalizing self-identification . . . located on other than exclusively psychological grounds'.[13] Martin problematizes 1970s' notions of identity politics by interrogating the categorizing itself of lesbian autobiography for effacing the intersecting forces of race, class and gender. What all this recent work has in common is the conviction that what matters is precisely who is speaking, and who is being spoken for.

The politics of the subject, as an arena of exploration for both feminists and deconstructionists, has currently displaced meta-critical commentary on their separate methodologies and possible mutual intersections. The issue of identity is precisely the ground on which feminism and deconstruction part company, for deconstruction aims to undo essential selfhood where feminism recognizes the political necessity of affirming subjective agency. In deconstruction, identity has no priority or authority; subjectivity is the inevitable aftermath of a play of cultural forces; it never precedes, but is only constituted in language. Feminist critics who have worked to theorize a female subject, like Nancy K. Miller or Teresa de Lauretis, do so because even if representation is only a fiction, it is a necessary illusion upon which men have capitalized for centuries and to which women currently view access as crucial. (Barbara Christian and Jane Tompkins make similar points in *Gender and Theory*, although their stances toward theory differ from Miller's and de Lauretis's.[14]) To transcend the impasse sketched above, and to read texts like Jamaica Kincaid's *At The Bottom of the River*, feminist and deconstructionist readings must both give way to new critical articulations of subjectivity, some of them as yet unnamed.

'Girl'/'Blackness'/'At the Bottom of the River'

Three stories in Kincaid's collection, taken together, constitute a multivalent pronouncement on identity, and provide the occasion for shifting the terms of the debate to a new register. 'Girl', with which the collection opens, and 'Blackness' serve as companion pieces, articulating sometimes surprising attitudes toward gender and race as determinants of identity. These stories remind us that individual identity can be understood as unresolved contradiction, as the complex, mediating position between cultural determinism and the open-ended possibility that language offers. 'Girl', which seems to aim in its title either toward an essential definition or toward the designation of an individual girl, singular and self-contained, is in fact no more than a series of socially prescribed 'do's and don't's', spoken in what seems to be a mother's voice. Girl, then, we are told playfully, or gender, is not who you are but what you do: this is how you 'wash the white clothes on Monday and put them on the stone heap', 'cook pumpkin fritters in very hot sweet oil', 'make a good medicine for a cold', 'grow okra', how you must 'try to walk like a lady instead of the slut you are so bent on becoming' (pp. 3, 5, 4). The prescription for 'girl' in this text is wholly culturally specific yet cross-culturally resonant, because the social construction of femininity – domestic skills, manners and decorum, control of sexuality – is operative both in and beyond the Caribbean context. Girl, or gender, is a series of learned behaviors that are manipulable, as the initiating voice instructs: 'This is how to bully a man; this is how a man bullies you; this is how to love a man, and if this doesn't work there are other ways, and if they don't work don't feel too bad about giving up' (p. 5). Like Brave Orchid's 'talk-story' in Maxine Hong Kingston's *The Woman Warrior*, the unnamed teacher's lesson imparts a double message. It both enjoins and warns, both colludes with the culture that delimits a girl and sides with her in some subversion of that culture: 'Always squeeze bread to make sure it's fresh; *but what if the baker won't let me feel the bread?* you mean to say that after all you are really going to be the kind of woman who the baker won't let near the bread?' (p. 5). The playful tone of 'Girl', the humor with which gender is limited to how you enact (and escape) certain inherited catechisms of behavior rather than who you are, makes an important statement about the relative involvement of gender in what Kincaid will later call, in a story propelled by the insistent first-person 'I' missing in 'Girl', 'my individual self' (p. 47).

'Blackness', by contrast, speaks of something bigger than the self, something large enough to obscure it, absorb it, something ineluctably determining in the constitution of 'my nature' (p. 48): 'The blackness fills up a small room, a large field, an island, my own being. . . . The blackness cannot be separated from me but often I can stand outside it . . . The blackness is not my blood, though it flows through my veins' (p. 46). Although the story may be literally about the fall of night, it must also be read as an allegory of race-as-identity: even if we insist upon reading the story literally, it can only work if the narrator is black. (In fact the literal plane of the story only emerges after the allegory is worked through, because the title confrontationally foregrounds race rather than dusk; in fact, another story is called less ambiguously 'In the Night'.) The dominant trope of this story, as the quotation above demonstrates, is paradox: that 'blackness' both erases the self and allows it a place to hide; that blackness both makes identity more difficult and makes it possible at all. Where 'Girl' reads the imposition of gender as funny, or at the very least not life-threatening, 'Blackness' reads race as a profound determinant of identity which is, like the night that envelops her, both annihilating and liberating. 'In the blackness, then, I have been erased. I can no longer say my own name. I can no longer point to myself and say "I." In the black- ness my voice is silent. First, then, I have been my individual self, carefully banishing randomness from my existence, then I am swallowed up in the blackness so that I am one with it' (p. 47). Racial identity provides a sense of belonging, because she does not know who she is when she is all alone – 'what is my nature, then?' (p. 48) – yet that individual specificity apart from race alienates but also exhilarates her: 'How frightened I became once on looking down to see an oddly shaped, ash-colored object that I did not recognize at once to be a small part of my own foot. And how powerful I then found that moment, so that I was not at one with myself and I felt myself separate, like a brittle substance dashed and shattered, each separate part without knowledge of the other separate parts' (p. 48). The paradox here is that Kincaid gives us two oscillating configurations of an identity that is never stable or totalized: a notion of identity as contestation between the 'brittle substance' of an 'I' 'dashed and shattered' and the easeful suspension of selfhood under the fall of a defining darkness.

Clearly Kincaid's texts defy any prefabricated intersection of race, class and gender, and in their richness and density also prefigure the limits and necessary closures imposed by even this latest critical triad. The last story in the collection, 'At the Bottom of the River', ends with a meditation on aspects of identity that are outside even race, class and gender, and that cannot be explained by even that recent opening up of critical categories to broader political concerns. The last pages of the story by a black Carib- bean woman writer address the problem of identity both politically and privately, not forcing an opposition between them, leaving them inextri- cably linked. Kincaid even assigns to her speculative subject the classic pose of a figure regarding itself in a mirror: 'I saw myself clearly, as if I were looking through a pane of glass' (p. 79). Before the basin that reflects her image, the narrator 'stoops down and touches the deepest bottom' (p. 79), and the truths she uncovers are not necessarily housed in a gendered, racially marked body. This subject speaks from a place she cannot yet name:

> I stood up on the edge of the basin and felt myself move. But what self? For I had no feet, or hands, or head, or heart. It was as if those things – my feet, my hands, my head, my heart – having once been there, were now stripped away, as if I had been dipped again and again, over and over, in a large vat filled with some precious elements and were now reduced to something I yet had no name for. I had no name for what I had become, so new was it to me. . . . I stood as if I were a prism, many-sided and transparent, refracting and reflecting light as it reached me, light that could never be destroyed. And how beautiful I became. (p. 80)

Here fragmentation is no longer threatening. The brittle and shattered ego which willingly sought to resolve itself in blackness becomes a many-faceted prism, neither unified nor essential, but capable of endless refraction of a range of colors. In the last passage the narrator discovers some aspect of what it means to be human, 'perishable and transient', which is neither a function merely of race or sex or class and their intersections, but which nonetheless allows her to assume speaking subjectivity: 'my name filling up my mouth' (p. 82). Where no one is naming her – that is, where identity is exempt from hierarchical imposition, relational definition, or even critical fiat – she finds the exuberant space to name herself. Kincaid's story prefigures a moment when a spectrum of things will matter just as much to us as the race, class, and gender of the person who is speaking.

NOTES

1 We restrict ourselves necessarily here to the topic of feminism and deconstruction, but a parallel gendering occurs in the pairing of feminism and psychoanalysis. We allude, of course, to Juliet Mitchell's *Psychoanalysis and Feminism*, and to Jean Strouse's collection, *Women and Analysis*, but Jane Gallop's title is even more to the point: *The Daughter's Seduction: Feminism and Psychoanalysis*.

2   Bartkowski 1980; Derrida 1985 (for Kamuf); Miller 1986; Derrida 1982 (McDonald); Derrida 1976 (Spivak); Johnson 1980; Jacobus 1982; Jardine 1985. Duyfhuizen assumes, in his opening formulation, that feminist critics have learned their deconstruction from the Yale School, but in fact the feminist deconstructors we list are all trained in French and engage directly with Derrida.

3   Showalter 1983: 142.

4   Boone 1989: 159.

5   We are indebted to Linda Kauffman for pointing out Jardine's inflated rhetoric and her claims to the absolute uniqueness of her enterprise, which clearly contributes to Duyfhuizen's idealization of her project.

6   Spivak 1983: 169-95.

7   Willis 1988: 40.

8   Ibid.: 39.

9   In *The Ear of the Other* (1985), for example, Derrida takes on Nietzsche as a test case, as 'putative source and inspiration' of Nazi ideology, in Christopher Norris's words, to explore the moral and political implications of Nietzsche's text for contradictory future readings. This is an especially delicate operation for Derrida, as Nietzsche has also served as the source and inspiration of deconstruction. See Norris 1986: 61.

10 'Apartheid. . . . It is to the lowest degree, the last of a series, but also that which comes along at the end of a history, or in the last analysis, to carry out the law of some process and reveal the thing's truth, here finishing off the essence of evil, the worst, the essence at its very worst – as if there were something like a racism par excellence, the most racist of racisms' (Gates 1986: 330).

11 Derrida 1986; McClintock and Nixon 1986.

12 Spivak 1986: 262-80.

13 Martin 1988: 82.

14 Christian 1989; Tompkins 1989.

REFERENCES

Bartkowski, Frances 1980. 'Feminism and deconstruction: "a union forever deferred" ', *Enclitic*, 4. 2: 70-7.

Boone, Joseph Allen 1989. 'Of me(n) and feminism: who(se) is the sex that writes?', in *Gender and Theory: Dialogues on Feminist Criticism*, ed. Linda Kauffman. Oxford and New York: Basil Blackwell: 158-80.

Christian, Barbara 1989. 'The race for theory', in *Gender and Theory: Dialogues on Feminist Criticism*, ed. Linda Kauffman. Oxford and New York: Basil Blackwell: 225-37.

Culler, Jonathan 1982. *On Deconstruction: Theory and Criticism after Structuralism*. Ithaca: Cornell University Press.

de Lauretis, Teresa 1984. *Alice Doesn't: Feminism, Semiotics, Cinema*. Bloomington: Indiana University Press.

Derrida, Jacques 1976. *Of Grammatology*. Trans. Gayatri Chakravorty Spivak. Baltimore: Johns Hopkins University Press.

Derrida, Jacques 1982. 'Choreographies': interview by Christie V. McDonald, *Diacritics*, 12 (Summer): 66-76.

Derrida, Jacques 1985. *The Ear of the Other: Otobiography, Transference, Translation: Texts and Discussions*. Trans. Avital Ronell. New York: Schocken.

Derrida, Jacques 1986. 'Racism's last word', *'Race,' Writing and Difference*, ed. Henry Louis Gates. Chicago: University of Chicago Press: 329-38.

Derrida, Jacques 1987. 'Women in the beehive', in Jardine and Smith 1987: 189-203.

Diacritics. Special issue: 'Cherchez la femme', 12 (Summer 1982).

Duyfhuizen, Bernard 1984. 'Review essay: deconstruction and feminist literary theory', *Tulsa Studies in Women's Literature*, 3.1/2 (Spring/Fall): 159-69.

Gallop, Jane 1982. *The Daughter's Seduction: Feminism and Psychoanalysis*. Ithaca: Cornell University Press.

Gates, Henry Louis 1986. *'Race,' Writing, and Difference*. Chicago: University of Chicago Press.

Jacobus, Mary 1982. 'Is there a woman in this text?', *New Literary History*, 14: 117-41.

Jacobus, Mary 1979. *Women Writing and Writing About Women*. London: Croom Helm.

Jardine, Alice 1985. *Gynesis: Configurations of Woman and Modernity*. Ithaca: Cornell University Press.

Jardine, Alice and Smith, Paul (eds) 1987. *Men in Feminism*. New York and London: Methuen.

Johnson, Barbara 1980. *The Critical Difference: Essays in the Contemporary Rhetoric of Reading*. Baltimore: Johns Hopkins University Press.

Kauffman, Linda (ed.) 1989. *Gender and Theory: Dialogues on Feminist Criticism*. Oxford and New York: Basil Blackwell.

Kincaid, Jamaica 1985. *At The Bottom of the River*. New York: Random House.

McClintock, Anne and Nixon, Rob 1986. *'Race', Writing and Difference*, ed. Henry Louis Gates. Chicago: University of Chicago Press: 339-53.

Martin, Biddy 1988. 'Lesbian identity and autobiographical difference[s]', in *Life/Lines: Theorizing Women's Autobiography*, ed. Bella Brodzki and Celeste Schenck. Ithaca: Cornell University Press.

Miller, Nancy 1986. 'Arachnologies', in *The Poetics of Gender*. New York: Columbia University Press.

Mitchell, Juliet 1975. *Psychoanalysis and Feminism*. New York: Vintage.

Norris, Christopher 1986. 'Deconstruction against itself: Derrida and Nietzsche', *Diacritics* (Winter): 61-9.

Schor, Naomi 1987. 'This essentialism which is not one: coming to grips with Irigaray', paper given at Grinnell College, Conference on 'Reading and Writing the Female Body', October 1987.

Showalter, Elaine 1983. 'Critical cross-dressing: male feminists and the woman of the year', *Raritan*, 3.2 (Fall): 130-49.

Spivak, Gayatri Chakravorty 1983. 'Displacement and the discourse of woman', in *Displacement: Derrida and After*, ed. Mark Krupnick. Bloomington: Indiana University Press.

Spivak, Gayatri Chakravorty 1986. 'Three women's texts and a critique of imperialism', in *'Race,' Writing and Difference*, ed. Henry Louis Gates. Chicago: University of Chicago Press.

Strouse, Jean 1985. *Women and Analysis*. Boston: G. K. Hall.

Tompkins, Jane 1989. 'Me and my shadow', in *Gender and Theory: Dialogues on Feminist Criticism*, ed. Linda Kauffman. Oxford and New York: Basil Blackwell: 121-39.

Willis, Sharon 1988. 'Feminism's interrupted genealogies: Alice Jardine's *Gynesis: Configurations of Woman and Modernity*', *Diacritics*, 18 (Spring): 29-41.

Part III

Theories of the Body Politic: Global Perspectives

Like Brodzki and Schenck, Alice Parker is also interested in new conceptualizations of subjectivity. In 'Writing against Writing and other disruptions in recent French lesbian texts', she shows how French and Canadian lesbian writers are theorizing the lesbian, deconstructing the term 'woman', and developing new tropes and figures - like that of the hologram - to suggest the kaleidoscopic potential of gender, freed from bipolar habits of discursivity. Parker relates these writers' experiments to *écriture féminine*, showing how the term 'lesbian' marks the difference within feminism and foregrounds heterosexism within culture. For the lesbian writers Parker discusses, an ex-centric relationship to their culture manifests itself in four subversive writing strategies: corruption, interruption, disruption, and eruption. These strategies serve lesbian critiques of heterosexism, post-colonial imperialism, and male phallic economies.

In 'Phallic reflections and other ways of thinking', Amitai F. Avi-ram agrees that lesbian writing is a valuable mode of subversion, but he is skeptical about the power of writing, texts, and language to initiate revolution. In order to dramatize precisely what he thinks those who wish to revolt are up against, Avi-ram formulates his own concept of Phallic Man, obsessed with power, domination, and destruction, and unable to see either women, gay men, other races, or Third World cultures as anything but 'other-than-himself'. Intersubjectivity is thus foreclosed by phallic man's obsessions, neuroses, and violence.

In 'The political is the personal: the construction of identity in Nadine Gordimer's *Burger's Daughter*', Elizabeth A. Meese focuses on the novel's power to defamiliarize our constructions of identity - racial, sexual, familial, and political. How, Meese asks, can she define the place, South Africa; the place of women; or the place of a white woman writer like Gordimer? How does one who does not wish to be the One, engage the Other? Gordimer attacks white privilege, subordinates women's liberation to black liberation, and records betrayals within the Communist Party. The burger's daughter must rewrite the traditional oppositions of black/white, evil/good, master/

slave to escape false consciousness. She must also rewrite her personal identity in relation to collective identity in order to contribute to the revolutionary effort. Meese questions her own place as a white feminist literary critic, and asks what place we as readers should assume among the novel's revolutionary 'subjects'.

In 'Negotiating subject positions in an uneven world', R. Radhakrishnan contests the binary division of narrative in post-structuralist thought between history as representation and history as production. Writing as a 'male feminist, Third World, post-colonialist Indian subject', he records his personal and political responses to recent films about colonialism in order to illustrate the complexity of his multiple subject positions. He points out that the same complexity informs Meese's analysis of the black insurrectionists, of whites rethinking their values, and of Rosa Burger's competing preoccupations with womanhood, her family, and her country in Gordimer's novel. The fact that these subject positions and the narratives about them are grounded in history and are interrelated to other subject positions should, Radhakrishnan argues, displace absolutism and facilitate revolution.

11

Writing Against Writing and Other Disruptions in Recent French Lesbian Texts

Alice Parker

Writing really consists of unwriting.

Christiane Rochefort, *C'est bizarre, l'écriture*

A colonized knowledge and a truncated language.

Every woman knows that the interior of language contains a micro-language filled with glimpses and allusions that are specifically destined for her.

Claudine Herrmann, *Les Voleuses de langue*

Winged words are also clubs; language is a lure; paradise is also the inferno of discourse, no longer the confusion of language as in Babel, nor discord, but the grand ordinance, the putting into place of a strict sense, of a social sense.

And it is there, in the interval between locution and interlocution, that the conflict arises: the strange tearing, the tension in the movement that every human being makes from the particular to the general, when from the unique *I* of language without form, without frontiers, infinite, it becomes suddenly nothing or almost nothing - you, he, she: an interlocutor.

Monique Wittig, 'Le Lieu de l'action'

'i don't stop reading/deliring - excitation: what arouses the unrecorded in my skin.'

Nicole Brossard, *Lovhers*

In a recent talk the Québécoise writer, Nicole Brossard, stated that the woman writing positions herself 'against literature'.[1] The post-modern project of opening up the text to what she calls the 'inadmissible' repressed by dominant discourses in order to permit the free circulation of speech acts by lesbians and other marginalized groups is a revolutionary goal signaling a fundamental change in what Foucault called the 'episteme'. Such an epistemological shift would have to account for a newly conceptualized space of subjectivity, which, in depriviledging the mark of gender, opens into a u-topian field of post-colonial textuality. If lesbian works insist on the materiality of the body as text/text as body, it is because their project is intensely political. In Western culture, as Monique Wittig observed, the category of sex sticks to the body of woman; to wrench oneself free means reinventing words, language and discourse that mediate our relationship to history, to our selves and to each other.[2]

Lesbian texts play a particular role in current discussions of the problematics of sexual difference. Feminist theory factors gender and the material oppression of women into analyses of texts and discourses. As a difference within feminism, lesbian writing foregrounds the operations of heterosexism within culture. This includes the ideologies of love, marriage and the family, the institution of motherhood and reproduction, sexuality and the education of children as they are inflected in a phallic economy. All of these institutions and discourses have 'deformed' women's bodies and denied them ontological status. Thus lesbian writers heed Wittig's call 'to recite one's own body, to recite the body of the other [which] is to recite the words of which the book is made up. The fascination for writing the never previously written and the fascination for the unattained body proceed from the same desire.'[3] On a theoretical level lesbian works interrogate in Western metaphysics the founding of bipolar systems of conceptual thought in the paradigm of gender difference. They likewise offer a serious critique of the methods and therefore results of research in the social sciences ('les sciences humaines'), typically based upon an unproblematic understanding and acceptance of sexual difference. This means, as Monique Wittig asserts, that much 'scientific' information will have to be rejected, including the fundamental discoveries of psychoanalysis, until serious reconceptualization occurs.[4] Thus like the works of other marginal groups, lesbian works insist on a reading practice that keeps us politically alert, in this case to any reinscription of heterosexual privilege, and on a writing practice that disrupts narrative expectations, especially the grammar of gender relations.

Scenes of reading and writing in lesbian texts foreground gender, sexuality and the power relationship between them. It should be of concern to any theoretical enterprise which targets binarism that hetero-sexism infects every cultural institution and discourse. Why, as Foucault asked pointedly in his introduction to the memoir of Herculine Barbin, the nineteenth-century hermaphrodite, should there be one true sex for every human individual, and why, further, should truth-producing and truth-verifying mechanisms depend on such an outrageously hegemonic conception of the infinite play of sexual difference?[5] Jacques Derrida calls likewise for expanded categories of sexual difference, without, however, focusing on heterosexuality as an institution.[6] The lesbian reader/writer has an illicit (unreadable) relationship to culture. 'She' must force entry into the symbolic systems from which she is barred, subverting their discourses with traces of the covers she must don as she 'passes' from one arena to another.

If Woman has an exclusively negative valence according to psycho-analysis, being what is not spoken or represented, how much more proscriptive (inaccessible to writing) is the silence regarding lesbian experience. What Marie-Jo Bonnet calls the 'secret' in *Un Choix sans équivoque* ('An Unequivocal Choice'), 'has established itself outside of words, and in a certain way against words'. 'It is the space that we create to explore and experiment with what society denies, refuses and cannot digest.'[7] In the realm of the indigestible, lesbian texts locate themselves beyond the pale, in the uncanny. At the same time, the lesbian writer must be suspicious of the 'feminine' space privileged by post-structuralism variously called the unconscious, the imaginary (Lacan), the semiotic/chora (Kristeva), or the 'invagination' of a feminine practice of writing (Derrida). These spaces are used to represent an alterity from which we may retrieve what humanism and phallogocentrism repressed or margin-alized in the production of culture. Thus 'poetic language' (Kristeva) or 'écriture féminine' (Cixous) can be drawn out through rifts in the symbolic codes to which we are most often subjugated. However, for the lesbian reader/writer, doubly barred from symbolic processes that produce cultural meaning through language and socialization, the redistribution of signifying spaces falls out along the same heterosexual axes that have always oppressed 'her'.

A problematic status with regard to the symbolic contract can, however, generate rich texts. As Julia Kristeva observed of avant-garde texts and of the potential for negativity generated by feminism in 'La Femme ce n'est jamais ça' ('Woman is never that'),[8] the eccentric relationship of lesbian experience to the 'sociolect' can produce texts that are provocative and subversive, rich in dislocations of all kinds – pronouns, syntax, rhetorical figures, graphesis, intertextual plays and so on. How do these differ from other post-modern efforts to rewrite key literary conventions? In their critique of heterosexual codes lesbian texts add another level of interplay – an excess – to an already loaded scene of writing, thus precipitating out repressed ideology. Further, if traditional texts are auto-logical, referring always to the Same, circulating among men as Luce Irigaray asserts, then the only possibility for heterogeneity is to introduce radically disparate elements.[9] In 'How does one speak to literature?' (1977), Julia Kristeva writes (on Barthes): 'Desire causes the signifier to appear as heterogeneous and, inversely, indicates heterogeneity through and across the signifier. To posit that the subject is linked by its desire to the signifier is to say, therefore, that s/he has access through and across the signifier to what the symbolic does not make explicit, even if it translates it: instinctual drives, historical contradictions.'[10] The most occulted of all desire is surely lesbian desire, which 'through and across the signifier' is likely to unhinge the least suspecting text.

Corruption

Lesbian writing (and reading) is by definition corrupt. It holds no promise, however, for the male voyeur who could be anyone with a reading knowledge of nineteenth-century appropriations of lesbian materials.[11] In examining new theoretical strategies I am bracketing definitions of lesbian experience [what persons are included or excluded from the category 'lesbian', and the admissible contours of a lesbian life]. The discourse that privileges such concerns (a conscious, centered subject, free to will or direct her experience) has been carefully interrogated by Barthes, Foucault and Derrida, to mention only the fathers. What does interest me is how the term 'lesbian' functions in texts and in discourses, in its absence as well as in its inscription as a sign, and what other terms it displaces or calls into question.

Corruption is a particular kind of rupture with(in) an authorizing discourse and which the operations of post-structuralist thought do not necessarily engage. The problematics of author, subject, presence, origin, etc. occasion significant dislocations in interpretive strategies, but leave certain ideological constructions intact, precisely those that excluded from subjectivity groups that never had access to language. Thus it makes 'sense' to a feminist reader when Kristeva refers to the abyss between the sexes ('La Femme,' p. 22) that no communication can breach. But what of a voice that can speak from neither side: we might call that voice 'lesbian'. We know why Eve got into such trouble: she took Adam's apple. But who knows what Eve and the serpent might signify, because this is only the pre-text, at the least an unlikely (corrupt) pair.[12] We know that it is only at points of stress or maximum vulnerability – that erotic little heel which, long before Achilles, Cretan women painted red – where meaning can surface. It will carry traces of the depths or secret spaces from which it emerged, and of the trajectory of its passage from there to here and back again, because there is no locus for a 'lesbian' desire, no house, no church, no public or private space it can call home, or from which one can call it home as you call home a soul that has strayed from its body, by chanting its name.

A lesbian practice of writing that has had some success by inscribing not just a problematical relationship to culture but a defiant one is the rewriting of texts from the canon, which I shall explore further on. Another strategy is what I might call being as raunchy as the boys, which comes perilously close in some women writers (e.g. Erica Jong) to 'being' one of the boys. A third is the practice of pornography itself, which aligns a lesbian writer like Christiane Rochefort with such avant-garde practices as those of Genêt, Bataille and Burroughs. *Quand tu vas chez les femmes* (1982) is a study in abjection, but without the pathos that Kristeva accords the term in *The Powers of Horror*.[13] 'Let me be your slave,' cries the male narrator (a teacher!) to his idol, Malaure (my Laura), a photographer, who obligingly whips him and keeps a visual record of his con-trite postures. The corruption is here a travesty and a parody in a troubling but comic mode: political markers are scattered through the text, as when the narrator notes: 'I sometimes have the impression that Malaure is more intelligent than I; her thought flies to the conclusion in a single movement, while mine has to walk through, from one proposition to another.' And guessing his 'train' of thought she answers, 'It's because I am a woman' (p. 147). Thrown back upon his 'own' thoughts and the pitiful state of his body – dishwater hands and 'the negligence in which I was left down there', he 'collapses, sobbing, against her – but she didn't catch me, slipped away, I fell on my knees, she laughed, I missed the ground – I missed the Mother' (p. 148). This is in fact a text in drag. Like most pornography it centers on power, and on who will laugh last. The reader certainly finds small comfort in the appropriations that have been staged, given the fact that the ideological systems that tie sexuality and power remain intact. 'Naked, stripped of everything, I laugh myself to death and I am dying of it, I laugh my last instant, I will arrive my Lord before You, in joy. To do what? To make chocolate' (p. 195). Finis.

The anomalous status of the lesbian or radical feminist text makes it subject to/productive of another kind of rupture. These are internal ruptures within a system that Claudine Herrmann in *Les Voleuses de langue* called a 'colonized knowledge and a truncated language'.[14] But what seemed by definition in 1976 a radical place, the place of woman, from which to launch the thieving excursions into the father's language, no longer provides dependable footing: 'C'est en restant à ma place que j'ai tenté de rédiger ce travail' (p. 165). The notion of a fixed place, be it eccentric or marginal, does little to problematize the ideology of location, which at its worst can systematically dispossess a whole people, as we see in South Africa and in Guatemala where again a native majority is totally disempowered. Thus in working toward more fruitful paradigms we may not want to dismantle what Adrienne Rich calls a 'politics of location', which permits us to account for our place on the map and in history.[15] This means, as Gayatri Spivak observes, assuming full responsibility for the subject position we have been assigned.[16] For a North American it means a self-critical appraisal of the extent to which 'white feelings remain at the center' (Rich, p. 231), a refusal to countenance post-colonial imperialism, a refusal to speak for the Third World, coupled with an effort to provide a space in which Third-World peoples can be heard. For a lesbian it means validating all of the subject positions she occupies, while investigating other spaces from which social codes may be profitably criticized and/or dismantled.

In evaluating her subject position the lesbian feminist has to assume her covers as well as the modalities of passing that permit her to function in society. As complex strategies these can undermine the symbolic contract rather than reinforce invisibility. Literary inventions can likewise empower the writer to grant full ludic potential to the project of repealing/ rewriting the social text, dismantling the ideologies which support, for example, the exchange of women, the 'sexage' that appropriates women's work,[17] sexual service, procreation and property stewardship. Interventions in the scenes of reading and writing may also create new possibilities for relationships among 'subjects' by inventing women who can love themselves although they are positioned in language as objects, and further, who can love each other. 'Society, culture, discourse will be recognized as *sexed* and not like a universal monopoly of one sex which fails to acknowledge the imprint of the body and its morphology on imaginary and symbolic creations.'[18]

Interruption

A significant collective project for lesbian writers has been to contextualize the culture that history has denied them through a narrative that validates a lesbian tradition as well as the present materiality of lesbian lives. In addition to the overviews of historians and theorists like Jeannette Foster, Lillian Faderman, Marie-Jo Bonnet, Judy Grahn and Mary Daly, fiction writers like Monique Wittig and Nicole Brossard incorporate litanies of real and imagined names in their texts, a practice referred to by the latter as 'cortex' (corps/texte).[19] Others create theatrical pieces that re-stage stories such as those of Gertrude and Alice, or Freud's Dora.[20] This text has to be written and rewritten as the work of retrieval goes on so that forebears and peers who have been silenced and rendered invisible can once again surface in the text. The tools have been progressively refined as lesbian writers learn from other women writers and theorists how to inscribe the supplement of sexual difference. For example, Monique Wittig studies the work of Natalie Sarraute for insights into how the social system works through language in her continuing effort to analyze the symbolic function of pronouns. Sarraute offers her a model of two conflicting contracts in the relationship between the speaker (*je*) and the word (*parole*).[21] The interruption occurs in the progression from free wordplay and limitless undifferentiated potential of the subject to the insertion of the subject into a social system based on interrogation and interlocution. Such a discursive model permits Sarraute and Wittig to sidestep the developmental (oedipal) model of psychoanalysis, although obviously the two are conceptually analogous in their efforts to account for the insertion of the subject into discourse.

In the same article devoted to Sarraute, again referring to a problematics of location, Wittig states that the paradise and the hell of discourse are 'not the confusion of languages as in Babel, nor discord, but the grand ordering, the putting into place of a strict sense, of a social sense'.[22] Read this way, the chasm opens up not between the sexes but between locution and interlocution. The abyss occurs between a first language in which 'sense has not yet come, which is available to all, which any one can in turn take, use, curve toward a sense', where there are 'neither men nor women nor races nor oppression, nor anything but what can be named measure by measure, word by word', and another sort of pact introduced by the concept of interlocution. This is where the constitutive power of language takes over, before the I even opens its mouth to speak. As soon as the other [interlocutor] advances in its own words, as Sarraute observes, 'something emanates from it . . . like a fluid . . . like rays . . . under the influence of which it [the I] undergoes an operation in the process of which it is given a form, a body, a sex, an age. It is adorned with a sign like a mathematical formula summarizing a long development.'[23] Thus, notes Wittig:

> it is there in the interval between locution and interlocution that the conflict arises: the strange tearing, the tension in the movement from the particular to the general that every human being makes when from the unique I of language without form or frontiers, infinite, it becomes suddenly nothing or almost nothing, a you, he, she . . . an interlocutor.[24]

This drastic reduction or 'fall' is of great interest to women, and particularly to lesbians, if, as Wittig (following Sarraute) asserts, the problem is in the form of the contract: 'Every social actor uses this weapon of commonplaces (*lieux communs*) whatever his/her situation; it is the decadent form of the reciprocity that founded the contract of exchange.' There is no place outside the contract, however; the only place to rewrite it is in literature.[25]

Readers are familiar with at least some of the u-topian enterprises of Monique Wittig, whose project is to challenge overtly the tyranny of the 'mark of gender'.[26] Rather like Proust's homosexual subject which she analyzes in 'The Trojan Horse', the term 'lesbian' in her work functions as a war machine.[27] In a series of radical texts Wittig stages take-overs of the state (*Les Guérillères*), of the dictionary (*Brouillon pour un diction-naire des amantes*), of such seminal literary pieces as *The Divine Comedy* (*Virgile, Non*) and *Don Quixote* (*Le Voyage sans fin*).[28] She uses language to unsettle the pivotal terms of discourse. Focusing her attention on pronouns in her early works, she pursues her project to rewrite the body (*Le Corps lesbien*) and 'lesbianize' the language that mediates our perception of it. In accord with her project to deconstruct gender as the site of phallocentric ideology, Monique Wittig offers us varied operations on the sociolect/ideolect ranging from the socialization of children (*L'Opoponax*) to the elaboration of both dystopic and utopic visions of a gender-free future.[29] Thus each of Wittig's works from *Les Guérillères* (1969) on calls radically into question the constitutive and the epistemological functions of texts in writing the body. Entries under 'Language' and 'Word' in the dictionary she wrote with Sande Zeig show how the body can be reinscribed avoiding rigid, repressive syntax and fixed meanings (pp. 150; 173–4).

Hélène Cixous early (1975) designed the neologisms 'sext' and 'sextual' in order to emphasize the perception that textual space is always, already gendered.[30] Language has traditionally conflated sexual and genital, and has privileged the visual; the injunction to 'write' the body is a desire to recover and reassemble the missing pieces and senses, and to inscribe a new materiality in the text. Nicole Brossard states: 'It is with the whole surface of my skin that I work, that I seize an unedited version of reality.' Proceeding from the assumption that 'woman' is a male fantasy, radical French writers have been trying to 'put into words the ontological intuition and daily emotion we have of ourselves'.[31] But here they encounter an obstacle. Although sexual difference is a determining factor in the production of literary texts,[32] 'woman' paradoxically is barred from language and can only be represented as missing. She is not just castrated; she is absent from the symbolic order (Freud and Lacan). 'She' is the other, the not said, the not represented (Kristeva).

Writers have rushed to explore this negative valence or 'dark continent' (obviously analogous to other colonized spaces), to fill in the silence or 'lack' with feminist desire. This is an act of survival: Madeleine Gagnon points out that women of the past reacted to the fetishized female body constructed by the discourse of the fathers by attacking it with hysteria;[33] today young women are countering the violence of advertising with anorexia. Michèle Causse calls our condition a masochistic triad: castration (lack); violation (sexual service); the labor of childbirth (of the son, the substitute penis).[34] Translations from the material world come always already laden with cultural messages or codes; the best we can do from within the symbolic order from which we speak is to be as clear as possible about our angle of vision and the ground on which we are obliged to stand. Hélène Cixous and Luce Irigaray have been exploring, under the rubric 'écriture féminine', what it means to write for/as a woman. It is not just that the subject is multiple and speaks to us polyphonically; language in turn speaks through the subject polysemically, producing meaning through many kinds of processes.

Monique Wittig, following the early lead of Simone de Beauvoir, investigated how culture produces woman as a gendered object, and further, how the ideology of phallogocentrism affects the subject position of woman.[35] It is not enough to write 'as a woman', if the discursive structures that traditionally exclude 'woman' as 'subject' remain intact. Gagnon pointed out that one has to 'be' male in the inherited discourse to recognize and affirm oneself female. One of the projects of French feminist writers has been to slough off their old skins, the bodies assigned them by the fathers. Using a process dubbed variously gynesis, gynesthesia, gyn/ecology, writers use invention and imagination to inscribe a significant Absence. First, Michèle Causse notes, following the phenomenologists, one must see oneself reflected in the mirror of the other (woman).[36] 'Ecriture féminine' explores female libidinal economy, the (presumably) as-yet-ungendered pre-oedipal ground designated masculine by Freud and Lacan, and as an 'other' bisexuality by Cixous. In her sensuous prose Cixous recreates the space categorized by Freud as 'polymorphous', introducing new materials and structures into her work.

Monique Wittig, who rejects psychoanalysis, locates her utopian project in theory, myth, epic, and fantasy, unsettling and rewriting major cultural texts. In a recent article Wittig describes the assault on gender in her works as a series of operations on the personal pronoun, especially the first- and second-person subject pronouns which provide entry for the interlocutor into discourse. Her point is to accord the woman speaker, reduced traditionally to the realm of the particular, access to the universal.[37] If the body, a primary source of information about relationships between 'self' and 'world', can only be 'known' through the mediation of language, and if bodies are as subject to ideology as is the state, we shall have to rewrite every cultural text, displacing the 'I'/eye as authoritative, dispassionate observer: 'The j/e with a bar in *The Lesbian Body*', Wittig writes, 'is an *I* become so powerful that it can attack the order of heterosexuality in texts and assault so-called love, the heroes of love, and lesbianize them.' Wittig uses the lesbian subject to 'modify language at the lexical level', which 'would upset the structure itself and its functioning', as well as 'change the relation of words at the metaphorical level'. Her project is to 'change the coloration of words in relation to each other and their tonality. It is a transformation that would affect the conceptual-philosophical level and the political one as well as the poetic one.'[38]

Hetero/sexism is supported by a monosexual discourse (Derrida, Irigaray) in which the sender and receiver are presumed male, although objects exchanged may be female. In this scheme, the Name of the Father (Nom, non) activates a symbolic system (Lacan) into which male and female children are inserted as soon as they have access to language. Here Woman literally has no place. Her role, as Jane Gallop illustrated in *The Daughter's Seduction*, is ambiguous, seducer/seduced by her father.[39] In displacing subjectivity which is traditionally centered and gendered, the daughter may escape from the oedipal trap. Wittig uses the category 'lesbian' to dislodge categories of gender that keep the daughter from speaking in her own body. Similarly, she foregrounds the ideology that empowers the institution of mothering (*Dictionnaire*) through which the phallus covertly exercises its authority over the daughters, and topples the phallus from its centered position as privileged signifier, stripping it of its powerful mantle of metaphors and symbols. Already, in 1969, her Amazon odyssey (*Les Guérillères*) rematerialized the text, substituting new signs, incantations, naming procedures and graphesis for the language of the fathers, which, Wittig alleged is 'killing' us. *The Lesbian Body* went much further, deconstructing the fetishized, plastic body named female by the fathers. Unlike Cixous, Wittig does not 'feminize' the body with ecstatic paeons to breasts, hair, milk, classical mythic references and symbols like water and evocations of oceanic experiences. She refuses to extol conception, gestation and mothering. Rather, she takes the whole body apart, piece by piece, refusing to privilege particular organs, dissolving boundaries between inside and outside and visual indicators. The space she opens up for us is radically new.

In *Virgile, Non*, her rewriting of Dante's *Divine Comedy*, Wittig warns writers who continue to mark out the feminine according to metaphysical conventions that their vision of paradise, the flow of words from heaven, will 'disappear like an inverse hemorrage' (p. 64). Figures of style will not get you to heaven; 'don't let yourself get carried away with words, because it will not be without impunity' (p. 65). 'I will thus have to vomit it up on the spot, my handsome paradise, until I articulate no word that is not literal' (p. 66). Foregrounding both herself as subject and the scene of lesbian writing, she finally understands that she must write the libretto herself for the incomparable music she hears in her periodic approaches to paradise (p. 48). But first she must write her way through a lesbian taxonomy of hell and limbo, the material 'reality' of women's torments and deformities. The only way to paradise is to write it – if not, everything will be brutally erased (p. 22). And where could it be but San Francisco, the limbo of lesbian bars and the promise of heaven? In Wittig's celestial kitchen, which one could easily mistake for Golden Gate Park, preparations are under way for a huge lesbian picnic: 'certain angels have rolled up their sleeves' (p. 138).

Interruption: breaking and entering. To 'steal' the father's tongue, for Wittig, means entering consecrated texts without invitation, staging scenes of metaphorical and conceptual take-over, stressing the grammar and syntax to foreground concealed ideology and make new imagining possible. This includes rethinking categories of the real, the symbolic and the fictional, and blurring their boundaries.[40] Into her work figures, images and texts are reborn through a process of re-citation, which, like the journey of Quichotte and Panza in *The Constant Journey* (1985), is 'without end'. Writing is the resurrection, the word made flesh and the flesh made word, but with what a difference! The divine and hapless Quixote in Wittig's dramatic text changes gender with a flick of the pen, the knight errant redresses the wrongs of prose fiction. In promulgating 'new doctrines and new genres of existence', the spectator is positioned, at the end of the play, to re-evaluate the authorizing power of all texts, norms, sanity and insanity.[41] The revised signifying potential of the Quixote figure alters our perception of human destiny: through a *reductio ad absurdum* of the gendered subject as both hero and anti-hero Wittig can deconstruct the epic discourse on which Western prose narrative is founded (founders). The sword and the pen lose the privilege of gender.

All of her utopian/dystopian visions unsettle previous boundaries. Rather than separating herself from male discourse she uses topoi like the heroic (male) couple and the circles of hell to (re)present women's deformities under phallogocentrism, and to suggest alternatives. Wittig was one of the first to recognize that the body of woman is always already overdetermined, colonized, so that all of our cultural texts bear an unacknowledged burden of phallic fantasy and will to power. A curious story entitled 'One Day My Prince Will Come' had projected a physical counterpart to the exclusion of women from culture and language in their more privileged operations – access to universality and ontology. Here the women are reduced to tumescent objects without limbs or mobility, cared for like hothouse flowers in a garden of obscene delights in which every sense is supersaturated.[42]

Pornography is only the most blatant of the narrative crimes against woman. Rosalind Coward's book on the production of female desire by late capitalism intent on conscripting female pleasure for its own marketing needs (*Female Desires: How They are Sought, Bought and Packaged*) tells the same story.[43] The narrator in Canadian writer Jovette Marchessault's 'Lesbian Chronicle' demonstrates how the principle of gender functions to produce female 'anti-bodies' – the cure for hysteria.[44] Recognition ('only one or two drops of recognition will revive the dead body') and revolt lead her to the singular project of 'incarnating' herself (p. 68). Having moved from the path on which she had been trained to walk, she finds herself in a different kind of space. 'It took me an incredible amount of time merely to recognize my own hand stretched out in front of me. It took another incredibly long time merely to comprehend that I could speak, draw, and move my body and my limbs all by myself' (p. 69).

The project of these writers is to move us beyond repressive, oppositional paradigms toward new reading and writing practices. They show us how the term 'lesbian' can be made to function in discourse, what space/time and other less ponderable dimensions it occupies or opens up to, how it affects understanding and sensibility, what other terms it displaces. In calling gender as a cultural construct into question, radical French writers problematize not only bipolarities of which the prototypical pair is male/female (and in France the corollary cultural imperative, 'vive la différence'), but also the ideological pressures of heterosexism. They dislodge boundaries that marked the traditional heterosexual couple and patriarchal family with their inherited morass of eighteenth- and nineteenth-century bourgeois socio-cultural, economic and ethical discourses. These writers are fully aware of the process by which alien terms and rifts in the discourses unsettle the ideological systems that support them, and the resulting potential for re-producing norms and therefore meaning.

Disruption

The right-wing protest that the destruction of the nuclear family as a cultural and political unit has eroded all traditional values is right on target. Of course, what has really happened is that the 'men', fathers and sons, are bailing out and leaving the 'women' and children with their minimal earning power to manage resources at the domestic level. One could say this re-presents the final paroxysm of the ideologies of heterosexism and the family which privilege (accord power to) a single term, the male, who as patriarch is the exclusive subject and name of the family's productive capacity as an economic unit and as a unit of social meaning. So, 'he' takes his capital, the phallus, the privileged signifier, and pulls out. And now, without a companion, sexual partner or home, he is left with a terrific array of destructive toys, all modeled after an ideology of masculine needs and 'pleasures' that sound like rape, rape of women and children, often sanctioned by marriage and civil authority, rape of the environment, of outer space and the species that co-inhabit the earth. French theorists continue to insist that it all 'takes place' in language.

In *Parler n'est jamais neutre*, Luce Irigaray studies carefully the extent to which speaking, language, texts and discourse are always already sexed (male), 'andrological'.[45] Even psychoanalysis 'resubmits the unconscious to the most fundamental laws of consciousness . . . A theory of sexuality, it ignores the sexual determinations of its theory' (p. 285). It continues to order its truth in the name of its God, the Phallus (p. 291). In this system 'woman does not appear or at most signifies as a non-man, with only negative specificity, with only aporetic difference. . . . According to such a logic man/woman really only forms *one* notion, dichotomized and hierarchical' (p. 288). Irigaray theorizes that a female specificity can in fact be written, taking as its point of departure an-other logic, an-other mechanics, an-other ideality and iconic system, which she elaborates in the last three essays of the book, 'The language of man,' 'The limits of transfer,' and 'Is the subject of science sexed?'

Given the omnipresence of the phallus as privileged signifier, and the already-(hetero)sexed modality of discourse, a significant project has been to re-imagine what happens to the female child when she first encounters the symbolic order. Jocelyne François's *Joue-nous 'España'*, ('Play "España" for Us') is an attempt, like Wittig's *Opoponax*, to write a portrait of the artist as a young girl.[46] And like the latter, it was awarded a prestigious literary prize (Prix Femina, 1980) by judges who surely misread the text. Juxtaposed are images of women bearing in their heavy bodies the stigmata of culture and time, rooted to the earth in a provincial town from which there is no escape (pp. 9-10), and a young girl trying to find alternate codes by which to plot her life. Smiling, she recalls the 'conjugated voices' of her parents, saying 'Play "España" for us!' (p. 11). They were her 'partners in the field of force; . . . nothing had attenuated with the years, neither of us disarmed' (pp. 11-12). One of the movements of the text will be to deconstruct family ideology. Another will be to recapture early gestures of defiance and to open her text to the grammar and inflections of a specifically lesbian desire and relationship to the larger social body. This last project she had attempted with a good deal less success in two previous novels (*Les Bonheurs*, 1982, and *Les Amantes*, 1978). The work closes on the androgynous figure of a Chinese mortuary statue, a resting traveler, at once strong and gentle and ready for death, a model of her desire. She will never again play 'España', she says, but 'there remains the music that precedes instruments, which contains, clustered in silence, sounds that we alone may recognize' (pp. 218–19).

The writers I am examining (and those for whom I do not have space merit another chapter) occupy different theoretical positions, each of which constitutes a special kind of disruption. François is one of the least obviously political. In her latest novel, *The Story of Volubilis*, François displaces all relational boundaries in conjunction with her lesbian couple, beginning with the body, the many dimensions of human creative and engendering potential, including children, the creation of home, love and art.[47] Like Margaret Atwood, François refuses to be called a feminist, not because she is apolitical, but because she rejects political categories designed by others, in this case one which operates on an unproblematical assumption of gender. François uses the term 'lesbian' as an entrée into a particular reading and writing practice, as a key for decoding signs which might otherwise appear indecipherable like the ruins at Volubilis in present-day Morocco. Essentially, her work presents us with a hermeneutical or interpretive strategy. What she has us ponder is how the term 'lesbian' affects reading, writing, and textual production.

François has designed for us a textual study in consonance and dissidence, a lyrical e-vocation of desire played out in the brutally luminous landscape of her adopted country, the Vaucluse region of Provence in southern France. Potentially destructive and creative fields of energy are charted with meticulous attention to detail in a series of intertwining relationships among lovers, children, friends, the house and the town, and finally the Provençal landscape. These pull on each other with the fatality and often the violence of the Mistral, the cold wind that funnels down the Rhône valley from the Alps, turning the sky a deep violet blue. The texts of the children's lives continue to be played out on the mother's body. Dissident voices of son, son-in-law and an expatriate couple periodically escaping Paris almost unsettle the difficultly wrought harmony of art, life, landscape and work.

Informing the subtext is the absurd question: How can one be a

lesbian? While skirting the more obvious political problem of the relationship of gender as a cultural construction to sexual choice, the work tries to
respond to this query. Corollary questions are: how does language look at
a life; what chances do we have of leading the life of which we dream, of
dreaming the life we choose? In other words, how does discourse validate
or deny the life we think we are free to choose? As Freud and the post-
Freudians note, we are born twice, once of our mother, and once of our
father, into language, a difficult and dangerous transition for those of us
who will try to fit into the female gender, and against which we may
choose to protect ourselves by the discursive doubling which is lesbian.
So, we might ask, with François, especially in her earlier book on growing
up lesbian, *Play España for Us*, what chances do the privileged discourses
of our culture give us of choosing lesbian; what does choosing lesbian do
to/for the discourse within which we function even provisionally?

In *The Story of Volubilis* (Volubilis alluding both to the archaeological
site to which the lovers in her novel dream of returning, and, with a small
'v', to the morning glory flowers which the narrator's daughter lovingly
re-attaches to the house after they are battered by a summer storm),
François finds two sensitive points from which the discourse may be
treated, through language (poetry) and landscape (painting). Her two
lesbians are thus a poet and a painter; they work through a process of
continuous repetition and review (re-construction). The little Provençal
town permits them to strip themselves of many of their cultural bearings
in a systematic, artistically-controlled regression, not a talking cure but a
working one. The strategic retreat in Provence opens up a space that the
narrator and her newly constituted family thought they would have to go
to Volubilis in North Africa to find, and which they imagined only an
archaeological process could uncover.

The book takes as its point of construction a single phrase: What opens
upon pain is not lost. The sentence, separated into its components, identifies the different parts of the novel, beginning with a relative pronoun in
the nominative case. Immediately the boundaries and categories begin to
be redrawn. The town, the hills beyond, the house itself, have a potential
for life as great as that of any 'human' being. The women live poorly, on
the edge of penury, with disaster imminent in the form of destruction
from without by nuclear holocaust, the seduction of a new love affair that
tempts each of them at least once, threatening their internal code and the
precious journey on which they embarked so long ago, for they are now
past the middle of their lives, and the sheer difficulty of rekindling the

stoves each day is enough to daunt their courage. Perhaps even more dangerous are the dramas that rage about them, especially those of two of the young adult children, who must be dealt with lovingly but respectfully as they try to design lives for themselves, and be rescued periodically when their psychic resources run out.

François uses a third-person narration that becomes so intimate that the distance between first and third-person narration disappears. Little by little we are absorbed into a text that subtly changes all traditional assumptions of the relationships of social and cultural grammar. It is not easy to dig oneself out from one's discursive assumptions, comfortable, comforting truisms about the nature of reality and of communication. Sometimes, François writes, the invention of her daily life does not work at all, and then she and her lover, like sinking ships on an indifferent sea, can find no signal at all that functions (p. 149). Since no outsider can ever know our story, as we cannot know those of our children, but merely help them maintain a level of courage necessary to keep on designing and living them, we cannot ever be 'present' enough (p. 144). This conception of presence does not imply stasis or the linearity of traditional narrative, but rather the tuned-in quality of poetic language. It is essentially a suppression of the ego, of rules that impose a meta-distance on the dailiness of existence: 'all the same you have to come back down into the shadows of things, into the maze of streets, to eye level', she writes. 'Our height is walking level' (p. 142). When things seem to be in their places one must continuously wonder what these places are, and from what height.

The archaeological site figures here like a narrative one invents for an ancient civilization when one has lost all of the major codes. The term 'lesbian' signals the process by means of which the exploration occurs, uncovering layers of cultural sedimentation, attempting to recover and reassemble a life. One is reminded of the title poem of Adrienne Rich's collection, *Diving into the Wreck*.[48] For François, Volubilis represents a privileged moment when one can 'see distinctly the thread that joins things and beings' (p. 73). 'To go to Volubilis will be like erasing the foot prints, smoothing the earth all around, forgetting the incessant comings and goings to advance toward elsewhere, toward otherwise. Perhaps' (p. 73). This is a return ('to her origins of ignorance and fertility'). It conflates the vanished civilization and the morning glory that seems like a promise of grace in the world that has yet to be imagined. Why pay so much attention to reconceptualizing the family, and especially to inserting the lesbian family into the discourse on Western social structures? Since

Montesquieu in the eighteenth century the patriarchal family had func-
tioned as the micromodel for society and, especially, as the channel
through which authority flowed down to women and children. This is
why it is so difficult even today to get convictions on abuse charges; it
calls into question the entire concept of the state and its systems of control.

To theorize gender is to problematize man and woman as cultural
products. For Wittig and for François, in the latter only as a subtext, man
and the heterosexual couple are signs of danger. While Wittig rejects
mothering as an institution, François is content to revise the ideology that
supports it. Nicole Brossard seems untroubled by gender; she simply
expands the categories of man and woman, and the multiple possibilities
of their relationships until the symbolic system called the 'Name of the
Father' with the phallus as its privileged signifier is stressed to the point of
precipitating out new signs. As the narrator in François's novel observes,
she would like to find another word for family, one that has never before
'served'. 'She will surely invent one' (p. 23).

In Quebec, Marie-Claire Blais's somber novels target the naive optimism
of modernism which did not foresee that in the late twentieth century our
cruelty would have become 'immanent, functional, tied to the destructive
mechanisms' of our culture. How, she asks, do we deal with Dostoevski's
question, why the misfortunes of the world rest always on innocence.[49]
Visions d'Anna presents a series of polylogues, in which the voices slide
into each other, a world in which text and context have lost their
bearings, are 'drifting away' like Anna and her friends ('dériver' in
French means both drift and derive). We follow them into the lower
depths of post-modern sensibility and text, as they refuse to 'penetrate this
shameful old tapestry the world has become, the debility of their language'
(p. 33). Blais marks out difference in terms of class and category, problematizing myths of destiny and control. She recodes the master–slave dialectic
in terms of late-capitalist imperialism in which the earth has become a
continuous war zone. In their arrogance the rulers do not suffer from
Anna's incurable sickness, the indigestible blood of all those who are
slaughtered and tortured (pp. 65-6). Drifting through the materiality of
the world of the dispossessed, Anna (like her friends), 'a collection of
intense details that could be called a life', floats 'toward a better world
from which men would be banished' (pp. 70, 68).

The world that positions the phallus, unambiguously associated with
the male sexual organ, on the side of the assassins, makes survival itself a
form of repression (pp. 141, 162). It is always, already too late to

welcome a new life (p. 151). The only way to write this story is in Anna's 'obscure, impenetrable signs'; this is the only access to her inner life, like the rigid writing on Indian temples (p. 152). There is no renewal in Anna's return, when she leaves the isolation of her wanderings and the island of her room to permit a final embrace by her mother. Unlike the optimistic excursions of writers like Irigaray and Cixous into the feminine unconscious, neither the recurring signs nor the voices in Blais's novel promise any utopian source of rebirth. Perhaps this is because Blais grounds her texts unflinchingly in the cruel materiality wrought by the technocratic supports and the belligerence of late capitalism, late communism and the military dictatorships which are all essentially phallocentric in their basic structures and ideologies.

For Blais the enemy is interior as well as exterior, female as well as male. Death is all around, not just in the instinctual pulsations identified by Freud. In a recent play, *Winter Sleep*, Blais puts a dead man in the center of the script in which a 'reversible woman' plays a series of thankless roles – a woman, a make-up artist, a bourgeois mother, a man with a register who tallies things up and orders new slaughters: 'On your feet, to the fields, get your arms and kill everything alive! Don't leave anything; kill them all: forests, flies, women, children . . .' (p. 29). There are echoes of national anthems, French and American. The ensuing *danse macabre* is at once a beggar's opera and so intimate a reflection of 'everyday reality' as to create sensations of acute dis-ease. How else could a lesbian portray the pain of her life and the anguish of the nuclear age in which we live?

Eruption

A compatriot of Marie-Claire Blais, Nicole Brossard positions her writing project on the boundaries of genre, gender and thought itself. Like Wittig, Brossard meditates on gender, and how to tease out what is hidden in language and thought that produces hierarchies and the abuse of power. As a writer she has an advantage: she can slow down the act of writing in order to observe the mechanisms of thought.[50] 'I have even', she writes, 'learned to anticipate the blanks, to hear them without having to make myself altogether an echo.' These white spaces 'are in fact so filled with thoughts, words, sensations, hesitations and audacity that one can only translate the whole thing by a tautology, another blank, this one visual'

(p. 51). 'It is in the white space that anyone writes, trembles, dies and is reborn. Before and after everything is all right, because there is the text. And it fills a life quite well, a text! And every text is exemplary also because it bears witness to the process of thought, in its most simple expression as in its most exploratory trajectory' (p. 51). 'Reality', Brossard declares, 'is an apparent certitude that the textual real takes apart' (p. 68). Brossard's operation on 'reality' takes two forms: the equation of love and language, and the demonstration that writing as text permits the writer to 'think thought' (p. 75). The point is for the mind to confront the unspeakable, and what in our body confines us to the inadmissible in the realm of the symbolic (p. 88).

As Shoshana Felman writes of the dialogic relationship between the psychoanalytic and the performative in her book on Don Juan and J. L. Austin, *Le Scandale du corps parlant* (*The Literary Speech Act*), 'The real is not the negative reflection – the symmetrical opposite – of the specular: the two are *knotted together*. But the specular does not exhaust the real. The self-reflexiveness of consciousness, the linguistic self-referentiality of subjectivity no longer refer to an identity, but to a referential residue, to a performative excess.'[51] What psychoanalytic and performative theory have both discovered is enacted as language effects, a sort of 'writing on the real' (pp. 93, 94). The speech act destroys the dichotomy between the body and language; as Lacan observed, 'a body is speech arising as such.'[52] Speech acts record desire insofar as they 'do things with words', as the deceptively simple title of Austin's essays suggests (*How To Do Things With Words*). This 'doing' sets in motion an excess which inheres in language as its ludic potential. It is just such a game of performative excess that we see in many contemporary lesbian works. As Austin himself wrote: 'to feel the firm ground of prejudice slipping away is exhilarating.'[53]

Brossard opens her texts to novel inscriptions of desire and to what she calls a 'hologrammatic' coding of the body. As early as 1974, *french kiss* mapped out a new geography of the body/text/urban landscape.[54] The title is obviously provocative; Brossard proposes new alignments of the body as text and text as body, turning 'us outside in behind the window-dressing which was our programming' (p. 114). 'Ride astride grammar', declares the first sentence, a challenge that is answered in the body of the work by a variety of typefaces, white spaces, a cartoon sequence, as well as textual innovations and improvisations and figures, especially a figure that recurs in her writing: the hologram. The last sentence echoes the first, following a paragraph that begins 'What's left for our story is to break up and be lost. *Expenditure* for a sign.' The 'sightseeing' in which the reader has been engaged has 'dislocated cosmogony' – a necessary prelude to a new kind of writing. After chapter breaks from 'Once' to 'Twenty Times' Brossard slows down to comment on the title: 'A wish: to abolish walls between mouths' (p. 57). Tongue in cheek or somewhere else Brossard suggests: 'Flip out under one's pal', but then concludes 'She rides eager astride the delible ink' (p. 122). In between are extraordinary pages in which 'Understanding is a sojourn. The story I have to tell, the furthest reaches, a version of love' (p. 100). It is also 'A journey/a reading'; 'Let's say she feels like a fiction laboratory' (pp. 96, 97).

picture theory (1982), with another English title, again explores the possibility of inscribing the body hologrammatically in the text.[55] 'Skin/link: yes the tongue could be reconstituted in three dimensions beginning with the part called pleasure where the lesbian body, tongue and energy are fused . . .' (p. 188). Word plays, foreign phrases and conscious intertextual allusions, neologisms and textual inter/ruptions and cor/ruptions, poems and prose, destroy linearity as they question master discourses and binarity, including male/female polarity. 'Utopia would be a fiction from which the generic body of the thinking woman would emerge' (p. 165). *picture theory* foregrounds surfaces like *skin* and *screen*, making them into tri-dimensional fields, so that the plane is not just inscribed in space but charged with energy like 'meteorites in the text' (p. 130); skin merges with spin and screen with scream to displace boundaries and categories which, like the hologram, unsettle stereoscopic vision.

A lesbian version of love is of course the discourse that unsettles all the others. A key project of Brossard is her 'lesbian triptych', *L'Amèr* (1977), *Le Sens apparent* (1980), and *Amantes* (1980).[56] As Barbara Godard notes in the preface to her translation of the third volume, *Lovhers*, Brossard uses doubling, paradox and the figure of the spiral to convey 'the mobility and multiplicity, the indeterminacy of the lesbian text' (p. 9). Texts here grow out of other texts in a rich lesbian tradition from Renée Vivien (reborn with the century) and Gertrude Stein to the present generation of radical feminists. Citing Wittig, Brossard reminds us that if we cannot remember (re-member), we must invent (p. 45; Wittig 1969: 127). The female body, written by the text, may be tortured as a phrase is tortured, and as women have been tortured forever under

patriarchy (p. 51), 'the open veins of biographies' (p. 40), or dismembered
(p. 100). Or the excess may move toward ecstasy, an excess of intelligence, of desire encoded in the spiral of the chambered nautilus. The
mixture of prose and poetry is laden with word plays, intertextual plays,
and inventions of all sorts, as in the early refrain: 'I do not stop reading',
(JE N'ARRÊTE PAS DE LIRE) where 'de lire' means 'reading', 'delirium',
and 'un-reading'.

At the center of a rich scene of feminist writing in Quebec, Nicole
Brossard is at once the most radical, experimental practitioner and the
most productive, with more than twenty books since 1965. Early associated with the 'language' poets, her continuous subject is writing itself,
her constant love affair is with the word, which makes all of her work
sensual, erotic and performative. What does it enact? The Brossardian
text eludes categories as poetry speaks theory, and fiction theorizes
reading/writing practices. Recurring figures like the horizon or 'aerial
letter' defy laws of gravity and syntax; poetic rhythms and images renew
the imaginary and the symbolic, opening up a space for the lesbian writing
subject to enjoy herself (jouir).[57] A 'white light' profiles a 'double
impression' (the unspeakable/unwritten) that radiates, ignites, inscribes
itself in newly rounded characters, with a movement that shimmers like
beauty, making the world vacillate (p. 130). 'Initiating and initiated
texts', (p. 8), Brossard's work encodes the lesbian body and lesbian desire,
exciting and inciting the reader to 'imperil reality, like an invitation to
knowledge' (*Amantes*, p. 12). Always attentive to the potential for
reading/writing practices to transform subjectivity, the social text and the
imaginary, Brossard's latest fiction, *Le Désert mauve*, is a project in
(lesbian) self-translation, or trans-literation. Translation, as Liana Borghi
explains, is literally a 'corps-à-corps' with the text, a physical as well as a
creative re-production.[58] Brossard plays in the work with doubling (to the
'sixth' sense) pairs of figures: the lesbian lovers, of which one is also a
mother-daughter unit; the women who seduce each other and call for
(lesbian) daughters, who when the time comes will re-discover their
affinities; the 'writer' and 'translator' who produce mirror texts; the
desert, listed in the translator's notebook as a 'dimension', at once rawly
material and abstract, anatomical, through effects of light and ecology; the
time/space of night and dawn; the photograph portfolio of the faceless
'long man' hidden in the middle of the book and of the translator's notebook, and the revolver that is secreted away in a drawer or glove compart-
ment; the engineer's explosion that foretells nuclear holocaust, and the

dawn that 'bends reality toward the light'.[59] Although the fifteen-year-old narrator must deal too young with the death that stalks us (if we forget to be vigilant), and she cannot (yet) suffer intimacy, the mauve horizon is a promise that our voices, lesbian voices, will continue to translate scenes of a continuously spiraling energy. The lesbian writer, facing a text, is always/already (her) double; in her attempt to write the double impression of a double version (Brossard's terms), she no longer needs the copulative 'and', only versions (turnings) of 'fiction dormant in its surface hole . . . devouring the apparent sense', a 'delirium' (unreading) 'history, rending the surface story'.[60]

Like Wittig, Brossard is concerned with 'a structural change in language, in its nerves, its framing'.[61] Why language? The writers I have been exploring share the post-structuralist view that what humanistic thought called reality and nature can only be approached through language, and that to effect change in the dominant discourse as the scene of ideological oppression is the first order of business. I like to think that French lesbian writers on both sides of the Atlantic are engaged in projects that complement those of Cixous and others exploring 'écriture féminine', which inscribes subjectively a space hitherto uncharted through a sort of systematic regression to the sources of thought and feeling, and those of French theorists and writers who refuse to be called feminists. Of these Julia Kristeva is the most problematic, seemingly rejecting both women and lesbians. As a reader/writer I must keep in mind my difference as a woman/lesbian/feminist while bearing equally in mind historical proscriptions and ideological pressures on the terms. Thus I refuse to choose between writing with a difference, what Mary Daly calls 'cerebral spinning' and what Judy Grahn calls 'Another mother tongue', and the post-structuralist critique of binary structures which must continue to question the paradigmatic status of gender marking.[62] Rather than an eclectic methodology which I see as apolitical, I prefer to view my position as heterogeneous and polyvalent.

Kristeva interests me precisely because of her radical interrogation of linguistics, psychoanalysis and feminism. She helps us analyze the ways in which discourse can be subverted, the ways in which symbolic structures function to exclude woman, and the possibility of gaining access to the Imaginary (semiotic, Chora). We need to follow her project closely since she is engaged in it as a woman; her subject and subject position are marked so that as she wanders at the edge of thought she takes us with her. Writing of the difficulty of gaining access to childhood in Western thought, she evokes the 'confrontation of thought with what it is not, wandering to/at limits of the thinkable'.[63] The study of childhood, the maternal bond, and infantile language – where the child and parent telescope – is precisely the project for/of a woman. By definition the woman has a difficult relationship to the other (object) and to love (p. 475). The preconditions for language acquisition, 'topological latencies', the entrance into syntax, the 'symbolic space of designation of the body itself' (p. 490) are of special interest to the (woman) writer.

Brossard sees us entering an era of simulation in which we will slide, weightless, on the surface of reality. Writing in the feminine will take place, if we can use such an expression, in an other world. The term 'lesbian' opens up the discursive space that permits the writer to (re)think thought; in writing against writing, in journeys through writing, we no longer need our genders as we don identities which are continuously displaced like the image of the hologram on the retina. 'It is the consciousness of the plural I that gives access to the word, to desire, to the project and to writing.'[64] Let us leave this plurality without categories that could presently be named, its ludic potential intact, polymorphous, and as Wittig tried to imagine the lesbian body, eroticized or tuned to life rather than death in every cell, membrane and member. 'A body, a text, which send me echoes of a territory I have lost and that I seek . . . Territory of the mother, which is to say that if this heterogeneous body, if this risk-taking text are givers of sense, of identity or of pleasure [*jouissance*], it will be in an altogether different way than a "Name of the Father".'[65] Brossard's spiral rejoins Kristeva's voyage, which must be undertaken continuously, on location or even without a location. 'The ruse of the female voyager, contrary to the Hellenic ruse, consists in not having a "chez soi," in considering every home a place . . . of the Other, and exasperated by its fixity to refuse it', to continually displace it, to remake it, to dissolve it.[66] Let us imagine the lesbian, the woman, as a space from which to relativize and to radicalize all textual and theoretical enter-prises. It is a space rather than a location from which new meanings may continuously e-merge.

NOTES

1 I have translated all of the epigraphs except the last, which comes from *Lovhers*, Barbara Godard's translation of *Amantes*, p. 20 (see notes 19 and 44). The French texts follow:

'Ecrire consiste vraiment à désécrire.' (Christiane Rochefort)

'Un savoir colonisé et un langage truqué.'

'Toute femme sait qu'il existe à l'intérieur du langage un micro-langage bourré de clins d'oeil et d'allusion qui lui est spécifiquement destiné.' (Claudine Herrmann)

'Les paroles ailées sont aussi des matraques, le langage est un leurre, le paradis c'est aussi l'enfer des discours, non plus la confusion des langues comme à Babel, ni la discorde, mais le grand ordonnancement, la mise au pas d'un sens strict, d'un sens social.'

'Et c'est là dans l'intervalle entre la locution et l'interlocution que le conflit surgit: l'étrange déchirement, la tension dans le mouvement du particulier au général que fait tout être humain, quand de *je* unique de la langue, sans formes, sans frontières, infini, il devient tout à coup rien ou presque rien, tu, vous, il, elle . . . un interlocuteur.' (Monique Wittig)

'je n'arrête pas de lire - excitation: ce qui me suscite inédit dans ma peau.' (Nicole Brossard)

Nicole Brossard spoke at the South Atlantic Modern Language Association meeting in November 1986. My translation.

2   Wittig 1982a: 68. I will be relying heavily on Wittig as a lesbian theorist, and on Brossard as a theorist of writing. Where possible I have used standard translations. For secondary material on Wittig see the 'spécial Monique Wittig' issue of *Vlasta*, 4 (1985).

3   Wittig 1975: 10.

4   Wittig 1982b: 83.

5   Foucault 1980: vii-xi.

6   Derrida 1984: 15: 'But there is another neutralization which can simply neutralize the sexual opposition, and not sexual difference, liberating the field of sexuality for a very *different* sexuality, a more multiple one. At that point there would be no more sexes . . . there would be one sex for each time. One sex for each gift.'

7   Bonnet 1981: 227; 229.

8   Kristeva 1974: 23-4. This was an interview with the 'Psychanalyse et Politique' group of the MLF, later collected in *Polylogue*.

9   Irigaray 1985: 282-91.

10   Kristeva 1980: 116.

11   Following Diderot's 'trouvaille', the wonderful discovery suggested by Mme d'Epinay that the lesbian Mother Superior in *La Religieuse* should cry out to her confessor: 'My father, I am *damned*' (my emphasis), although Diderot believed neither in hell nor God, and thought lesbianism a psycho-physiological disturbance, there was a whole series of 'lesbian' novels by male authors, culminating in Baudelaire's portrayal of 'les femmes damnées'. These images are so persuasive that twentieth-century critics continue to read the work of Renée Vivien, the first authentic 'lesbian' writer since Sappho, through a screen of Baudelairean/decadent aesthetics. See Parker 1986a and 1986b.

12   See Stone 1976: 198-223.

13   Rochefort 1982; Kristeva 1982. Kristeva calls this work her 'descent into the hell of naming, that is to say of signifiable identity' (p. 207).

14   Herrmann 1976: 9.

15 Rich 1986: 210-31.
16 Spivak 1988.
17 On the appropriation of women and the term 'sexage' see Guillaumin 1978: 5-30, esp. 21.
18 Irigaray 1984: 63-73, esp. 70-2.
19 Used throughout her work, the term 'cortex' foregrounds the lesbian body and intertext for Brossard; see Barbara Godard's introduction to *Lovhers* (Montreal: Guernica, 1986): 8.
20 Marchessault 1984; Cixous 1976. Lesbian feminist theatre, alive and well in Paris and Montreal, deserves another chapter.
21 Wittig 1984a: 69-75, esp. 71-5.
22 Ibid.: 74.
23 Sarraute 1980: 91.
24 Wittig 1984a: 74.
25 Ibid.: 75.
26 Wittig 1985a: 3-12.
27 Wittig 1984b: 45-9.
28 Wittig 1969; 1976 (with Sande Zeig); 1985b; 1985c.
29 Wittig 1964. *L'Opoponax* was awarded the prestigious Prix Médicis by critics who certainly did not read it as a lesbian novel.
30 Cixous 1975: 39-54; trans. in *Signs*, 1 (1976): 875-99; esp. 885.
31 Brossard 1983: 34; 36.
32 Johnson 1980: 33.
33 Gagnon 1977: 64.
34 Causse 1983: 14. A major lacuna in this essay is an appraisal of Michèle Causse's own writing, which I hope to remedy when I collect the pieces for a book on radical feminist and lesbian writers working in France and Canada.
35 Wittig 1982b: 75-84.
36 Causse 1983: 19.
37 Wittig 1985a: 5-6.
38 Ibid.: 11.
39 Gallop 1982.
40 Wittig 1975: 9-10.
41 See Wittig 1985c: 44-52.
42 Wittig 1978: 31-9. One of the only untranslated pieces.
43 Coward 1984/5.
44 Marchessault 1985: 67.
45 Irigaray 1985: 282.
46 François 1980.
47 François 1986.
48 Rich 1973: 22-4.
49 Blais 1982: 42. Blais is a prolific novelist whose award-winning *Une Saison dans la vie d'Emmanuel* (1965) was followed by eleven other novels, numerous plays and two books of poetry.
50 Brossard 1984b: 51.
51 Felman 1983: 81.

52 Cited by Felman 1980: 94.
53 Austin 1975: 61; cited by Felman 1980: 121.
54 Brossard 1974b. I use the English translation by Patricia Claxton (Toronto: The Coach House Press, 1986) for citations.
55 Brossard 1982. My translations.
56 Brossard 1980a. I use the French edition for references which follow, and my own translations.
57 An important collection of theoretical texts, *La Lettre aérienne* (Brossard 1985) has just been translated by Marlene Wildeman (*The Aerial Letter*, Toronto: The Women's Press, 1988). See Brossard's collection of poems and texts, *Double Impression* (1984a: 130-2).
58 In a private interview with the Italian publisher and writer.
59 Brossard 1987; inscribed on the title page: 'pour faire pencher la lumière du côté de la réalité', reversing a phrase on p. 14, 'j'appuyais sur mes pensées pour qu'elles penchent la réalité du côté de la lumière.'
60 Brossard 1980b: 76.
61 Wittig 1985a: 7.
62 Daly 1978. See the last chapter: 'Spinning: cosmic tapestries'; Grahn 1984: *passim*.
63 Kristeva, 'Noms de lieu', in Kristeva 1977: 472.
64 Brossard 1983: 97.
65 Kristeva, 'Polylogue' in Kristeva 1977: 177.
66 Kristeva, 'D'Ithaca à New York', in Kristeva 1977: 515, 495.

REFERENCES

Austin, J. L. 1975. *How To Do Things With Words*. Cambridge: Harvard University Press (2nd edn).

Blais, Marie-Claire 1982. *Visions d'Anna*. Paris: Gallimard.

Bonnet, Marie-Jo 1981. *Un Choix sans équivoque*. Paris: Denoel.

Brossard, Nicole 1974. *french kiss*. Montreal: Les Quinze. Trans. Patricia Claxton, Toronto: The Coach House Press, 1986.

Brossard, Nicole 1977. *L'Amèr*. Montreal: Les Quinze.

Brossard, Nicole 1980a. *Amantes*. Montreal: Les Quinze. Trans. Barbara Godard (*Lovhers*), Montreal: Guernica, 1986.

Brossard, Nicole 1980b. *Le Sens apparent*. Paris: Flammarion.

Brossard, Nicole 1982. *picture theory*. Montreal: Nouvelle Optique.

Brossard, Nicole 1983. 'Rencontre avec Nicole Brossard.' *Vlasta*, 1: 32-9.

Brossard, Nicole 1984a. *Double Impression*. Montreal: l'Hexagone.

Brossard, Nicole 1984b. *Journal intime*. Montreal: Les Herbes rouges.

Brossard, Nicole 1985. *La Lettre aérienne*. Montreal: les éditions du remue-menage. Trans. Marlene Wildeman (*The Aerial Letter*), Toronto: The Women's Press, 1988.

Brossard, Nicole 1987. *Le Désert mauve*. Montreal: l'Hexagone.

Causse, Michèle 1983. 'Le Monde comme volonté et comme représentation', *Vlasta*, 1: 10-25.

Cixous, Hélène 1975. 'Le Rire de la Méduse', *L'Arc*: 39-54.

Cixous, Hélène 1976. 'Portrait de Dora', in *Théâtre*. Paris: des femmes.

Coward, Rosalind 1984/5. *Female Desires: How They Are Sought, Bought and Packaged*. New York: Grove Press, 1985; London: Paladin, 1984.

Daly, Mary 1978. *Gyn/Ecology*. Boston: Beacon Press.

Derrida, Jacques 1984. 'Women in the Beehive: A seminar with Jacques Derrida', *subjects/objects*, 2: 5-19.

Felman, Shoshana 1983. *The Literary Speech Act: Don Juan with J. L. Austin or Seduction in Two Languages*. Ithaca, NY: Cornell University Press.

Foucault, Michel (ed.) 1980. Introduction to *Herculine Barbin, Being the Recently Discovered Memoirs of a Nineteenth-Century Hermaphrodite*, vii-xvii. Trans. Richard McDougall. New York: Pantheon Books.

François, Jocelyne 1978. *Les Amantes*. Paris: Mercure de France.

François, Jocelyne 1980. *Joue-nous 'España'*. Paris: Mercure de France.

François, Jocelyne 1982. *Les Bonheurs*. Paris: Mercure de France.

François, Jocelyne 1986. *Histoire de Volubilis*. Paris: Mercure de France.

Gagnon, Madeleine 1977. 'Mon Corps dans l'écriture', in H. Cixous, M. Gagnon and A. Leclerc, *La Venue à l'écriture*. Paris: Union générale d'éditions.

Gallop, Jane 1982. *The Daughter's Seduction: Feminism and Psychoanalysis*. Ithaca, NY: Cornell University Press.

Grahn, Judy 1984. *Another Mother Tongue*. Boston: Beacon Press.

Guillaumin, Colette 1978. 'Pratique du pouvoir et idée de Nature', *Questions féministes*, 2: 5-30.

Herrmann, Claudine 1976. *Les Voleuses de langue*. Paris: des femmes.

Irigaray, Luce 1984. 'L'Amour de soi', in *Ethique de la différence sexuelle*: 63-73. Paris: Editions de Minuit.

Irigaray, Luce 1985. 'Le Langage de l'homme', in *Parler n'est jamais neutre*. Paris: Editions de Minuit: 282-91.

Johnson, Barbara 1980. *The Critical Difference*. Baltimore: Johns Hopkins University Press.

Kristeva, Julia 1977. *Polylogue*. Paris: Editions du Seuil.

Kristeva, Julia 1980. *Desire in Language*. Trans. Thomas Gora, Alice Jardine, and Leon Roudiez. New York: Columbia University Press

Kristeva, Julia 1982. *The Powers of Horror*. Trans. Leon Roudiez. New York: Columbia University Press.

Marchessault, Jovette 1984. *Alice & Gertrude, Natalie & Renée et ce cher Ernest*. Montreal: Les Editions de la pleine lune.

Marchessault, Jovette 1985. *Lesbian Triptych*. Trans. Yvonne Klein. Toronto: The Women's Press. *Tryptique lesbien*. Ottawa: Les Editions de la pleine lune, 1980.

Parker, Alice 1986a. 'Did/Erotica: Diderot's contribution to the history of sexuality', in *Diderot Studies 22*. Geneva: Droz.

Parker, Alice 1986b. 'Renée Vivien in the Night Garden of the Spirit', in *Aspects of Fantasy*, ed. William Coyle. Westport, CO: Greenwood Press.

Rich, Adrienne 1973. *Diving into the Wreck*. New York: W. W. Norton.

Rich, Adrienne 1986. 'Notes toward a politics of location', in *Blood, Bread and Poetry*. New York: W. W. Norton: 210-31.

Rochefort, Christiane 1971. *C'est bizarre l'écriture*. Paris: Grasset.

Rochefort, Christiane 1982. *Quand tu vas chez les femmes*. Paris: Grasset.

Sarraute, Nathalie 1980. *L'Usage de la parole*. Paris: Gallimard.

Spivak, Gayatri Chakravorty 1988. Response to 'The Differences Within: Feminism and Critical Theory'. Amsterdam: John Benjamins.

Stone, Merlin 1976. 'Unraveling the myth of Adam and Eve', in *When God Was a Woman*. New York: Harcourt, Brace, Jovanovich: 198-223.

Wittig, Monique 1964. *L'Opoponax*. Paris: Editions de Minuit.

Wittig, Monique 1969. *Les Guérillères*. Paris: Editions de Minuit.

Wittig, Monique 1975. *The Lesbian Body*. Trans. David LeVay of *Le Corps lesbien*. New York: Morrow.

Wittig, Monique 1976. *Brouillon pour un dictionnaire des amantes*. (With Sande Zeig.) Paris: Grasset.

Wittig, Monique 1978. 'Un Jour mon prince viendra', *Questions féministes*, 2: 31-9.

Wittig, Monique 1982a. 'The category of sex', *Feminist Issues*, 2: 63-8.

Wittig, Monique 1982b. 'On ne naît pas femme', *Questions féministes*, 8: 75-84.

Wittig, Monique 1984a. 'Le Lieu de l'action', *Digraphe*, 32: 69-75.

Wittig, Monique 1984b. 'The Trojan Horse', *Feminist Issues*, 4: 45-9.

Wittig, Monique 1985a. 'The mark of gender', *Feminist Issues*, 5: 3-12.

Wittig, Monique 1985b. *Virgile, Non*. Paris: Editions de Minuit.

Wittig, Monique 1985c. *Le Voyage sans fin* (*The Constant Journey*). Special Supplement to *Vlasta*, 4.

12

Phallic Reflections and Other Ways of Thinking

Amitai F. Avi-ram

Alice Parker's essay, 'Writing against writing and other disruptions in recent French lesbian texts', presents a theoretical framework which Parker makes most explicit near the end: 'What humanistic thought called reality and nature can only be approached through language, and . . . to effect change in the dominant discourse as the scene of ideological oppression is the first order of business' (p. 233). Parker emphasizes repeatedly the articulation of the (apparently) unspoken or unspeakable in lesbian texts and the (apparently) unique challenge that these lesbian texts pose to conventional thought and its inherent prejudices. This challenge takes the forms she enumerates of corruption, disruption, interruption, and eruption.

What follows is an effort to respond to Parker's essay by sketching out a rudimentary theory of my own. This theory will attempt to place in a larger perspective the interrelations between the dominant discourse (and other exercises of power) and discourses that challenge that power, including, but not limited to, lesbian discourse. In so doing, I question Parker's assumption of a neat identification between 'male' (as a 'biological' category of perception) and 'phallic' (as a category of social power), and I also question the ultimate value of directing revolution against the notion of gender itself rather than against the notion of gender as we have come to use it. At the same time, I hope to challenge what I see as Parker's and her authors' assumption of privilege for the lesbian writer as somehow the essence of revolution. As I see it, lesbian writing may partake in a complex and many-sided structure of revolution, just as it also complies with and contributes to systems of power.

An essential habit in the Western tradition of ideas is to explain things in the real world by tracing them to some cause or reducing them to a principle that is somehow prior or original. Thus we try to explain various realities, psychic and social, by tracing them to language. If we could only change that language, then we could change our world and attack the sources of pain and suffering at their roots.

But this is only one way of thinking, and while it is the dominant mode of criticism today, it is nevertheless inadequate. The inadequacies of cause-and-effect logic as the basis of theory have been exposed in such fields as advanced physics, psychoanalysis, sociology, and anthropology, as well as art and literary criticism. There is at least one other possible way of thinking, one which I shall remind us of even though I shall soon abandon it in order consciously, if temporarily, to pursue the usual course of cause-and-effect myth. This way of thinking does not have a name, but it has something to do with systems. A cause-and-effect critic, observing some correspondence between social and linguistic patterns, and also observing that her salary is paid for services as a language-and-literature scholar, will find it useful and interesting to say that the social patterns are determined by the linguistic, and that in order to change the social one must first change the linguistic, which of course can be done with the aid of her services. The alternative is a critic like myself, one who finds himself writing from outside of academic institutions altogether. I too see correspondences between language and society, but I maintain that language and society are all of a piece, as are many other features of the people in question – all somehow bearing the mark of their kinship within the whole system of human social life. Change, I would argue, can and should be effected at every possible point in the life of the society. One must enter a revolution with endless patience and boundless hope, and with very low expectations for the immediate future. One cannot expect to find a 'center' to attack and to destroy in order to effect a revolution, because there is no one cause for society's structure. Rather, everyone is contributing a little to its evil as well as its good, and the critic must be aware of his or her own complicity in that very plot, that structure, of good and evil.

Having said as much, I'd like to indulge in a fictitious, if instructive, narrative, to trace a line of descent, as it were, that would seem to give an accounting of the evil against which we are struggling. I do so without footnotes and without committing myself to the façade of objectivity. Since at the moment my salary is not paid by a university, I feel I have an exhilarating sense of freedom and must cherish and exploit it.

It is hard to imagine the origin of Western industrialized society's power-hunger, but it puts all those not pursuing domination in the unchosen position of either having to imitate the power-hungry and compete for power (in order to maintain self-determination), or of submitting. When power-hunger manifests itself on the individual level, it sets up a cycle that is not only self-sustaining but self-aggravating. The man knows – probably already as a little boy – that his body generally, and his sexuality in particular, are the place of his mortality and his vulnerability to others. In his quest for power, he must rid himself of this vulnerability and make himself as invulnerable, as steely, as possible. He therefore sacrifices his sexuality (penis, cock) for a symbol that resembles it but that is not really sexual and thus not vulnerable. The man trades his sexual body in for missiles, tall buildings, and money; hence his mania to replace the human body with machines and the warm but aging brain with the cold computer. These replacements, which are essential to industrial and post-industrial societies, have as their aim not pleasure but power, and thus their ultimate motivation is some wild and unceasing terror.

Phallic Man thus tries to protect himself from the vulnerability of his body by a substitution that is, in effect, a self-castration. Think of an investment banker who makes a six-figure income but who does nothing but work and who has no erotic life. For such a man, all the desires and feelings that are being suppressed in the name of success cannot simply disappear – as he might wish them to – and yet of course he doesn't wish them to disappear because they are part of his being and he must in some way love them. Rather, they become displaced, especially on to the body of the woman.

The woman thus represents to such a man not only his fiction of her sexuality, which can have any sort of relation to the woman's real sexuality or none at all, but also the man's own sexuality, his own body. The woman is over-sexualized, for she must represent to the man all of human sexuality and the entire sphere of the body – of vulnerability, of emotions, of feelings. Since Phallic Man always knows, without speaking it consciously, that to him the woman means his own body, he uses the power acquired by this very substitution in order further to repress the woman. His original psychic repression, faced with the image of the woman as the return of the repressed, now becomes external, political repression. He objectifies and rationalizes this repression by hypothesizing the woman's inferiority and untrustworthiness, but at the same time he cannot hear the woman's own voice or even see her own body as the focus of her subjectivity because his assignment of meaning to her, a kind of metonymy, interferes with any further learning or awareness. He even thinks that she is speaking when he has already forced her to be silent, and he suffers other gross distortions of perception.

As if all this oppression were not enough, Phallic Man also transfers the responsibility for his castration from himself onto the woman, who for him takes on the image of the castrated person, one who usually hides her terrible desire to castrate the man in revenge. (Medusa's head comes to mind.) The view of the woman as castrated is thus not prior to man's oppression of woman, but comes hand-in-hand with it. And, of course, we are speaking here not merely of a momentary phase in a boy's childhood development but rather of an obsession continuously repeated – having a controlling place in space as well as in time. The man is terrified of the woman not because she is a castrator but because he has castrated himself and displaces his crisis and culpability on to her. This terror gives way to a defensive and self-pitying rage which motivates revenge in the forms of misogyny and rape.

Finally, the man uses the image of the woman in order to create the phallic signifier out of the binary opposition of his sex and hers. This cannot be the origin of all masculine neurosis and social sexism, as Lacan has supposed, since such a theory would naturalize the perception of woman as castrated, which is by no means self-evident fact. Rather, it comes out of the need to transcend the vulnerable penis by replacing it with a signifier, the phallus. As deconstruction demonstrates, this pair of opposites is also necessarily hierarchical, since the castrated woman, the inverse of the positive signifier (phallus), has only been created secondarily in order to make the phallus different from something else, and therefore viable for meaning.

This annihilation of the woman's subjectivity in order to make her serve the purposes of phallic signification is blatant in Lacan. I have never found any evidence whatsoever in Lacan's work that he thinks that this system is anything but universal and therefore natural. (See, for example, Lacan's *Lettre d'amour*.) Lacan's more liberating, earlier politics of psychoanalysis, insisting that nothing be considered natural and that the patient be led to speak his or her truth without social 'adjustment', requires him to engage in a certain double-talk about it – but we need not be fooled. One need not therefore discard all of Lacan, who offers many partial truths. But when we use his terms and refer to him by the word 'psychoanalysis', we should not deceive ourselves.

If women serve these multiple functions within Phallic Man's symbolic universe – castrated, castrating, both different and inferior – lesbians are seen as a terrible challenge to the whole complex system. A lesbian does not desire men sexually, and therefore has no incentive to place herself at the mercy of his domination in order to find some basic satisfaction. Rather, a lesbian loves other women and therefore raises to view (if one looks in her direction) the possibility – the reality – of a woman being all-important to herself and to another woman, of her meaning residing not in her service to the signification of the phallus but rather in her own lived reality.

Indeed, Phallic Man's greatest defense is to efface the lesbian altogether. To him, she is invisible. Although rape is always an option in Phallic Man's program of domination of women in general, against lesbians in particular he tends to choose the technique of denial or obliteration. Since Phallic Man's quest for power has enabled him to control the dominating discourses and media, lesbians are made to feel isolated and 'queer'. As opposed to gay men in this society, who are directly threatened with gruesome violence and annihilation at every step, but who can also pose as members of the dominating group of men, lesbians are both ignored and also barred from the group in power. Whereas direct violence is probably the chief source of oppression for gay men, isolation, loss of identity, and depression are used to threaten and to undermine the power of lesbians.

The substitution essential to Phallic Man's quest for power brings him into a strange relation not only with women and gay men but also with men of other races and cultures. Analyses of racism have often concentrated on the use of black men or the 'darker races' for a purpose similar to that of women – as a group in opposition against which the dominant group, white men, can define themselves. Nevertheless, this does not explain why darkness of skin should be privileged above other possible signifiers, nor does it explain the arbitrariness with which races are defined and revised over time. For example, the German Nazis overtly and consciously racialized Jews as Other in order to obliterate their identity as Germans, Frenchmen, etc. In the United States in the decades since the Second World War, Jews have become progressively de-racialized. We must understand the same process as having occurred and continuing to occur against black and Hispanic people in the United States, against Arabs in France, and so forth.

Men of these 'minority' cultural backgrounds, however much they participate in and comply with the hegemonic empires into which they are forced to enter through a process of colonization, are not quite as culturally prepared, and therefore not quite as eager, to sacrifice basic pleasure for the sake of power, nor to trade in their bodies for dominating symbols and technologies. The encounter between imperial 'progressives' and men of 'minority' cultures has given rise to an unfortunate confusion as to the real meaning of the 'macho' ethic, which for many Latin men, at least, means not the oppression of women but a sense of an integral role of the male in the community's complex economy of responsibility, care, and pleasure.

These men have refused to castrate themselves. Phallic Man bars these men who resist his system from social, economic, and political power, for they threaten his phallic man's economy – a threat that could, he fears, include less exploitation, more free time, less capital accumulation, slower industrial 'progress', and more equal wages from top to bottom – in other words, more pleasure for all. When and if men from these cultures become fully indoctrinated into the phallic system – against the great odds of their continual exclusion from its material advantages – then they will presumably become de-racialized as the Jews have become (in part) in the United States. Nevertheless, this is unlikely because of resistance on both sides. Even the Jews show an ambivalence in relation to their assimilation that marks the odd disparities in their politics, some Jews being among the most vocal leaders of liberation movements, while others lead massacres against indigenous Arabs in Israel and burn poor tenants out of their homes in New York.

In the meantime, so long as black and Hispanic men continue to seek a living wage in order to have a satisfying life with their loved ones in their communities, rather than to accumulate capital in order to have power over the masses of the world, Phallic Man will continue to despise them out of envy, because they still have what he has willfully given up, and they continue to be a living demonstration to him of what he could be if he gave up his quest for power and confronted his motivating terror. In reaction, Phallic Man makes sure that these other men cannot accumulate capital; he even prevents them from earning the minimum wage.

Instead of breaking his neurotic pattern, Phallic Man directs his rage against these men through such acts as lynching. Lynching is not simply violence or injustice. Lynching is a ritual whose every element is deeply significant. The over-sexualizing of the black man by the white men, demonstrated in the ever-present accusation of the black man's seduction or 'disrespect' towards a white woman, leads to the ritual massacre and dismemberment of the black man's body, including, of course, castration. White men's feeling of sexual lack, their use of a black man for ritual castration, and their subsequent sense of sexual re-empowerment, is well presented in Audre Lorde's poem on the lynching of Emmett Till, 'After-images', as well as in Gwendolyn Brooks's 'A Bronzeville Mother Loiters . . .'. In such works by great black women poets, the real meanings of lynching and race hatred come through; but for Phallic Man, the differences between himself and his objects of hatred are repressed and replaced by an arbitrary color-code.

If the retention of male sexuality is what the 'darker races' represent to Phallic Man, gay men *a fortiori* threaten him, not with the *difference* in their sexuality but precisely because the *strength* and *intensity* of their erotic feelings cannot be denied. Gay men avow their nonconformity to the dominant structuring of sexuality, which has nothing to do with pleasure or desire. Phallic Man's hatred of gay men does not arise because he sees gay men as the same as women or as traitors against male superiority - or at least not because of these things alone. He associates gay men with women out of a desire to assert the sexual inferiority of gay men, a kind of impulse to castrate, because he is afraid that gay men are in some way more in touch with maleness - that is, with their own bodies, feelings, and desires - than he is. Ironically, like so many other aspects of the oppressive hegemony, the shared oppression of gay men and women has in turn given them a stronger awareness of their common cause and their common humanity.

In general, then, Phallic Man is always asserting the inferiority of whomever he designates as the Other and is always disempowering the Other. The Other, in turn, as subject rather than as other, has entirely different goals, such as peace, freedom, and pleasure, which do not fit easily into the phallic categories of power and submission. At the same time that Phallic Man uses the Other, he is also continually trying to destroy the possibility of another's subjectivity. Thus inadvertently Phallic Man is always threatening to destroy the otherness of the Other - the very source of the Other's value to him. Because Phallic Man has developed a discourse of power, there is no place in that discourse for the other person's subjectivity except as imagined by Phallic Man. Thus, the Other is only what Phallic Man invents him or her to be.

Unconsciously, Phallic Man knows this - in the psychoanalytic sense that the patient already knows his whole truth but cannot speak it or bring it to verbal consciousness. Phallic Man knows that the Other is really a mere figment of his own symbolic system and therefore not a real other but a product of himself. He knows that the Other is, beyond a thin and fragile illusion, nothing but a distorted reflection of the Same. He also knows that the woman as he sees her is the displacement of his own sexuality, and that he therefore cannot see through to the real woman, the real other person. He is utterly alone with himself in the world, because he cannot see beyond himself. And, since the Other is really just the Same veiled by some thin tissue of fictitious difference, Phallic Man has no way of finally grounding the difference that makes his symbolic self meaningful. Because all the beings that he uses to define himself are mere fictions and projections of himself, Phallic Man knows in his heart that he is meaningless and that his power is based on self-delusion. His manic clinging to that self-delusion leads him to constant threats and violence against other people. This manic energy expressed as violent brute force is in turn what hinders other people from successfully and completely exploding his self-delusion once and for all.

There are notable correspondences between Phallic Man's effect individually and his effect internationally. Indeed, the military-industrial complex in the United States can be viewed as a collection of phallic men, or as a collective Phallic Man. In its economic and political interactions, other nations and other peoples are always viewed as 'the Other'. The United States continuously undermines the will of people in poorer countries who seek to control their own domestic economies and to determine their own political destinies. It does so both through such economic manipulations as the creation of Third World debt and through direct military force. The current crisis in the world economy is the result of the American empire's efforts to eliminate Third-World economic independence and by the consequent loss of markets for high-priced US goods. But by eliminating the competition, the US also eliminated the buyers. Since the principle of the American empire's economic power is not superiority of production but control over world markets, this decline in markets has proved to be disastrous – both for the US and for all the nations that depend on it. Nevertheless, despite the United States' drive to crush countries like, for example, Nicaragua to prevent it from expressing its own political and economic choices, the Nicaraguans continue to resist. Cuba, moreover, demonstrates that it is possible to survive and to produce without consuming US products.

Throughout this essay, I have spoken of Phallic Man and have traced elements of phallic discourse as if there were other men and other discourses. Throughout, I have suggested intersubjectivity as the experience foreclosed by the phallic replacement of symbol-for-body and the subsequent projection, subjugation, and annihilation of the Other. This theory has been useful in showing the thematic resemblance of diverse phenomena in social structures, global economics, and literature. It also helps to explain the striking note of self-pity we so often hear in the discourses of the most powerful. The theory raises a number of problems, however, which I can only begin to sketch here.

First of all, what determines who is phallic and who is not? And what leads to the phallic replacement to begin with? What is that shadow terror against which the sacrifice of the real body is a defense? Once the phallic economy is in place, it fills the subject with the terror of scarcity and loss, and therefore with the drive for exclusive power. A circle of fear and domination is in place; the question of origin no longer matters.

Since 'modern' industrialized societies use the discourses of power and are engaged in a phallic economy, the individual does not choose to be or to submit to Phallic Man. Rather, the individual is subjected to the social system into which he or she is placed. Can a woman be a Phallic Man? Yes; many women participating in the phallic economy are. But the symbolic economy demands especially that men fill this role, while the role of Other is reserved for women. It is, however, possible, indeed most common, to play more than one role.

Like Alice Parker, I too have an ex-centric interest in the discourses on the family. The organization of human life into 'families', in which the relation of mother to child is considered most original, pure, exclusive, and in some sense utopian, contributes to the perpetuation of the phallic economy. While it is wrong to see the family as the root and cause of all evil, the deification of the mother-child relationship pervades not only the rhetoric of the imperialist right but also that of psychoanalysis, including that of Julia Kristeva. We do not seem to be able to recognize that other social organizations do in fact exist, that in other cultures the relations of parents to children are communal and partake of a wholly different economy. While a Euro-North-American mother will tend to say 'my children', a Hopi mother, for example, will say 'our children'. In the Hopi language, moreover, the same word applies to 'father' as to 'uncle'. By contrast, the Euro-American family is a focus of quite inhuman pressure. In philosophical and psychoanalytic investigations, we must remember that the 'natural' originary point of 'human' psychic life is actually culturally specific and learned behavior. And that behavior affects our politics, our economies, our religions, and even our methods of criticism.

The combination of the relatively extreme individualistic orientation of 'modern' Euro-American societies with the extraordinary pressures placed exclusively upon the mother-child relationship may give rise to a terror of loss – loss of the mother, loss of control and power – in both sexes, but especially in boys and men, who understand that they cannot replicate the sacred dyad by becoming mothers themselves. Thus, if we were to imitate the causal reductionism of psychoanalytic and other philosophic traditions, we would have to say that Phallic Man's quest for power can be traced to an original womb-envy.

For Lacan, it is redundant to speak of 'phallic discourse', since the *origin* of *human* language is the phallus. That is, the child acquires language in direct response to the introduction into his (I say 'his' purposely here) blissful dyad with the mother of the father's presence, or, by extension, the presence of anything in the outside world that the mother desires beyond her child. The phallus is the metonymic symbol of that desire, and the child thenceforth learns to manipulate symbols in order imaginatively to control the loss of his mother and to stand in the place of her desire, to inhabit the phallus. As a result of this set of experiences, men are *by nature*, as linguistic creatures, subject to the perpetual fear of castration, and women are by nature to be seen as castrated and lacking. Also as a result, every individual is placed in a continual struggle towards a desire that cannot be fulfilled. The suffering of the human race is the suffering of the human animal subjected to the demands of the Symbolic Order.

Julia Kristeva follows Lacan's view of the essentially phallic nature of language. In *La Révolution du langage poétique* she attempts to show how poetry allows the non-linguistic, or pre-linguistic, or 'semiotic' (an unfortunately confusing term), to express itself through rhythms and disruptions of standard prose structures. Whether we choose to appropriate or to repudiate Kristeva, we must be cautious, as Parker points out. If what Kristeva says is true, then it is true of all poetry, of all art, in short of any self-conscious manipulation of symbols in which attention is given to the material qualities of the signifiers rather than exclusively to their referential values (for example, the color of blue paint rather than the water depicted). At the same time, these material qualities are precisely what *cannot* mean; they are what is *not* language. Thus the idea of a liberating, 'semiotic' language would be a contradiction in terms.

The idea that poetic or other artistic forms, their non-representational, material qualities, free the experiencer of art from the confining rationality of meaningful language is not terribly new. Kristeva's laborious derivation of this notion from a theory of infancy participates once more in the mythic elevation of the mother-child relationship and in the mythic purity and perfection of babyhood. We seem still to be thinking, as Wordsworth did, that the infant is somehow godlike and sublime and that the growth of the human individual is a wretched fall from grace. It is unlikely that sexism, racism, and imperialist oppression will be destroyed by means of the resuscitation of this basically Christian mythology.

And although Lacan's 'La signification du phallus' and related theories of the introduction of the Symbolic Order into the individual are revealing metaphors, it is equally unlikely that language is so essentially phallic in nature. If phallic discourse becomes familiar to us from our earliest familial experiences, this is because the family and the discourse belong to the same, culture-specific, economy of power.

Thus such theories as Lacan's, like the theories of literary critics, probably exaggerate the importance of language in human experience. Of course language is very important, and it seems to be the essence of what we call consciousness – the ability to articulate experience symbolically. But a great deal that we know about ourselves, each other, and the world, is not spoken right away, or even ever spoken. And whereas the linguistic element in the experience of literary art is obviously weighty, it is much less important in the experience of dance, music, and other arts. Although one may wish to talk another person into appreciating music one loves, one's most engaged experience of the music itself is in singing it, not so much in becoming a sod to its high requiem, but rather in wishing to embody the music, to *be* it. As Heidegger would say, that is when the listener really comes into being.

But let's stick with language for now. If intersubjectivity is what phallic discourse most threatens to destroy, then one wonders whether there is such a thing as intersubjective discourse. Actually, post-modern criticism and Lacan have shown us that all discourse is in some way intersubjective, in that it speaks through the subject from some other place, some other, prior subject. The question is whether one then tries to forget where it is coming from and tries to give it the unified look of authority – phallic discourse – or whether one celebrates its otherness and allows that otherness to give oneself a sense of being, like the being one achieves in appreciating music one loves. One finds such a being-in-the-other informing the pleasure of Gertrude Stein's texts, including the play of identities in her apparently relatively conventional *Autobiography of Alice B.*

Toklas. Likewise, Audre Lorde's 'biomythography', *Zami: A New Spelling of My Name*, tells the process of its own creation as the writing of a richly inhabited and fertile disunity, a first-person character.

I touch briefly on these two works as two among many examples of revolutionary art that speaks to an audience not limited to a class or professional elite. And here is where I feel the strongest difference from Alice Parker and the greatest urgency to respond to her essay. Either because of Parker's presentation of the French and French Canadian writers' works, or perhaps because of the works themselves, the essay's methods and materials seem to me to contradict its apparent aim – to 'effect change in the dominant discourse as the scene of ideological oppression'.

The rhetoric in both Parker's essay and in the writers she quotes is useful in exposing sexist, racist, and imperialistic – in short, phallic – rhetoric. At the same time, she no longer wants to be dependent on the phallic text for her critique. (Of course, aspects of the texts in question still fall into this category. For example, Christiane Rochefort's *Quand tu vas chez les femmes* sounds to me like a caricature of Petrarch's extremely egocentric and phallocentric relation to Laura.) Still, on the whole, the efforts represented in and by Parker's essay move away from such critical dependence and towards an autonomous, even self-generating, *essentially* lesbian rhetoric.

But in fact one cannot define or understand a term like 'lesbian' *except in a larger context that is already given*, unless one appeals to a fallacious *essence*. Such a notion would expose us not only to the limits of intellectual dialogue but to naturalized ideology and prejudice, the very things feminism is against. The net result is not a revolution in language but a more technical, class-coded language that is less accessible and less empowering to those who are not already in a professional intellectual elite.

One of the most important goals of an artist in literature is to make the literature articulate an experience so that others can benefit from its articulation. It is extremely important for lesbian experience to be brought into writing more fully. But this does not mean that lesbians have, and have had, no words for their experiences. Typically, it is rather the bourgeois medium of 'high' literature, and especially the professional medium of literary criticism, that has excluded such articulations in order to uphold the myths of its class and social alliances. Although these discourses, too, must change, it is a class-centric and potentially counter-revolutionary mistake to make such high claims for the importance of language over experience.

Here I return to my opening comments. Pronouns may be important but they are not pivotally revolutionary. I have criticized Lacan and Kristeva, moreover, in response to the ease with which especially Kristeva's ideas can be appropriated so as to allow one to mystify language and to look for 'the body' in its signs and figures. Cixous similarly tends towards such mystification, indeed reification. While championing a particular revolutionary position, one must still guard against enshrining one's own position as somehow either beyond language and language's unavoidable separation from the body, or beyond complicity in the prevailing power-structure. Revolutionary challenges are possible and necessary without recourse to such religious thinking.

In response to Parker's presentation of lesbian perspectives and lesbian experience as things that have never been articulated, I still do not know what she means by that or by 'the body' in this context. I have thus attempted the foregoing analysis of Phallic Man, a theory of who speaks, how, and why. I have also tried to do justice to the complexity of a theory of genders as they operate in our society. The idea that revolution would effectly wipe out genders seems to me simplistic. It is based on assumptions about the meaning and nature of genders that remain unchallenged even when attacked. A more promising revolutionary project would be to continue to understand and to criticize the *meaning* of genders in relation to power in our society, and to move from that analysis toward the imaginary space of art.

REFERENCES

Brooks, Gwendolyn 1963. 'A Bronzeville Mother Loiters in Mississippi. Meanwhile, a Mississippi Mother Burns Bacon', in *Selected Poems*. New York: Harper & Row.
Kristeva, Julia 1974. *La Révolution du langage poétique*. Paris: Editions du Seuil.
Lacan, Jacques 1971. 'La signification du phallus', in *Ecrits II*. Paris: Editions du Seuil.
Lacan, Jacques 1975. 'Lettre d'amour', in *Seminaire. Livre XX. Encore*. Paris: Editions du Seuil.
Lorde, Audre 1982a. 'Afterimages', in *Chosen Poems - Old and New*. New York: W. W. Norton.
Lorde, Audre 1982b. *Zami: A New Spelling of My Name. Biomythography by Audre Lorde*. Trumansburg, New York: Crossing Press.
Rochefort, Christiane 1982. *Quand tu vas chez les femmes*. Paris: Grasset.
Stein, Gertrude 1933. *The Autobiography of Alice B. Toklas*. New York: Random House.

13

The Political is the Personal: The Construction of Identity in Nadine Gordimer's *Burger's Daughter*

Elizabeth A. Meese

> Your freedom and mine cannot be separated. I will return.
>
> Nelson Mandela, quoted in Winnie Mandela,
> *Part of My Soul Went with Him*

> [F]or three hundred and fifty years and more, we have been not merely rubbing shoulders but truly in contact with one another, despite the laws, despite everything that has kept us apart; there is a whole area of life where we know each other. And I really say the word *know*. Yes, we know each other in ways that are not expressed. We know the different hypocrisies that come out of our actions and our speeches: indeed we know each other in the sense that we can read between the lines.
>
> Nadine Gordimer, 'The Clash'

That 'the personal is the political' has been a caveat of the contemporary feminist movement, a maxim authorizing the private, subjective experiences of the individual woman to be read in terms of or for its significance with respect to larger issues, or to stand as/for 'the issues' of contemporary society. The microstructure of experience and the macrostructure of political forces are made synonymous, the former dignified, given the significance and readability presumed to belong to the political space of 'public' life. This was an important move in the late 1960s, perhaps at any time. But the valorization of the personal is a gesture which, if elevated to law-in-itself, may become an exclusionary principle inhibiting other political actions - outside the private sphere, in the rest of or in other parts of the world. The maxim is a curious one, since it does not rewrite an/other rule, its obverse, about the individual and political positioning, a point Terry Eagleton reminds us of in his observation: 'Nor is it adequate to *identify* the personal and political: that the personal is political is profoundly true, but there is an important sense in which the personal is also personal and the political political. Political struggle cannot be *reduced* to the personal, or vice versa.'[1] What then is the excess, the 'more than' the personal which constitutes The Political (not as reduction) or the-political-taken-personally? And what is the 'more than' or 'other than' the political which constitutes The Personal in this non-identification which Eagleton suggests? Something sounds like the 'truth' in his initial statement, as in that liberating maxim (or maxim of liberation) from the women's movement, but both leave unspecified the critical elaboration of this complex relationship, the site of struggle in/between the self and the world – the working out of which might help us live in the tension.

For almost forty years, Nadine Gordimer has engaged the problem of race in South Africa from the personal, political and artistic perspective. The conundrum, 'Where do whites fit in?', the title of an essay from 1959,[2] has provided a structuring principle for artistic elaboration. The question and Gordimer's method of exploration articulate the terms of her fiction – works that offer lessons on how to negotiate that act of reading between the lines in a racially complex society of imbricated freedoms, how to approach the question of who one is *vis-à-vis* 'the other', and what is required in view of the identity one claims and the subject position one inhabits (chosen or not). Further, a consideration of her works elucidates the difficulty of differentiating 'the personal' from 'the political' and 'the political' from 'the artistic'.

When Gordimer published this brief essay (a short note, really), she had only written some short stories and two novels. She asks questions of enduring personal and political importance for white readers, as objects of future black rule and, I would hope, to prospective black rulers of 'the New Africa'. She rejects 'nowhere' as the answer to the title question, and proposes something more like 'any place we can'. There is something embarrassing in the encounter with this white woman's words, words that could be mine, as she tries to speak honestly about her 'place' with respect to racial crime and racial capital in South Africa, her native land. She foregrounds those most difficult questions which lurk in the background – how can a white person stay? In the absence of ever being able to expect that intangible sense of emotional participation, of belonging, 'What are we to do? Shall we go? Shall we leave Africa?' (p. 327) – questions the characters in her fiction will continue to ask in the decades to come. The posing of such questions involves taking responsibility, not perhaps, as Lazarus points out, *for revolution*, but *for* being *against apartheid*.[3] In an interview she expands this view: 'what you *can* do is work among your own people to change them, because if white people are to survive in the true sense, which doesn't merely mean saving their necks, it means learning to live in a new way, then they must rethink all their values. It is on this rethinking of values that white-consciousness is founded.'[4] It is a taking of responsibility in the form of 'cultural con-scienciation'[5] for what has been made, if not actually by us as whites, certainly at least in our name. Her own retrospective self-critique makes it clear that her earlier 'humanistic' or 'individualistic attitude', which could, in light of the opening opposition, be called the 'personal' approach, was inadequate to combat an unyielding white supremacist regime: 'I felt that all I needed, in my own behavior, was to ignore and defy the color bar. In other words my own attitude toward blacks seemed to be sufficient action. I didn't see that it was pretty meaningless until much later.'[6] Rather, she discovers that the 'essential gesture' for black and white writers alike in South Africa 'is a revolutionary gesture',[7] the nature of which for each, however, is marked by their different positions relative to the 'bar' (as line, law, institution and mark of subjectivity).

How, before the revolution (which must and will come), can a white person leave, when 'to leave' means leaving responsibility in the hands of those who are less responsible (in the instance of white segregationists) or less able to oppose it (the black majority which needs to work for revolution)? But then how, before the revolution, can one stay? Gordimer's white characters continue, obsessively, to ask and to answer this question.[8] My reflections are always haunted by the idea that if you are alive in South Africa, you 'fit in' the Old Africa. I do not want to conduct the kind of inquisition that Gordimer so justly resents: 'When abroad, you often disappoint interviewers: you are there, and not in jail in your own country. And since you are not – why are you not? Aha . . . does this mean you have not written the book you should have written? Can you imagine this kind of self-righteous inquisition being directed against a John Updike for not having made the trauma of America's Vietnam war the theme of his work?'[9] Because her culture is inseparable from mine, it is my own position, the position of feminism, as much as Gordimer's, I wish to interrogate. Nonetheless, I believe in some other way that this matter of 'taking responsibility' involves one's life and one's death – another inseparable, inescapable pair – where and how to live and to die. Against such a recognition, and in the name of this responsibility,

Gordimer writes: 'You must give yourself the freedom to write as if you were dead. It is very difficult, and nobody can carry it out to the hundredth degree because you are still alive.' [10]

Gordimer recognizes the privilege inherent in posing the question of where and how one is to live. At the same time that the white South African suffers the responsibility of choosing his or her 'place' in South Africa, the 'other' South Africans have only restricted choices, no choice at all, with respect to geo-political positioning, or as the title of Zoë Wicomb's book declares, *You Can't Get Lost in Cape Town*.[11] In the aftermath of the 1976 Soweto uprising, Gordimer realizes that death – as choice, descriptor, invocation – marks this particular moment in the development of political consciousness: 'We whites do not know how to deal with the fact of this death when children, in full knowledge of what can happen to them, continue to go out to meet it at the hands of the law, for which we are solely responsible, whether we support white supremacy, or, opposing, have failed to unseat it.'[12] In Soweto, black children who are born for life find death, that non-choice for the living having become life's only choice.

In her seventh novel, *Burger's Daughter*,[13] published in 1979, Nadine Gordimer explores the growth and development of a white woman as responsible or revolutionary 'subject'. She takes her character Rosa Burger from adolescence to young womanhood, under what one might think are optimal circumstances for the production of a political consciousness capable of unseating apartheid. As the novel's epigraph from Claude Lévi-Strauss suggests – 'I am the place in which something has occurred' – Rosa Burger is one such place; South Africa, Gordimer's text (the discursive space of which begins by marking itself off there), the author herself, and ultimately the reader are other 'places,' sites for/of production and performance. Who this subject is, where the place and what the thing that has 'taken place', the reader is to discover by reading between the lines of this textual complex of interlocking relationships.

The novel opens with a description of people waiting outside a prison. Perspectives for viewing are numerous – passengers from buses that must have passed by, the warder who tries not to see, others who wait, the scene's omniscient narrator, perhaps more than one preparer of reports, constructing identities for Rosemarie Burger, Rosa Burger, Lionel Burger's daughter, schoolgirl on the first hockey team, promising student, daughter of her imprisoned mother Cathy Burger. She wonders, *'When they saw me outside the prison, what did they see?'* (p. 13) – the omni-directional question of the subject being constituted in the illusory identity-fixing scrutiny of the mirror stage: 'I shall never know [what they saw]. It's all concocted. I saw – see – that profile in a hand-held mirror directed towards another mirror' (p. 14). Rosa sees herself 'in place, outside the prison', but her attention is not focused on the public spectacle that she is and of which she is a/part. She stands in front of the prison and menstruates for the first time, becoming a woman, who, as Abdul JanMohamed puts it, is more/other than a daughter: 'Thus her simultaneous yet unconnected existence as an object of public scrutiny and as a locus of private experience reflects her predicament as a bifurcated social being' (p. 129). In her version of the story, Rosa focuses on her bio-sexual identity, the biological fact of her womanhood, turning her private, internal experience into a public one where 'the internal landscape of my mysterious body turns me inside out, so that in that public place on that public occasion . . . I am within that monthly crisis of destruction, the purging, tearing, draining of my own structure. I am my womb' (pp. 15-16). She tells us in retrospect that it matters little whose identity story we read – theirs or hers – as 'both would seem equally concocted' (p. 16).

Rosa articulates the arbitrariness of subject-construction, identity, and discursivity. How inconsequential (both everything and nothing) it is to be standing 'before the law' – the prison gate of white supremacy, the periodicity of menstruation marking her womanhood, or the father's law in language. Rosa explains: 'And if I were really telling, instead of talking to you in my mind the way I find I do . . . One is never talking to oneself, always one is addressed to someone. Suddenly, without knowing the reason, at different stages in one's life, one is addressing this person or that all the time, even dreams are performed before an audience. I see that' (p. 16). The performative displaces the constative (to the extent that one ever plays a/part the other), making it difficult to know either the self or the other as 'subject', the irony of which is apparent in South African society which devotes itself to the elaboration of absolute, precise differentiations.[14] The novel becomes a space where conflicting discourses, competing ideologies, are performed for all readers to regard, where discursivity takes (its) place.

Gordimer replays the fusions of the opening scene when Rosa's friend Conrad observes that the personal and political horrors of her family circle are indistinguishable in origin: '– Disease, drowning, arrests, imprisonments. . . . – It didn't make any difference' (p. 41). Her mother died from multiple sclerosis, her father died in prison, her brother drowned in the backyard pool. To Conrad, the losses are indistinct as to cause – dead is dead: 'But the Lionel Burgers of this world – personal horrors and political ones are the same to you. You live through them all. On the same level. And whatever happens – no matter what happens' (p. 42). The contrasting memories of Conrad and Rosa as children at twelve point up a difference in the tenor of their family dramas: Rosa recalls the political memory of the Sharpeville Massacre as its aftermath works itself out in her home; Conrad remembers the consuming personal obsession of his oedipal preoccupation with his mother and her lover. These differences continue in adulthood, as his friends plan to go to sea in a hand-made boat and hers, lacking passports to support such fantasies, go to prison (p. 50); their uncommitted (or only personally committed) lives, as experienced on the French Riviera, epitomize 'the bourgeois fate, alternate to Lionel's: to eat without hunger, mate without desire' (p. 117). Trying to put herself in Conrad's 'place', Rosa realizes that her family circle was characterized by non-possession; all members existed only in relation to the political cause, the father and mother functions, assumed by many and extended to numerous dependents in a revised sense of kinship.

Lionel Burger's household, with its pool, black servants, black 'son' 'Baasie', and steak barbecues, embodies the domestication of white revolutionary South African politics in the 1950s. In response to Conrad's challenge that 'Saint-Simon and Fourier and Marx and Lenin and Luxemburg whose namesake you are' (p. 47) provide no rationale for personal existence, no *raison d'être*, Rosa elaborates the indistinguishability in white communist households of the ostensible opposition of the personal and the political: 'If Lionel and my mother . . . if the concepts of our life, our relationships, we children accepted from them were those of Marx and Lenin, they'd already become natural and personal by the time they reached me. D'you see? It was all on the same level at which you – I – children learn to eat with a knife and fork, go to church if their parents do (p. 50). The revolutionary cause, articulated in that utopic monolith The Future, its own form of immortality, stands in opposition to Conrad's elevation of 'I' against 'we' in the face of Rosa's question, 'What do you do when something terrible happens?' (p. 52) Rosa projects her father's reading of Conrad, another fix on the difference between the personal and the political: 'Lionel Burger probably saw in you the closed circuit of self; for him, such a life must be in need of a conduit towards meaning, which posited: outside self. That's where the tension that makes it possible to live lay, for him; between self and others; between the present and creation of something called the future' (p. 86). Thus, Gordimer makes the case for the collective identity and structural relationships revolution requires and which Rosa, while searching for personal identity in *relation* to collective purpose, must re-write in her own name just as one re-enacts the family drama in the progress of generations.

Her struggle is with the political made personal: 'didn't you understand, everything that child, that girl did was out of what is between daughter and mother, daughter and brother, daughter and father. . . . I was struggling with a monstrous resentment against the claim – not of the Communist party! – of blood, shared genes, the semen from which I had issued and the body in which I had grown' (p. 62). Rosa also struggles with the personal made political; she believes that it is Lionel Burger the man, her father, not a 'God' or a 'devil' of revolutionary politics (p. 18), and Cathy Burger, her mother, with whom she must contend. Everyone concocts identities for Lionel Burger; they see him in ways that Rosa does not or cannot in her effort to see herself by seeing him: 'And who are they to have decided – the law did not allow them to photograph *him* – in their descriptions of him in the dock, in the way he listened to evidence against him, in the expression with which he met the public gallery or greeted friends there, that they knew what he was, when I don't know that I do' (p. 145). Part of what Rosa fails to see is that, because the tenets of white communism have been 'naturalized' in the family, they are as inseparable for her in the effort to 'identify' herself as they were for her father or mother. Likewise, the natural becomes the unnatural, or is it the other way around? At seventeen, Rosa is 'engaged' to an imprisoned communist so that she can act as a go-between, carrying supplies and messages in and out of prison. She is 'used' by adults to further the struggle: 'it was natural' (p. 65). But then 'use', in relation to such a compelling goal, is only that, the use value someone or something has for revolutionary success.

The dichotomy is most confounded in the death of a tramp in the park where Rosa eats her lunch in anonymous pleasure. He looked alive, even in death, a life-like statue of a man, his legs crossed 'conversationally' (p. 78). This is Rosa's first experience of death. Her family losses were somehow 'obscured . . . by sorrow and explained by accident, illness, or imprisonment' (p. 79). But this anonymous death comes unfiltered through responsibility or explanation; it eludes discursive captivity: 'this death was the mystery itself. . . . we die because we live, yes, and there was no way for me to understand what I was walking away from in the park' (p. 79). This death is the remainder, what is left after the revolution eliminates skin and class privilege, needless death and suffering. About this death the revolution has nothing to say: 'Justice, equality, the brotherhood of man, human dignity - but *it will still be there*' (p. 80). Hence the irony of Marisa Kgosana's comment when Lionel receives the life sentence: 'whose life, theirs or his?' (p. 154) In South Africa, where 'life means life' (p. 28), a life sentence is also a death sentence.

The question of where and how one should live or die encompasses the issues of choice and betrayal. Even Lionel Burger is a betrayer in the eyes of some: the man who, according to the Afrikan nationalist Brandt Vermeulen, could have been prime minister (p. 186) turns traitor, betraying 'the heritage of his people', the 'white man's power' (p. 61). With Lionel Burger's death, her mother and brother already dead, Rosa is set free. She is free 'to be anonymous, to be like other people' (p. 77); to experience the loneliness of living 'without social responsibility' (p. 77) - to live as she desires (p. 246). She must undertake the burden of Wang Yang-ming's proclamation which Gordimer places at the opening of the novel's second part: '*To know and not to act is not to know*' (p. 213). To assume this freedom is to accept the 'death sentence'.

Despite Rosa's ultimate imprisonment carried in the verbs of the novel's opening sentences, and the inescapable answer to Claire's question of what choice (no choice) one has, Rosa is also free to act the part of the betrayer, as she escapes the demands of the Terblanches, feeling 'the need to get away from something obscene - and afraid to wound him - them - by showing it' (p. 111). She runs from Dick's splotchy cancer-marked hands and Claire's peeling eczema, implicated in their political demands. As Rosa comments to the absent Conrad: 'Even animals have the instinct to turn from suffering. The sense to run away. . . . A sickness not to be able to ignore that condition of a healthy, ordinary life: other people's suffering' (p. 73). Thus Gordimer marks her character's turning point, the decisive moment, with another turning away in the scene with the donkey. Just as she rejects the demands of the Terblanches, Rosa fails to act on her own sense that she can and must intervene to stop the suffering.

The black man beating the donkey, a vision welding all participants into one form, provides a significant moment in Rosa's search for a direction. The event holds the history of human suffering before her - from thumbscrews to solitary confinement, the ability to inflict it and the capacity to endure it. The full weight of agony presents itself in the black location, 'in the "place" that isn't on the map' (p. 209), unnamed and un'known'. Reflecting on the scene, Gordimer explains that 'the image catalyses all the other forms of suffering - the suffering man inflicts on man - into an intense awareness of the problem of suffering itself, the pure phenomenon, gathering up in her mind the atrocities committed by East and West. Her contemplation of the central human fact of suffering - and possible responses to it other than her father's chosen one - preoccupies her throughout the book.' [15] Rosa remotivates her need to choose, through the space of the novel as an extended meditation on suffering. She recovers suffering in all the forms in which she has experienced it, and comes to terms with the problem of responsible self-positioning.

In a sense Gordimer's question of what is the place of whites in South Africa (given in this novel to Katya: 'how will they fit in, white people?' [p. 249]) is conflated with what is 'woman's place'. That is, in *Burger's Daughter* we can read these as correlative questions. Rosa is offered an identity - as comrade-daughter (the communist family), South African white (state), cultural product (language and history), corporeal subject (menstruating girl turned woman). Her problem is how to be Burger's daughter and more, other - how to be white but not the master, colonizer - finding a representation which permits a non-hierarchical play of difference. In her address to Conrad, she explains the difference in her relation to identity, when, 'far from poring over the navel of a single identity (yes, a dig at you, Conrad)', she, through political activity, 'sees the necessity of many' (p. 112). What happens in a society like South Africa when the construction of the 'truth' of your white identity (unlike the master's) is *not* formed by the reflection/recognition given you by your slave, as daughter to the father, woman to society?

In this context, the scene of the women's meeting deserves some comment. Over the years, various interviewers have asked Gordimer about her views of feminism which she insists on regarding as secondary to the struggles against apartheid and for revolution. Seeing herself as fortunate, while other women are not, she resists generalizing because 'other women do have these struggles', and regards women's situation 'as part of the whole question of human rights and disaffected groups in various societies'. [16] Obviously Gordimer believes in feminism, but feminism is not her highest priority: 'Black women have so many terrible disabilities that they share in common with men - the oppression of racism - that the whole feminist movement means something quite different there. Unless feminism is seen as merely part of the general struggle for black liberation, and the struggle of all, white and black, against racial oppression, it has no validity in South Africa, in any view.'[17] She shares the view of many women of color who are multiply oppressed. Theirs is a compelling position, although Gordimer repeatedly represents feminism through trivializing examples:

> the white man and the white woman have much more in common than the white woman and the black woman, despite their difference in sex. Similarly, the black man and the black woman have much more in common than the black man and the white man. Their attitude toward life is much more similar. The basis of color cuts right through the sisterhood or brotherhood of sex. It boils down to the old issue of prejudice and the suppression of blacks by both sexes, to the way that they are forced to live. . . . Thus, the loyalty to your sex is secondary to the loyalty to your race. That's why Women's Liberation is, I think, a farce in South Africa. It's a bit ridiculous when you see white girls at the University campaigning for Women's Liberation because they're kicked out of some frater-nity-type club or because they can't get into bars the way men do. Who cares? A black woman has got things to worry about much more serious than these piffling issues. White women have the vote; no black, male or female, has.[18]

Why Gordimer only characterizes feminism in such terms is implicit in the circularity of the opposition she uses.

Gordimer's critique of white privilege requires her to place the black woman first, limited though her understanding may be concerning who the 'black woman' is and what she wants and what that 'first place' might be. It is the gesture that saves her in the endless struggle against her subject position, her racial privilege – what she as a white woman in South Africa *has* but does not necessarily *want*. The danger in this missionary-like position is that we might only always answer for and from ourselves. In a world where whites can't trust themselves, the test of one's political commitments under apartheid has to be addressed through the questions: What does it do for blacks? How, when, and under what conditions? We cannot allow ourselves to ask how beneficial feminism might be for whites until racial consciencization has taken place. Thus, the scene of the women's meeting in Flora Donaldson's living room, where racist white women insist on coopting black women, urging them 'SMILE AND SAY

THANKS' to promote racial understanding, or ' "our Bantu women must pull together with us" ' for road safety, is captured finally in the injunction: 'We don't need to bring politics into the fellowship of women' (p. 203). While the construction of a hierarchy of the oppressed is a defeating exercise, South Africa demands unrelenting attention to apartheid/revolution, and to feminism only to the extent that politics and the 'fellowship of women' might be made synonymous. Acting it out before us, Gordimer sums up her position, along with that of Rosa and other white communists: 'the oppression of black women [is] primarily by race and only secondarily by sex discrimination' (p. 199).

Gordimer offers feminist readers more than an opportunity to take a critical look at their political interests. Considering Gordimer's female characters' position in the scheme of competing loyalties, Sheila Roberts provides the following summary:

> I would say that the female characters in her novels are all more troubled about their moral position as citizens in a racist country than they are about their position as women relating to men. Not that these two positions do not interlock at times: they do. Nevertheless, in those novels with female protagonists the strongest focus is not on their status as women but on the moral validity of action as women in various circumstances in an overall political inheritance.[19]

Gordimer's novels are valuable to us as feminists precisely for the way in which she figures women negotiating the relationship of their subject position in the context of race and class conflict, for the awareness of their interconnectedness, required in an intertwined emergence, for political effectiveness.

As feminists are invited to scrutinize their ideological positions, Rosa reviews a history of betrayals within and issuing from the Communist Party, seeking a multi-dimensional record of the past, as opposed to a one-dimensional political polemic. She wants to differentiate herself from her father, and other party members, who wait in prison or at home for 'The Future' (p. 112), as something already known and specified. Observing, 'I would like once and for all to match the facts with what I ought to know' (p. 111), Rosa searches for a founding epistemology and authorizing text upon which her present and future can be built. Like the alternative Afrikaner (and Western) mythos of God, family and country, the language of revolution requires redefinition and reclamation before

Rosa can act with personal/political purpose. Engaging the personally and rhetorically obscure 'difference between the truth and the facts', Rosa indicts the language of struggle:

> My father's biographer, respectfully coaxing me onto the stepping stones of the official vocabulary – words, nothing but dead words, abstractions: that's not where reality is, you flung at me – national democratic revolution, ideological integration, revolutionary impera- tive, minority domination, liberation alliance, unity of the people, infiltration, incursion, viable agency for change, reformist option, armed tactics, mass political mobilization of the people in a combi- nation of legal, semi-legal and clandestine methods. (p. 142)

And the 'reality' Rosa recalls is the alleged and unlikely suicide of 'Baasie''s father in prison, and telling her father at a prison visit that her clandestine activities had been successfully completed. Such events, while in the service of political interests, stand in contradistinction to the 'propositions of the faithful' which she understands 'personally', 'in a way theory doesn't explain' (p. 151).

Rosa's revision of political history is inseparable from her relationship with her father; her analytic gesture performs the operation feminism wants in its yoking of the personal and the political: 'In 1956 when the Soviet tanks came into Budapest I was his little girl, dog-paddling to him with my black brother Baasie, the two of us reaching for him as a place where no fear, hurt or pain existed. And later, when he was in jail and I began to think back, even I . . . could not have found the way to ask him – in spite of all these things: do you still believe in the future? The same Future? Just as you always did?' (p. 115) Rosa questions the very process of revolution, how one knows it is over, foreclosed or carried on indepen- dently: 'It is complete only for Lionel Burger; he has done all he had to do and that, in his case, happened to imply a death in prison as part of the process. It does not occur to them [other CP members] that it could be complete for themselves, for me' (p. 113). She enacts Gordimer's more complex awareness that, in this continuing political process, the moment of the Future when South Africa's black majority has been freed, enfran- chised, and assumes political power, will not necessarily be the Future revolution took as its end, that 'revolution' is not a moment the beginning and ending of which we can necessarily ever be certain. Where did it start? Has it concluded? A similar analysis might be offered with respect to Rosa Burger's freedom and the South African revolution outside the novel.

If communism's totalizing vision of The Future is shaken loose, diversified, the strategies required for social change of necessity change also. Thus, *Burger's Daughter* concerns the translation of one generation's struggle into the terms of the next: the children educate the parents. Specifically, the novel chronicles the shift from revolution as conceived by the African National Congress under the influence of white communists to revolution designed and directed by blacks alone through the Black Consciousness Movement. The political 'place' of the South African people against apartheid is articulated in the space between these two positions. First, there is Rosa's reflection on what her father lived for: '*The future* he was living for until the day he died can be achieved only by black people with the involvement of the small group of white revolutionaries who have solved the contradiction between black consciousness and class consciousness, and qualify to make unconditional common cause with the struggle for full liberation, e.g., a national and social revolution' (p. 126). Second, the extended living-room debate concerning class and race struggle challenges the view of the 1950s and early 1960s, prevailing then and lingering still in what might be called an undecided third moment (the remainder of the discourse on apartheid).[20] The young black man, Dhladhla, articulates the position of black solidarity: 'Whites, whatever you are, it doesn't matter, It's no difference. You can tell them – Afrikaners, liberals, Communists. We don't accept anything from anybody. We take' (p. 157); 'All collaboration with whites has always ended in exploitation of blacks' (p. 159); 'He doesn't live black, what does he know what a black man needs? He's only going to *tell* him –' (p. 159). The rhetoric of Black Consciousness, in its capacity to ossify otherwise fluid positions, to construct opposition among those against apartheid, functions analogously to other political discourses. Rosa reflects: 'I've heard all the black clichés before. I am aware that, like the ones the faithful use, they are an attempt to habituate ordinary communication to overwhelming meanings in human existence' (p. 328). But political rhetorics work; they are powerful in their capacity to construct motivating narratives: 'They become enormous lies incarcerating enormous truths' (p. 328).

Dhladhla has a keen fix on the 'no-place' for whites in the new South Africa. In his view, they work from different centers of interest. The white man 'goes [to prison] for his ideas about me, I go for my ideas about myself' (p. 159). His assessment of Lionel Burger's action is that: 'He knows what he was doing in jail. A white knows what he must do if he doesn't like what he is. That's his business. We only know what we must do ourselves' (p. 160). Similarly, in response to Orde Greer's embarrassing question as to what the radical young black man would do if he were white, Dhladhla responds: 'I don't think about that' (p. 167). Whites in South Africa must find their own ways of taking responsibility. Rosa is on the other side of a dialectic, having rejected the master–slave relationship of the white colonial to the black African. What she does not realize is that once she makes this move, there is no longer a choice. In a comment which sounds the death knell to Conrad's existential isolation and which Rosa at the time cannot accept, the pitiful Claire Terblanche articulates the non-choice position of the daughters of South African white communists: 'Yes . . . I suppose if you want to look at it like that . . . But no! Rosa! What choice? Rosa? In this country, under this system, looking at the way blacks live – what has the choice to do with parents? What else could you choose?' (p. 127) Perhaps Claire expresses the political-as-apolitical: what must be chosen irrespective of the personal. Lionel Burger takes this position in his final trial when he speaks in terms of a definitional reversal of guilt and innocence as determined by the state, versus responsibility to one's countrymen: 'I would be guilty if I were innocent of working to destroy racism in my country. If I'm guilty of that innocence the police will not be the ones with the right to apprehend me' (p. 133). She reflects on the difference between the position of black and white communists of her father's generation and that of the black nationalists represented by Dhladhla and the students: 'in that house where I grew up there was no guilt because it was believed it was as a ruling class and not a colour that whites assumed responsibility. It wasn't something bleached into the flesh' (p. 161). In the Black Consciousness Movement's reconceptualization of revolution, the class struggle is perceived as 'white nonsense', in place of which racism and capitalism will be eliminated through 'a race struggle' (p. 163) – requiring black unity that whites, in their own self-interest, speaking for the interest of 'humanity' (another suspicious generic rivaling 'man' and 'mankind'), have historically opposed.

Rosa needs to re-write the Manichaean black/white: evil/good: slave/master opposition, to escape the false consciousness of romanticizing or fearing blackness. Orde Greer's embarrassing question is her question, is Gordimer's and mine too: 'What would you do if you were me? *What is to be done?'* (p. 172). For the moment, in her search for an answer to this undecidable, nagging question, Rosa settles on the idea that, for her parents, connections between people result from believing in the connections; they are a matter of faith. She reflects on her family as follows: 'Lionel – my mother and father – people in that house, had a connection with blacks that was completely personal. In this way, their Communism was the antithesis of anti-individualism. . . . At last there was nothing between this skin and that . . . it was a human conspiracy, above all other kinds' (p. 172). Rosa's encounter with 'Baasie' casts another light on her theory of skin and (in)difference. Rosa finds herself caught between the personal indictment of her black child-friend and the political indictment of the state apparatus. The sibling relationship of Rosa and Zwelinzima Vulindlela ('Baasie') proves transitory, as white sister and black brother betray one another. He rejects his Afrikaans name 'Baasie' ('little master' or 'boss') and asserts his African name, Zwelinzima, 'suffering land' (p. 318), indicting Burger as another white engaged in the 'takeover' of blacks.[21] Zwelinzima shares his complaint with the Soweto Students Representative Council: the Burgers of South Africa get accolades for their role in the liberation movement, while the African leaders, like Zwelinzima's father, victim of the alleged prison suicide, are discredited and erased from history. Rosa fights back, sharing in the betrayal as she accuses Zwelinzima of remaining a safe distance from serious struggle. Cooke offers the following view of the scene:

> She shows her acceptance of a different bond between them as their taunts reach their nastiest pitch. They seem to be 'poking with a stick at some creature writhing between them,' an image which recalls the brutal mule beating that led Rosa to leave the country. Her conversation with Baasie prompts her return by calling up the brutality inherent in any relationship between privileged whites and dispossessed blacks. Rosa's acceptance of hate as well as love – monstrous detachment and excessive identification – in her bond with Baasie makes the woman we see at the close of *Burger's Daughter*.[22]

While this is certainly a pivotal scene, the power of which recurs, it is not yet the moment of Rosa's turning back to South Africa. The Rosa of the novel's close has (re)negotiated the age-old opposition played out in this interaction, where black and white each takes up the assigned part: 'In one night we had succeeded in manoeuvering ourselves into the position

their history books back home have ready for us – him bitter; me guilty'
(p. 330).

Rosa, like all of us (even when we think we are not choosing), must
make her choice, one no less viable because the terms and motive differ or
because it is the choice she was socialized by her communist family to
make. Rosa assumes her 'place' in her own name, a 'place' redefined in
relation both to her father and Black Consciousness, a point Stephen
Clingman makes as well: 'for her the fact of suffering is paramount rather
than any question of ideology. . . . But she is acting in the spirit of her
father's tradition and reconnecting with his heritage. . . . Fusing the
needs of the present with the traditions of the past there is a strong revolutionary alignment in the novel.'[23] After Black Consciousness, after the
Soweto uprising, political alignments in South Africa are never quite the
same again.[24] Or as Gordimer herself explains:

> when Rosa begins to talk to her father, at the end – I paraphrase –
> 'You knew what the children have discovered, you knew that it
> would come from the people, as Lenin predicted,' Well, here it
> came, indeed, not from the fathers of the people but from their
> children. Which is also, of course, a kind of reversal of what has
> happened to her; it's a turning over of predestination. She struggles
> against what she inherited from the father, embraces and struggles;
> and here you have a generation that turns the tables and takes the
> initiative.[25]

Rosa assumes her destiny, as Lionel Burger's daughter, by accepting the
responsibility to act, but her way of getting there – through Black Consciousness, the reformulation of communist ideology, the man on the
park bench, the donkey, the old woman on the Riviera – is her own, in
recognition that life, even the life of pleasure, is subject to that final
sentence: speaking existentially we all end up at the same 'place'. Clingman makes a good case for the view that 'for Rosa Burger in her way, and
for Gordimer's novel in its own, there is the affirmation of an historical
synthesis of the inheritance of Lionel Burger in its post-Soweto form. The
revolutionary "subject" of Burger's Daughter has been constructed.'[26]

Yet there is also a certain formalized uncertainty, the ambiguity at the
heart of each individual, that Gordimer through her mode of narration
attempts to articulate, but to leave in its state of mystery. It is the
mystery, the off-the-center, the expression of the not-to-be-discovered,

rather than 'absolute' character, Identity-itself, which interests her and serves as a model for characterization and strategy of narration. Jan-Mohamed aptly describes Gordimer's approach in contrast with white colonial writers: 'unlike the subjectivity in the works of Cary and Dinesen, which derives its intensity from the desire to maintain a coherent self, in Gordimer's fiction it is a product of her willingness to embrace incoherence in order to root out unconscious biases and desires.'[27] Gordimer writes against interpretation – not so much to thwart the reader but to capture what the writer sees, much of which she does not understand (in the sense of finally deciding the proper direction and strategy for South African revolution) and can only speculate about through her characters' performance of alternatives. Through the novel, she poses a conflict which she regards as 'central to civilized man's existence' and summarizes as follows: 'what is a meaningful life? Is there a cause greater than the gift of life itself? Can one fulfill oneself simply by earning a living, falling in love, marrying and producing the next generation, with no concern for anyone outside the family circle? Conversely, can one fulfill oneself while sacrificing personal emotional preoccupations, ambitions, joys and sorrows – what is generally accepted as the pursuit of happiness – to the selflessness exacted by faith in a cause greater than oneself?'[28] Rosa redefines the terms of her action, although the specific theory (in)forming that redefinition remains vague and the action itself unspecified.

Rosa's visit to see 'The Lady and the Unicorn' tapestries in the Musée de Cluny, an important and beautiful scene which is never discussed, can be read emblematically, like the tapestries themselves; here the scene marks the character's final turn back to South Africa upon her realization that 'No one can defect' (p. 332). In the first tapestry which, with the sixth, interests Gordimer most, the spectators gaze at the unicorn and the lady. The unicorn is like the illusion of identity, the always ever illusory identity: 'This is the creature that has never been' (p. 304); '*O dieses ist das Tier das es nicht gibt*' (p. 340). Recalling the mirror reflections constructing Rosa's identity at the novel's opening (p. 14), we see the unicorn regard the tiny 'naturalized' image of himself in the Lady's hand-held mirror – a unicorn without a horn. In another closed circuit of mirroring self-(re)presentation, the Lady's oval face imitates the mirror, her hair twisted up in a braid like the unicorn's horn (or his horn like her hair?), both constructed 'to imitate a spiral' (p. 340). Clearly Gordimer has studied the tapestries carefully; the visit to the Cluny is positioned near the novel's end, to (re)figure from another perspective, Rosa's dilemma and ours. As Gordimer explains, the six tapestries represent the five senses, but we are left with the uncertainty of the sixth, thought by art critics to convey 'a deep moral significance'[29] concerning the renunciation of the passions as they are depicted in the previous panels.

The sixth tapestry is known by the legend inscribed over the Lady's tent canopy, '*A mon seul désir*' (p. 341). Here Rosa Burger turns away from being Bernard Chabalier's mistress who is 'not accountable to the Future', free to meditate on the unicorn, 'A mythical creature. *Un paradis inventé*' (p. 304). The tapestry's interpreter, Erlande-Brandenburg, translates the French by analogy to the Latin inscription '*Liberum arbitrium*', noting 'We know what the philosophers meant by "free will": for Socrates and Plato it was the natural disposition to behave rightly, which we lose because, through our senses, we become the slaves of our passions. . . . "*á mon seul désir*", that is, "in accordance only with my will".'[30] While we may 'know' what the philosophers meant (a point open to question), we can place alongside it the novel's second epigraph where 'knowing' in this state of free will only reveals itself as knowledge when we act it (out). At the Cluny, like the earlier visit to see the paintings by Bonnard, for whom 'It's as if nothing has ever happened' (p. 287), Rosa, as 'the place in which something has occurred', contemplates the juxtaposition of the utopic with the 'real': 'An old and lovely world, gardens and gentle beauties among gentle beasts. Such harmony and sensual peace in the age of the thumbscrew and dungeon' (p. 341). Her identity is conflated with that of the Lady, the unicorn and South Africa (about which 'there is nothing left to fear' [p. 341]) as she 'Sits gazing, this creature that has never been' (p. 341). And, like the lady in the tapestry, Rosa renounces her life of pleasure to (re)turn to her 'place' in South Africa, a move which lends weight to Boyers's assessment that 'Politics here is conceived simultaneously as a choice and a vocation, a fate and an ambitiously forbidding object of desire.'[31] Leaving behind her lover Chabalier, the sensuous pleasures of food, herbs, light, love's caresses in exile, she goes home to prison, where even her prison cell is described in terms of the beauty of a spot of light, a pleasure worth relating and thus worth censoring.

Under the pretense of pursuing her 'hobby', Rosa (re)figures the unicorn tapestries, the scenes from Bonnard, the boat made by Conrad's friends, and the landscape of the Riviera, in 'naive imaginary landscapes that could rouse no suspicions that she might be incorporating plans of the lay-out of the prison etc. - it represented, in a number of versions, a village covering a hill with a castle on the apex, a wood in the foreground, the sea behind. The stone of the houses seemed to give a lot of trouble: it was tried out in pinks, greys, even brownish orange. She had been more successful with the gay flags on the battlements of the castle and the bright sails of tiny boats, although through some failure of perspective they were sailing straight for the tower' (p. 355). Again scene and significance coalesce as past pleasures are recuperated for use in new codes for political purpose, another kind of *'paradis inventé'* (p. 287) which makes it possible 'to act', her synonym of 'to live' (p. 296). Thus, Gordimer gives us, even in the end, the simultaneously necessary personal solution to political action.

Burger's Daughter is, without question, a very political and a very personal work. Assessing Gordimer's achievement in the novel, Robert Boyers comments: 'She has, in fact, reconceived the very idea of private experience and created a form that can accommodate microscopic details of individual behavior and sentiment without suggesting for a moment that individuals are cut off from the collective consciousness and political situations characteristic of their societies.'[32] In their painful conversation, Rosa and 'Baasie', once 'sister' and 'brother', confront each other as 'other' (a position we can only say that 'Baasie' is able to assume through the power of Black Consciousness). Revealing the 'real' reason for his call and his anger, he says accusingly, 'You're different so I must be different too. You aren't white and I'm not black' (p. 321). What their names signify in the political sphere is the subject examined here; each one stands as an undeniable contradiction (which they seek to deny all the more vehemently) to the stark black/white dichotomy that drives the political rhetoric of race (the other black/white dichotomy). In this respect JanMohamed notes that Gordimer 'did not inherit the otherness of blacks as a *neutral* ontological fact, rather it was valorized for her in a manner that became profoundly problematic: "If you are [born] white, you begin from the premise of being white. Are they different because they are black? Or are they black because they are different?"'[33] The narrative circles around this and other undecided problematics, the questions left open in a revolutionary gesture (also the 'essential gesture' for the artist) that resists the closure of the revolutionary process by placing it in the service of a homogeneous narrative.

Although Gordimer insists, as she must, that 'As a novelist I am not interested in "reconciling" political ideologies',[34] still, her text is subversive: it too acts out what it knows. Specifically, she recuperates the banned and excluded, bringing together what cannot be seen through the capacity of literature to place side by side what apartheid insists on keeping separate.[35] She says concerning the Soweto Students Representative Council pamphlet, a historically banned publication by a banned organization, 'I reproduced the document exactly as it was, in all its naivety, leaving spelling mistakes and grammatical errors uncorrected, because I felt it expressed more eloquently and honestly than any pamphlet I could have invented, the spirit of the young people who wrote it'.[36] This loyalty to their spirit provides a way of guarding against the subject position she knows she occupies as a white South African. Furthermore, Gordimer's strategy of using what is at hand through unattributed quotation (Marx, Lenin, Slovo), the extensiveness of which Clingman documents well,[37] reinforces her role as historian, recoverer of forbidden words. Clingman observes:

> This functionalism . . . not only introduces the actual mood of the time (in the case of the SSRC pamphlet) but from the point of view of authorship it overrides the conventions of bourgeois property relations – in this sense 'ownership' of the documents or phrases used. The novel opts for use-value in preference to exchange-value: what is important is that the words are reproduced, and not the exchange of ownership rights denoted by the 'purchase' of textual attribution.[38]

Like the Burgers, Gordimer uses words as she needs them, in the interest of a larger political purpose which we are invited to 'know'.

In the effort to read both history and present conflict, Rosa becomes an analogue for the Barthesian reader: 'the space on which all the quotations that make up a writing are inscribed without any of them being lost; a text's unity lies not in its origin but in its destination',[39] but Gordimer makes of herself and us such reading spaces as well. Like Burger in the dock, and the revolutionary South African text, she redefines categories. Rosa in the timeless, undifferentiated pleasure of the Riviera, feels 'Like someone in prison' (p. 222), and at the novel's close, she enjoys the fellowship of the imprisoned women. My epigraph from Nelson Mandela[40] resonates with the pronominal ambiguity of Gordimer's first epigraph ('I am the space'). His freedom and mine, ours and theirs, black and white (although the context of his remarks might stipulate that I read his statement as addressed only to his black brothers and sisters), coalesce in desire and discursive space. Resembling Gordimer who writes as though dead, Rosa writes from prison to a dead audience (Conrad, who if he isn't dead might as well be, and her dead father), the ones that set her free to engage this writing. Ironically, the novel's last reader, Madame Bagnelli, receives a card from Rosa, the final line of which was censored, so she 'was never able to make it out' (p. 361). This closing line of the novel suggests an interesting reversal in which Rosa, who writes from prison, has 'made it out' and, in retrospect, is Gordimer's own signature anticipating the embargo, banning and ultimate unbanning of her novel in South Africa. But who can read Rosa's censored text? Is she destined to (be)come Burger's daughter – arrested, tried, jailed for life (death) on treason charges? Did she do or will she have done what 'they' (the communist family/the South African state) say she did? How, in us as readers, the ultimate 'place' of Gordimer's South African narrative, will Rosa's story be 'concocted', many more times in many more versions? How are we as readers finally to discover our places among its revolutionary 'subjects'?

NOTES

I want to express my appreciation for assistance received in support of this project from the University of Alabama Research Grants Committee, 1987.

 1   Eagleton 1983: 149.
 2   Gordimer 1959.
 3   Lazarus 1986-7: 155.
 4   Gordimer 1984: 30.
 5   Gordimer 1983a: 661.
 6   Gordimer 1983b: 93.
 7   Gordimer 1985: 147.
 8   Lazarus 1986-7: 131-4.
 9   Gordimer 1985: 138-9.
10   Gordimer 1983c: 58.
11   Wicomb 1987.
12   Gordimer 1976: 3.
13   Nadine Gordimer, *Burger's Daughter* (New York: Viking Press, 1979). All references are to this edition and have been placed in the text.
14   Cooke 1985: 13.
15   Gordimer 1980: 32.
16   Gordimer 1983b: 119.
17   Ibid.: 120.

18 Gordimer 1984: 19-20.
19 Roberts 1983: 45.
20 I mean this in the sense put forward by Jacques Derrida (1985: 290-9).
21 See Clingman 1986: 183.
22 Cooke 1985: 216.
23 Clingman 1986: 185.
24 See Winnie Mandela 1984: 118-28.
25 Gordimer 1981: 269.
26 Clingman 1986: 193.
27 JanMohamed 1983: 272-3.
28 Gordimer 1980: 17.
29 Erlande-Brandenburg 1979: 12.
30 Ibid.: 68.
31 Boyers 1984: 81.
32 Ibid.: 63.
33 JanMohamed 1983: 84.
34 Gordimer 1980: 29.
35 Gordimer 1985: 145.
36 Gordimer 1980: 30.
37 Clingman 1986: 186-8.
38 Clingman 1986: 187-8.
39 Barthes 1977: 148.
40 Winnie Mandela 1984: 148; from Nelson Mandela's response to P. W. Botha's offer of release in 1985 on the condition that he abandon political activity.

REFERENCES

Barthes, Roland 1977. *Image-Music-Text*. Trans. Stephen Heath. New York: Hill and Wang.

Boyers, Robert 1984. 'Public and private: on Burger's Daughter', *Salmagundi*, 62 (Winter): 62-93.

Clingman, Stephen 1986. *The Novels of Nadine Gordimer: History from the Inside*. London: Allen and Unwin.

Cooke, John 1985. *The Novels of Nadine Gordimer: Private Lives/Public Landscapes*. Baton Rouge and London: Louisiana University Press.

Derrida, Jacques 1985. 'Racism's last word', *Critical Inquiry*, 12: 290-9.

Eagleton, Terry 1983. *Literary Theory: An Introduction*. Minneapolis: University of Minnesota Press.

Erlande-Brandenburg, Alain 1979. *The Lady and the Unicorn/La Dame à la Licorne*. Paris: Editions de la Réunion des Musées Nationaux.

Gordimer, Nadine 1959. 'Where do whites fit in?', *Twentieth Century*, 165: 326-31.

Gordimer, Nadine 1976. 'Letter from South Africa', *New York Review of Books*. 9 December: 3-10.

Gordimer, Nadine 1979. *Burger's Daughter*. New York: Viking Press.

Gordimer, Nadine 1980. *What Happened to Burger's Daughter or How South African Censorship Works*. Emmarentia, SA: Taurus.

Gordimer, Nadine 1981. 'Interview with Nadine Gordimer.' (With Stephen Gray.) *Contemporary Literature*, 22: 263-71.

Gordimer, Nadine 1983a. 'Art and the State in South Africa', *The Nation*, 237 (24 December): 657-61.

Gordimer, Nadine 1983b. 'The art of fiction LXXVII: Nadine Gordimer'. (With Jannika Hurwitt). *Paris Review*, 78: 83-127.

Gordimer, Nadine 1983c. 'The Clash.' (With Diana Cooper-Clark.) *London Magazine*, NS 22.11 (February): 45-59.

Gordimer, Nadine 1984. 'A conversation with Nadine Gordimer' (with Robert Boyers, Clark Blaise, Terence Diggory, Jordan Elgrably), *Salmagundi*, 62: 3-31.

Gordimer, Nadine 1985. 'The essential gesture: writers and responsibility', *Granta*, 15: 137-51.

JanMohamed, Abdul R. 1983. *Manichean Aesthetics: The Politics of Literature in Colonial Africa*. Amherst: University of Massachusetts Press.

Lazarus, Neil 1986-7. 'Modernism and modernity: T. W. Adorno and contemporary white South African literature', *Cultural Critique*, 5: 131-55.

Mandela, Winnie 1984. *Part of My Soul Went with Him*. Ed. Anne Benjamin. New York and London. W. W. Norton.

Roberts, Sheila 1983. 'Nadine Gordimer's "family of women" ', *Theoria*, 60: 45-57.

Wicomb, Zoë 1987. *You Can't Get Lost in Cape Town*. New York: Pantheon.

14
Negotiating Subject Positions in an Uneven World

R. Radhakrishnan

Among the politically progressive aspects of post-structuralist thought has been its capacity to enable a dialogic and often contestatory articulation between 'history as representation' and 'history as production'. The pressure has been particularly severe on the form known as 'narrative', for now it has to tell a story or represent a reality as though it were a transcendental signified, and at the same time foreground this very activity of representation as an unnatural mode of production. The authority of the narrative is thus schizophrenically divided between a commitment to a truth value that is anterior to the narrative intervention and a formal allegiance that is internal to the narrative itself. In other words, having lost its instrumental transparency, narrative is forced into a meta-narrative speculation and reflexivity, thus calling into question the once putative bonding between 'narrative as meaning' and 'narrative as technique or form'. Our contemporary fictional and narrative scenario affords enough examples on the one hand of story tellers who dismiss meta-fictional reflexivity as precious and ultimately inane and life-denying, and on the other hand, of second-order fabricators who find narrative outmoded. The difficulty, in general, has been the lack of a space where the two modes could meet, negotiate, and generate through their mutual asymmetry an effective but a progressively complex and mediated sense of 'history' and 'reality'. In many ways, the contemporary political novel could well be that space, for what is 'political' demands a clear and unequivocal reference to reality and history, and contemporaneity insists that such a reference itself be subjected to auto-critique and protocols of 'self-enactment'. This already complicated situation is problematized further when we consider the heterogeneous, non-totalizable, and post-representational nature of contemporary reality that rejects the authority of a univocal narrative that emanates from a universal Subject of history.

The story we need to tell is of a world characterized by a non-synchronous and multi-temporal development: a world animated by plural subject positions that are simultaneous but not synchronic. On the one hand, those in dominant subject positions, like whites who are against apartheid in South Africa, are in the process of de-authorizing themselves and seeking affiliation with emerging revolutionary subjects. On the other hand, those in emerging revolutionary positions, like blacks in South Africa, are striving to affirm and legitimate themselves by creating their own 'insider space'. Whereas the dominant position requires acts of self-deconstruction, the subordinate position entails collective self-construction.

It is in this context that Nadine Gordimer's fictions are to be read and evaluated. We have the individual subject position of a white woman whose dedication to the abolition of apartheid has to route itself via an interrogation of its own positionality, for such a subject position, however supportive it may be of Black Consciousness, is still not a historical and existential inhabitant of that consciousness. The 'personal' and individual valence that Gordimer wishes to generate on behalf of herself and her fictions are out of sync with her given and filiative[1] political valence as a 'white'. Consequently, it is incumbent upon such a subject that it perennially divest itself of its own 'assigned'[2] position before it can legitimately ask the question: What role should I play in the revolutionary Black Consciousness? Gordimer's *Burger's Daughter* takes on this question in all its ramified complexity. 'The excellence of *Burger's Daughter*', as Abdul JanMohamed puts it, 'is due to a judicious combination of the relative simplicity of its plot, the elegance and appropriateness of its style, and the integrity, acuteness, and courage of Rosa Burger's attempt to define her "self".'[3] The attempts that Rosa Burger makes to thematize her own problematic and contradictory subject positionality are characterized by a certain psychological autonomy, but an autonomy that can only be relative to and ultimately determined by the larger political reality.

Elizabeth Meese's essay, 'The political is the personal: the construction of a revolutionary "subject" in Nadine Gordimer's *Burger's Daughter*', re-enacts, at a critical-interpretive but empathic distance, the agonies of a 'self' in search of an authentic position. Through an interpretive strategy that combines rigorous and highly nuanced textual readings with the capacity to move speculatively and critically out of the text into 'the world', Meese activates a readerly space where the reader is challenged to undertake the uneven and perilous task of 'self-consciencization'. As she asks in her conclusion to the essay: 'How, in us as readers, the ultimate "place" of Gordimer's South African narrative, will Rosa's story be "concocted", many more times in many more versions? How are we as readers finally to discover our places among its revolutionary "subjects"?' (p. 273) I am particularly grateful to Meese for the way in which she 'identifies' and foregrounds her own position as reader as a necessary prolegomenon to the act of critical intervention. To quote Meese again: Because her culture is inseparable from mine, it is my own position, the position of feminism, as much as Gordimer's, I wish to interrogate' (p. 255). I say I am grateful, since it is rare in the context of academic critical discourse for a professional critic to make constitutive references to her own 'person' and explicitly implicate the 'non-innocence' of her own position in the act of producing a critical reading. Meese's sense of self-implication also enables me, I would even say that it enjoins me, to disclose the ideological and intellectual underpinnings of my position as a male feminist, Third World, post-colonialist Indian subject deeply invested in post-structuralist practices. I will begin therefore with a brief critical analysis of three paradigmatic situations: one from my 'personal' life, one from literature, and one from history, all by way of denaturalizing my own position and of opening up a significant area where I may join the already inaugurated dialogue between Meese and Gordimer.

The first situation has to do with my critical reaction to the movie *Out of Africa*. Simply stated, I walked out of the theater after the first twenty minutes or so, in great anger and indignation. I just could not bear to see the history of an entire culture being frozen and fetishized into a spectacle so as to better serve as a backdrop for the emerging psychodrama of a white woman's sense of identity. It seemed to me that the effective histor-icization of the white woman's consciousness was unfolding into narrative within a privileged and privatized space, or, if you will, a *chronotope*, that pre-empted the narrative of black African consciousness. (The fact that Dinesen's Africa is not the same as Gordimer's is a valid point, but it does not in any fundamental way alter my argument here.) Given the macropolitical situation of Africa, an individual's psychodrama seemed to me particularly lacking in valence, all the more so since the individual concerned was 'white'. But I must confess to feeling very angry and confused with my own 'self' for having walked out with such an uncom-plicated and righteous sense of my own 'purity'. What exactly did my reaction signify? Certainly, a bias, but how did this bias rule out my potential sympathy for the white woman's subject position, especially when I call myself a 'male feminist'? Wasn't there enough space within the area known as my 'self' to accommodate both biases? Or perhaps it was all right to be unconcerned about the 'scotoma' in my visual field, given the world-historical conjunction between my own identity as a post-colonial Indian watching a film about a white woman's conquest of Africa. What I found difficult to justify (although I didn't feel all that guilty about it) was the ease with which I chose not to listen to a particular narrative. If my real complaint was that the film did not have room for multiple conflicting and contradictory narratives, was I not guilty of a similar insensitivity?

The second situation in its own way points up the impossibility of constructing a narrative that is heterogeneous, multiple, and differential enough to offer fair representation to multiple subject positions. I have in mind E. M. Forster's *Passage to India* and the built-in antagonism between Adela Quested's sense of 'subjecthood' and Aziz's sense of constituency. Given the asymmetry between the two predicaments, what can we demand of narrative and its commitment to a certain world and world-view? What or which world are we talking about? Here again is a text that places the reader in an anxious space where decisions and choices are not easy. There are two different subject positions each imbued with its own historicity and each a potentially adversarial and revolutionary agency relative to the dominant mode that holds it in captivity. On the one hand, the text deals with feminine sexuality in opposition to phallo-centric normativity, and on the other, with an emerging national con-sciousness in battle against the forces of colonialism. In each case, the personal element is part of a long *durée* which is not to be exhausted by any of its particular instances.[4] How is narrative to arbitrate between two macropolitical discourses and assign priorities? This is a problem that faces Nadine Gordimer too as she moves among Black Consciousness, feminism, and communism. First, there is the question concerning the transcendence of the 'personal' into the 'political', and second (and this is even more complicated), there is the problem of determining how differ-ent personal 'selves', such as black, white, male, female, etc., interact differently in their respective constituencies. For example, during the moments of the revolutionary emergence of a group consciousness, there is a solidarity of the personal with the political within the psyche of each 'self' that comprises that group (that is, in such historical junctures, the 'representative' and the 'individual' nature of the self become virtually the same), a solidarity that is communicable but not easily sharable or generalizable beyond that group.

This brings me to my last example, which is a scene from the film *Gandhi*: a scene so poignant that every time I see it, there are tears in my eyes. Gandhi is in prison, and his white Scottish comrade, the priest Charles F. Andrews, visits him. The two of them have been intimate fellow-travelers seeking paths to India's independence from British rule. As a matter of fact, in the literature that deals with the Indian independence struggle, C. F. Andrews is referred to as 'Deshbakth' or 'Patriot' Andrews in affectionate acknowledgment of his total solidarity with the Indian National Congress and its ideology. And yet, in this scene from the movie, Gandhi, from behind the bars, tells Charlie that the time has come for them to part, for from now on it is only Indians who can and should carry on the struggle. Charlie agrees and leaves after Gandhi assures him that in an ideal sense the two never are and never will be parted. This scene demonstrates both the historical finitude of subject positions and the extent to which 'given' subject positions can be critically transcended in search of new and different affiliations. To play a little on the polysemy of the word 'bar', Gandhi is behind 'bars' whereas Andrews is not. As Meese puts it in the context of the apartheid color bar, 'the "essential gesture" for black and white writers alike in South Africa "is a revolutionary gesture", the nature of which for each, however, is marked by their different positions relative to the "bar" (as line, law, institution and mark of subjectivity)' (p. 255).

The epigraph to *Burger's Daughter*, a quotation from Claude Lévi-Strauss, 'I am the place in which something has occurred', provides the reader with a historico-structuralist orientation to Rosa Burger's sense of identity and place. Meese's essay argues that

> Rosa Burger is one such place; South Africa, Gordimer's text (the discursive space of which begins by marking itself off there), the author herself, and ultimately the reader are other 'places', sites for/of production and performance. Who this subject is, where the place and what the thing that has 'taken place', the reader is to discover by reading between the lines of this textual complex of interlocking relationships. (p. 256)

A point well taken, for it seems to me that the tension between 'place' and 'what takes place in it' is essential to an understanding of historicity. I wish to argue that the structuralist rhetoric of 'positionality' does not have to result in empty allegorical readings of history, but instead can be used to sensitize our awareness of historical process as *chrono-topic*, to use Bakhtin's influential terminology.[5] If one's sense of identity in 'one's own time' endows the 'self' with a sense of personal authenticity, a spatialized perception of one's own personal identity leads to the realm of the 'political' which necessarily relativizes and/or sublates the *personal as such*.

As the very title of Meese's essay suggests, the personal-political nexus is of the utmost importance both to Gordimer and to Meese. Meese notes at the very beginning of her reading that ' "the personal is the political" has been a caveat of the contemporary feminist movement, a maxim authorizing the private, subjective experiences of the individual woman to be read in terms of or for its significance with respect to larger issues, or to stand as/for "the issues" of contemporary society. The microstructure of experience and the macrostructure of political forces are made synonymous, the former dignified, given the significance and readability presumed to belong to the political space of "public" life'; and yet, Meese is concerned that if the valorization of the personal as a gesture were 'elevated to law-in-itself, [it] may become an exclusionary principle inhibiting other political actions – outside the private sphere, in the rest of or in other parts of the world' (p. 253). Quoting Terry Eagleton, who reminds us that 'political struggle cannot be *reduced* to the personal, or vice versa', Meese goes on to ask the all-important question: 'What then is the excess, the "more than" the personal which constitutes The Political (not as reduction) or the-political-taken-personally? And what is the "more than" or "other than" the political which constitutes The Personal in this non-identification which Eagleton suggests?' What she suggests then is 'the critical elaboration of this complex relationship, the site of struggle in/between the self and the world – the working out of which might help us live in the tension' (p. 254). The truly difficult task, it seems to me, is 'to live in the tension', even live as tension without letting the 'living' simplify tension or allowing the tension to render the 'living' non-viable. I would like now to attempt a brief critical articulation of the kind that Meese is calling for.

The entire question of the conjunction of the personal and political partakes, to borrow from Althusser's structuralist-marxism, both of a general and omni-historical reality and a particular reality. In other words, one may posit that human social reality is always such that the personal and the political are co-implicated within a dialectically oriented symbiosis. But one could also state that the particular forms that this co-implication takes in different socio-political, economic, and cultural conjunctures have specific histories of their own. For example, given the political age of a group, that is, the duration of its history as an independent and autonomous group, the persons who constitute that group may feel differently about the ontological status of their individuation and the extent to which they feel their 'selves' to be explicitly politicized. Their conscious awareness of the manner in which they are 'ideologically interpellated' varies. The protocols which determine the relative weight of the political over the personal also varies, depending upon how well established the group is. Generally speaking, the perception of one's individual 'self' is hierarchically subsumed without any accompanying sense of personal impoverishment when the group is just becoming established, whereas the sense of individual autonomy is intensified when the group is firmly established as a dominant or hegemonic collectivity. To state this in the context of Rosa Burger, her sense of secure selfhood and subjectivity as a white is being made to respond sympathetically to a differently emerging historic self. Rosa's sense of her 'white self' is made aware of the untenability of the very collective identity of which she has been a part, and hence, her self is in double jeopardy: it is in an adversarial relationship with the hegemonic constituency that is her 'base', so to speak, while it cannot entirely claim the revolutionary Black Consciousness as its new base. Whereas, for Baasie, her black 'brother', his subjectivity and personal identity have already been parsed, as it were, within the developing revolutionary language, Rosa's dis-placed self is in search of an authentic constituency. The question that Rosa's self asks, 'Where do whites fit in?', can only be answered as an asymmetrical response to the black revolution. Indeed, the question 'Where do whites fit in?' is politically meaningless in the context of a black majority consciousness historicizing itself into effective political existence. The tricky task facing the 'white subject' engaged in 'self-consciencization' is one of articulation: a transformed articulation that has to divest itself of authority and privilege. There is the black insurrectionary subject position, there is the subject position of the 'white' 'rethinking all its values', and there is a common political space that subtends both these positions. In his essay 'Intellectuals in the post-colonial world', Edward Said makes a brilliant analysis of this unevenness: 'The tragedy of this experience, and indeed of all post-colonial questions, lies in the constitutive limitation imposed on any attempt to deal with relationships that are polarized, radically uneven, remembered differently. The spheres, the sites of intensity, the agendas, the constituencies in the metropolitan and ex-colonized worlds overlap only partially. The small area that is common does not, at this point, provide for more than what I'd like to call *a politics of blame*.'[6]

I am aware that the regimes of colonialism and apartheid are not the same. I am also aware that whereas Said's comments pertain to ex-colonized realities, the South African reality is still under apartheid, and yet Said's central point still holds. From a world-historical perspective, the white question, 'Can we stay on in South Africa?', is not, and in a sense, cannot be part of the progressive agenda *at this particular point*. And the irony is that this question intrinsically is an askable question that emanates from an existing perspective, albeit, a perspective deracinated from *its* hegemonic history. The really meaningful question, a question that can eventually lead to a post-apartheid cooperation across 'the bar', is: What forms of 'self-consciencization' should white consciousness practice in order to earn the merit to stay: *ascesis*, self de- and re-identification, a deracinated consciousness?

Gordimer does not spare her protagonist the intense agony of these questions. The problem confronting Rosa Burger, given her profoundly political upbringing, is that of choice. What sort of strategy and what kind of 'ontological anchorage' would be most honest and appropriate for the conscientious white consciousness in apartheid South Africa? How best can Rosa as *topos* coordinate the political with the personal? Gordimer's own personal realization has been that the personal approach is 'inadequate to combat an unyielding white supremacist regime'. The personal developed as such is in great danger of easy trivialization or privatization. The dictum 'the personal is the political' could atrophy into a form of inaction or into an all too easy acceptance of every form of the personal as the political. The personal as a result gets shielded from its responsibility to actualize itself in progressively political formations; instead, it is valorized in its very *status quo* as 'always already' political. The other problem with this formulation is that in letting the personal be its own dispensation, it forecloses the insight that the personal itself can only be part of an overall pattern of socialization where each self exists in a state of exo-topy (Bakhtin again) towards other selves within a mobile socio-political field where there is neither pure identity nor pure alterity. The fetishization of both 'living for one's self' and 'living for others' is the mediated expression of contradictions and overdeterminations within a structural totality where often the different regional logics are out of sync with one another.

But the irony in Rosa's case is the fact that she has indeed been brought up under Marxist-Leninist principles to valorize the political and the social over the personal. And this precisely is the problem: the doctrinaire internalization of communist tenets results in a curious blindness and insensitivity. As Meese observes shrewdly: 'Part of what Rosa fails to see is that, because the tenets of white communism have been "naturalized" in the family, they are as inseparable for her in the effort to "identify" herself as they were for her father or mother. Likewise, the natural becomes the unnatural, or is it the other way around?' (p. 259) Her analysis also makes the point that 'Lionel Burger's household, with its pool, black servants, black "son" "Baasie", and steak barbecues, embodies the domestication of white revolutionary South African politics in the 1950s' (p. 258). We now see that Rosa as 'place' is multiply coordinated and there are no easy ways to name or identify such a place. Rosa as 'place' is also a topographic detail within the utopic communist map, a map whose algebraic and programmatic sense of space has led to the loss, within the space, of an existential and phenomenological density. And besides, communism itself, in having naturalized itself, has lost touch with its own contingency. In other words, it has hardened into a master discourse of a Eurocentric radicality that does not sit well on the South African scene that is so strongly determined by race, not class.

The important issue that Meese raises here but does not elaborate is that of the formation of the revolutionary subject position. What is the modality of such a subject position and within what intellectual, cultural, and socio-political tradition of opposition is such a position being generated? What are the formal characteristics of the model and what are its master concepts and categories: marxist, feminist, African Nationalist, ethnic? What if a given subject position like Rosa's straddles multiple realities and modes: feminist, communist, anti-racist? Will a single model suffice or should the revolutionary subject resort to improper *bricolage*? In my response so far, in situating Rosa in an exclusively race-specific context, I have overlooked the feminist valence in her position. Is it conceivable then that the inordinate search for a personal 'self' that seems so solipsistic and retrogressive in the context of the politics of the revolutionary black consciousness might well be the appropriate demand of a legitimate 'insider' if we situate Rosa within the feminist model? Meese, as a feminist critic, is quick to perceive this dimension in *Burger's Daughter*:

In a sense Gordimer's question of what is the place of whites in South Africa . . . is conflated with what is 'woman's place'. That is, in *Burger's Daughter* we can read these as correlative questions. Rosa is offered an identity – as comrade-daughter (the communist

family), South African white (state), cultural product (language and
history), corporeal subject (menstruating girl turned woman). Her
problem is how to be Burger's daughter and more, other – how to be
white but not the master, colonizer – *finding a representation which
permits a non-hierarchical play of difference*. (p. 261; emphasis
mine)

How does this correlation of 'woman's space' with the 'white's place'
work? And, as a result of this correlation, what new critical 'place' is
produced where the two agendas may be said to meet, interrupt, and
throw each other into crisis? It is a particularly vexing question to answer
since one of the two agendas, 'woman's', world-historically speaking, is a
progressive one, whereas the other, 'white's', is, politically and world-
historically speaking, part of a dying order. Whereas 'woman's place'
carries with it an irrefragable moral authority that is affirmative and
future-oriented, the 'white's place' brings with it an auto-critical, deconstructive, and an ascetic ethic. And of course, both these 'places' are
'sub-places' within the 'place' known as Rosa. If the rationale of the
revolutionary subject is the production of knowledge as change and not as
adequation, on what terrain or axis should such a production take place,
that is, given the overdeterminations and contradictions inherent in Rosa
as structural *topos*? A sensitive topographical rendering of Rosa's positionality, it seems to me, should map her (and Gordimer too) multiply so
that the different factors that determine Rosa are correlated but not
rendered mutually identical, interchangeable, or structurally isomorphic.
For example, it is obvious that the woman's question in South Africa at
this particular time does not have the same urgent priority as the color
and race question, but this assignment of priorities is not immutable or
transcendent. There are clear indications in *Burger's Daughter* that the
woman's question is both part of and in excess of the race and color
question. The difficulty comes in when a single mono-thetic revolutionary
blueprint presumes to speak for an entire range of 'sub-constituencies'
that make up the constituency of the oppressed.[7] After all, given a general
history where 'there is no document of civilization which is not at the
same time a document of barbarism',[8] should not the different groups that
make up, however unevenly, the world of the oppressed seek an axial-
coalitional expression of themselves rather than look for fiercely regional
and autochthonous islands of self-fulfillment? One cannot but refer in this
context to the eloquent critique elaborated during the early days of

academic feminism in this country by Shulamith Firestone, who found that during the many revolutions in history (ethnic, Marxist, and Freudian revolutions), the 'woman's question' had always been subsumed within a larger agenda, but never articulated in and for itself. To go back then to the question I posed a little while ago: how is the correlation to be achieved? But first let us look at 'woman's place' as coordinated in Gordimer's text and Meese's sensitive interpretation of it.

I quote, for reasons of economy, from Meese's text as it interacts critically with the opening of *Burger's Daughter*:

> Rosa sees herself 'in place, outside the prison', but her attention is not focused on the public spectacle that she is and of which she is a/part. She stands in front of the prison and menstruates for the first time, becoming a woman, who, as JanMohamed puts it, is more/other than a daughter: 'Thus her simultaneous yet unconnected existence as an object of public scrutiny and as a locus of private experience reflects her predicament as a bifurcated social being.' In her version of the story, Rosa focuses on her bio-sexual identity, the biological fact of her womanhood, turning her private, internal experience into a public one where 'the internal landscape of my mysterious body turns me inside out, so that in that public place on that public occasion . . . I am within that monthly crisis of destruction, the purging, tearing, draining of my own structure. I am my womb.' She tells us in retrospect that it matters little whose identity story we read – theirs or hers – as 'both would seem equally concocted'. (p. 257)

And my question is: who is to decide or who can arrogate to herself the univocal authority to decide whose version has the maximum significance, that is, given the fact that they are all versions that are conscious and perspectival productions of meaning? Does or can one have the right to arbitrate against Rosa's 'focus on her bio-sexual identity' just because the macropolitical situation in South Africa has to do with race and color and not with 'becoming woman'? But, even given the incontrovertible race/color-specificity of the political situation in South Africa, how can any specific/particular subject position within that reality be expected *not to involve its own specific structure* in the act of hermeneutically understanding the macro-situation? To put it concretely in the context both of Rosa Burger and Gordimer: Indeed it is true that the larger South African oppression has to do with race, but how can Gordimer and Rosa Burger interpret this reality except *as women?* Would their readings not be suspect and disingenuous from any other positional base?[9] Would it make a difference if they were black women? But then, what about the position 'women' within the designation 'black women'? Are there then exemplary norms of blackness that preclude other determinations? And whose black norms are these – black men's? While post-structuralism teaches us that 'common reality' can only be understood through multiple and contradictory narratives, the politically aware reader has to choose positions that are either 'inside' or 'outside', despite her awareness that the very terms 'inside' and 'outside' can be deconstructed. Otherwise, Gordimer's/Rosa's narratives end up resembling Botha's.

Meese's critical study focuses on this 'dis-junction' quite appropriately. It is clear that Meese finds Gordimer's placing of feminism in the South African context quite unsatisfactory, but at the same time she is sensitive to the contradictory valences of Gordimer's own position as a white woman in that society. Writes Meese: 'Obviously Gordimer believes in feminism; but feminism is not her highest priority.' And again: 'She shares the view of many women of color who are multiply oppressed. Theirs is a compelling position, *although Gordimer repeatedly represents feminism through trivializing examples*' [pp. 261–2; my emphasis]. And further on: 'Gordimer's critique of white privilege requires her to place the black woman first, limited though her understanding may be concerning who the "black woman" is and what she wants and what that "first place" might be. *It is the gesture* [my emphasis] that saves her in the endless struggle against her subject position, her racial privilege – what she as a white woman in South Africa *has* but does not necessarily *want*' (p. 262). I particularly appreciate Meese's highly nuanced use of the word 'gesture', for in many ways what we are talking about here are some of the differences between substantive politics and gestural politics, and between representational politics and a post-representational sense of constituency. Gordimer can neither represent the black consciousness (this would be false representation), nor can she, in elucidating her subject position, *not talk* about it (such omission would be unconscionable). In a global situation where '*I cannot be you*' and yet I have the moral and the political need to join coalitional forces with *you*, it seems more urgent than ever to articulate theories of critical-political solidarity that would 'inmix' the 'substantive' with the 'gestural', and the 'representational' with the 'post-representational'. Moreover, feminism, ethnicity, the

'Third World', and many other constituencies share common enemies: racism, sexism, normative heterosexism, and ethno-phallogocentrism. All the more reason to invest in coalitional processes and *not to* dissipate energy in precious insider-fighting. There is a time to emphasize difference and a time to stress not 'identity' but similarity and 'co-axiality'.[10]

In conclusion, I revisit the scene where Rosa's 'becoming woman' is turned inside out. That scene in many ways is paradigmatic of what a post-structuralist feminism (or feminisms) can bring to the politicization of theory: an awareness of reality and history as 'liminal' and the need for 'liminal' thinking. The figural-political representation of the inside/outside as well as the private/public opposition goes to the very source of the problem which is binarity itself, and not merely some of the particular forms that this binarity takes on.[11] That scene, in my reading, demonstrates with surpassing intensity and eloquence, (a) that subject positions and the narratives that they produce about themselves are productions of reality that are in themselves historical (a point ably made by Mae Henderson in chapter 1 of the present volume, where she argues that even inter-textual and self-referential narratives are historically contextual); (b) that the second-order story of the subject position *qua* subject position and the story that it tells need to be understood together and in light of the reality of other subject positions and their narratives; (c) that the spatial nature of positions in general should allow for mobility among and across positions; and, finally, (d) that the binary historiography that we have 'received' needs to be problematized and in a sense 'transcended' so that critical thinking may respond both to the present and the permanent revolution in the present moment.

As for my subject position, it is cathected and politicized on the one hand by the desire for a worldliness that is 'between Culture and System' (Edward Said), and on the other, by an imperative to dwell within a tension as well as a 'contradiction without recourse', where different and heterogeneous agencies within the same 'subject' are perennially calling each other's absolutism into question.[12]

NOTES

1 My reference here is to Edward Said's notions of 'filiation' and 'affiliation', where 'filiation' represents given and received subject-positions and 'affiliation' signifies the capacity of the subject to displace and re-affiliate itself through the practice of a secular and oppositional criticism. See Said 1983.

2 The way subject positions are 'assigned' is an important aspect of Michel Foucault's genealogical archaeology that insists that 'subjects' are both 'constituting' and 'constituted', both agential and determined. See Foucault 1972 and 1970.

3 JanMohamed 1983: 126.

4 This is a conflated reference both to Braudel's notion of the *longue durée* as well as to the Althusserian thesis that particular histories and structures are interpellated in response to the authority of general structures. See Braudel 1980 and 1976. Also see Althusser 1969 and 1971, and Althusser and Balibar 1970.

5 Unlike most forms of Western European critical theory that are invested in bi-polar and binary modes of thinking, Bakhtin's critical philosophical anthropology consistently works for a dialectical nexus where 'opposites' negotiate with each other. The 'chronotope', for example, does away with the highly overdetermined space-time/structure-history opposition in order to inaugurate a study of the morphology of historical forms. See Bakhtin 1981.

6 Said 1986: 45.

7 Radhakrishnan 1987: 199-220.

8 Benjamin 1969: 256.

9 This is as much a political problem as it is a hermeneutic problem. How is the political to be actualized if not through interpretation, and, how can interpretation (after Martin Heidegger and Hans-Georg Gadamer) not implicate its own positionality and historicity in the act of producing knowledge and truth?

10 See my forthcoming essay, 'Toward an effective intellectual: Foucault or Gramsci?', in *Intellectuals and Social Change*, ed. Bruce Robbins. Minneapolis: University of Minnesota Press.

11 No one has taken on this task of thematizing, unmasking, and displacing *binarity as such* as brilliantly and relentlessly as Jacques Derrida, but it is interesting to see that these formal, second-order critiques do not sometimes sit well politically. I am referring in particular to Derrida's essay, 'Racism's last word', (Derrida 1985).

12 Gayatri Chakravorty Spivak's subject position as well as her choice of critical methodology as marxist-feminist-deconstructivist-post-colonialist-Indian-and-subaltern is exemplary of such a creative crisis. See Spivak 1987. See also my essay, 'Traveling theory and the professional intellectual: in search of a common world', in *Feminist Critical Negotiations*, ed. Elizabeth A. Meese and Alice Parker, forthcoming. See also Said 1983.

REFERENCES

Althusser, Louis 1969. *For Marx*. Harmondsworth: Penguin.

Althusser, Louis 1971. *Lenin and Philosophy and Other Essays*. Trans. Ben Brewster. London: New Left Books.

Althusser, Louis and Balibar, Etienne 1970. *Reading Capital*. London: New Left Books.

Bakhtin, Mikhail 1981. *The Dialogic Imagination: Four Essays*. Trans. Michael Holquist and Caryl Emerson. Austin: University of Texas Press.

Benjamin, Walter 1969. 'Theses on the philosophy of history', in *Illuminations*, ed. Hannah Arendt. New York: Schocken.

Braudel, Fernand 1976. *Afterthoughts on Material Civilization and Capitalism*. Baltimore: Johns Hopkins University Press.

Braudel, Fernand 1980. *On History*. Chicago and London: University of Chicago Press.

Derrida, Jacques 1974. *Of Grammatology*. Trans. Gayatri Chakravorty Spivak. London and Baltimore: Johns Hopkins University Press.

Derrida, Jacques 1981. *Dissemination*. Chicago: University of Chicago Press.

Derrida, Jacques 1985. 'Racism's last word', *Critical Inquiry*, 12.1 (Autumn): 290-9.

Forster, E. M. 1952. *A Passage to India*. New York: Harcourt, Brace and World.

Foucault, Michel 1966. *The Order of Things*. London: Tavistock.

Foucault, Michel 1972. *The Archaeology of Knowledge*. London: Tavistock.

JanMohamed, Abdul 1983. *Manichean Aesthetics: The Politics of Literature in Colonial Africa*. Amherst, MA: University of Massachusetts Press.

Radhakrishnan, R. 1987. 'Ethnic identity and post-structuralist différance', *Cultural Critique*, 6 (Spring): 199-220.

Said, Edward 1983. *The World, the Text, the Critic*. Cambridge, MA: Harvard University Press.

Said, Edward W. 1986. 'Intellectuals in the post-colonial world', *Salmagundi*, 70-71 (Spring-Summer): 44-81.

Spivak, Gayatri Chakravorty 1987. *In Other Worlds: Essays in Cultural Politics*. New York and London: Methuen.

Index

Martin, Biddy 202
Martin, Wallace 175, 183
Marx, Karl 97, 101, 150, 179, 258, 272
marxism 2, 7, 18, 90–122, 129, 139, 143, 152, 153, 154, 155, 168, 179, 180, 181, 183, 188, 281, 283, 284, 286
Marxism and Deconstruction (Ryan) 179–81
masculinist culture 93, 94, 96, 100, 102, 106
masculinist discourse 91, 92, 104, 118
masculinity 8, 55, 59, 64, 65, 66, 70, 71, 74, 80, 81, 181, 186, 220, 224, 243
masochism 219
Master and Man (Tolstoy) 61
mastery 8, 49, 103, 104, 110, 134, 153, 171, 184
matriarchy 19
'Meditations on History' (Williams) 7, 8, 11–16, 19–38, 39n.2, n.12, 41n.34, 45–9
Meese, Elizabeth A. 2, 209, 210, 277–8, 280–1, 289n.12
Mehlman, Jeffrey 176
Men in Feminism (Jardine and Smith eds) 93, 94, 127, 128, 135, 185–6, 195, 201
Messer-Davidow, Ellen 81, 87n.2
Metahistory (White) 169
Midnight's Children (Rushdie) 143–4, 153, 156, 158n.1
Mill, John Stuart 150
Miller, Arthur 166
Miller, J. Hillis 174
Miller, Nancy 176, 195, 202
Millett, Kate 124n.19
Milton, John 61
misogyny 243

Mitchell, Juliet 124n.15, 183, 205n.1
modernism 143, 144, 146, 166, 169, 171, 228
Moglen, Helene 83, 85–6, 87n.9
Mohrke, Helga 154
Montrelay, Michèle 150
Moore, Charles 141
Morrison, Toni 147–8, 151, 153
motherhood 188, 212, 221, 228, 248, 249, 250
mother(s) 19, 92, 215, 225, 226, 229, 232, 233, 234, 257, 258, 259, 260, 267, 284
multiplicity 2, 43, 45, 47, 69, 80, 119, 122, 144, 146, 147, 150, 151, 157, 169, 178, 210, 219, 228, 231, 279, 284, 285, 287
Mulvey, Laura 106, 107, 124n.15
myth 16, 19, 38, 93, 100, 104, 105, 129, 155, 220, 221, 228, 241, 250, 251, 270

The Name of the Rose (Eco) 144, 158n.1
Nancy, Jean-Luc 75n.31
narrative 7, 9, 13, 22, 27, 28, 38, 46, 48, 98, 112, 115, 116, 143, 146, 155, 156, 176, 189, 190, 197, 210, 212, 217, 222, 227, 241, 265, 268, 269, 271, 273, 276, 278, 279, 287, 288
Naylor, Gloria 43
Neal, Larry 10
New Criticism 59, 62, 79
Newman, Charles 141
Nietzsche, Friedrich W. 24, 106, 150, 178, 187, 206n.9
Nights at the Circus (Carter) 145
Nimis, Stephen 59
Nixon, Rob 201